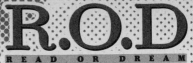

R.O.D

READ OR DREAM

We are Paper Sisters Detective Company

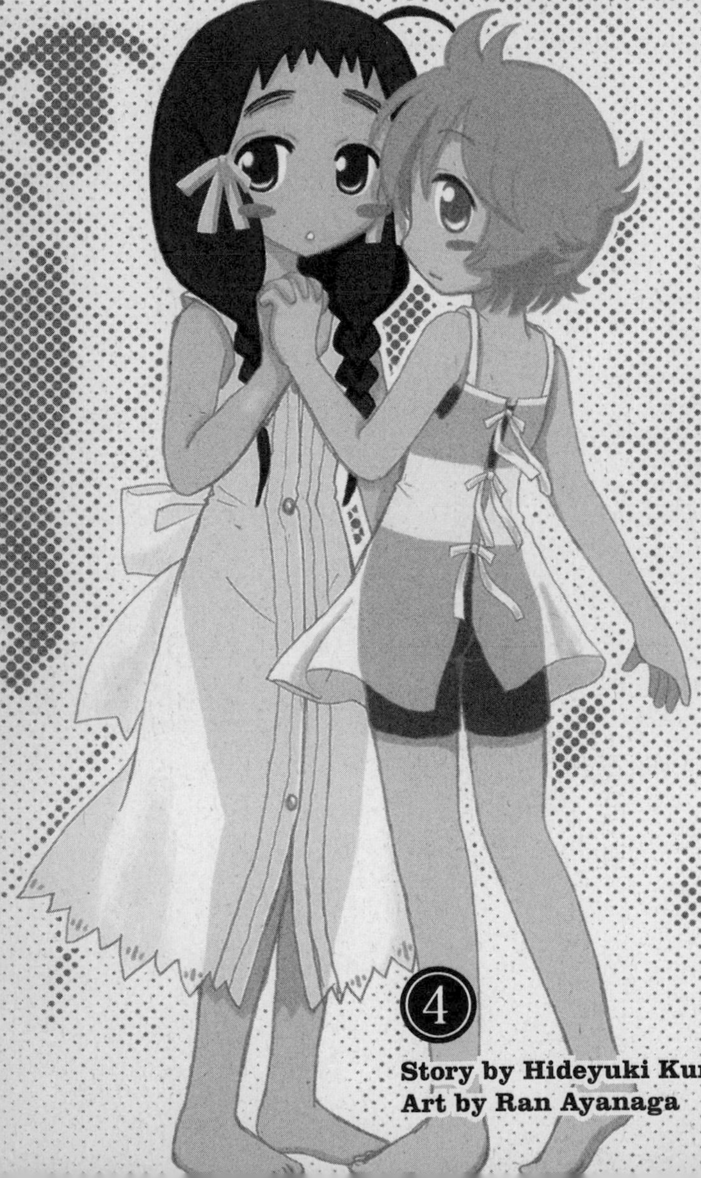

4

Story by Hideyuki Kurata
Art by Ran Ayanaga

R.O.D
R E A D   O R   D R E A M
We are Paper Sisters Detective Company

C O N T E N T S

Chapter 24 3

Chapter 25 27

Chapter 26 51

Chapter 27 75

Chapter 28 99

Chapter 29 123

Chapter 30 147

Chapter 31 171

The Final Chapter 195

Postscript 224

Bonus Story: Cleaning Up Demons with
Anita the Cleaner 226

CHAPTER 24

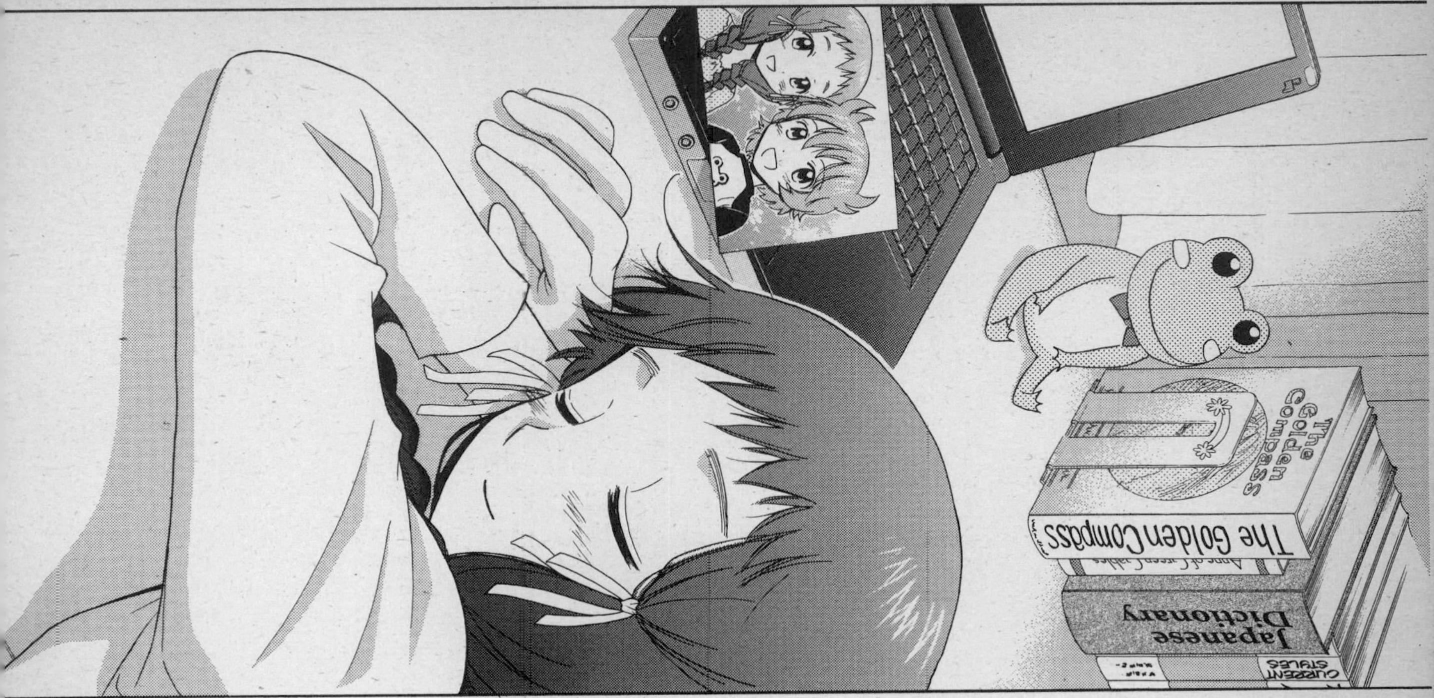
The Golden Compass
The Golden Compass
Anne of Green Gables
Japanese Dictionary
CURRENT STYLES

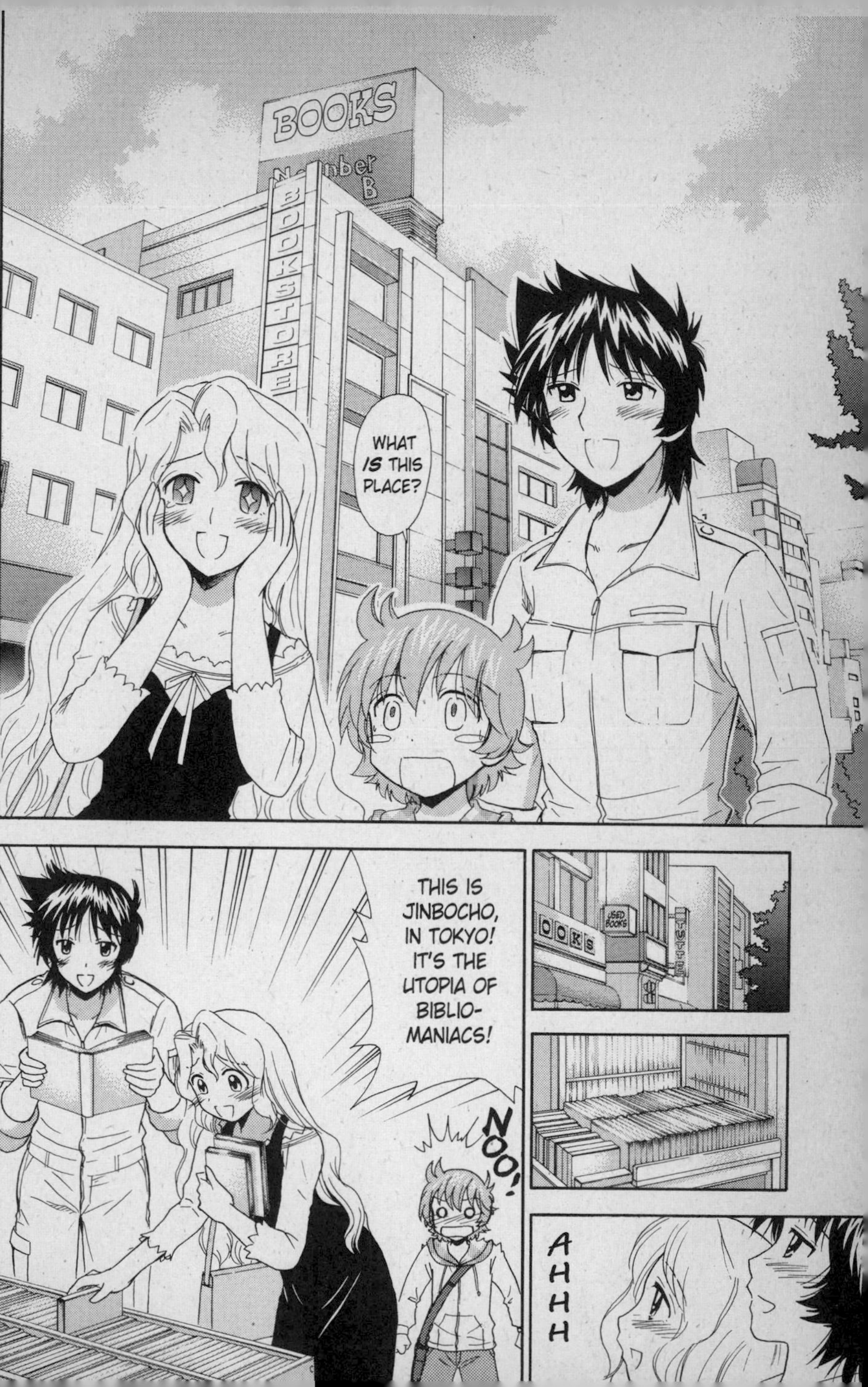
BOOKS
BOOKSTORE
WHAT *IS* THIS PLACE?
USED BOOKS
AHHH
THIS IS JINBOCHO, IN TOKYO! IT'S THE UTOPIA OF BIBLIO-MANIACS!
NOOO!

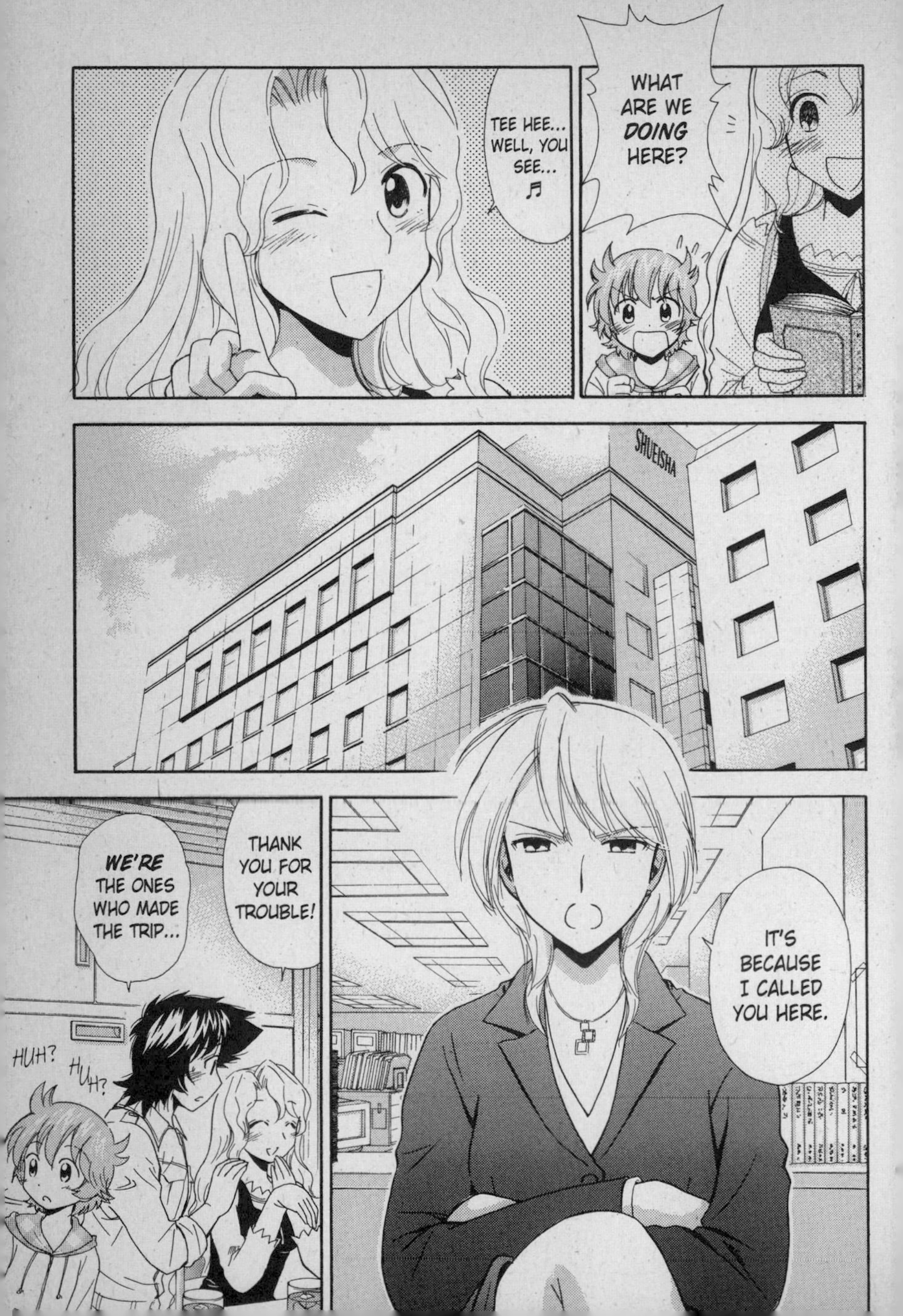
WHAT ARE WE *DOING* HERE?
TEE HEE... WELL, YOU SEE... ♬
SHUEISHA
IT'S BECAUSE I CALLED YOU HERE.
THANK YOU FOR YOUR TROUBLE!
WE'RE THE ONES WHO MADE THE TRIP...
HUH?
HUH?

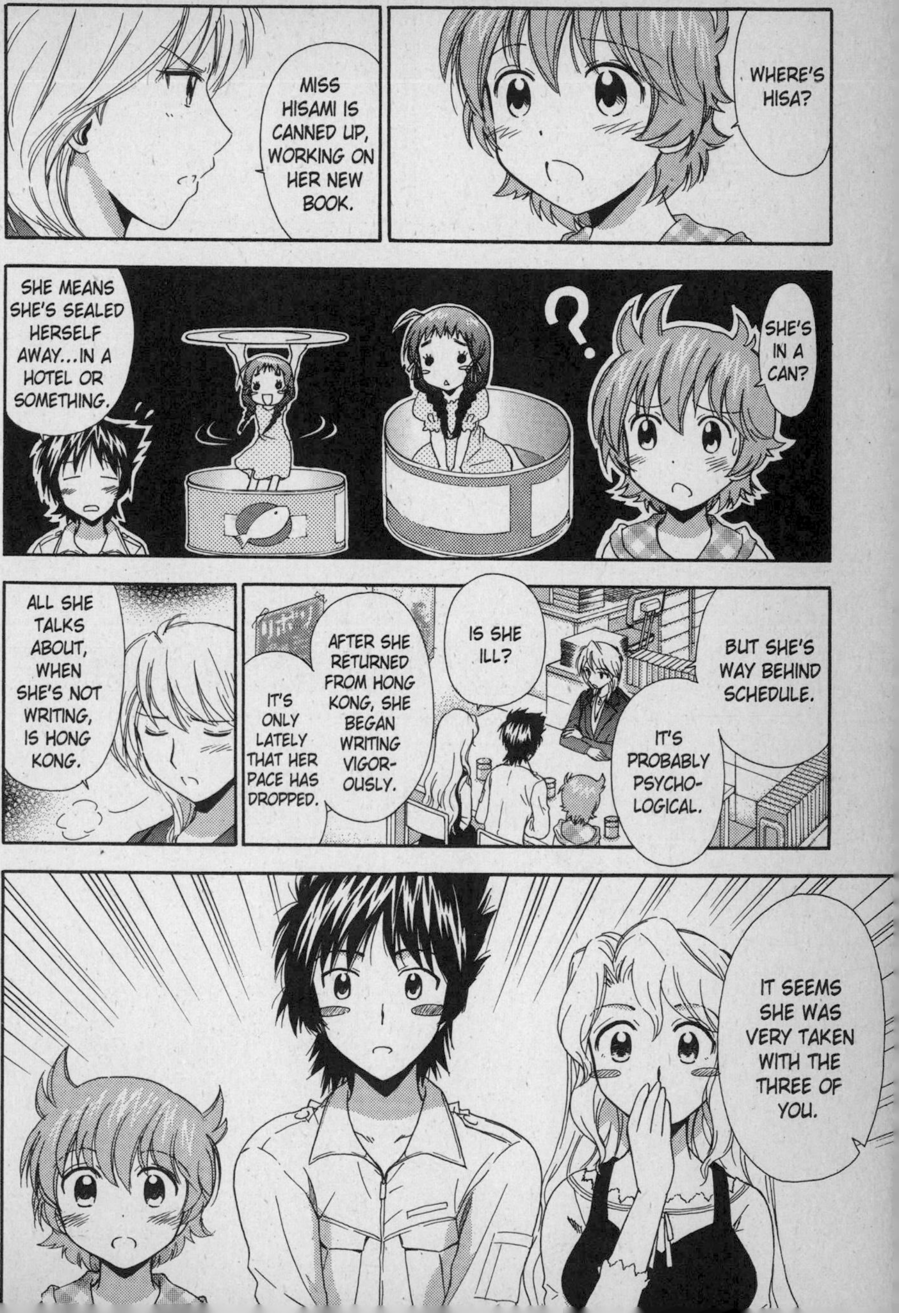
WHERE'S HISA?
MISS HISAMI IS CANNED UP, WORKING ON HER NEW BOOK.
SHE'S IN A CAN?
SHE MEANS SHE'S SEALED HERSELF AWAY...IN A HOTEL OR SOMETHING.
BUT SHE'S WAY BEHIND SCHEDULE.
IS SHE ILL?
IT'S PROBABLY PSYCHOLOGICAL.
AFTER SHE RETURNED FROM HONG KONG, SHE BEGAN WRITING VIGOROUSLY.
IT'S ONLY LATELY THAT HER PACE HAS DROPPED.
ALL SHE TALKS ABOUT, WHEN SHE'S NOT WRITING, IS HONG KONG.
IT SEEMS SHE WAS VERY TAKEN WITH THE THREE OF YOU.

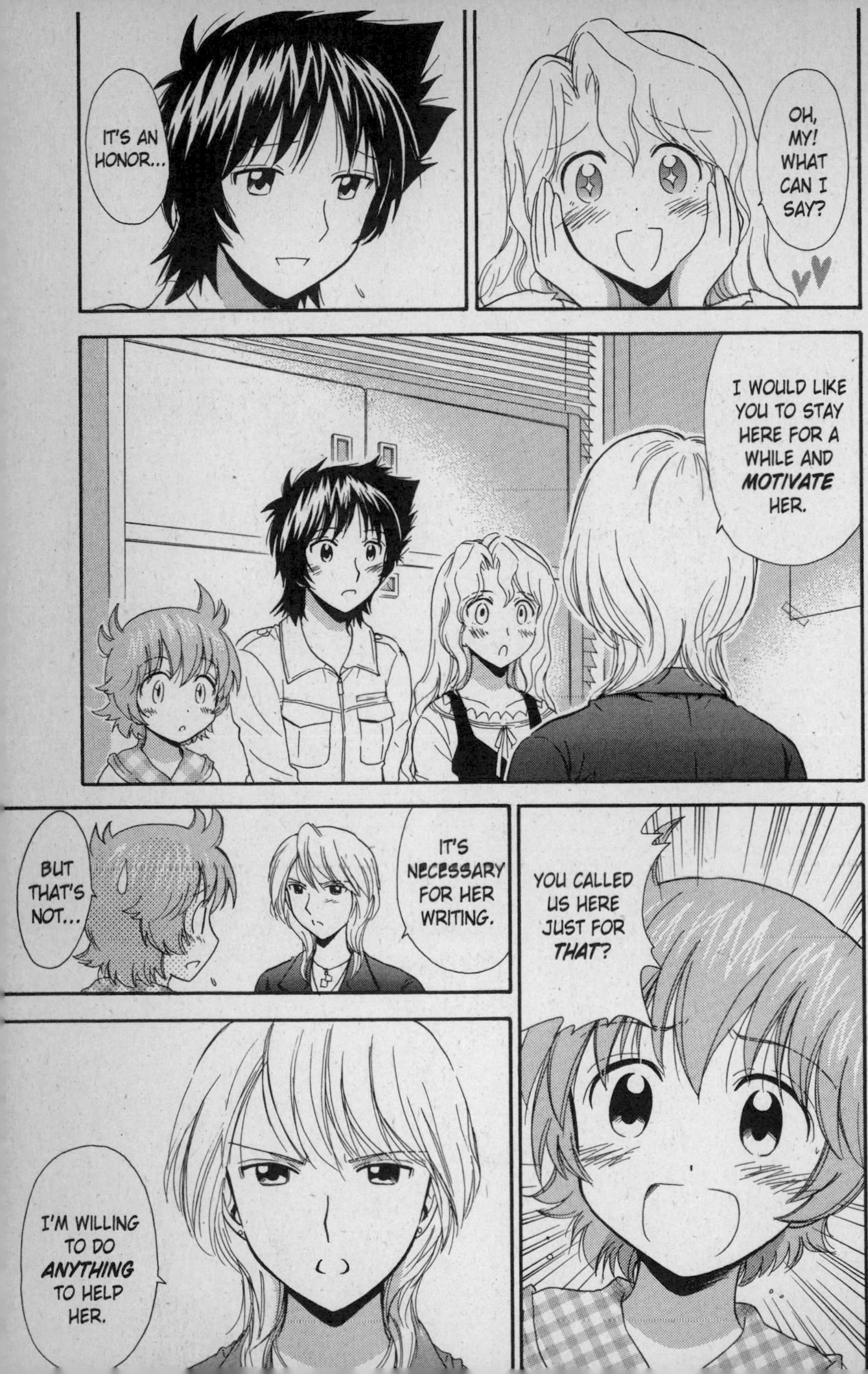
OH, MY! WHAT CAN I SAY?
IT'S AN HONOR...
I WOULD LIKE YOU TO STAY HERE FOR A WHILE AND *MOTIVATE* HER.
YOU CALLED US HERE JUST FOR *THAT*?
IT'S NECESSARY FOR HER WRITING.
BUT THAT'S NOT...
I'M WILLING TO DO *ANYTHING* TO HELP HER.

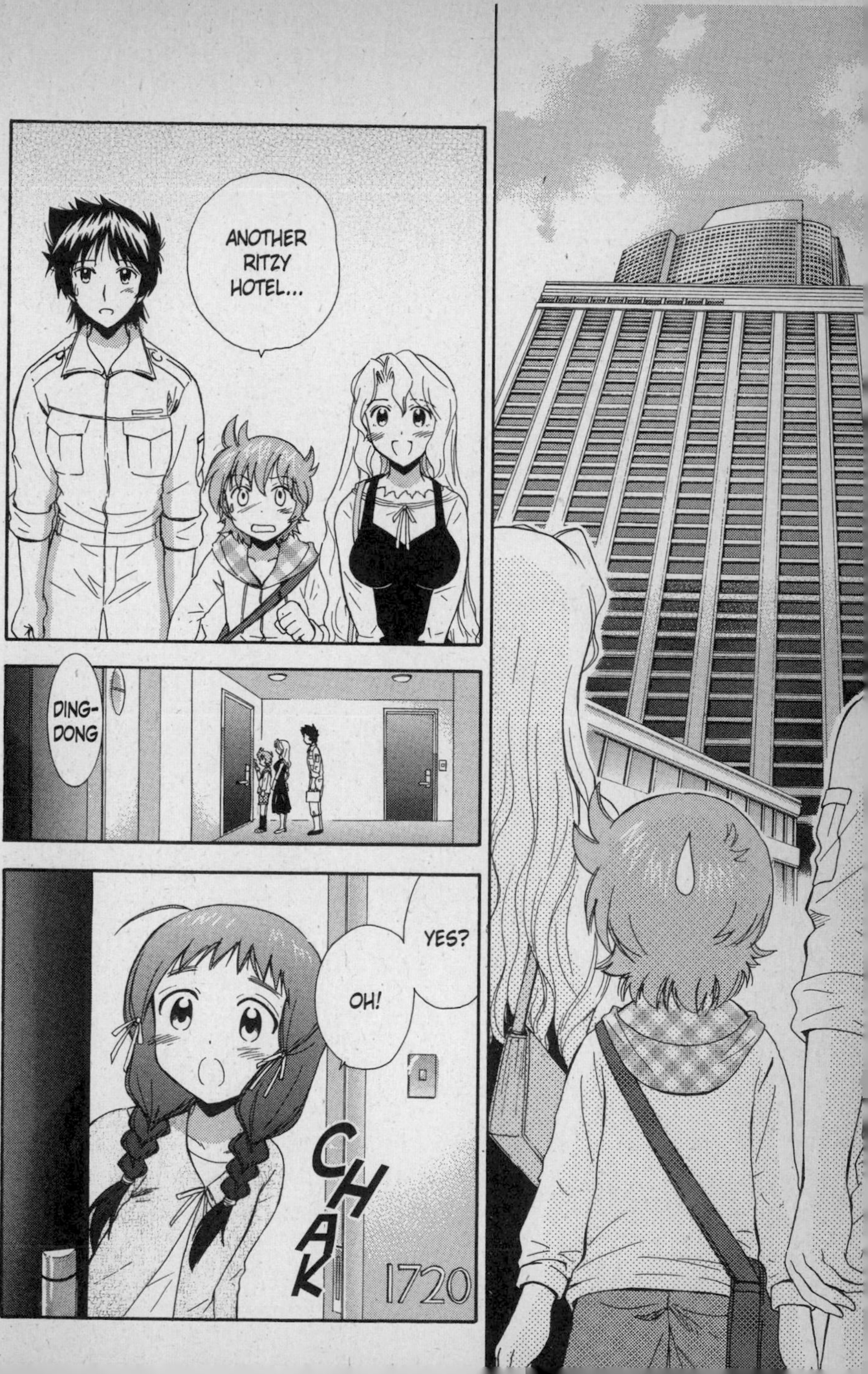
ANOTHER RITZY HOTEL...
DING-DONG
YES?
OH!
CHAK
1720

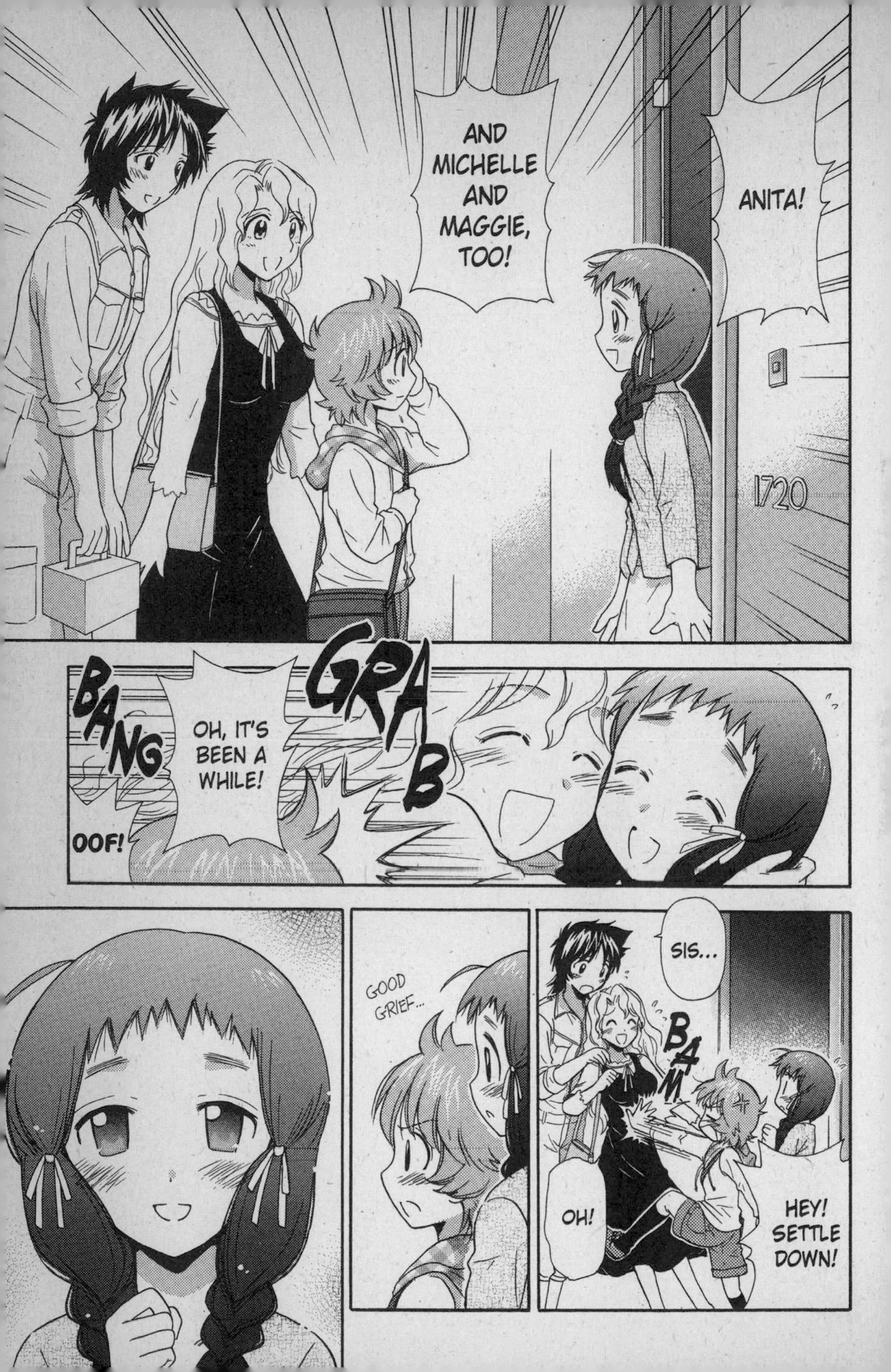
ANITA!
AND MICHELLE AND MAGGIE, TOO!
GRAB
OH, IT'S BEEN A WHILE!
BANG
OOF!
SIS...
BAM
HEY! SETTLE DOWN!
OH!
GOOD GRIEF...
1720

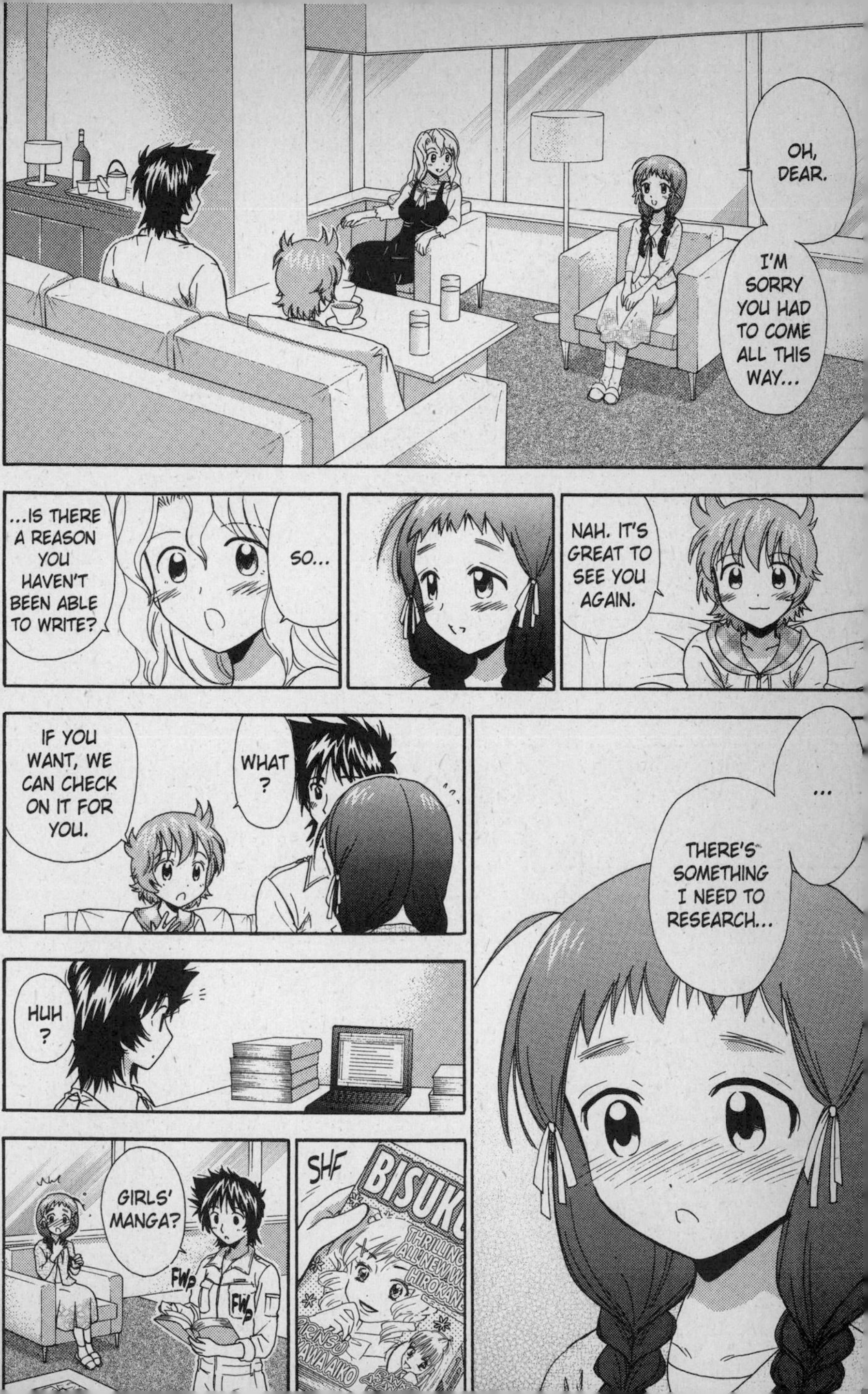
OH, DEAR.
I'M SORRY YOU HAD TO COME ALL THIS WAY...
NAH. IT'S GREAT TO SEE YOU AGAIN.
SO...
...IS THERE A REASON YOU HAVEN'T BEEN ABLE TO WRITE?
...
THERE'S SOMETHING I NEED TO RESEARCH...
WHAT?
IF YOU WANT, WE CAN CHECK ON IT FOR YOU.
HUH?
SHF
GIRLS' MANGA?
FWP
FWP

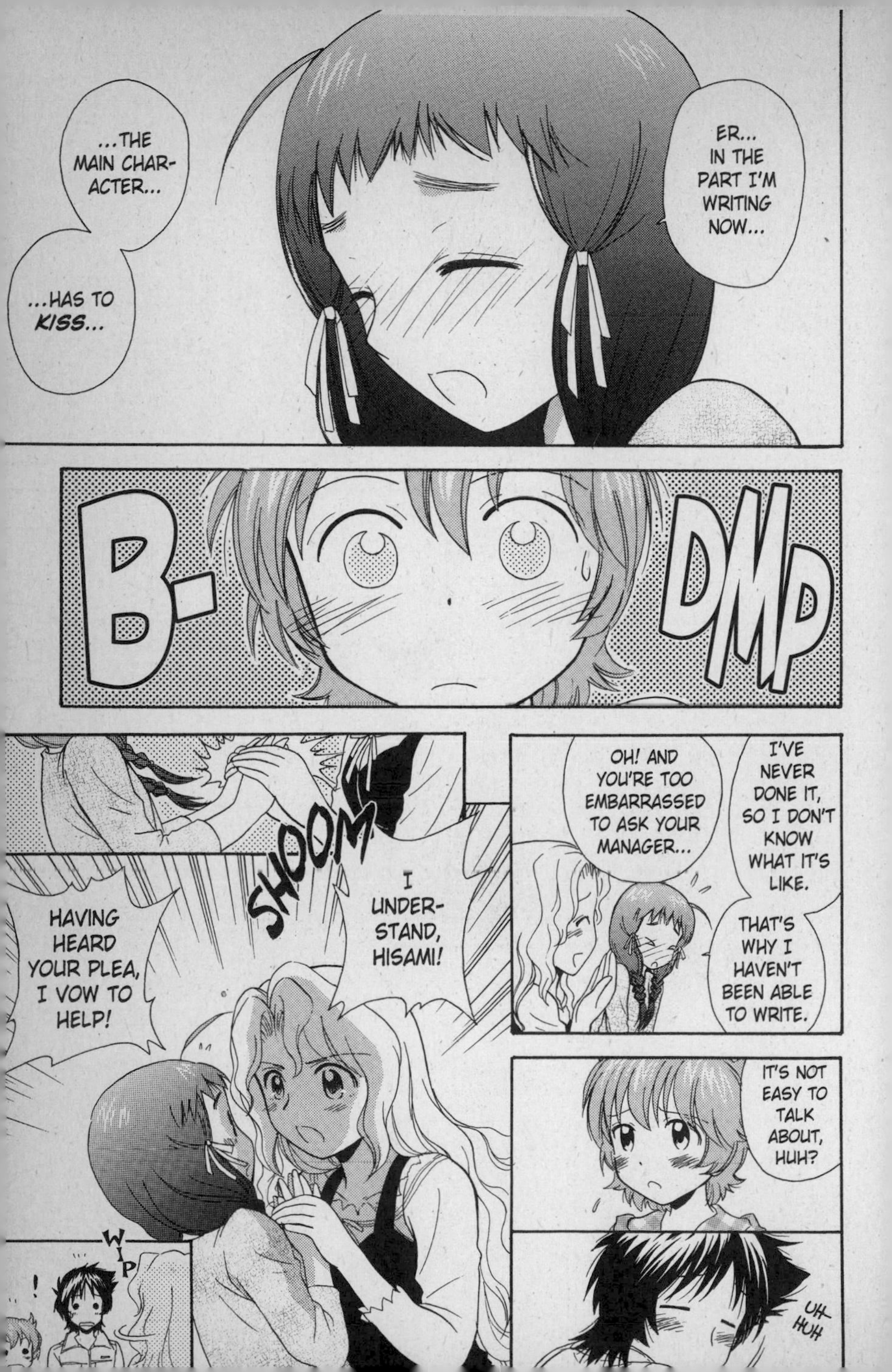
ER... IN THE PART I'M WRITING NOW...
...THE MAIN CHARACTER...
...HAS TO *KISS*...
B-DMP
I'VE NEVER DONE IT, SO I DON'T KNOW WHAT IT'S LIKE.
THAT'S WHY I HAVEN'T BEEN ABLE TO WRITE.
OH! AND YOU'RE TOO EMBARRASSED TO ASK YOUR MANAGER...
SHOOM
I UNDERSTAND, HISAMI!
HAVING HEARD YOUR PLEA, I VOW TO HELP!
IT'S NOT EASY TO TALK ABOUT, HUH?
UH HUH
WIP
!

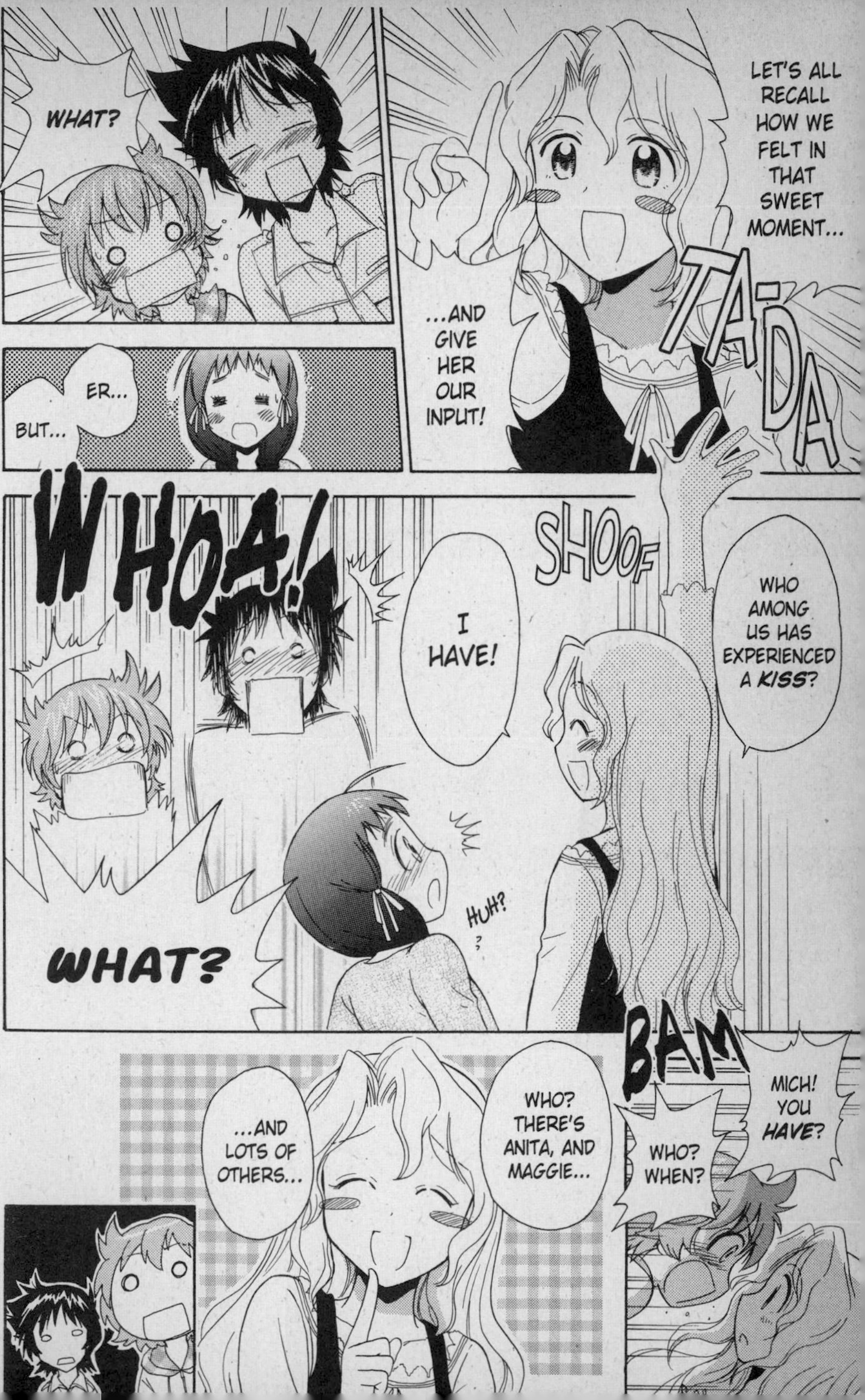
LET'S ALL RECALL HOW WE FELT IN THAT SWEET MOMENT...
TA-DA
...AND GIVE HER OUR INPUT!
WHAT?
ER...
BUT...
WHO AMONG US HAS EXPERIENCED A *KISS*?
SHOOF
I HAVE!
WHOA!
HUH?
WHAT?
BAM
MICH! YOU *HAVE*?
WHO? WHEN?
WHO? THERE'S ANITA, AND MAGGIE...
...AND LOTS OF OTHERS...

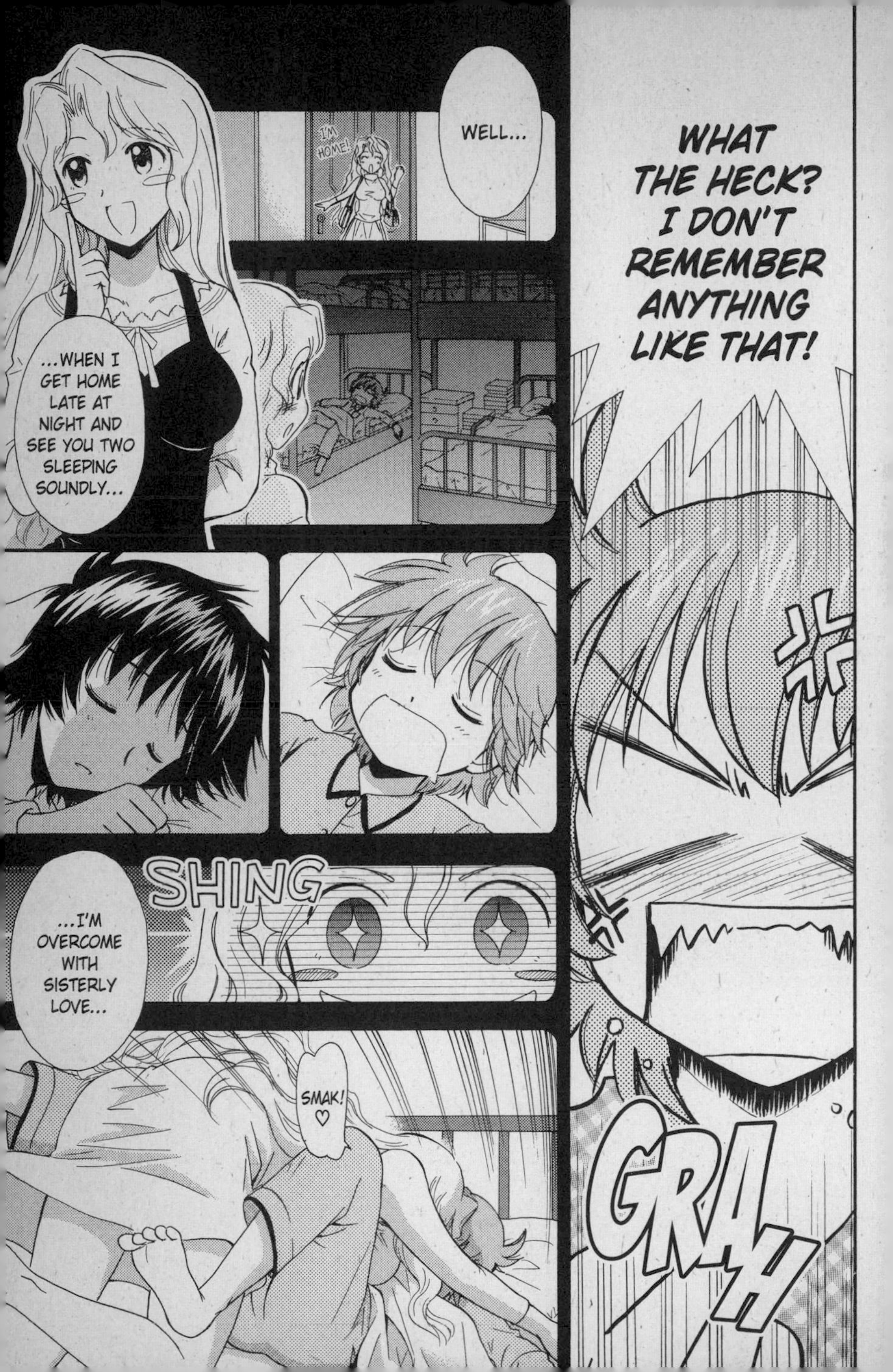
WHAT THE HECK? I DON'T REMEMBER ANYTHING LIKE THAT!
GRAH
I'M HOME!
WELL...
...WHEN I GET HOME LATE AT NIGHT AND SEE YOU TWO SLEEPING SOUNDLY...
SHING
...I'M OVERCOME WITH SISTERLY LOVE...
SMAK! ♡

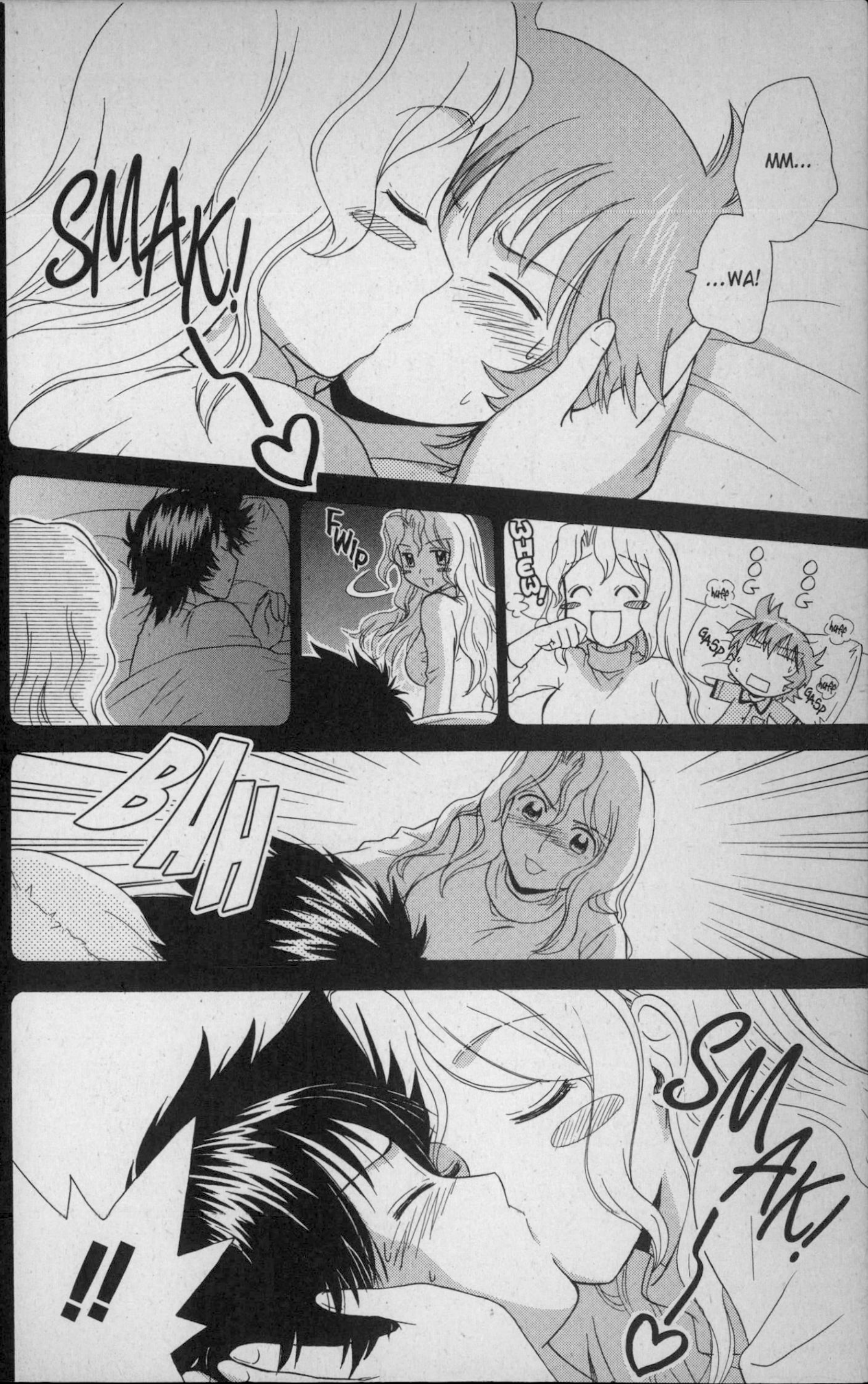
MM...
...WA!
SMAK!
WHEW!
haff
GASP
haff
haff
GASP
FWIP
BAH
SMAK!
!!

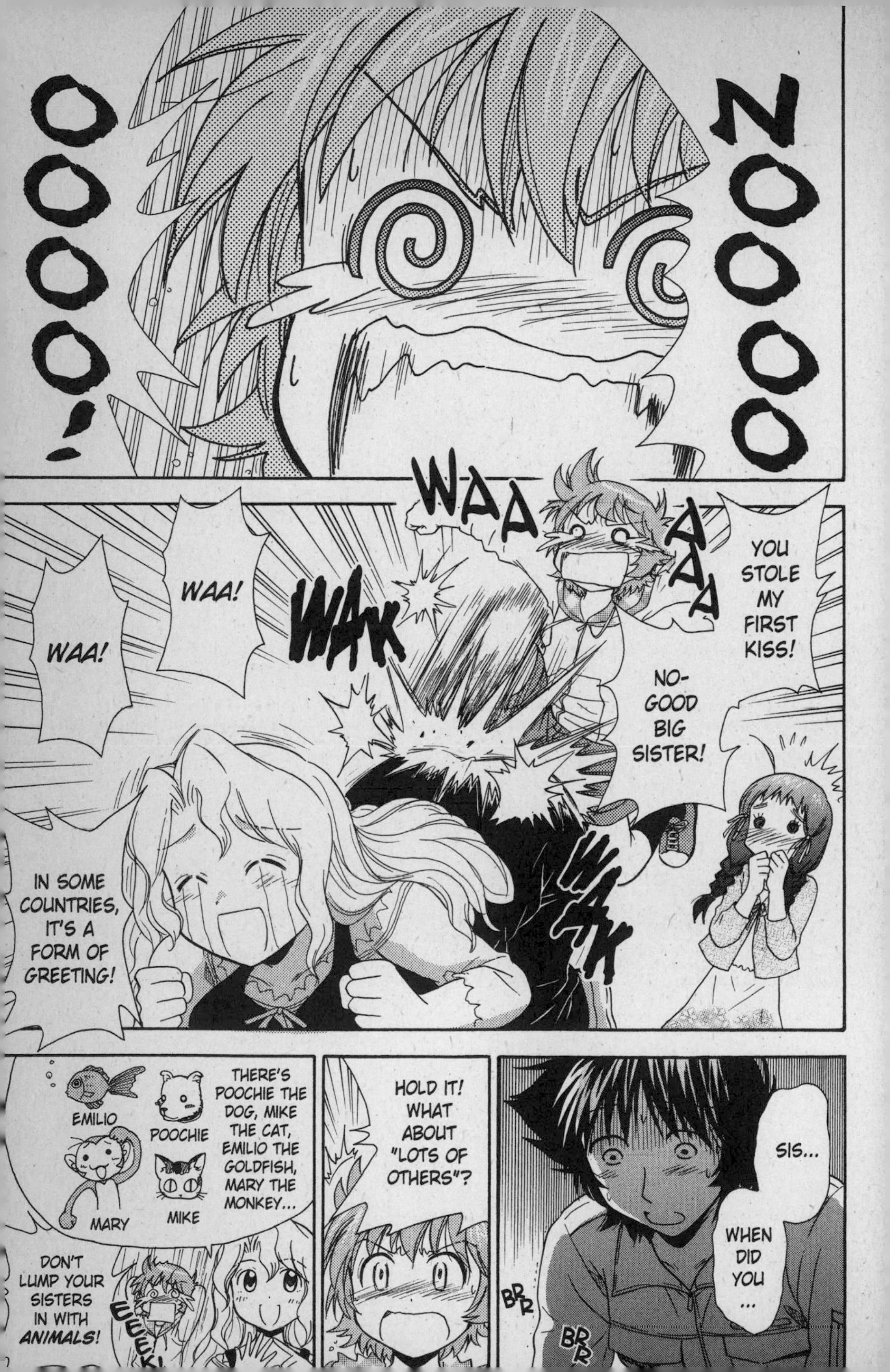
NOOOO
OOOO!
YOU STOLE MY FIRST KISS!
NO-GOOD BIG SISTER!
WAAAAA
WAK
WAK
WAA!
WAA!
IN SOME COUNTRIES, IT'S A FORM OF GREETING!
SIS...
WHEN DID YOU ...
BRR
BRR
HOLD IT! WHAT ABOUT "LOTS OF OTHERS"?
THERE'S POOCHIE THE DOG, MIKE THE CAT, EMILIO THE GOLDFISH, MARY THE MONKEY...
EMILIO
POOCHIE
MARY
MIKE
DON'T LUMP YOUR SISTERS IN WITH ANIMALS!
EEEEK!

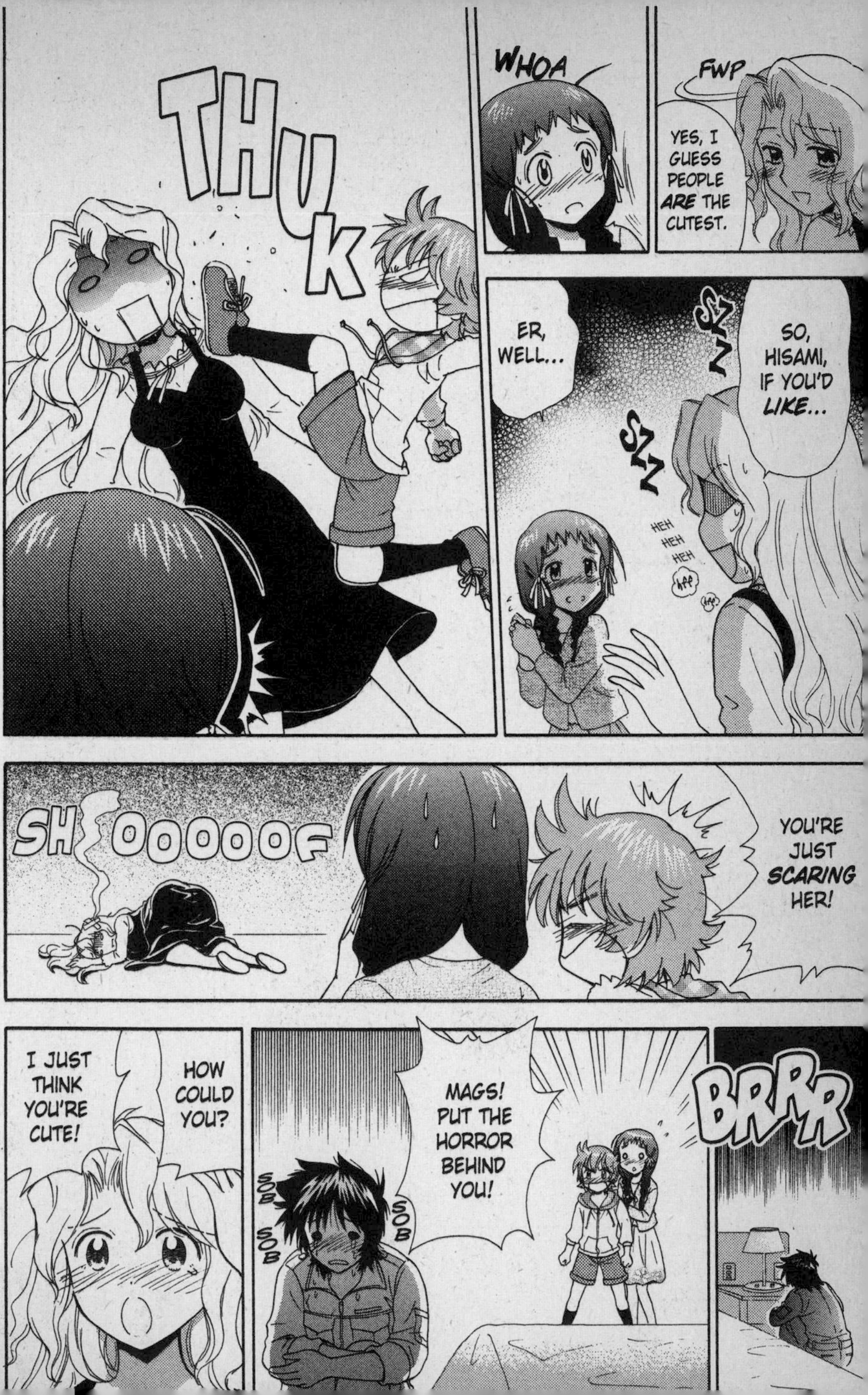
FWP
YES, I GUESS PEOPLE ARE THE CUTEST.
WHOA
SO, HISAMI, IF YOU'D LIKE...
SZZ
SZZ
HEH HEH HEH
ER, WELL...
THUK
YOU'RE JUST SCARING HER!
SHOOOOOF
BRRR
MAGS! PUT THE HORROR BEHIND YOU!
SOB SOB
SOB SOB
HOW COULD YOU?
I JUST THINK YOU'RE CUTE!

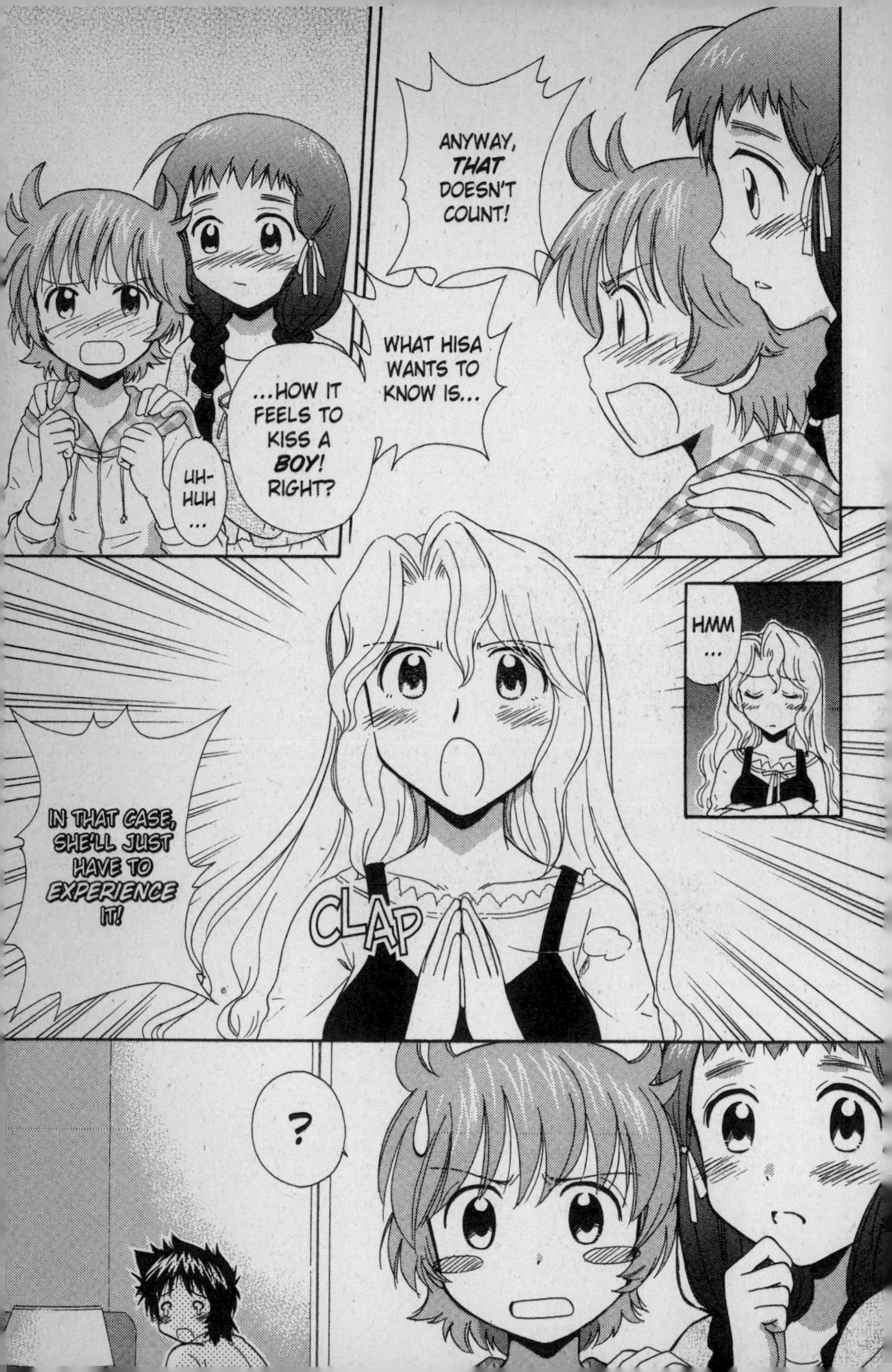
ANYWAY, THAT DOESN'T COUNT!
WHAT HISA WANTS TO KNOW IS...
...HOW IT FEELS TO KISS A BOY! RIGHT?
UH-HUH...
HMM...
IN THAT CASE, SHE'LL JUST HAVE TO EXPERIENCE IT!
CLAP
?

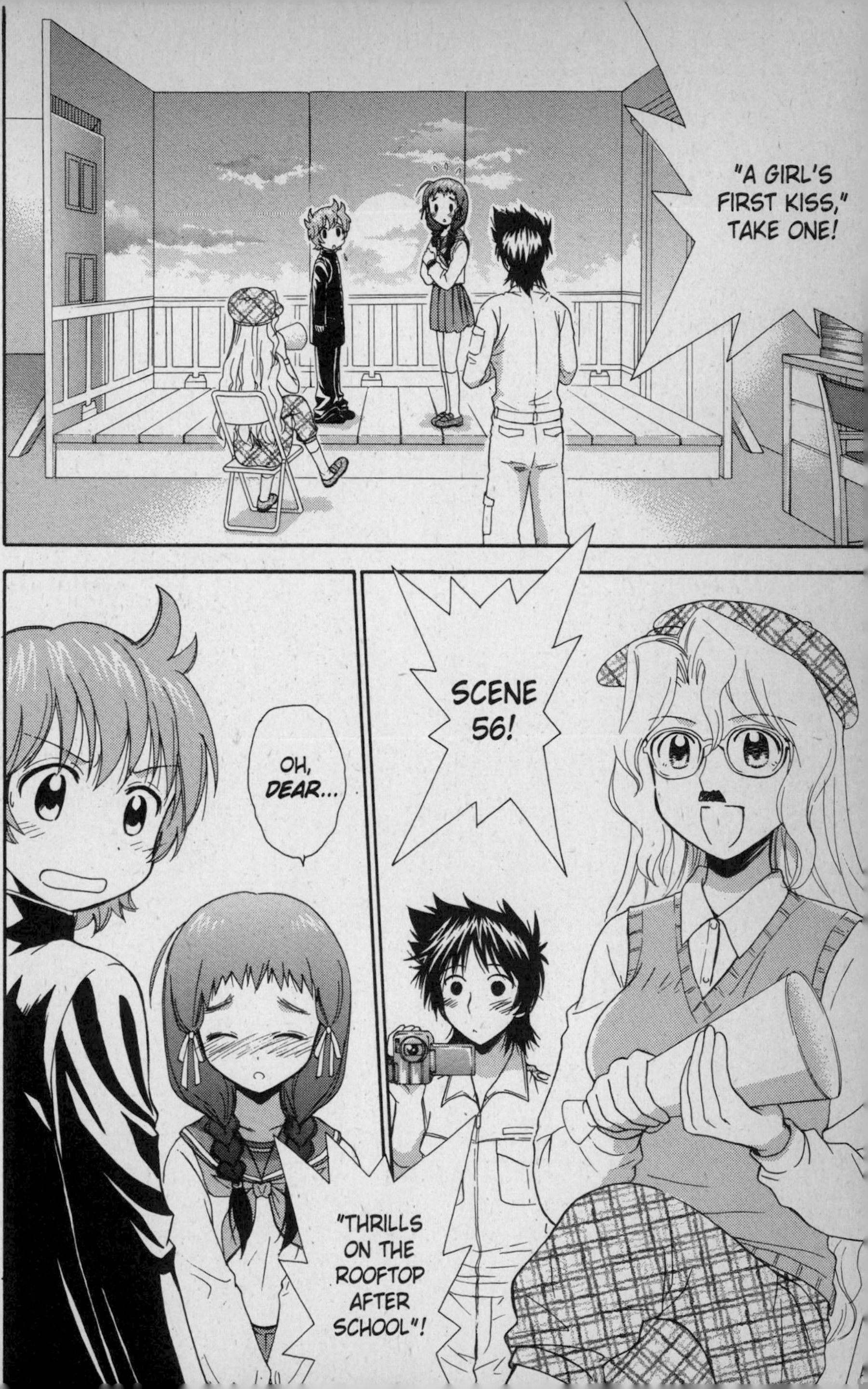
"A GIRL'S FIRST KISS," TAKE ONE!
SCENE 56!
"THRILLS ON THE ROOFTOP AFTER SCHOOL"!
OH, DEAR...

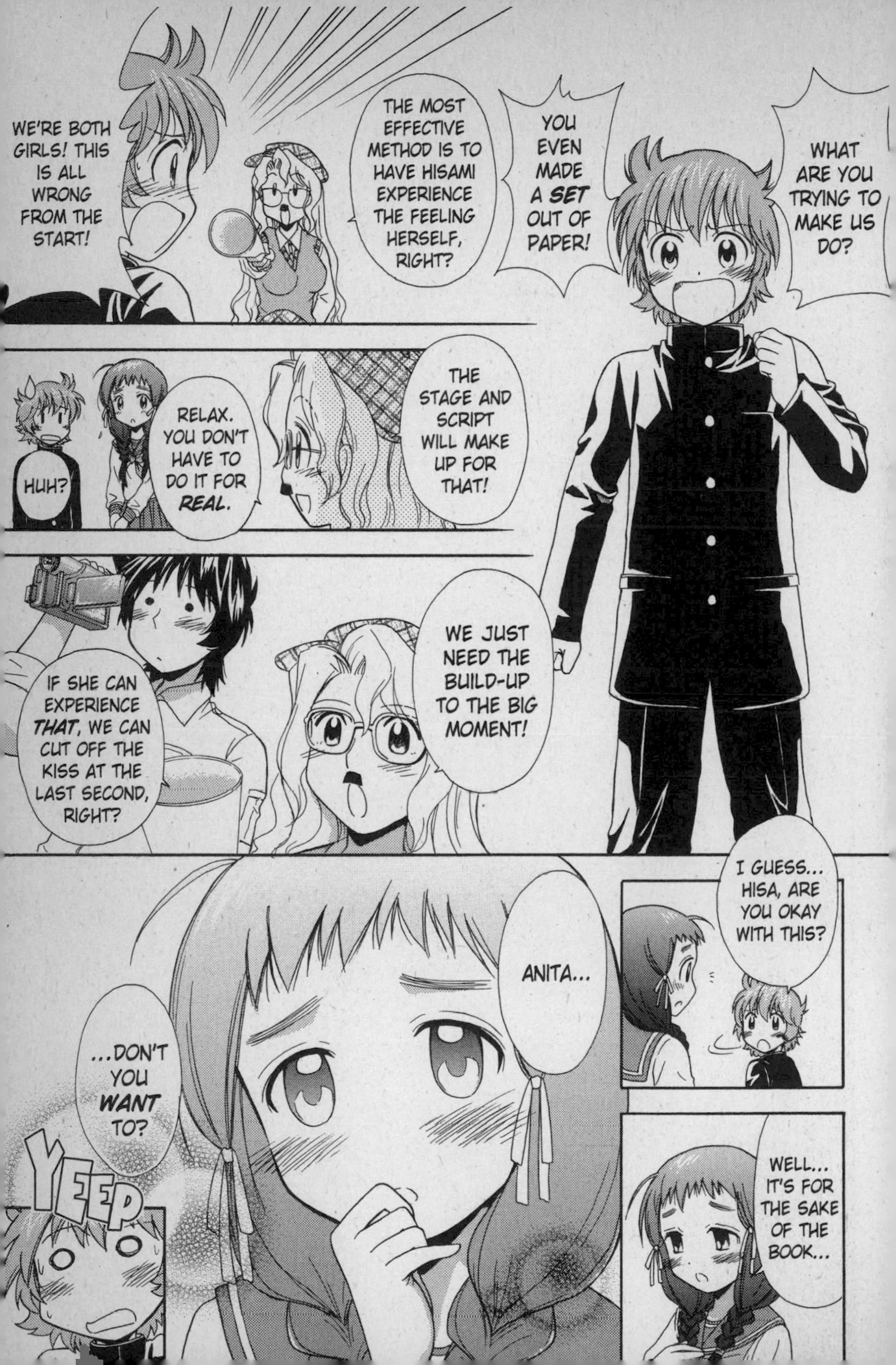
WHAT ARE YOU TRYING TO MAKE US DO?
YOU EVEN MADE A *SET* OUT OF PAPER!
THE MOST EFFECTIVE METHOD IS TO HAVE HISAMI EXPERIENCE THE FEELING HERSELF, RIGHT?
WE'RE BOTH GIRLS! THIS IS ALL WRONG FROM THE START!
THE STAGE AND SCRIPT WILL MAKE UP FOR THAT!
RELAX. YOU DON'T HAVE TO DO IT FOR *REAL.*
HUH?
WE JUST NEED THE BUILD-UP TO THE BIG MOMENT!
IF SHE CAN EXPERIENCE *THAT*, WE CAN CUT OFF THE KISS AT THE LAST SECOND, RIGHT?
I GUESS... HISA, ARE YOU OKAY WITH THIS?
WELL... IT'S FOR THE SAKE OF THE BOOK...
ANITA...
...DON'T YOU *WANT* TO?
YEEP

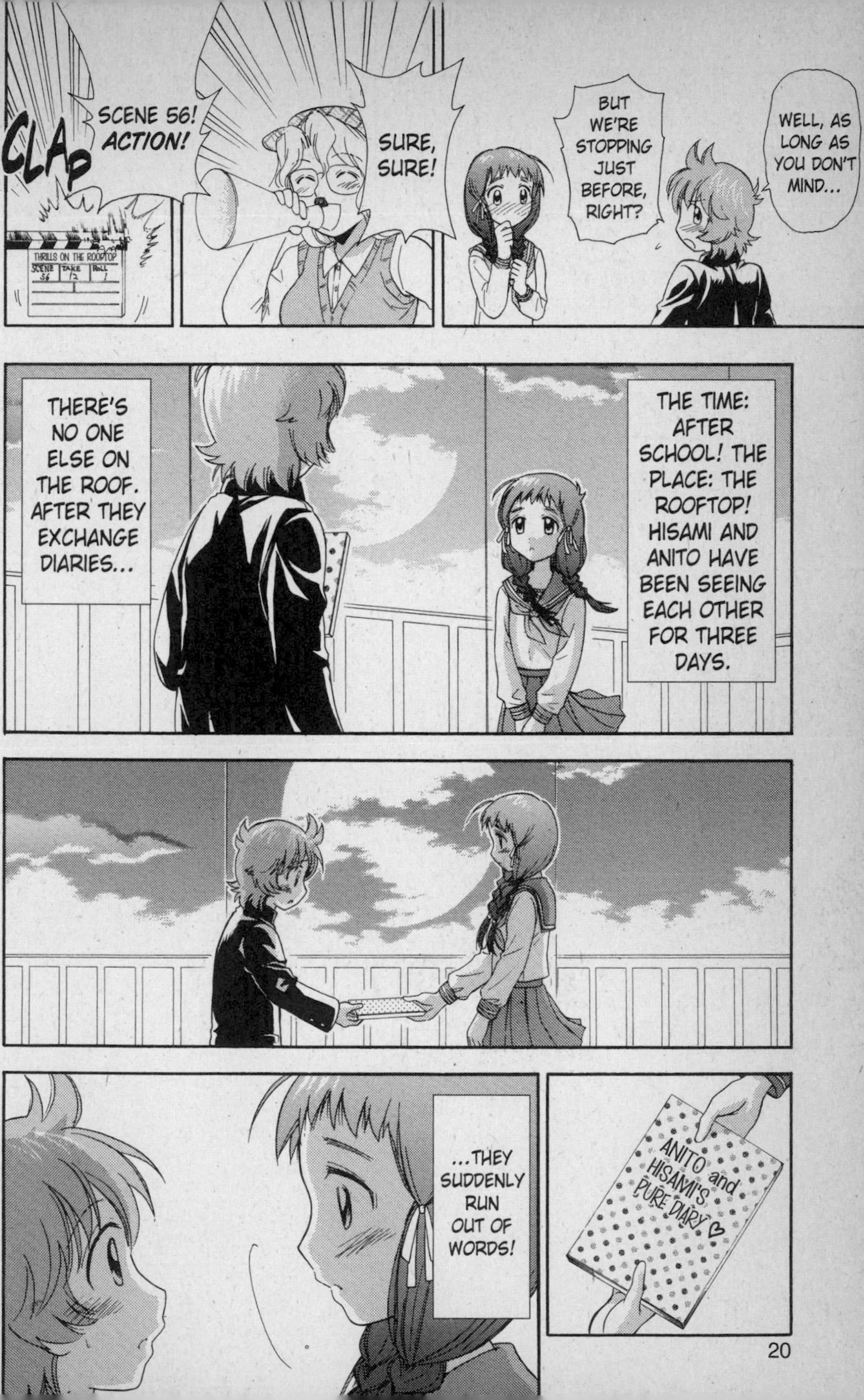
WELL, AS LONG AS YOU DON'T MIND...
BUT WE'RE STOPPING JUST BEFORE, RIGHT?
SURE, SURE!
SCENE 56! ACTION!
CLAP
THRILLS ON THE ROOFTOP
SCENE 56 TAKE 12 ROLL 1
THE TIME: AFTER SCHOOL! THE PLACE: THE ROOFTOP! HISAMI AND ANITO HAVE BEEN SEEING EACH OTHER FOR THREE DAYS.
THERE'S NO ONE ELSE ON THE ROOF. AFTER THEY EXCHANGE DIARIES...
ANITO and HISAMI'S PURE DIARY
...THEY SUDDENLY RUN OUT OF WORDS!

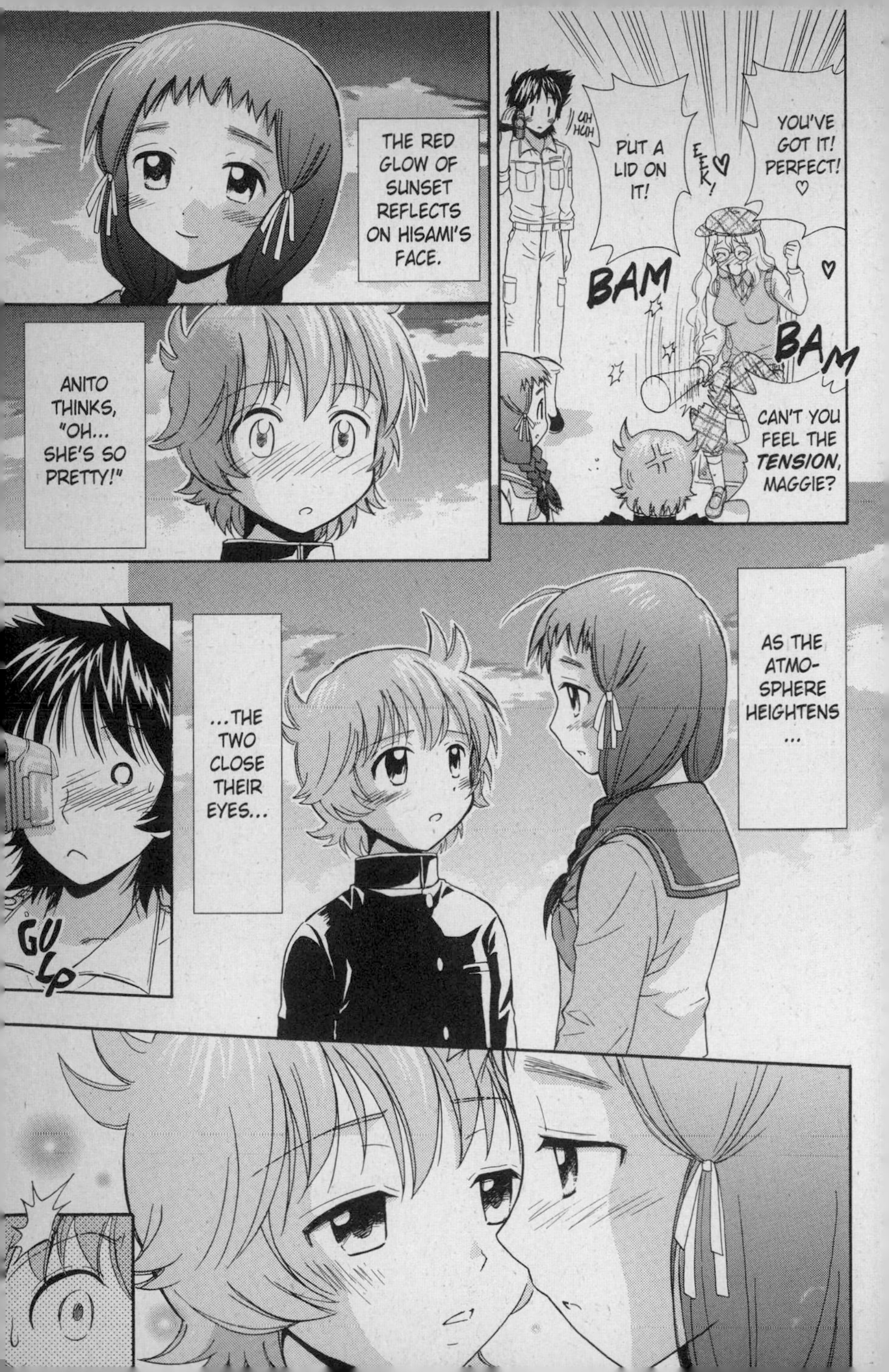
YOU'VE GOT IT! PERFECT! ♡
EEK! ♡
PUT A LID ON IT!
UH HUH
♡
BAM
BAM
CAN'T YOU FEEL THE TENSION, MAGGIE?
THE RED GLOW OF SUNSET REFLECTS ON HISAMI'S FACE.
ANITO THINKS, "OH... SHE'S SO PRETTY!"
AS THE ATMO-SPHERE HEIGHTENS ...
...THE TWO CLOSE THEIR EYES...
GULP

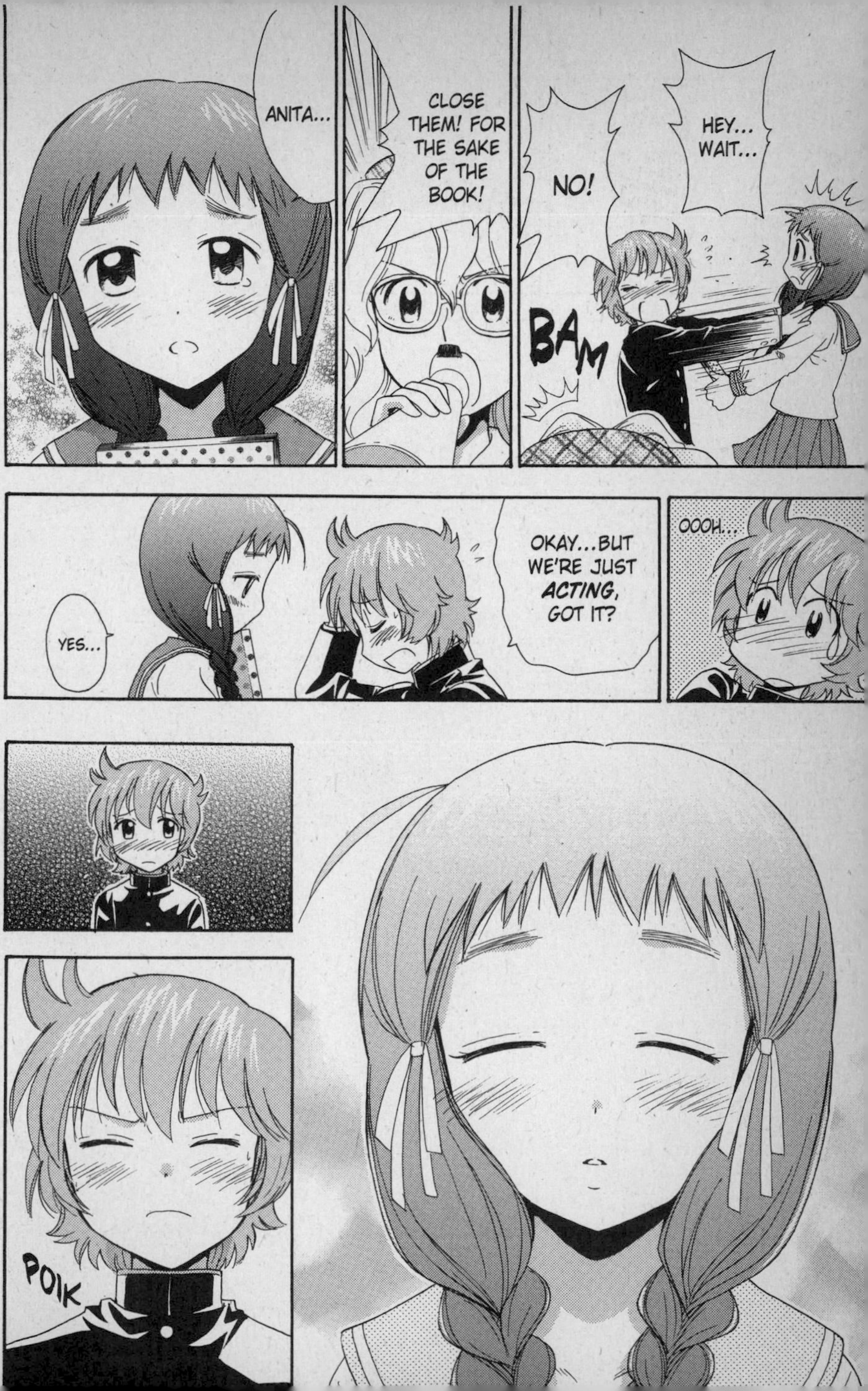
HEY... WAIT...
NO!
BAM
CLOSE THEM! FOR THE SAKE OF THE BOOK!
ANITA...
OOOH...
OKAY...BUT WE'RE JUST ACTING, GOT IT?
YES...
POIK

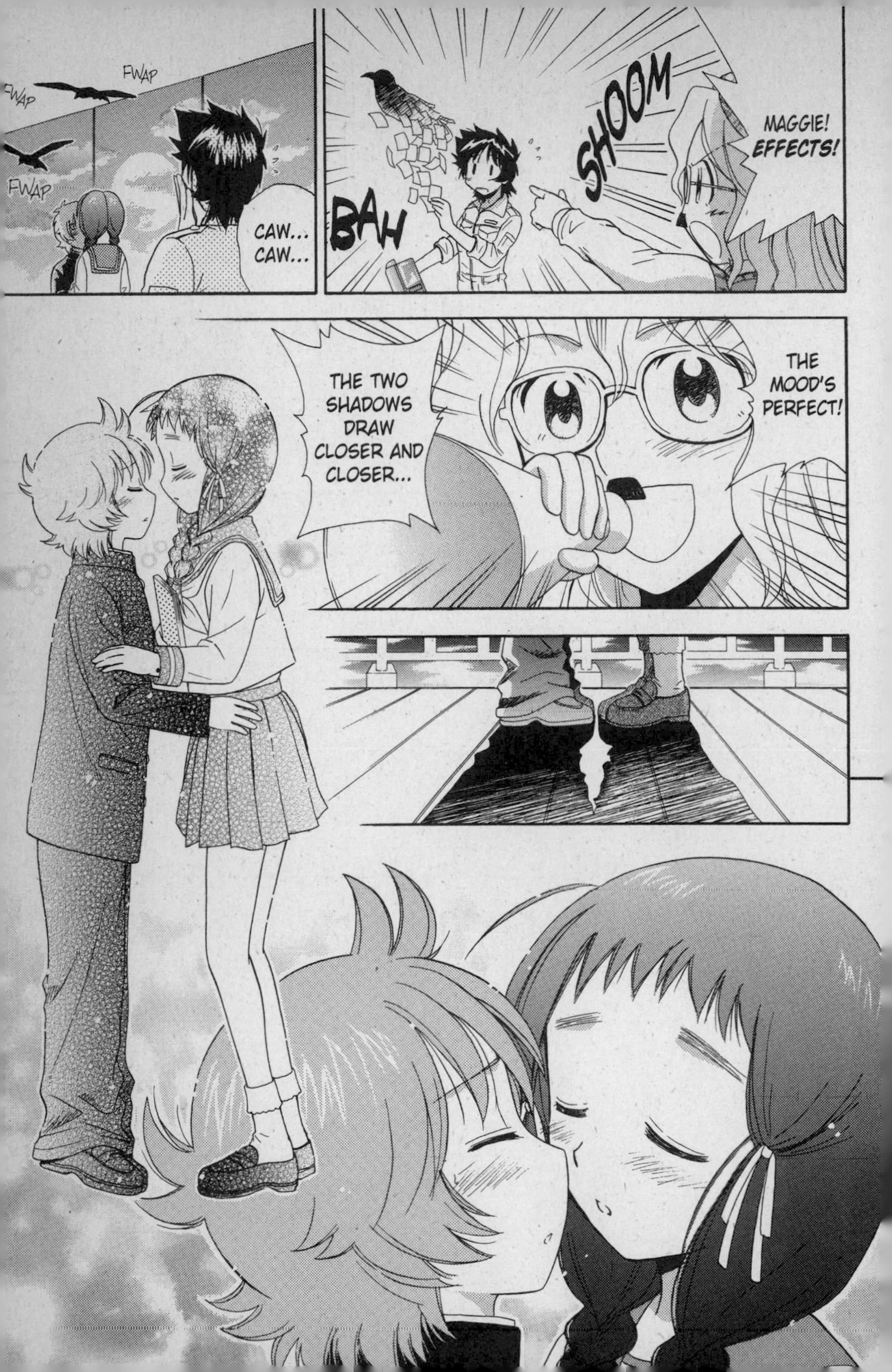
MAGGIE! EFFECTS!
SHOOM
BAH
FWAP
FWAP
FWAP
CAW... CAW...
THE MOOD'S PERFECT!
THE TWO SHADOWS DRAW CLOSER AND CLOSER...

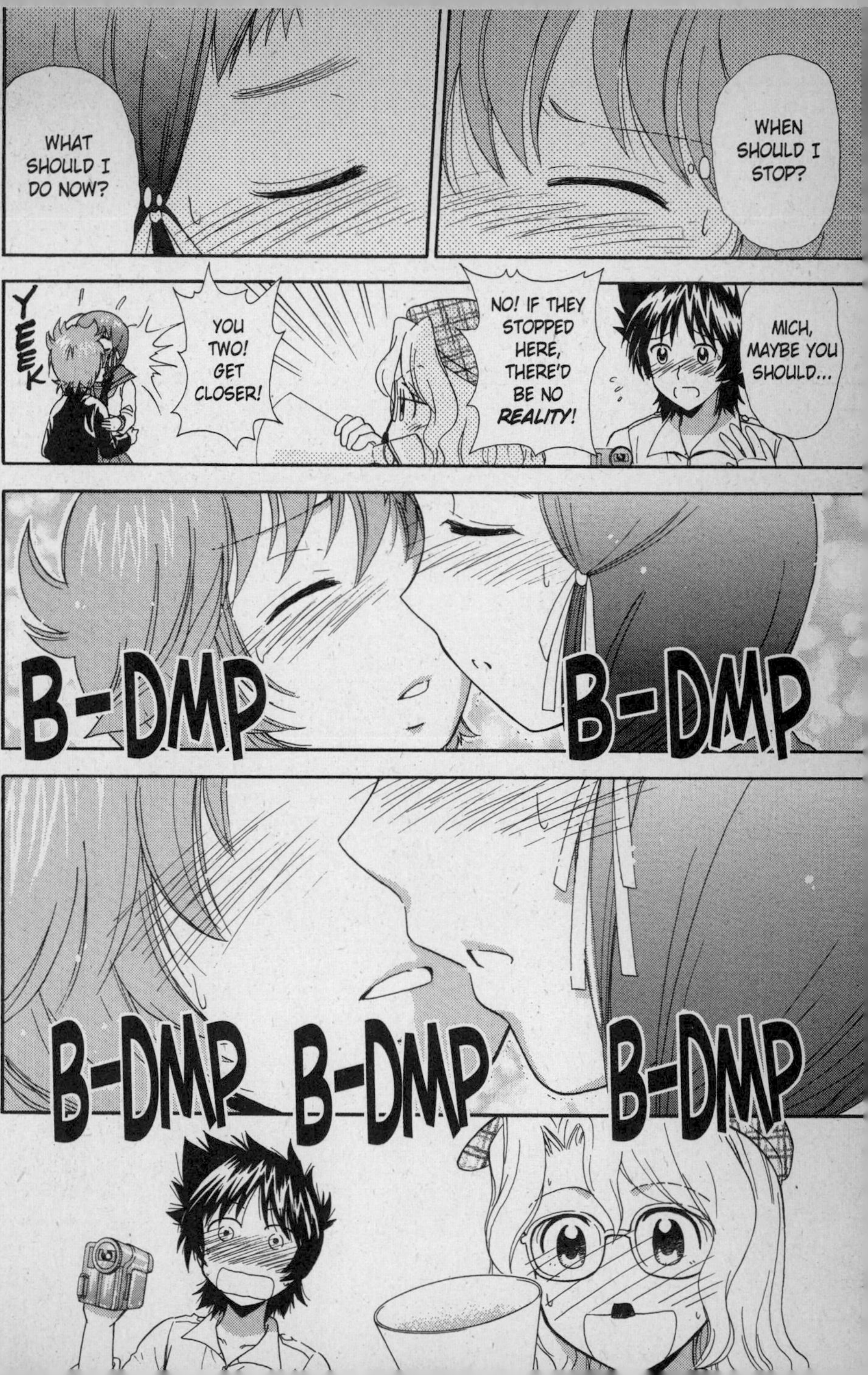
WHEN SHOULD I STOP?
WHAT SHOULD I DO NOW?
MICH, MAYBE YOU SHOULD...
NO! IF THEY STOPPED HERE, THERE'D BE NO *REALITY*!
YOU TWO! GET CLOSER!
YEEK
B-DMP
B-DMP
B-DMP
B-DMP
B-DMP

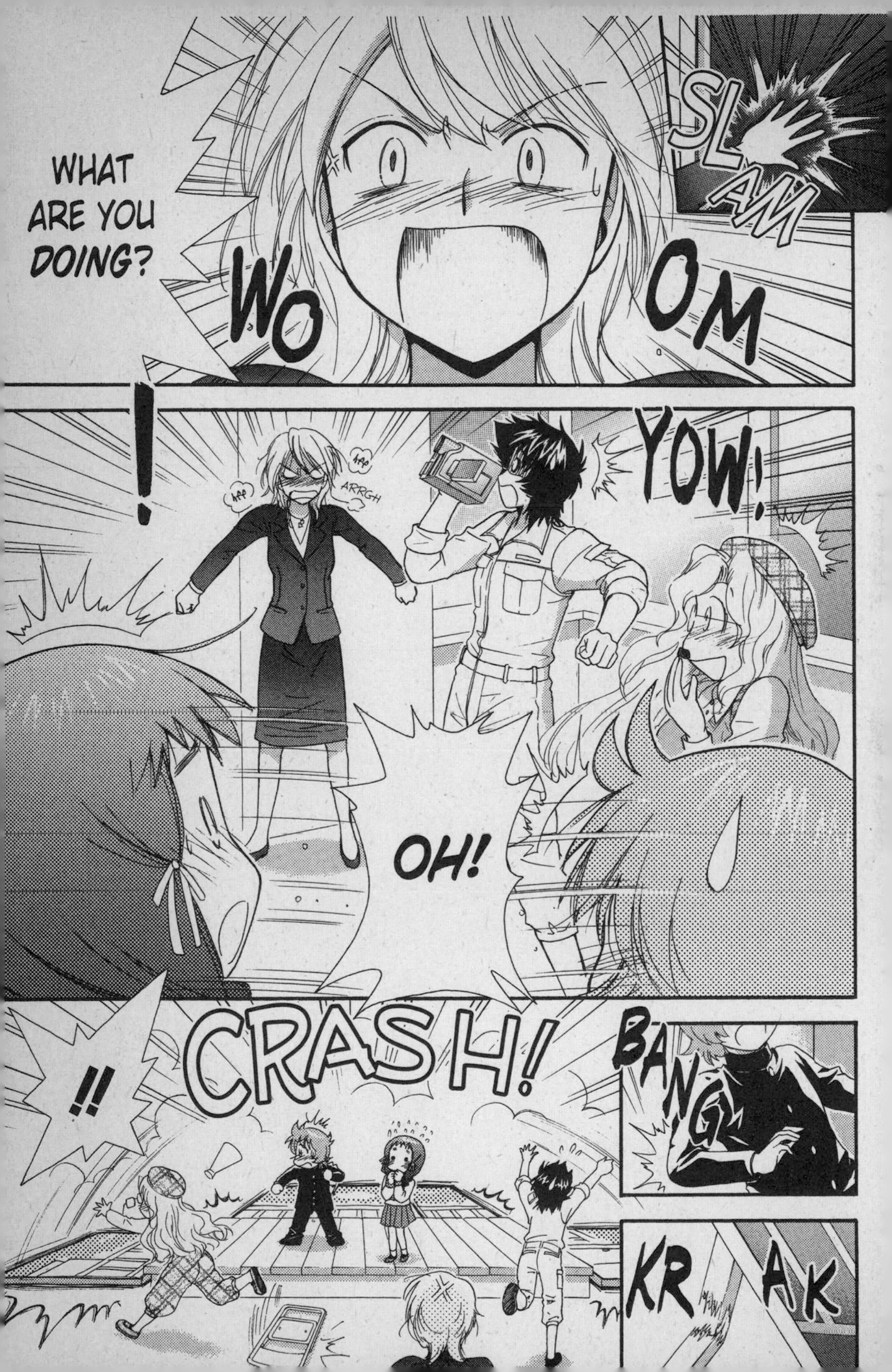
SLAM
WO OM
WHAT ARE YOU DOING?
YOW!
hff
ARRGH
hff
!
OH!
BANG
KRAK
CRASH!
!!

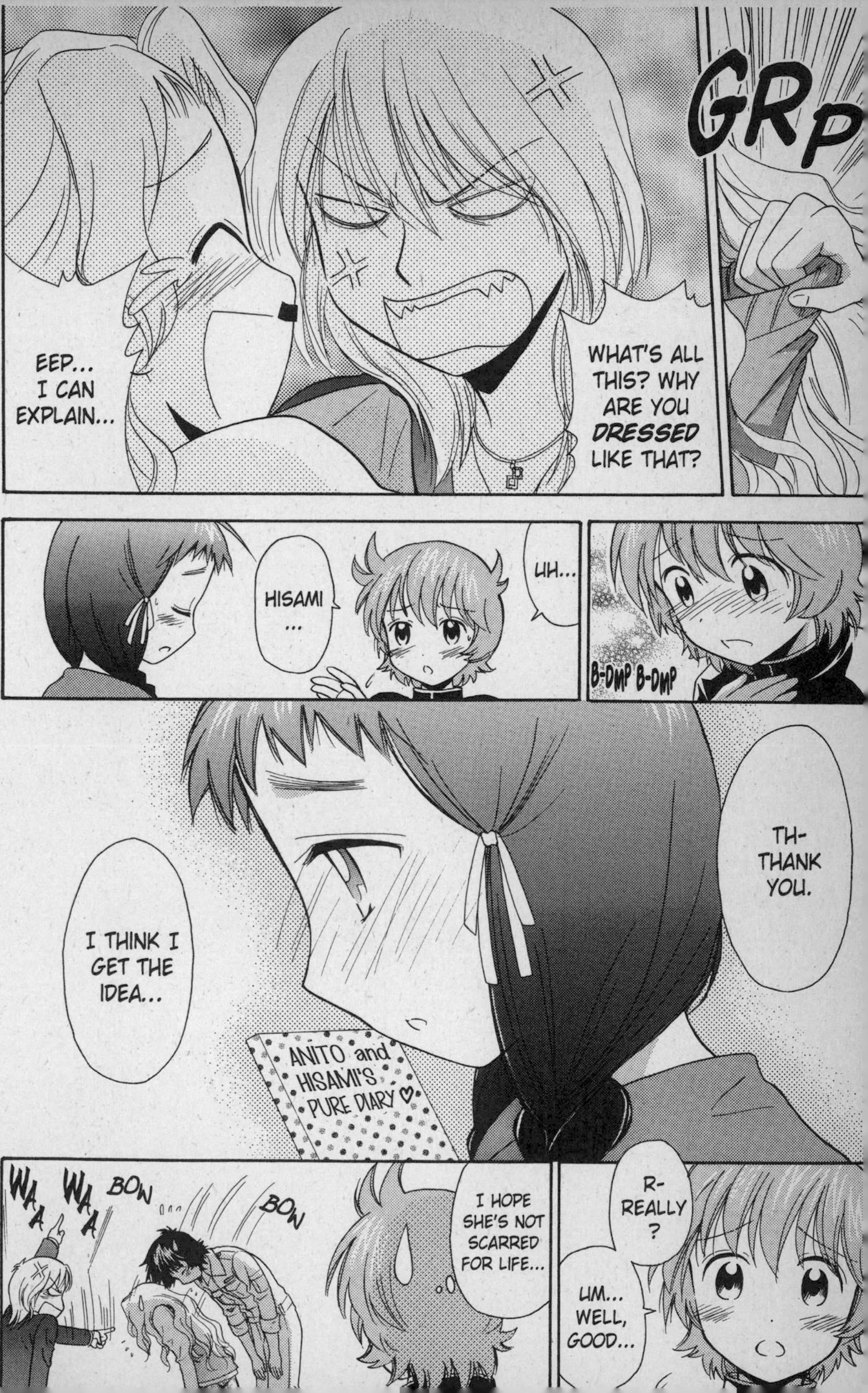
GRP
WHAT'S ALL THIS? WHY ARE YOU DRESSED LIKE THAT?
EEP... I CAN EXPLAIN...
B-DMP B-DMP
UH...
HISAMI ...
TH- THANK YOU.
ANITO and HISAMI'S PURE DIARY ♡
I THINK I GET THE IDEA...
R- REALLY ?
UM... WELL, GOOD...
I HOPE SHE'S NOT SCARRED FOR LIFE...
BOW
BOW
WAA
WAA

CHAPTER 25

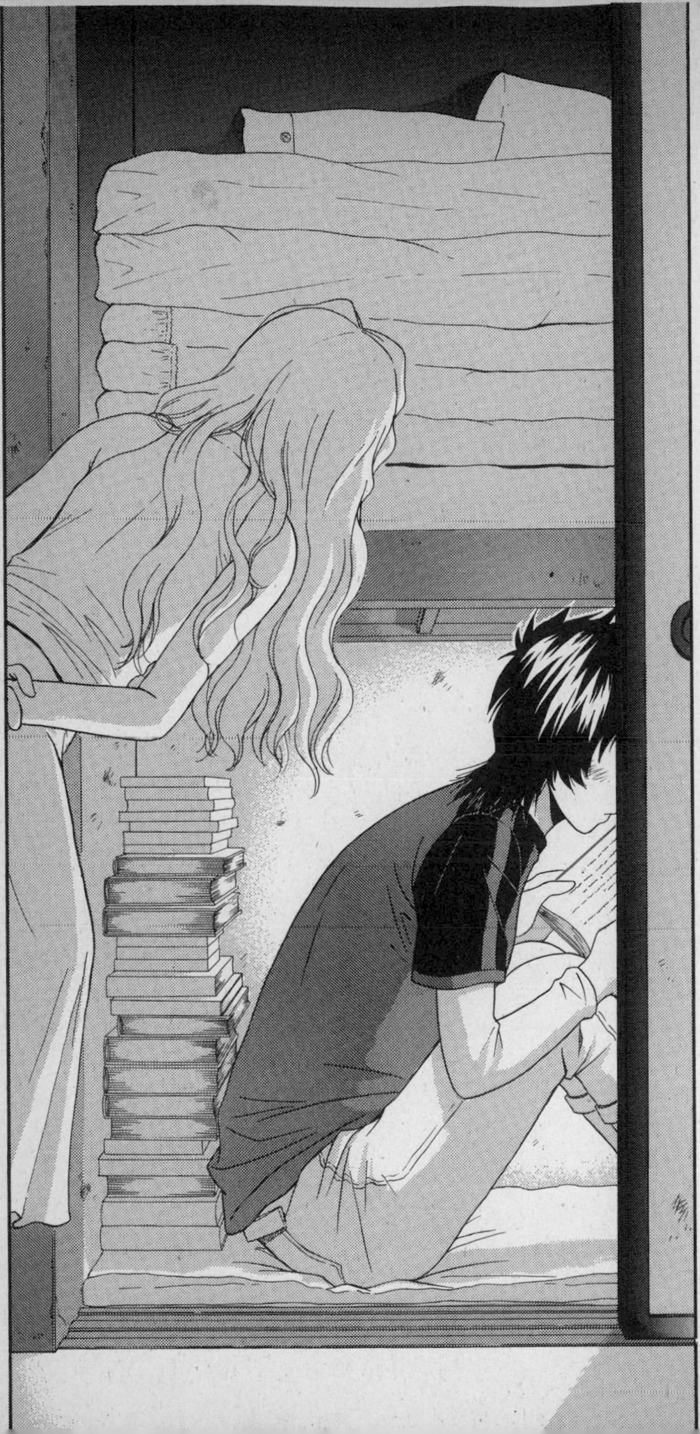

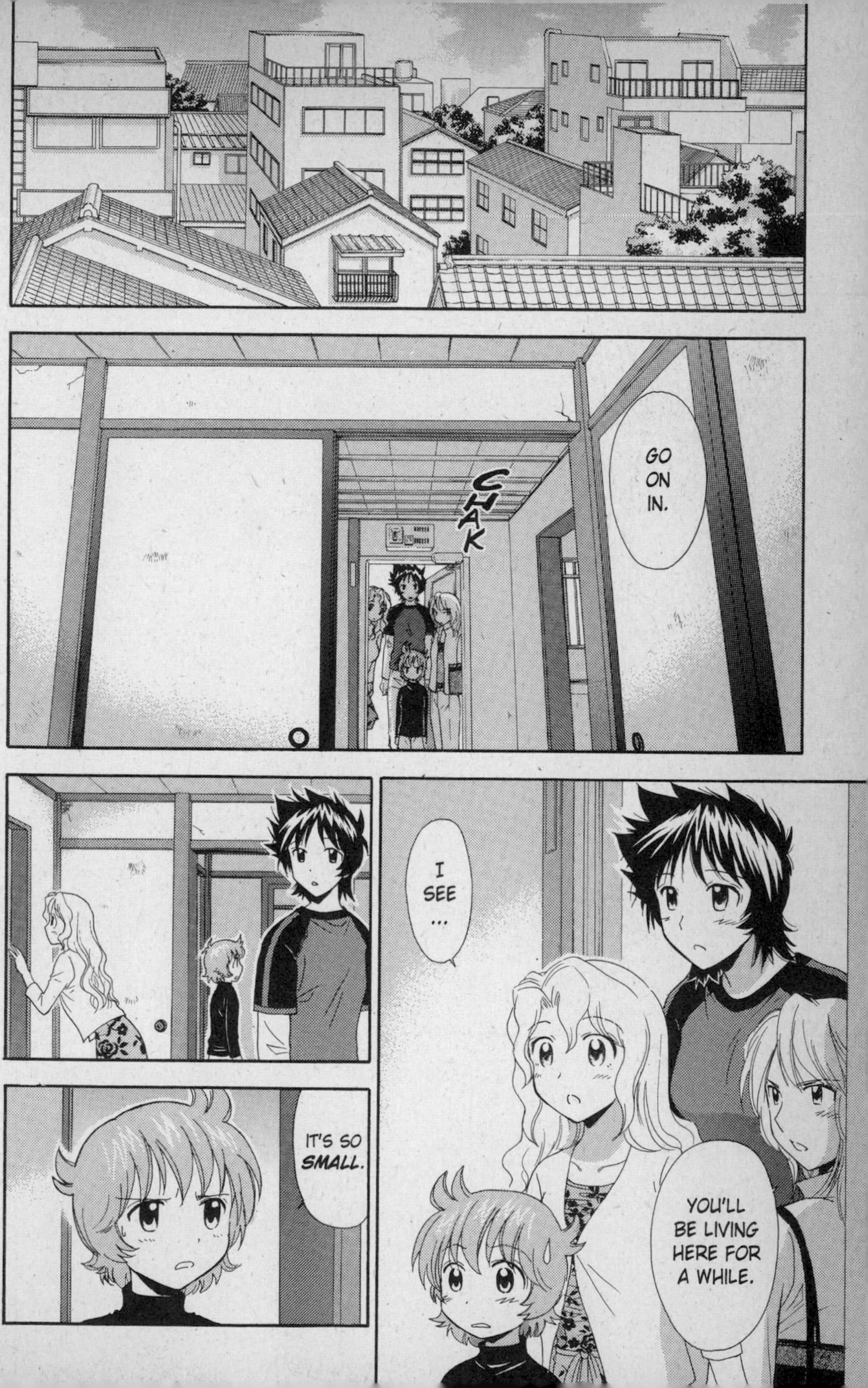
GO ON IN.
CHAK
I SEE ...
YOU'LL BE LIVING HERE FOR A WHILE.
IT'S SO SMALL.

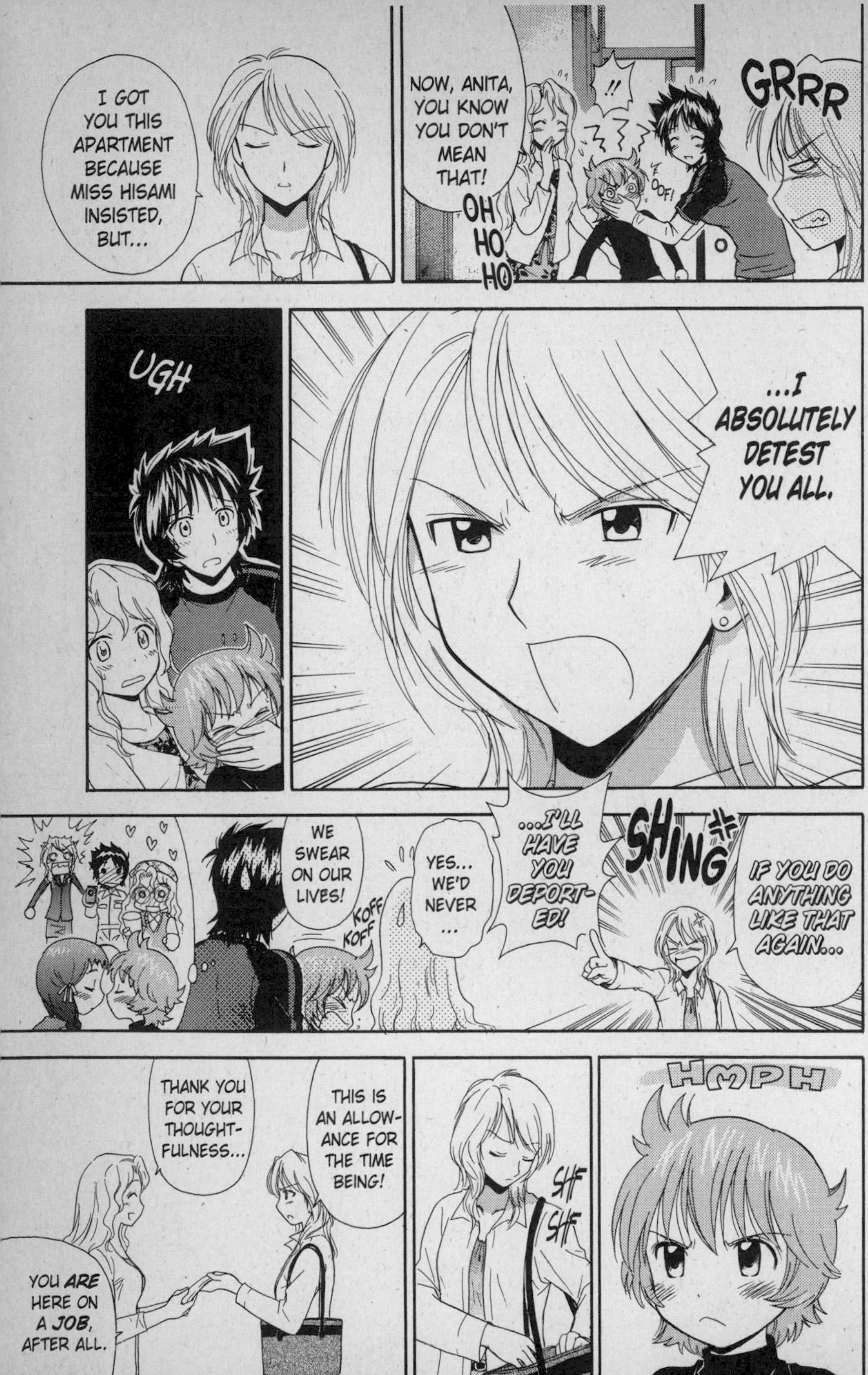
GRRR
NOW, ANITA, YOU KNOW YOU DON'T MEAN THAT!
OH HO HO
!!
OOF!
I GOT YOU THIS APARTMENT BECAUSE MISS HISAMI INSISTED, BUT...
...I ABSOLUTELY DETEST YOU ALL.
UGH
IF YOU DO ANYTHING LIKE THAT AGAIN...
SHING
...I'LL HAVE YOU DEPORT-ED!
YES... WE'D NEVER ...
KOFF KOFF
WE SWEAR ON OUR LIVES!
HMPH
SHF SHF
THIS IS AN ALLOW-ANCE FOR THE TIME BEING!
THANK YOU FOR YOUR THOUGHT-FULNESS...
YOU ARE HERE ON A JOB, AFTER ALL.

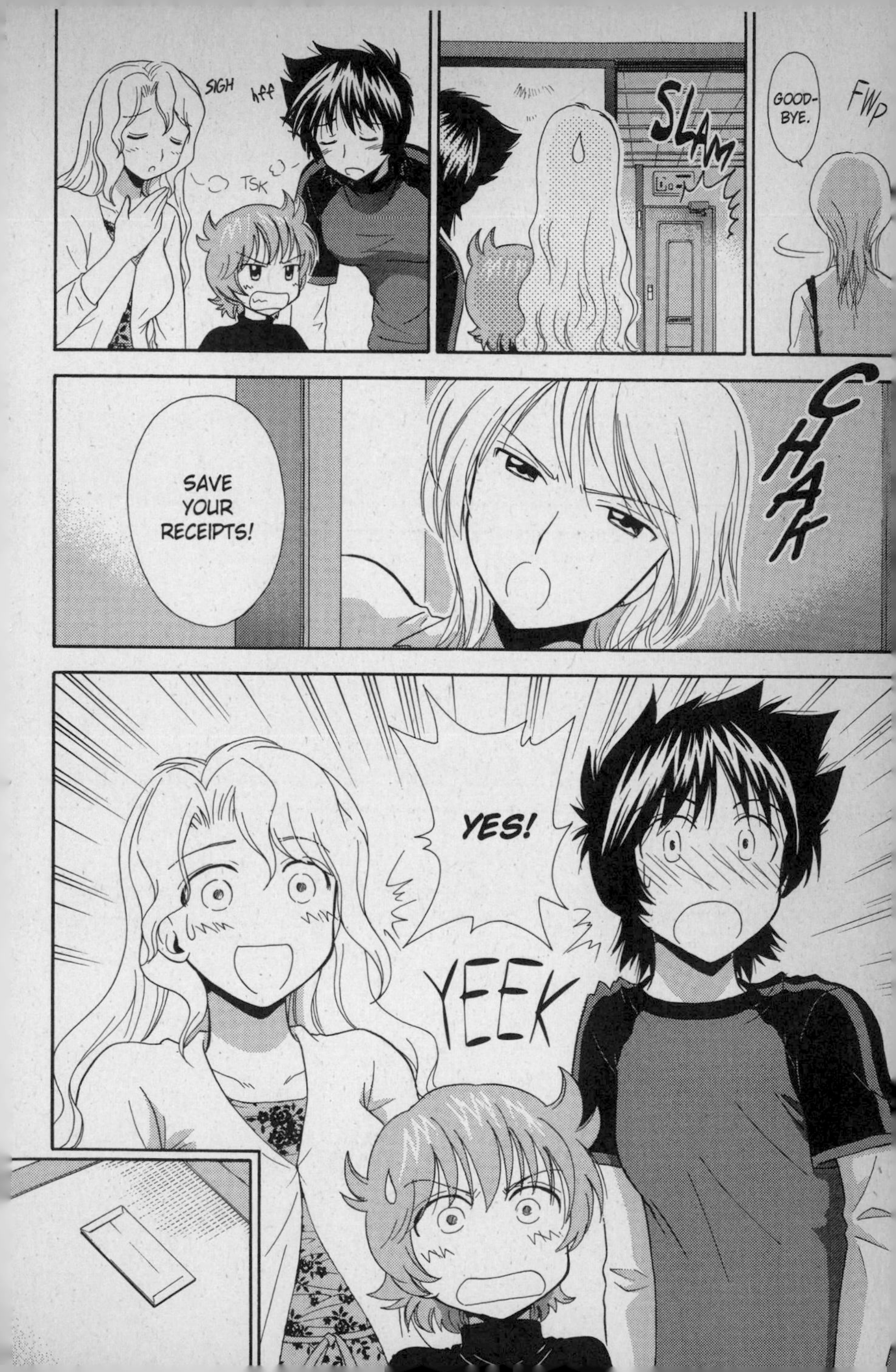
GOOD-BYE.
FWP
SLAM
SIGH
hff
TSK
CHAK
SAVE YOUR RECEIPTS!
YES!
YEEK

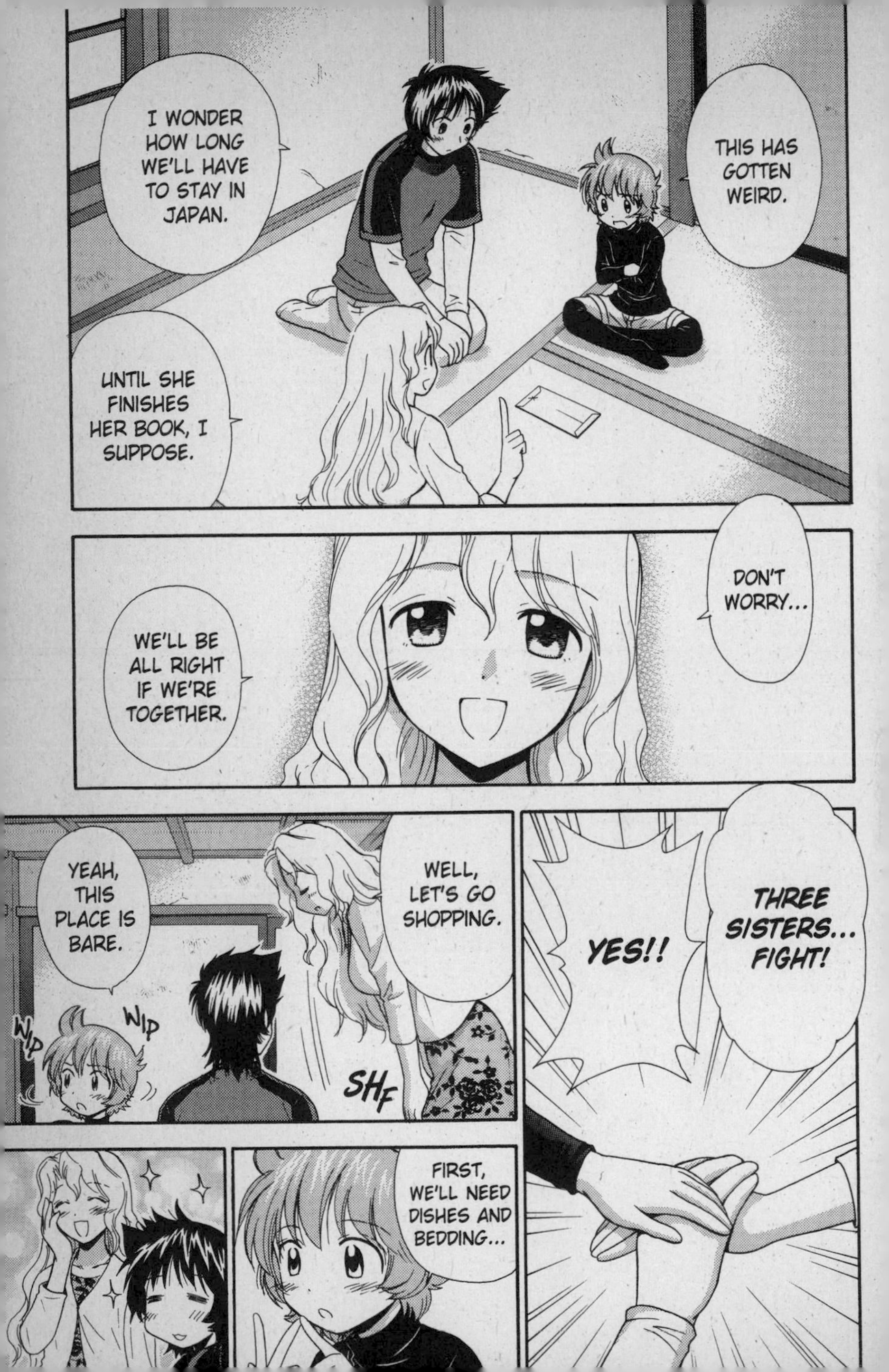
THIS HAS GOTTEN WEIRD.
I WONDER HOW LONG WE'LL HAVE TO STAY IN JAPAN.
UNTIL SHE FINISHES HER BOOK, I SUPPOSE.
DON'T WORRY...
WE'LL BE ALL RIGHT IF WE'RE TOGETHER.
THREE SISTERS... FIGHT!
YES!!
WELL, LET'S GO SHOPPING.
YEAH, THIS PLACE IS BARE.
SHF
WIP
WIP
FIRST, WE'LL NEED DISHES AND BEDDING...

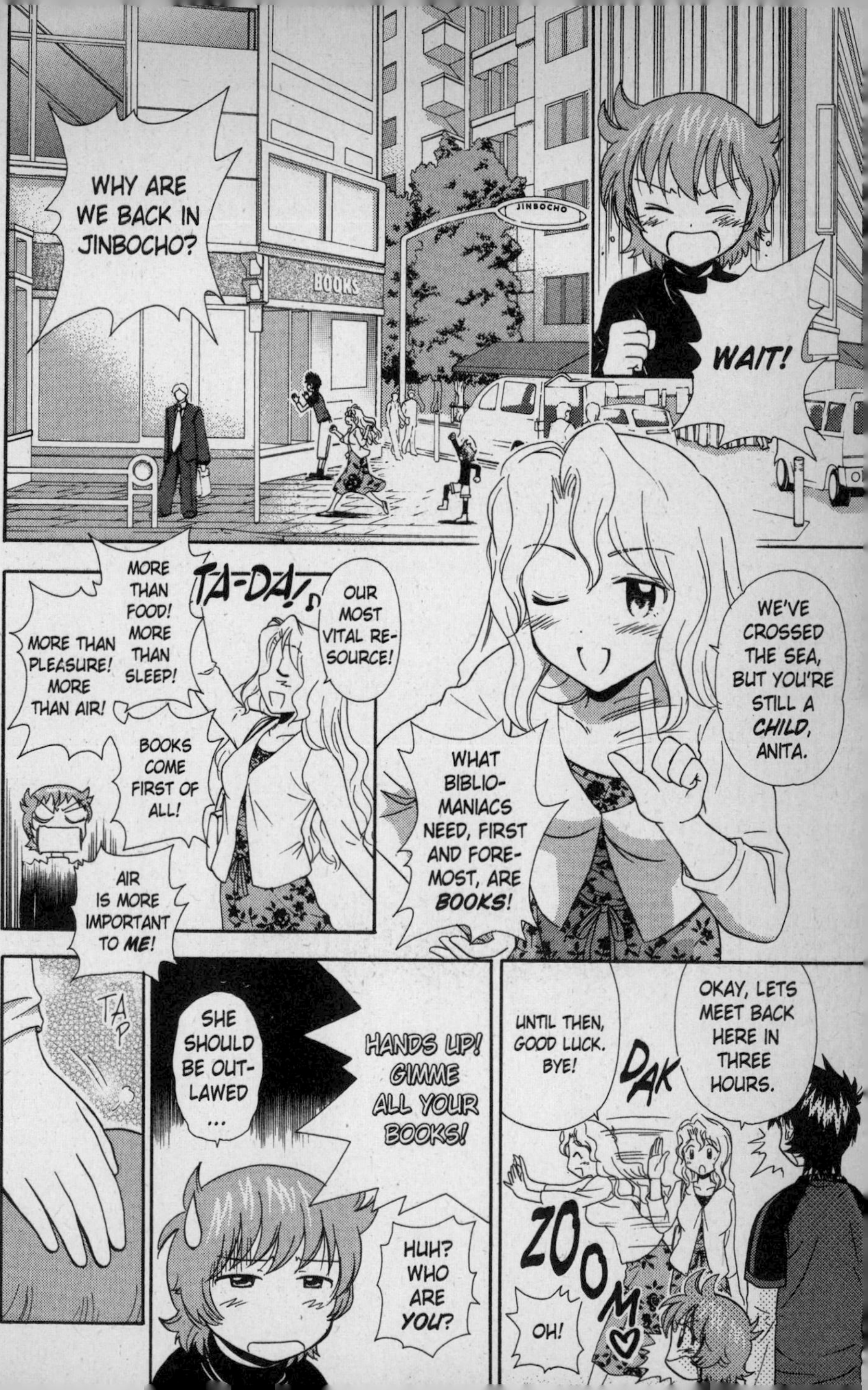

WAIT!
WHY ARE WE BACK IN JINBOCHO?
JINBOCHO
BOOKS
WE'VE CROSSED THE SEA, BUT YOU'RE STILL A *CHILD*, ANITA.
WHAT BIBLIO-MANIACS NEED, FIRST AND FORE-MOST, ARE *BOOKS*!
OUR MOST VITAL RE-SOURCE!
TA-DA!
MORE THAN FOOD! MORE THAN SLEEP!
MORE THAN PLEASURE! MORE THAN AIR!
BOOKS COME FIRST OF ALL!
AIR IS MORE IMPORTANT TO *ME*!
OKAY, LETS MEET BACK HERE IN THREE HOURS.
DAK
UNTIL THEN, GOOD LUCK. BYE!
ZOOM
OH!
HANDS UP! GIMME ALL YOUR BOOKS!
SHE SHOULD BE OUT-LAWED ...
HUH? WHO ARE *YOU*?
TAP

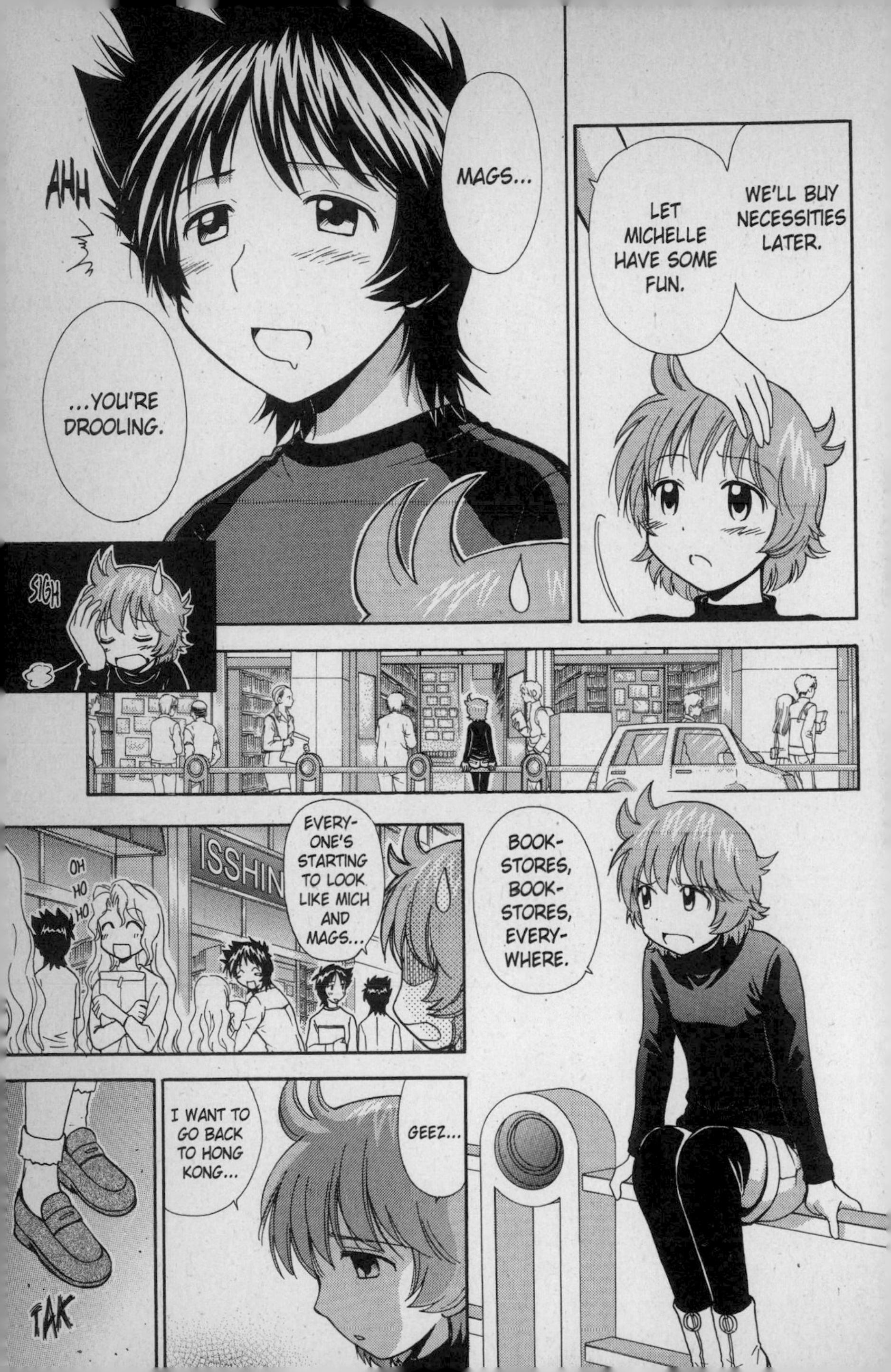
WE'LL BUY NECESSITIES LATER.
LET MICHELLE HAVE SOME FUN.
MAGS...
AHH
...YOU'RE DROOLING.
SIGH
BOOK-STORES, BOOK-STORES, EVERY-WHERE.
EVERY-ONE'S STARTING TO LOOK LIKE MICH AND MAGS...
ISSHIN
OH HO HO
GEEZ...
I WANT TO GO BACK TO HONG KONG...
TAK

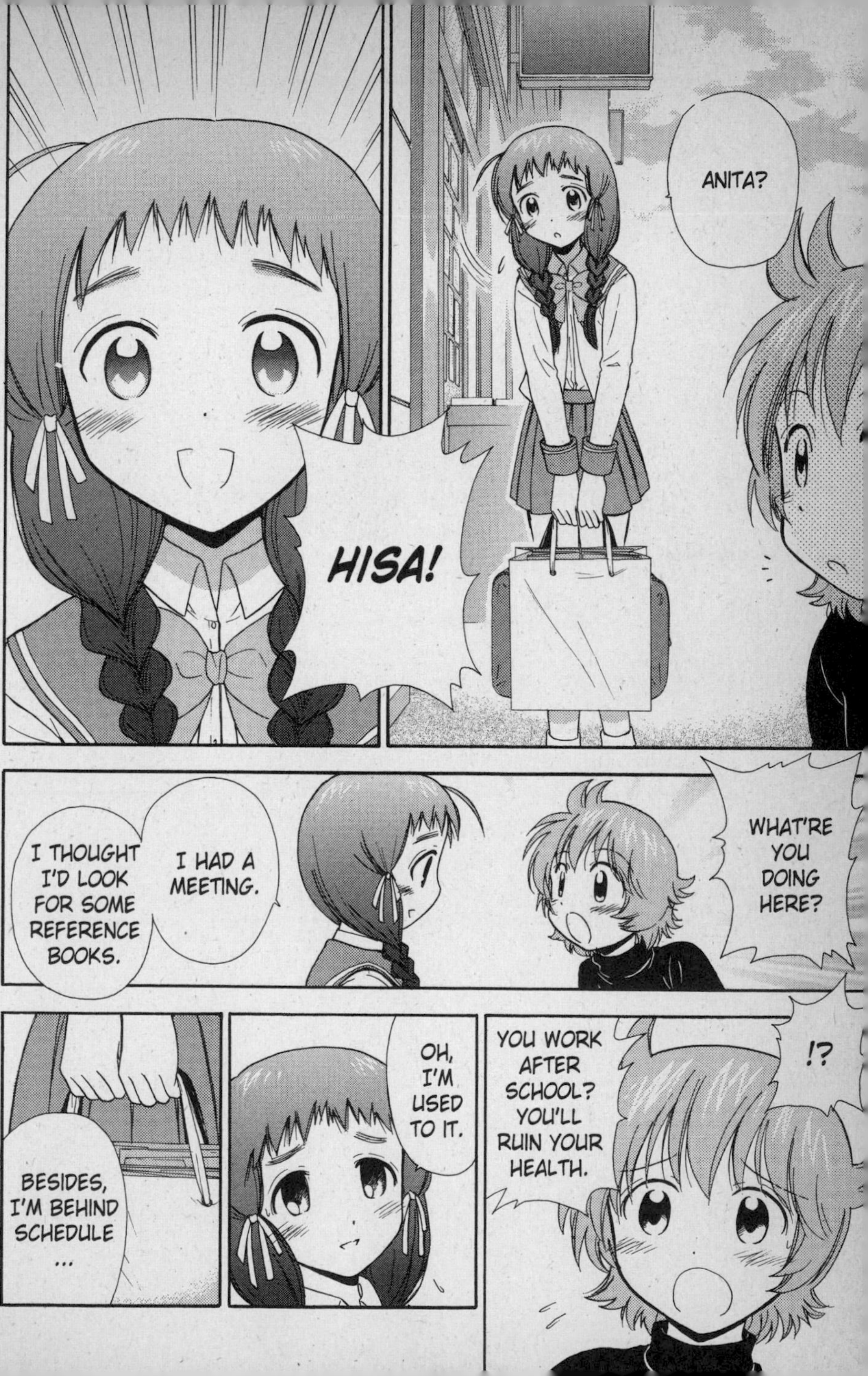
ANITA?
HISA!
WHAT'RE YOU DOING HERE?
I HAD A MEETING.
I THOUGHT I'D LOOK FOR SOME REFERENCE BOOKS.
!?
YOU WORK AFTER SCHOOL? YOU'LL RUIN YOUR HEALTH.
OH, I'M USED TO IT.
BESIDES, I'M BEHIND SCHEDULE ...

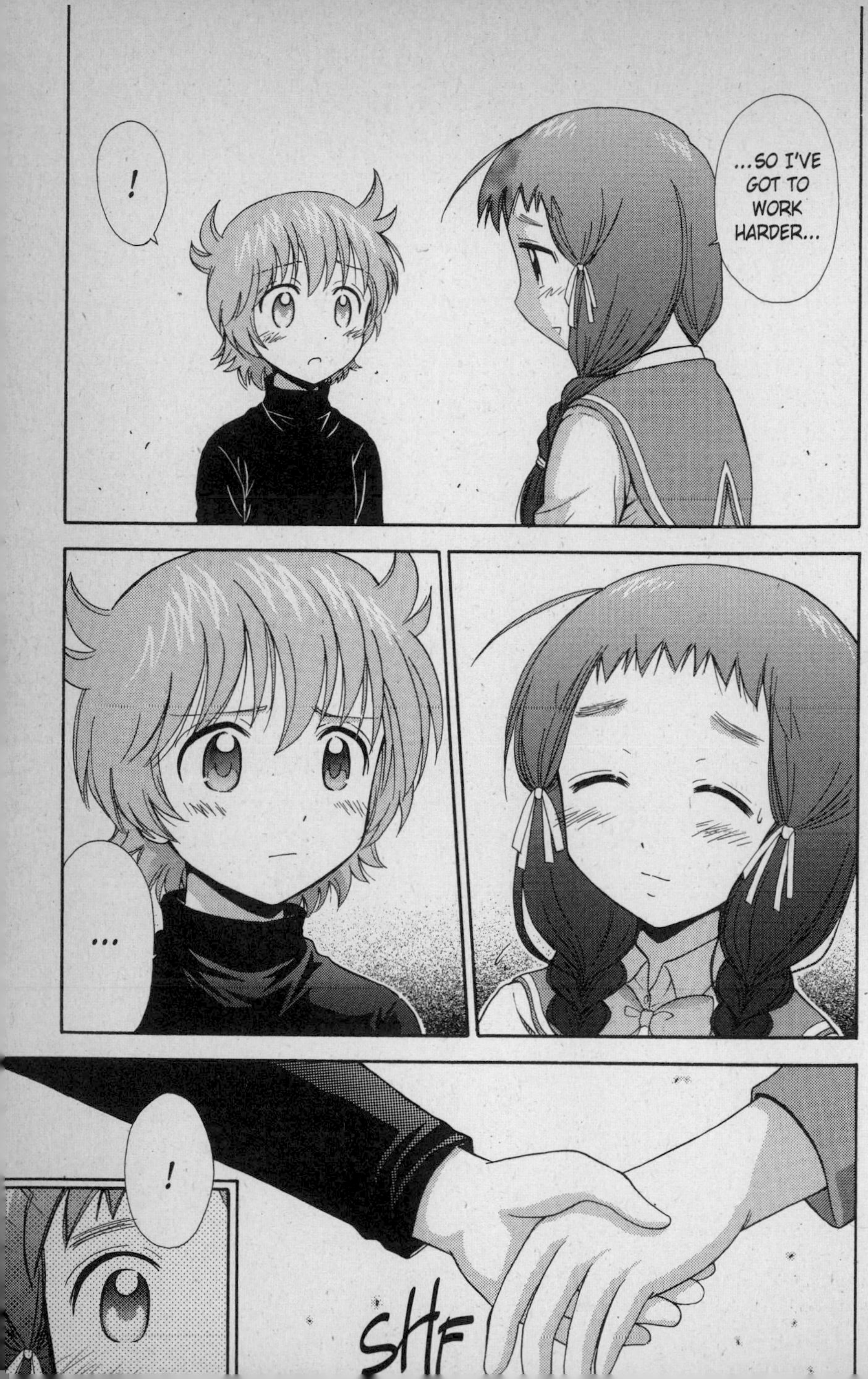

...SO I'VE GOT TO WORK HARDER...
!
...
!
SHF

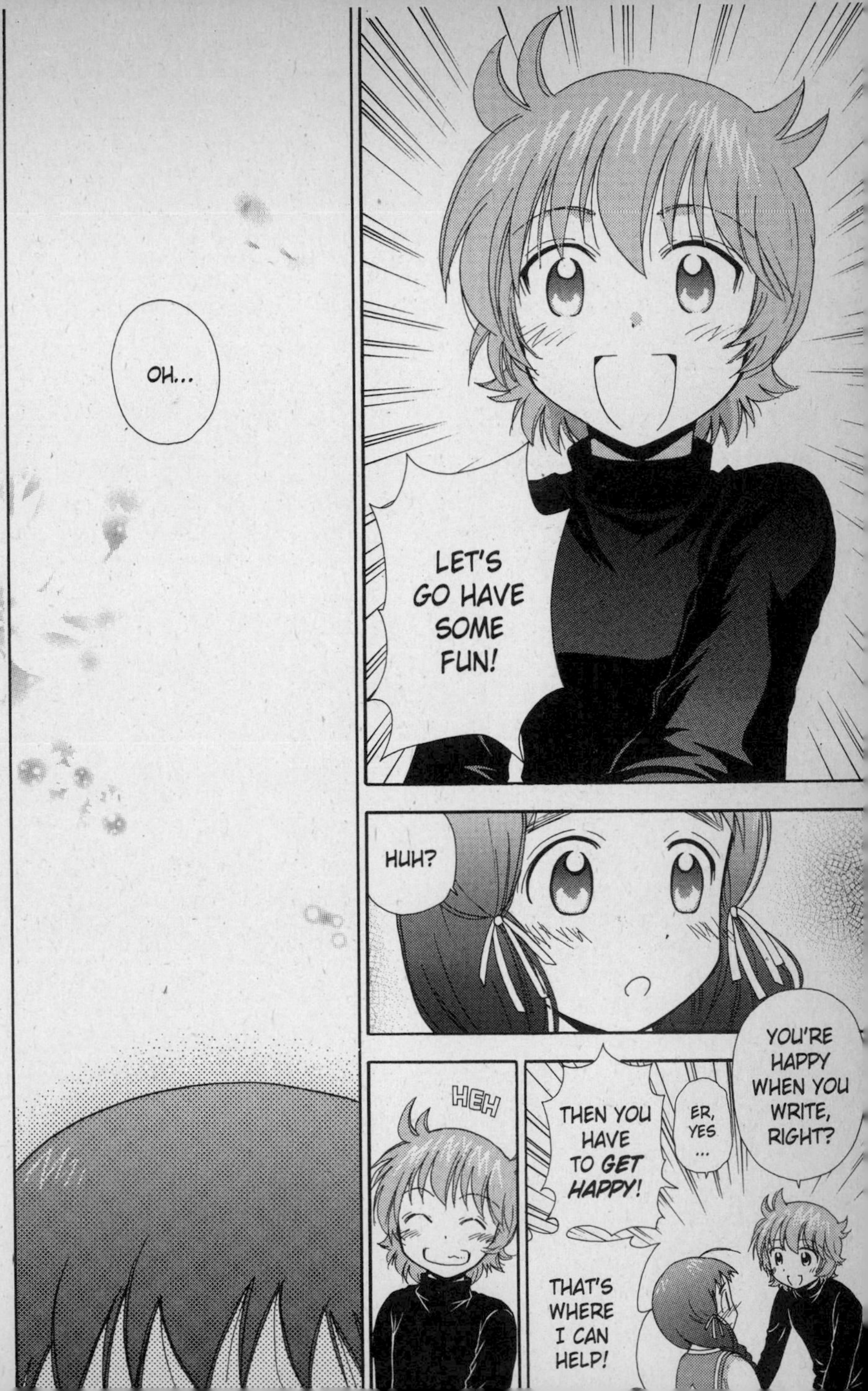
LET'S GO HAVE SOME FUN!
HUH?
YOU'RE HAPPY WHEN YOU WRITE, RIGHT?
ER, YES...
THEN YOU HAVE TO GET HAPPY!
THAT'S WHERE I CAN HELP!
HEH
OH...

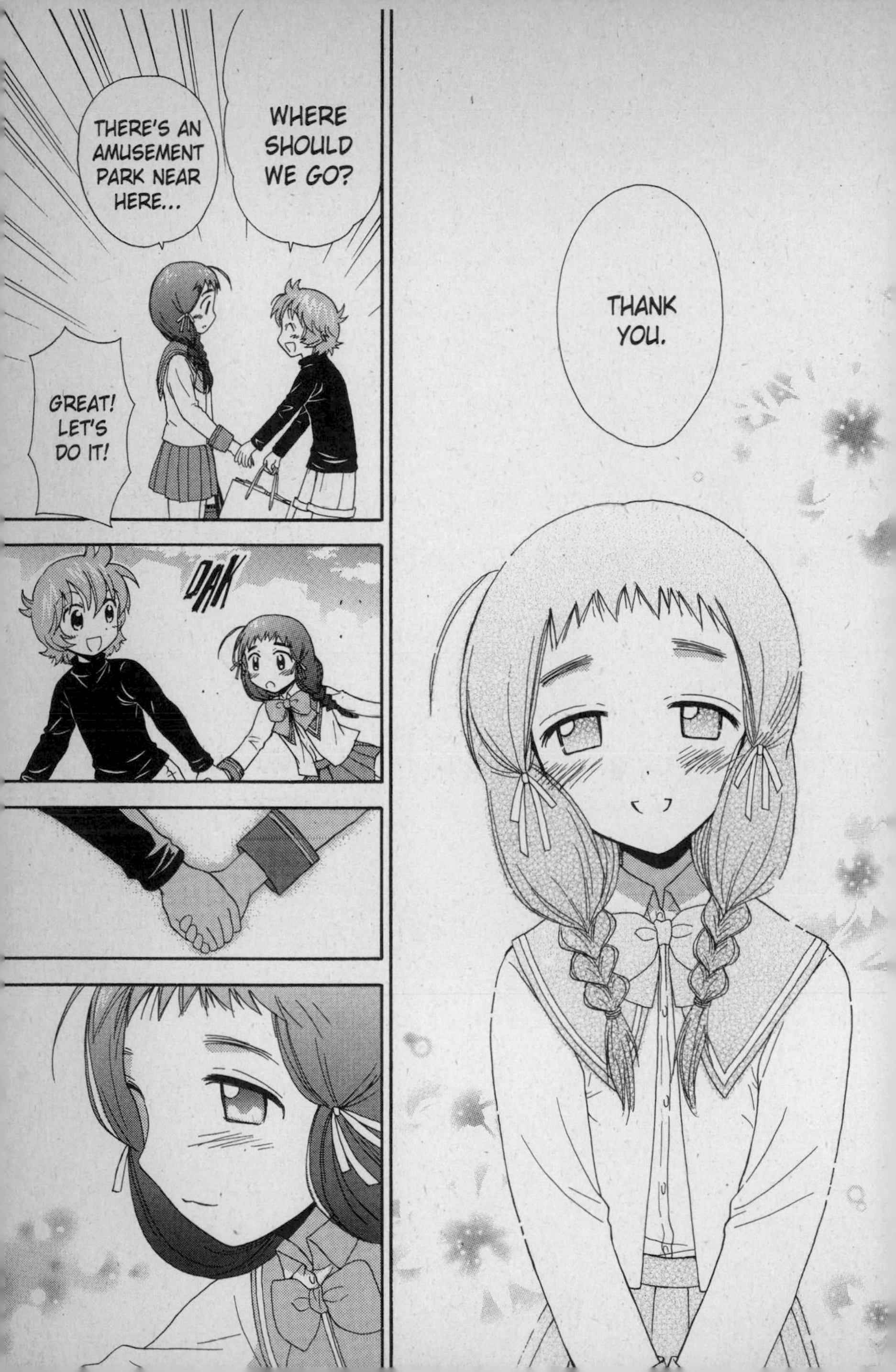
THANK YOU.
WHERE SHOULD WE GO?
THERE'S AN AMUSEMENT PARK NEAR HERE...
GREAT! LET'S DO IT!
DAK

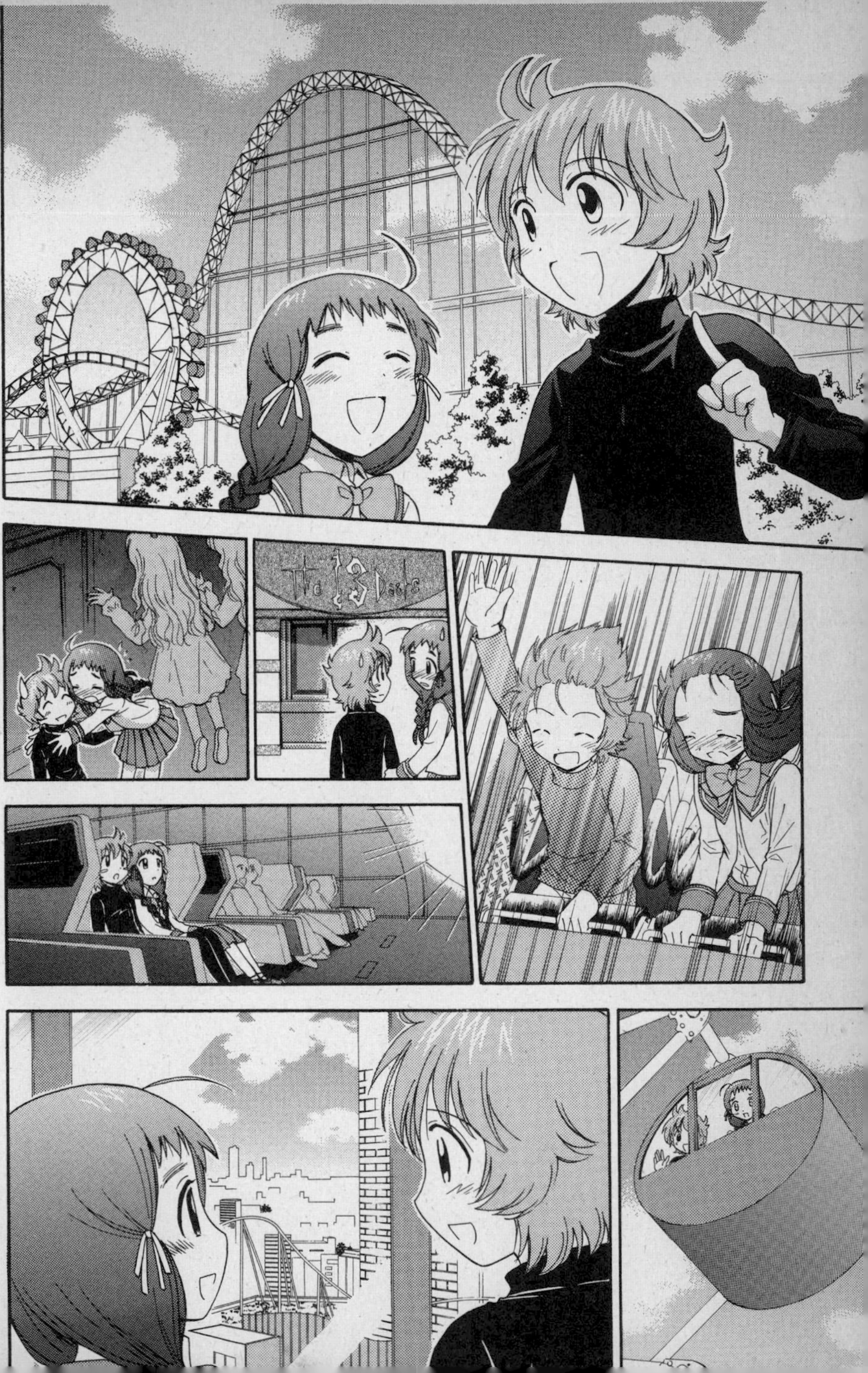
The 13 Doors

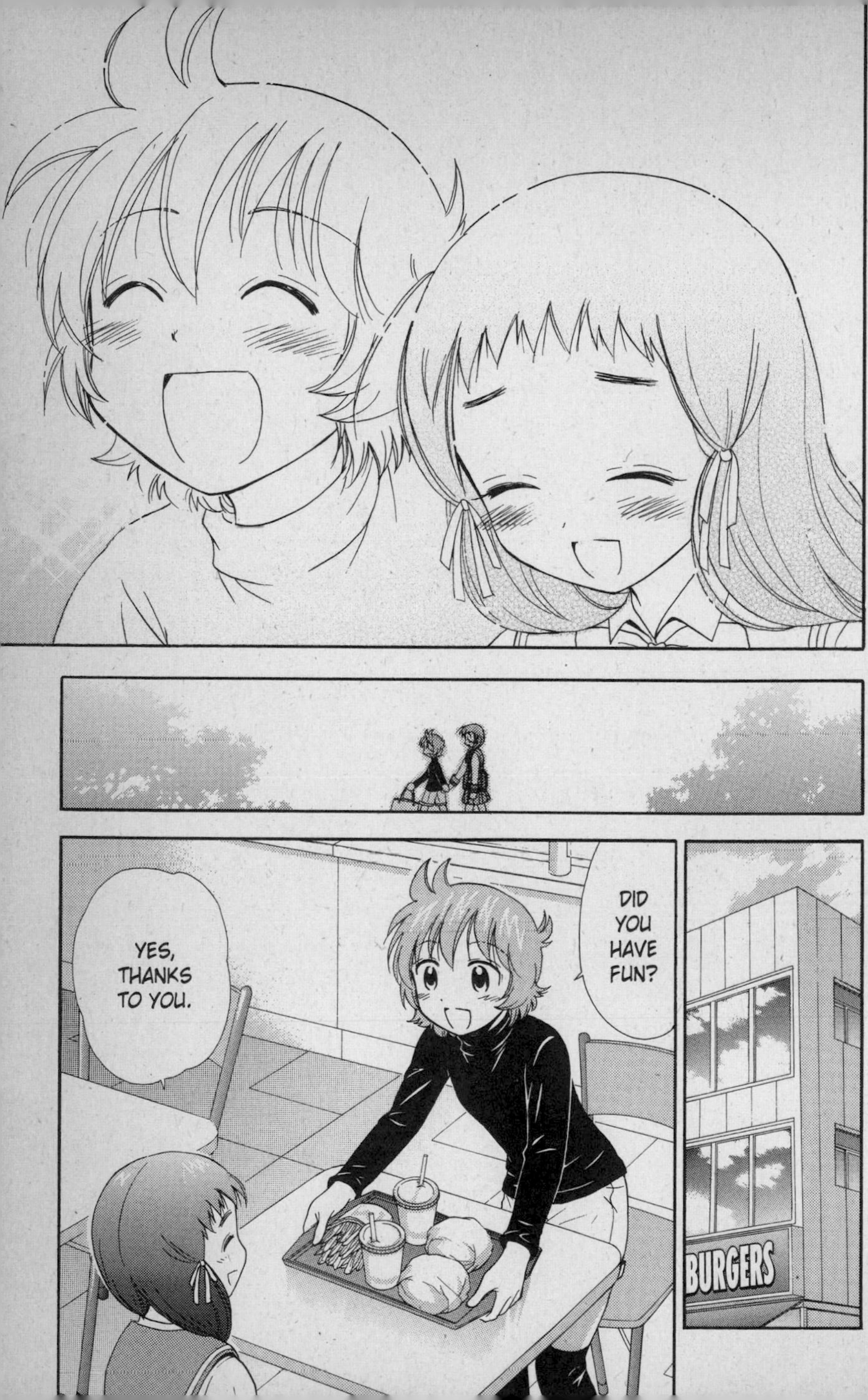
BURGERS
DID YOU HAVE FUN?
YES, THANKS TO YOU.

I'M SORRY...

...

FOR WHAT?

HUH?

OH... THAT'S OKAY.

FOR FORCING YOU TO STAY HERE...

...

BESIDES, IT'S WORK.

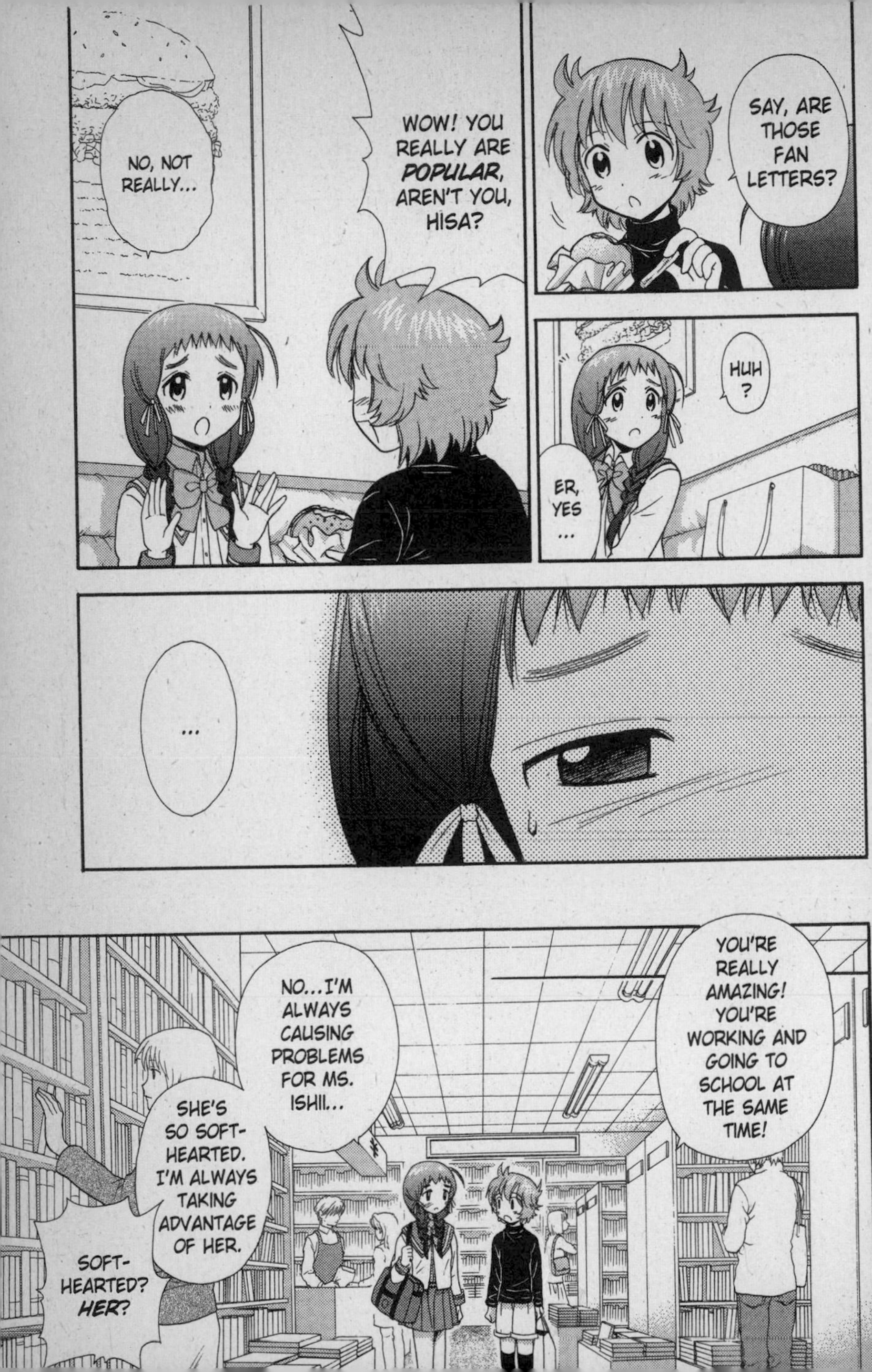
SAY, ARE THOSE FAN LETTERS?
HUH?
ER, YES...
WOW! YOU REALLY ARE *POPULAR*, AREN'T YOU, HISA?
NO, NOT REALLY...
...
YOU'RE REALLY AMAZING! YOU'RE WORKING AND GOING TO SCHOOL AT THE SAME TIME!
NO...I'M ALWAYS CAUSING PROBLEMS FOR MS. ISHII...
SHE'S SO SOFT-HEARTED. I'M ALWAYS TAKING ADVANTAGE OF HER.
SOFT-HEARTED? *HER*?

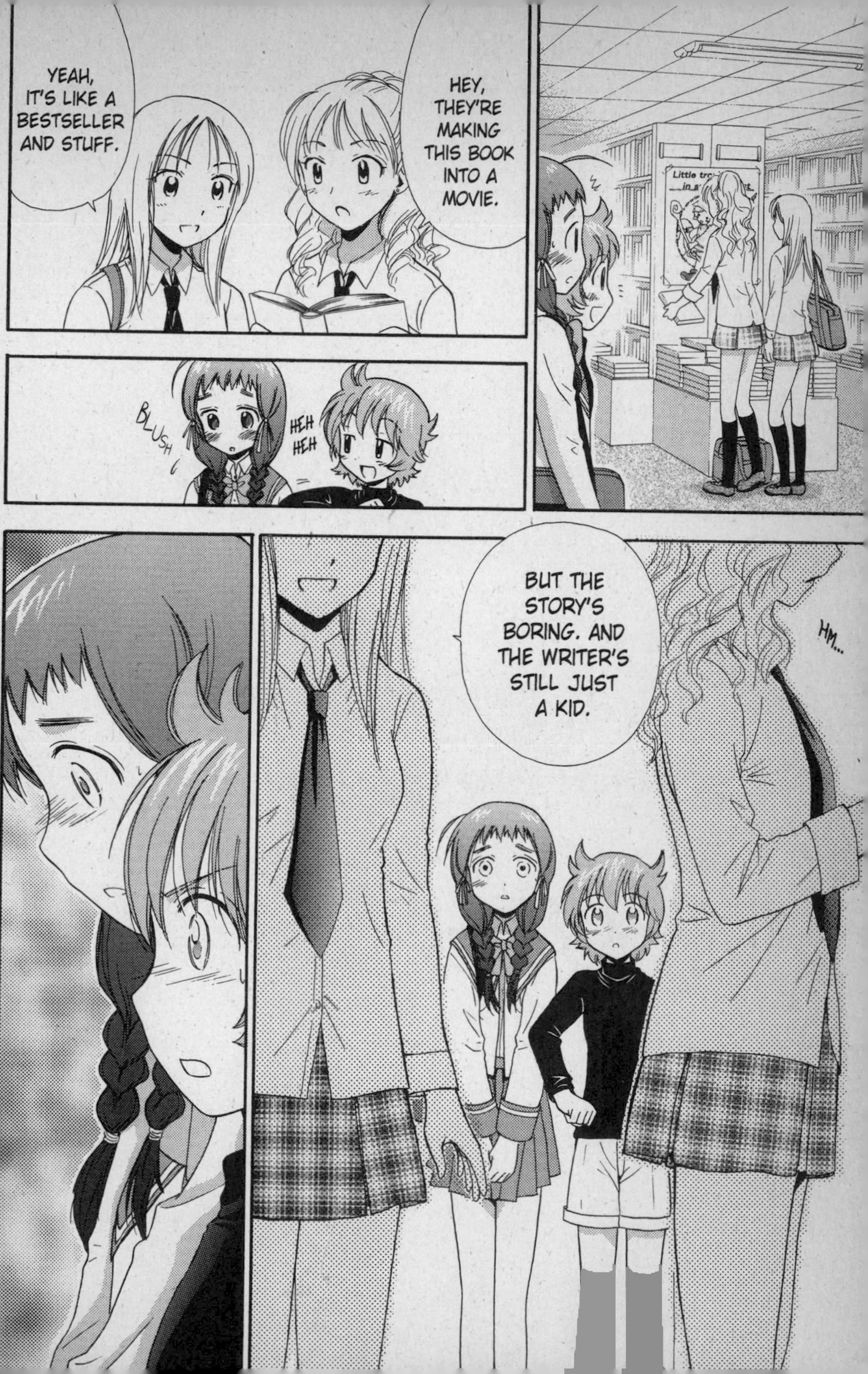
HEY, THEY'RE MAKING THIS BOOK INTO A MOVIE.
YEAH, IT'S LIKE A BESTSELLER AND STUFF.
HEH HEH
BLUSH
HM...
BUT THE STORY'S BORING. AND THE WRITER'S STILL JUST A KID.

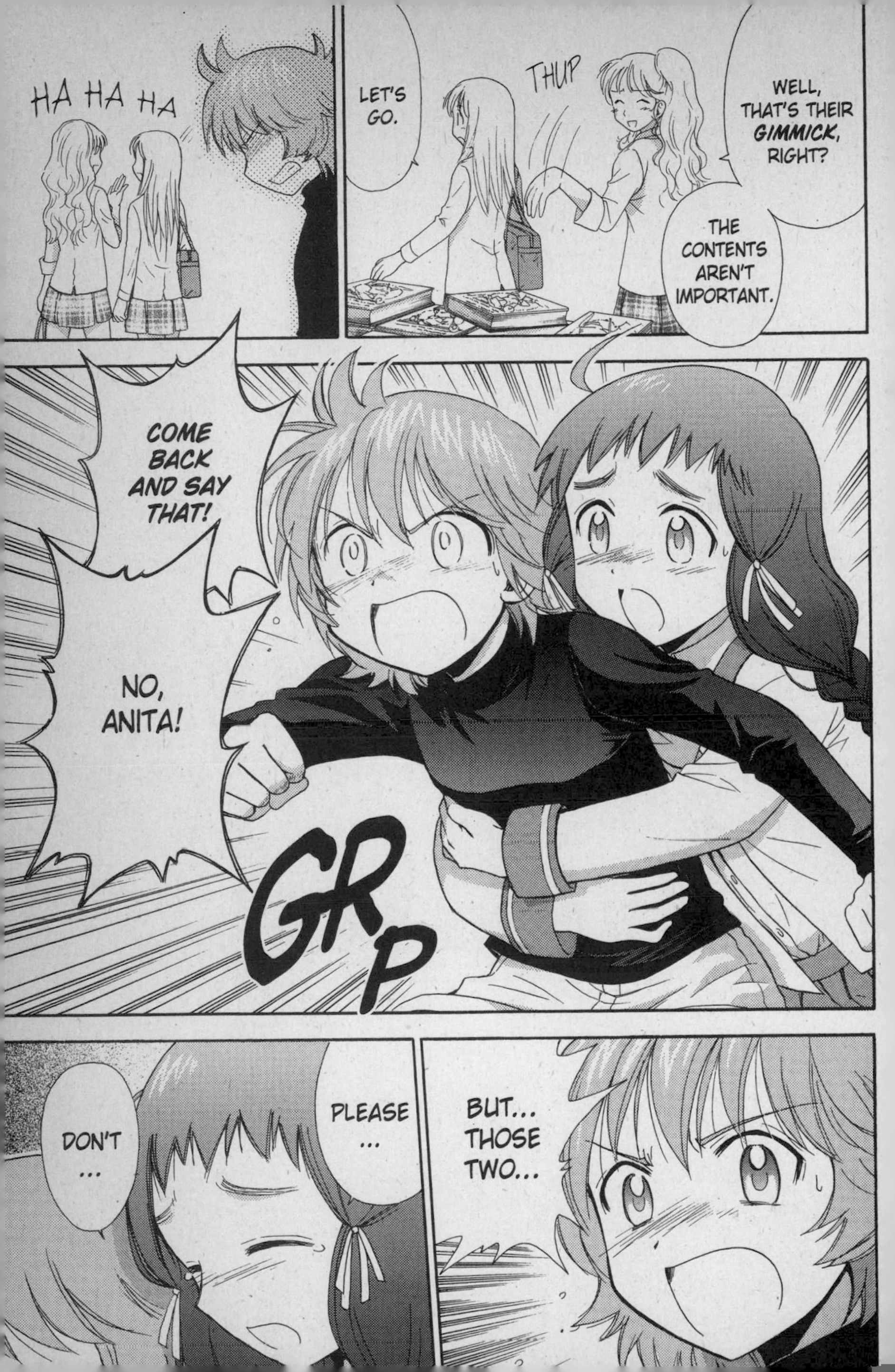
WELL, THAT'S THEIR GIMMICK, RIGHT?
THE CONTENTS AREN'T IMPORTANT.
THUP
LET'S GO.
HA HA HA
COME BACK AND SAY THAT!
NO, ANITA!
GRP
BUT... THOSE TWO...
PLEASE ...
DON'T ...

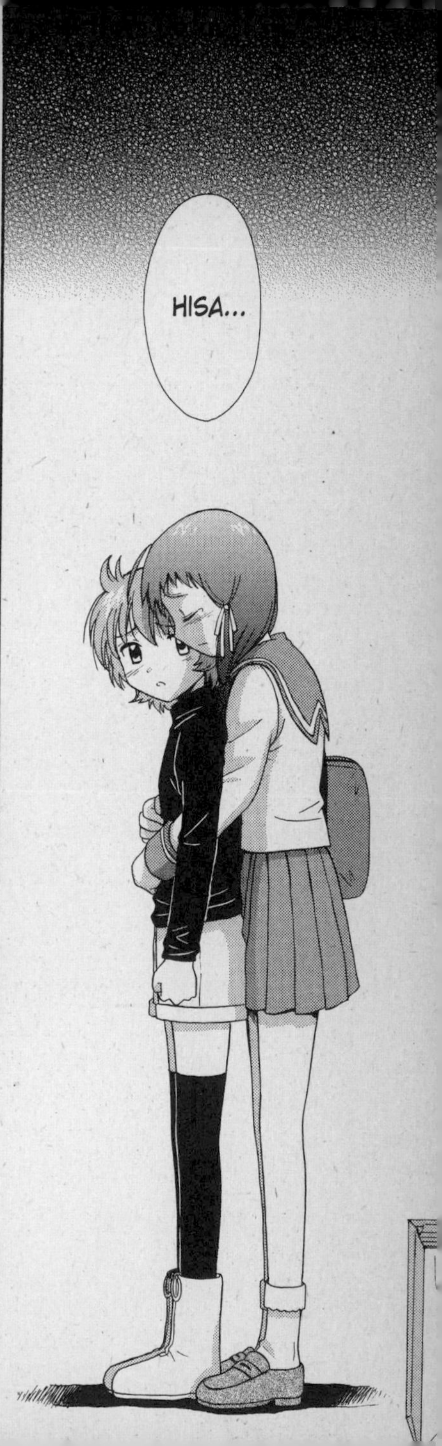
HISA...
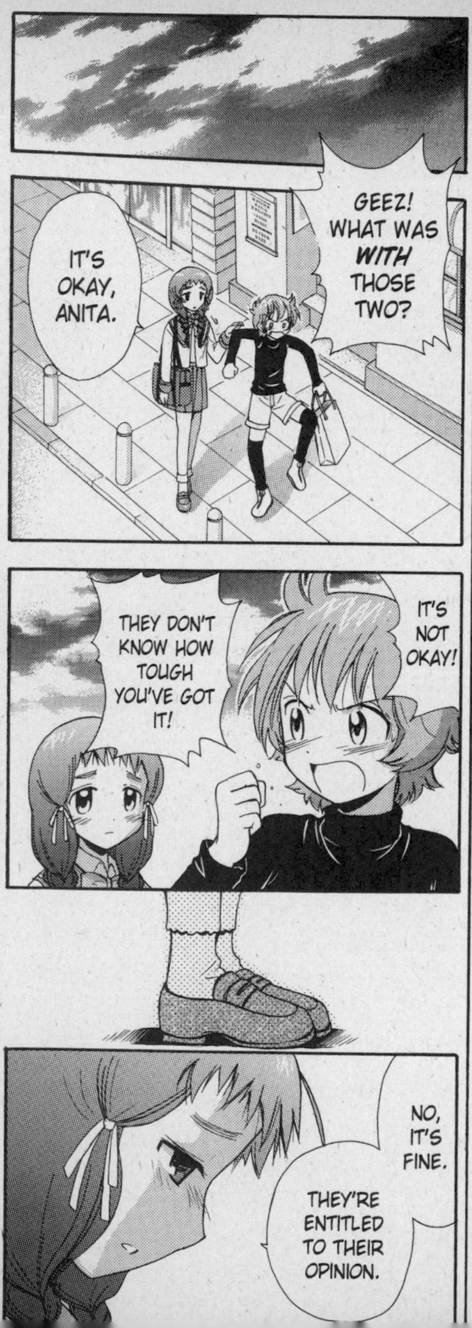
GEEZ! WHAT WAS *WITH* THOSE TWO?
IT'S OKAY, ANITA.
IT'S NOT OKAY!
THEY DON'T KNOW HOW TOUGH YOU'VE GOT IT!
NO, IT'S FINE.
THEY'RE ENTITLED TO THEIR OPINION.

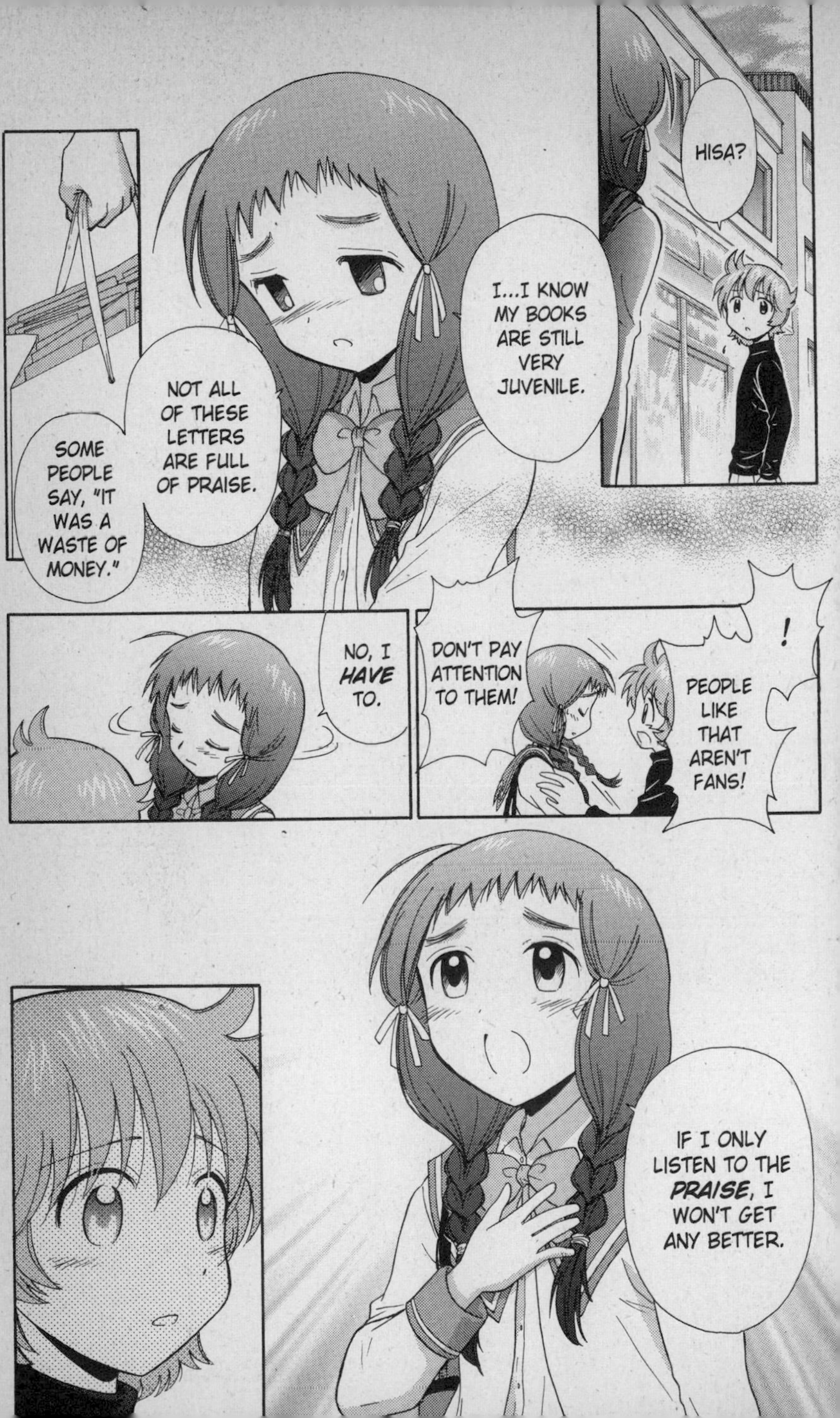
HISA?
I...I KNOW MY BOOKS ARE STILL VERY JUVENILE.
NOT ALL OF THESE LETTERS ARE FULL OF PRAISE.
SOME PEOPLE SAY, "IT WAS A WASTE OF MONEY."
!
DON'T PAY ATTENTION TO THEM!
PEOPLE LIKE THAT AREN'T FANS!
NO, I *HAVE* TO.
IF I ONLY LISTEN TO THE *PRAISE*, I WON'T GET ANY BETTER.

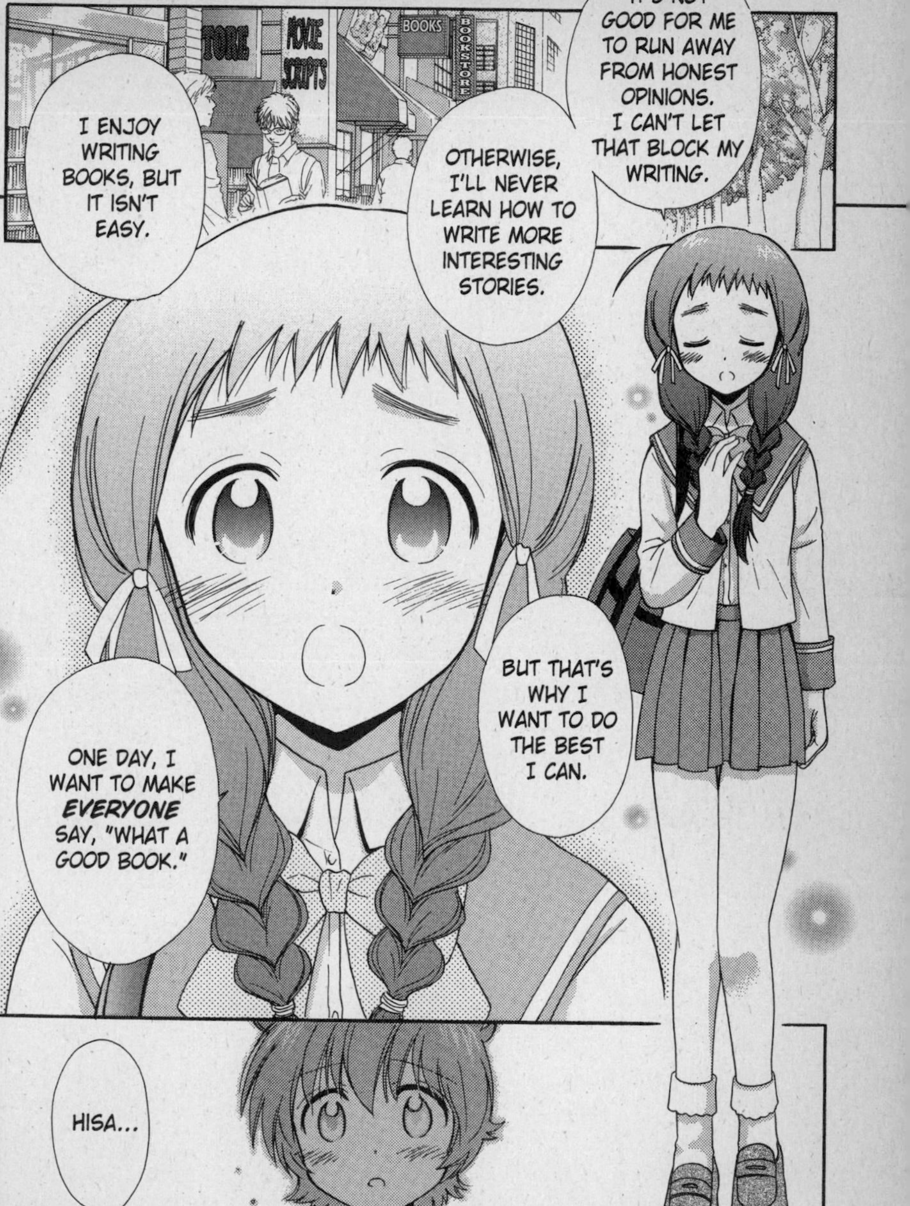
IT'S NOT GOOD FOR ME TO RUN AWAY FROM HONEST OPINIONS. I CAN'T LET THAT BLOCK MY WRITING.
OTHERWISE, I'LL NEVER LEARN HOW TO WRITE MORE INTERESTING STORIES.
I ENJOY WRITING BOOKS, BUT IT ISN'T EASY.
BOOKSTORE
BOOKS
MOVIE SCRIPTS
STORE
BUT THAT'S WHY I WANT TO DO THE BEST I CAN.
ONE DAY, I WANT TO MAKE ***EVERYONE*** SAY, "WHAT A GOOD BOOK."
HISA...

OH...
UH...
JUST
NOW...

ANITA?

I'M SORRY... I GUESS I SOUNDED IMPERTINENT.

NO WAY!

...YOU LOOKED SO MATURE...

BLUSH

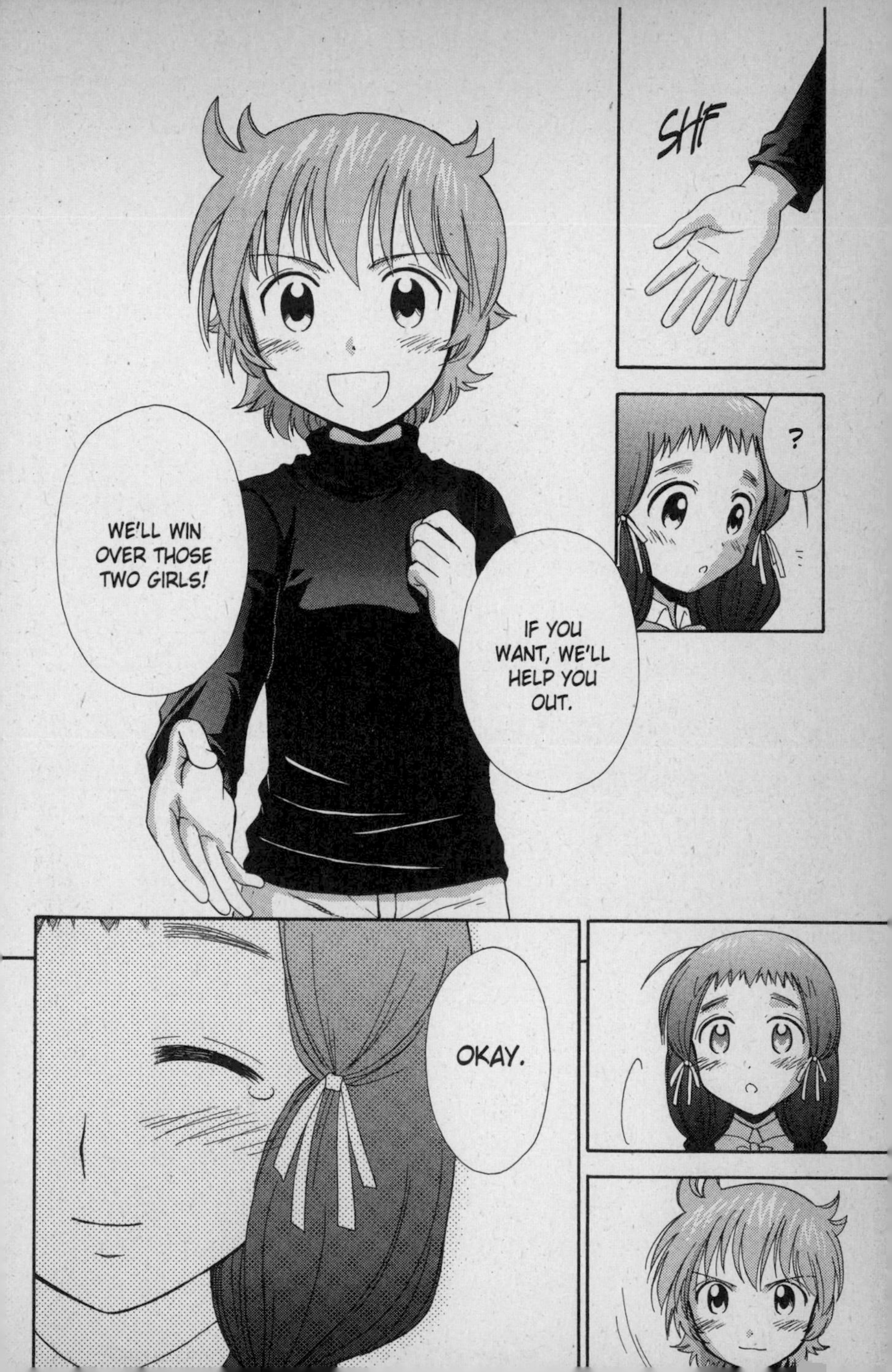
SHF
?
IF YOU WANT, WE'LL HELP YOU OUT.
WE'LL WIN OVER THOSE TWO GIRLS!
OKAY.

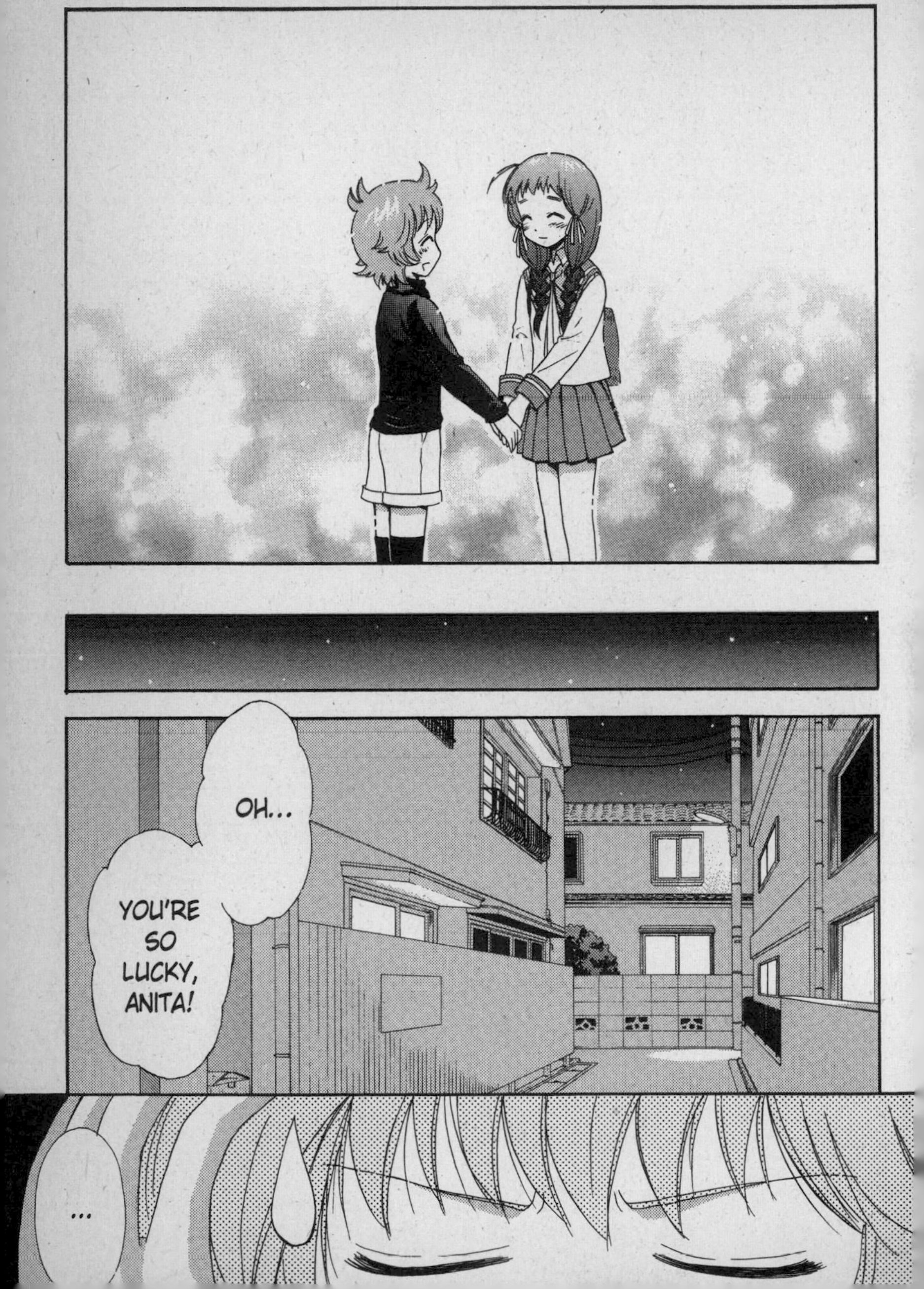
OH...
YOU'RE SO LUCKY, ANITA!
...

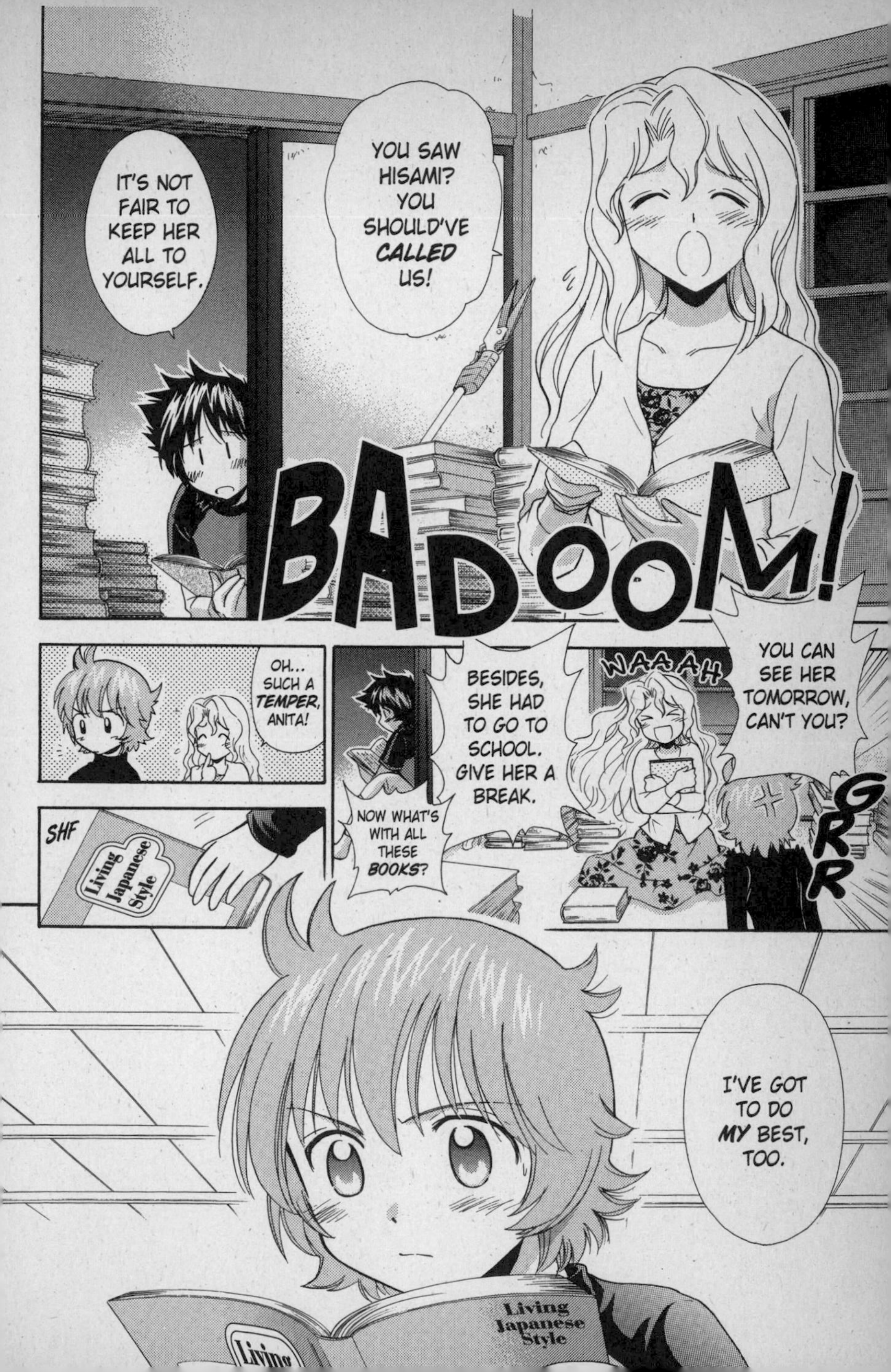
YOU SAW HISAMI? YOU SHOULD'VE CALLED US!
IT'S NOT FAIR TO KEEP HER ALL TO YOURSELF.
BADOOM!
YOU CAN SEE HER TOMORROW, CAN'T YOU?
GRR
WAAAH
BESIDES, SHE HAD TO GO TO SCHOOL. GIVE HER A BREAK.
NOW WHAT'S WITH ALL THESE BOOKS?
OH... SUCH A TEMPER, ANITA!
SHF
Living Japanese Style
I'VE GOT TO DO MY BEST, TOO.
Living Japanese Style
Living

CHAPTER 26

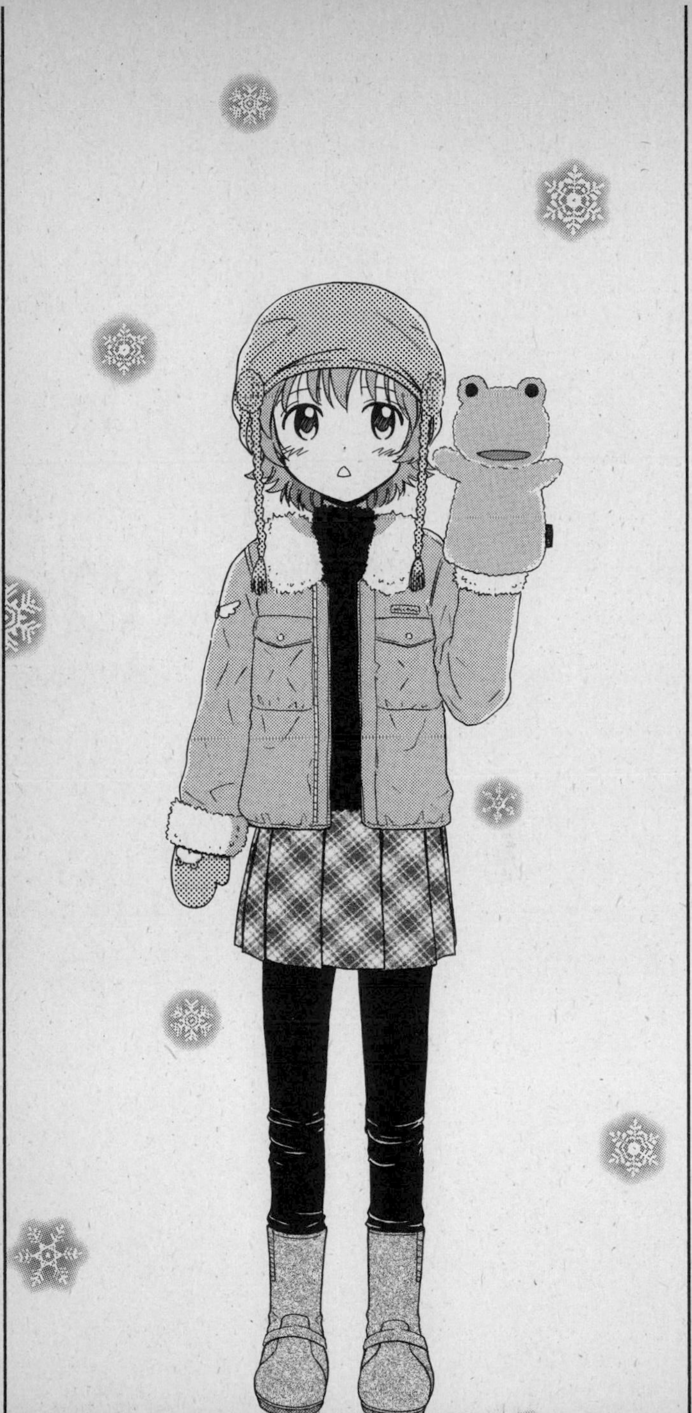

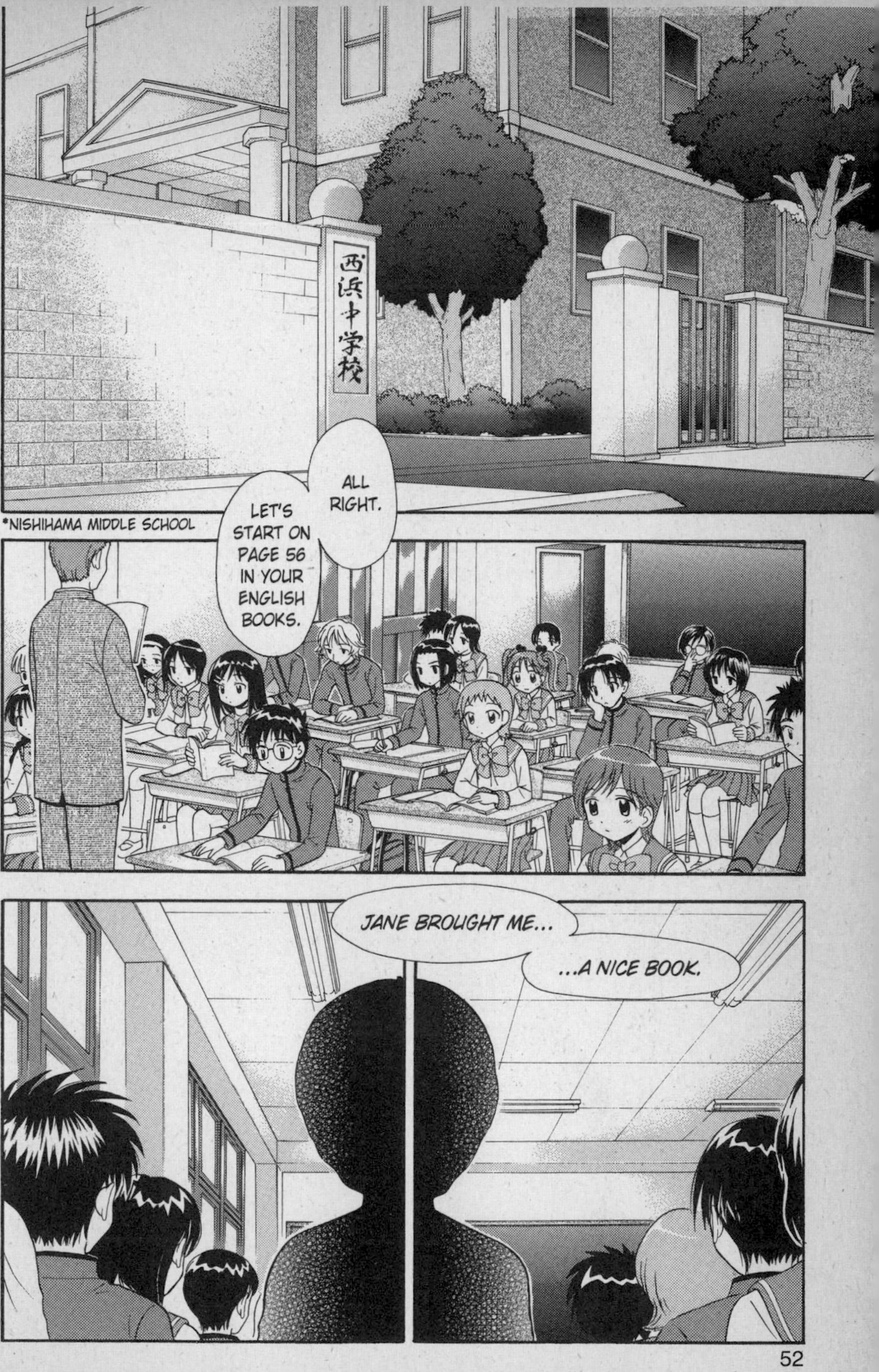
西浜中学校
ALL RIGHT.
LET'S START ON PAGE 56 IN YOUR ENGLISH BOOKS.
JANE BROUGHT ME...
...A NICE BOOK.
*NISHIHAMA MIDDLE SCHOOL

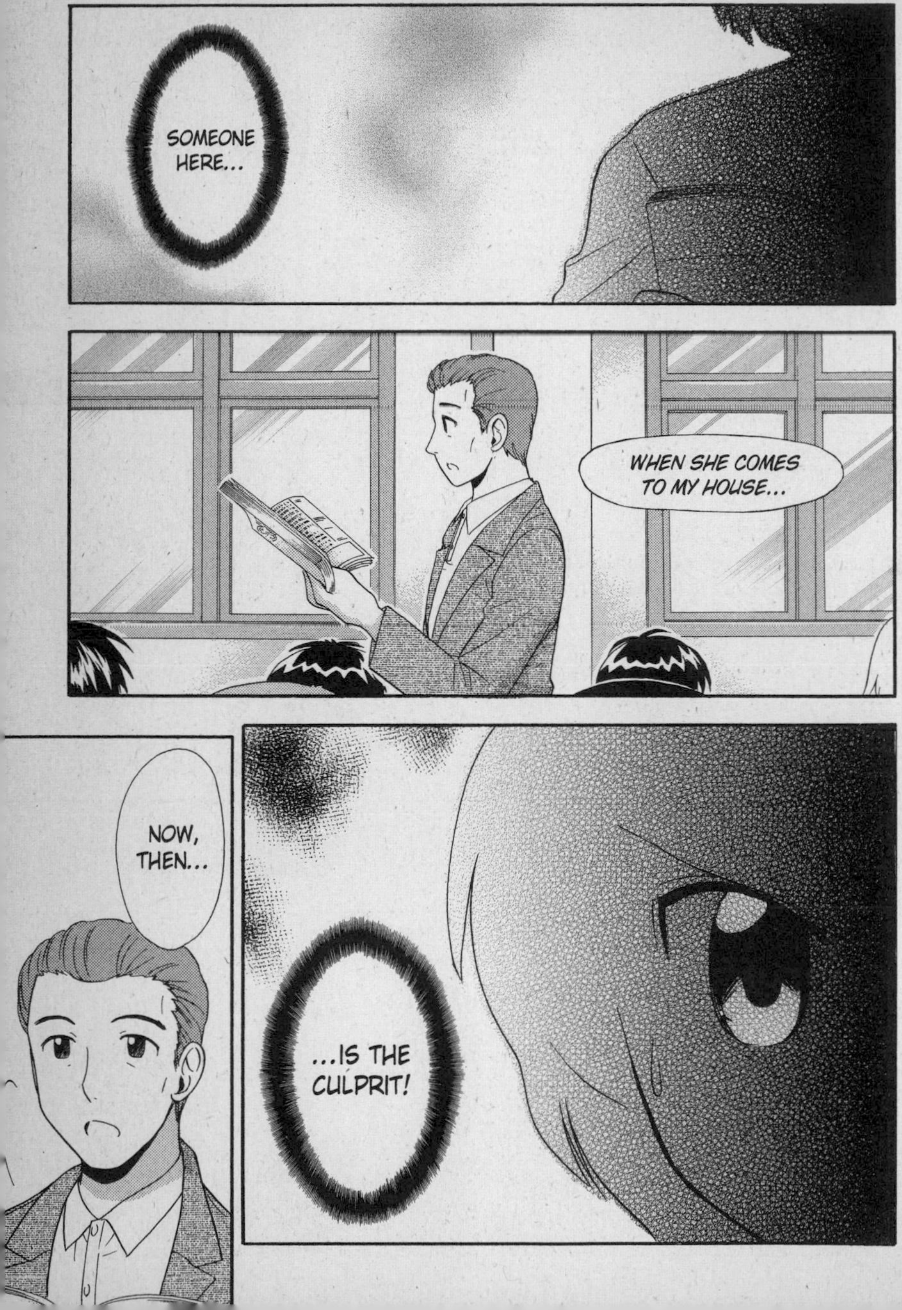
SOMEONE HERE...
WHEN SHE COMES TO MY HOUSE...
...IS THE CULPRIT!
NOW, THEN...

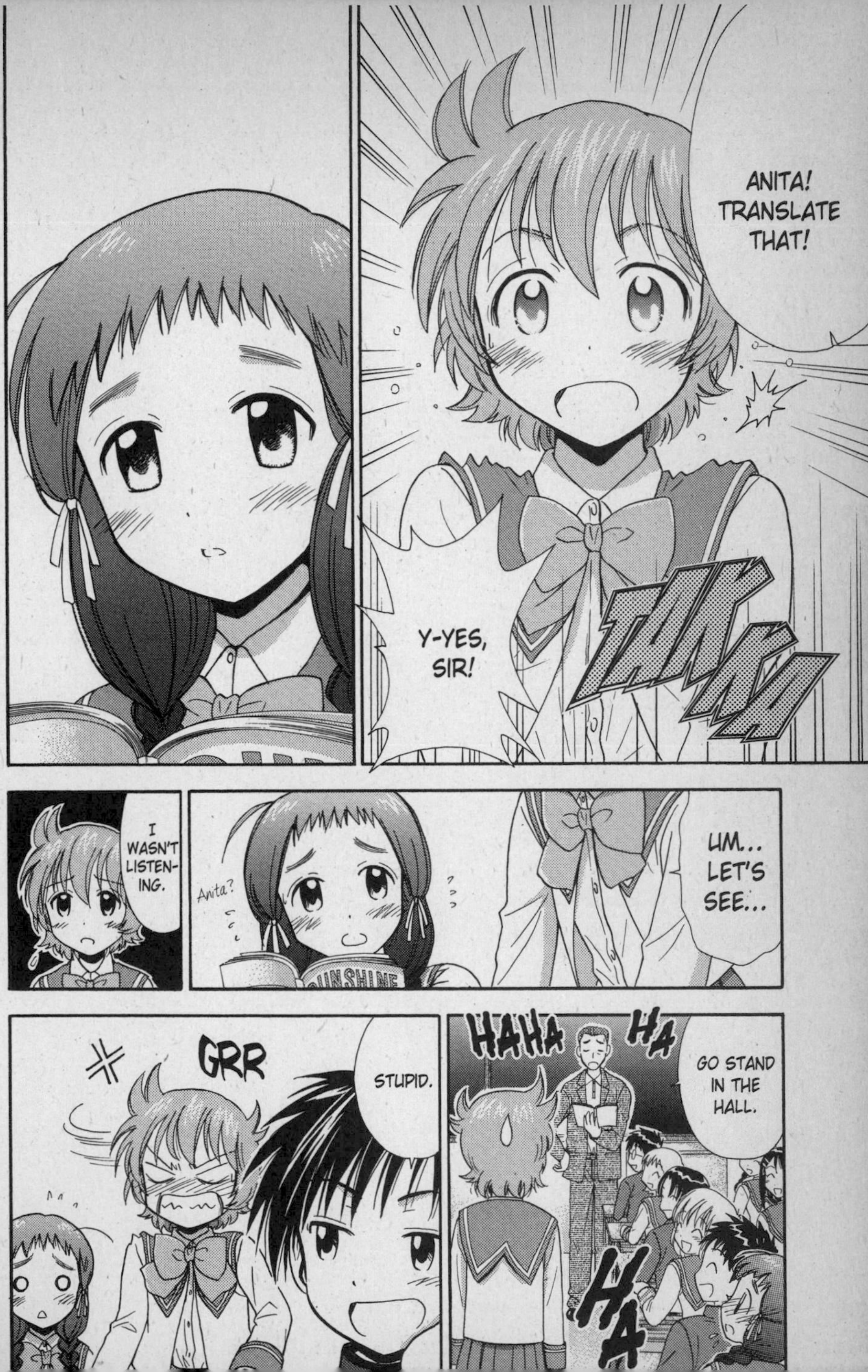
ANITA! TRANSLATE THAT!
Y-YES, SIR!
UM... LET'S SEE...
Anita?
I WASN'T LISTEN-ING.
HAHA
HA
GO STAND IN THE HALL.
HA
HA
STUPID.
GRR

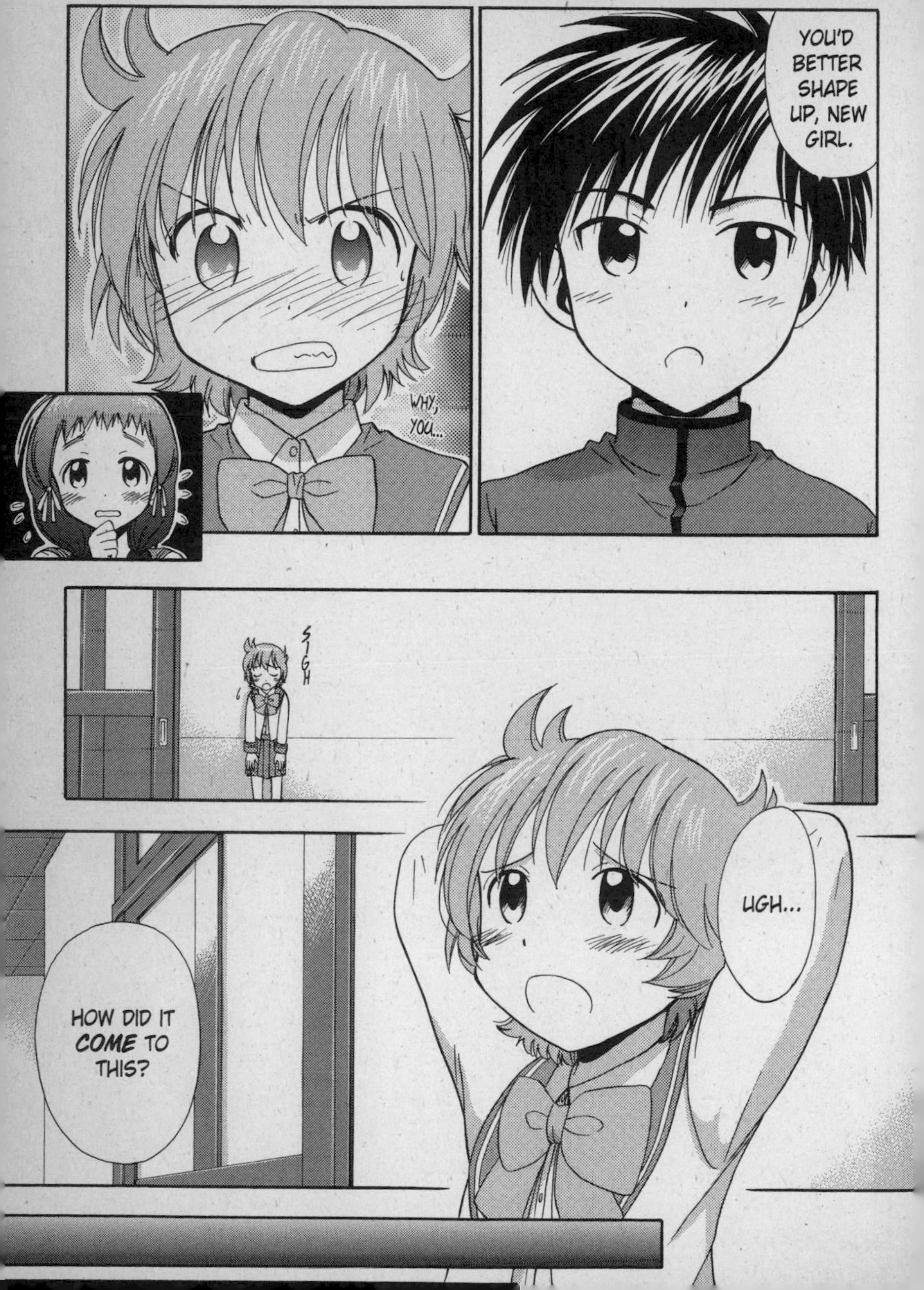
YOU'D BETTER SHAPE UP, NEW GIRL.
WHY, YOU...
SIGH
UGH...
HOW DID IT COME TO THIS?

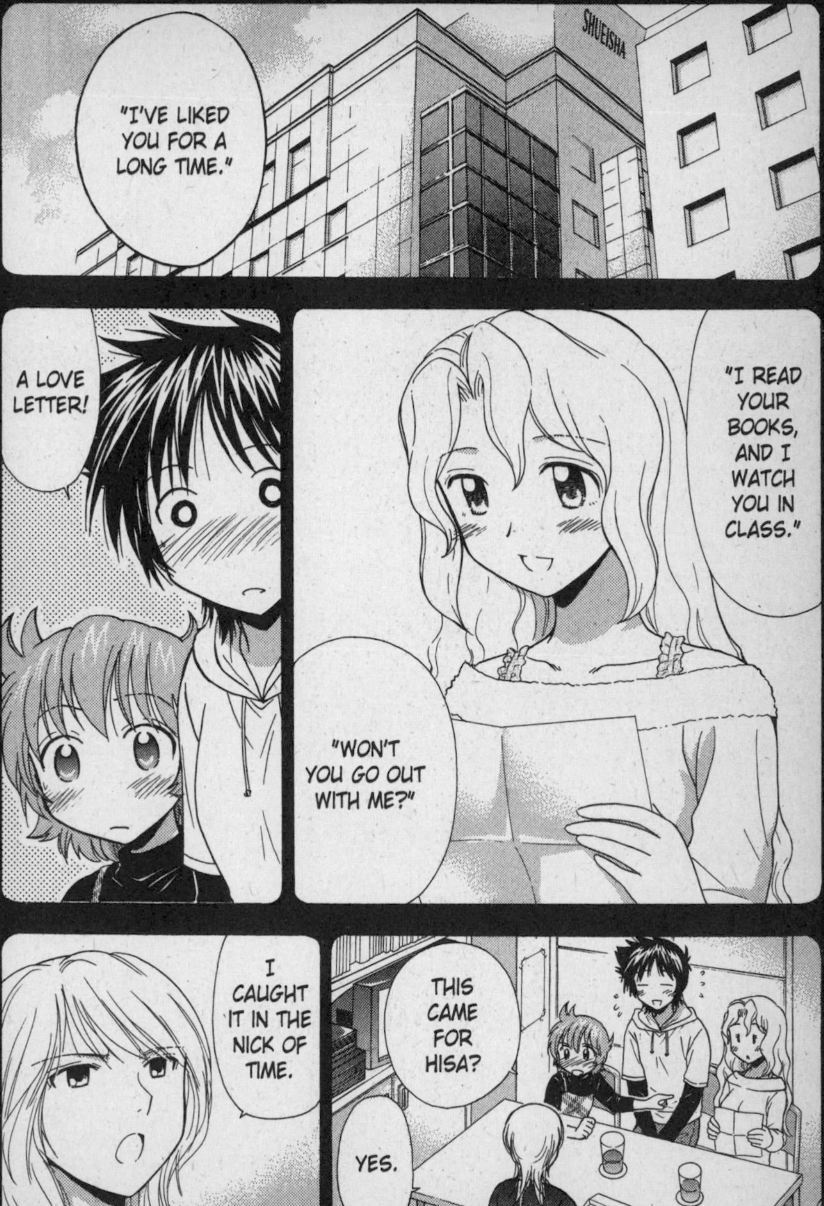
SHUEISHA
"I'VE LIKED YOU FOR A LONG TIME."
"I READ YOUR BOOKS, AND I WATCH YOU IN CLASS."
"WON'T YOU GO OUT WITH ME?"
A LOVE LETTER!
THIS CAME FOR HISA?
YES.
I CAUGHT IT IN THE NICK OF TIME.

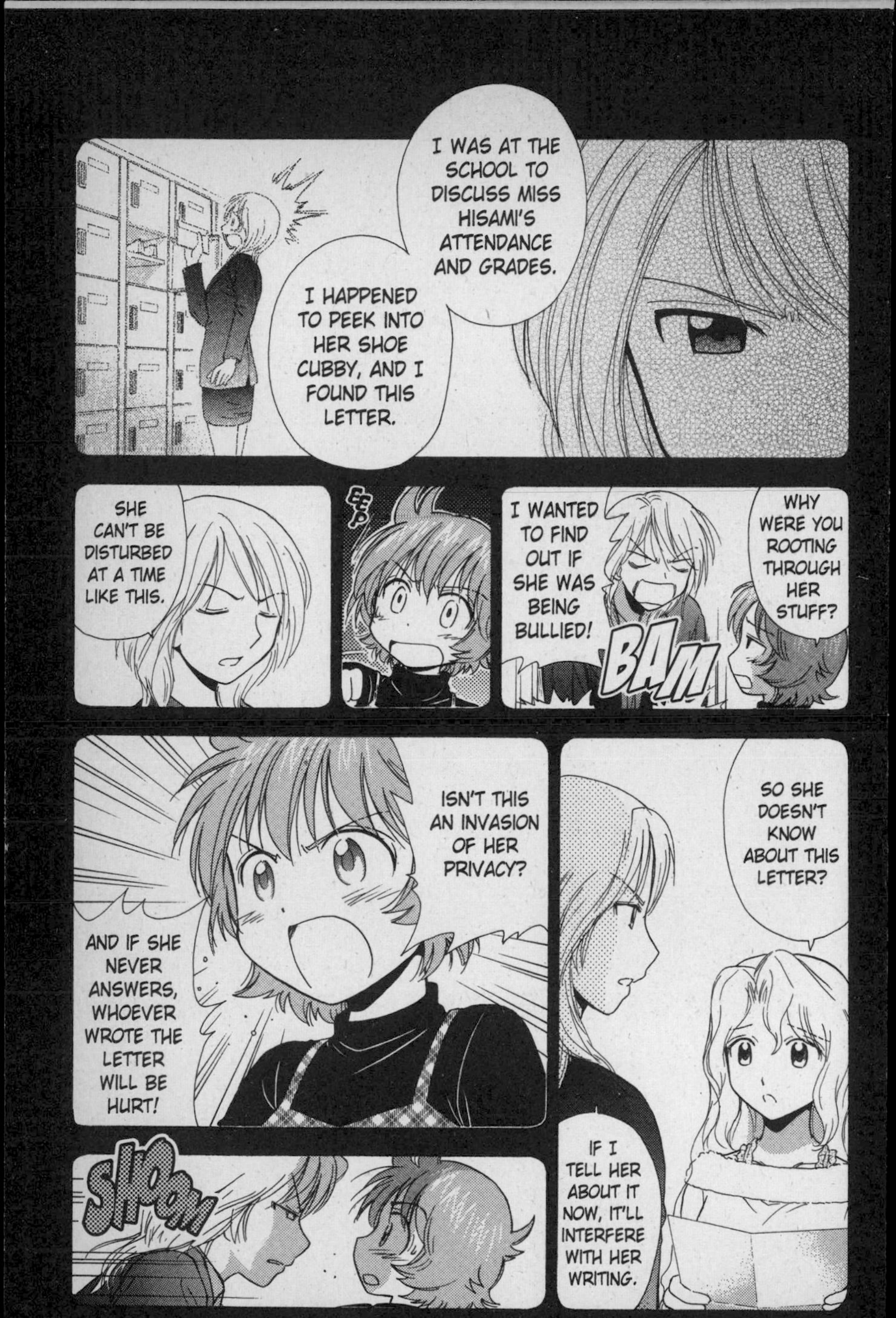
I WAS AT THE SCHOOL TO DISCUSS MISS HISAMI'S ATTENDANCE AND GRADES.
I HAPPENED TO PEEK INTO HER SHOE CUBBY, AND I FOUND THIS LETTER.
WHY WERE YOU ROOTING THROUGH HER STUFF?
I WANTED TO FIND OUT IF SHE WAS BEING BULLIED!
BAM
EEP
SHE CAN'T BE DISTURBED AT A TIME LIKE THIS.
SO SHE DOESN'T KNOW ABOUT THIS LETTER?
IF I TELL HER ABOUT IT NOW, IT'LL INTERFERE WITH HER WRITING.
ISN'T THIS AN INVASION OF HER PRIVACY?
AND IF SHE NEVER ANSWERS, WHOEVER WROTE THE LETTER WILL BE HURT!
SHOOM

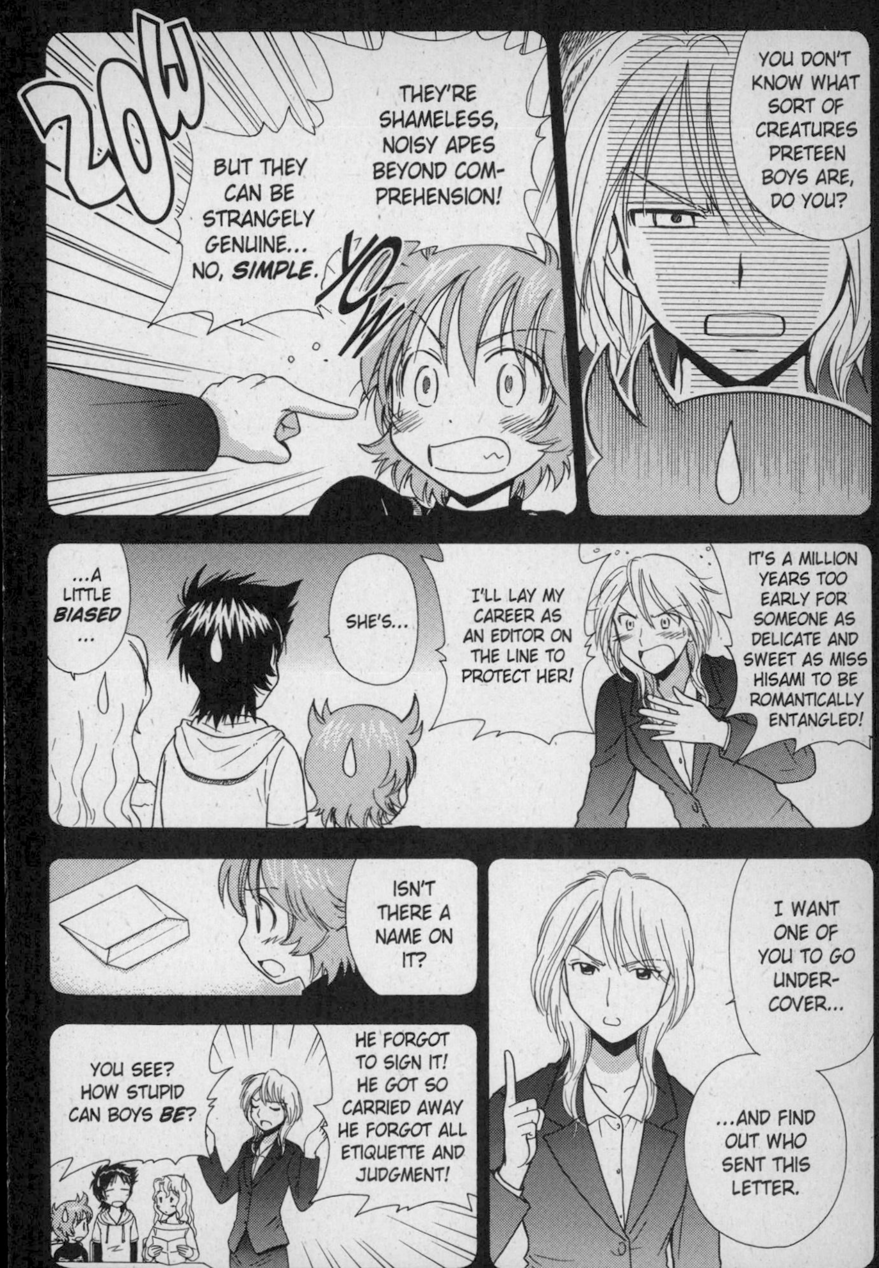
YOU DON'T KNOW WHAT SORT OF CREATURES PRETEEN BOYS ARE, DO YOU?
THEY'RE SHAMELESS, NOISY APES BEYOND COM-PREHENSION!
BUT THEY CAN BE STRANGELY GENUINE... NO, *SIMPLE*.
YOW
ZOW
IT'S A MILLION YEARS TOO EARLY FOR SOMEONE AS DELICATE AND SWEET AS MISS HISAMI TO BE ROMANTICALLY ENTANGLED!
I'LL LAY MY CAREER AS AN EDITOR ON THE LINE TO PROTECT HER!
SHE'S...
...A LITTLE *BIASED*...
I WANT ONE OF YOU TO GO UNDER-COVER...
...AND FIND OUT WHO SENT THIS LETTER.
ISN'T THERE A NAME ON IT?
HE FORGOT TO SIGN IT! HE GOT SO CARRIED AWAY HE FORGOT ALL ETIQUETTE AND JUDGMENT!
YOU SEE? HOW STUPID CAN BOYS *BE*?

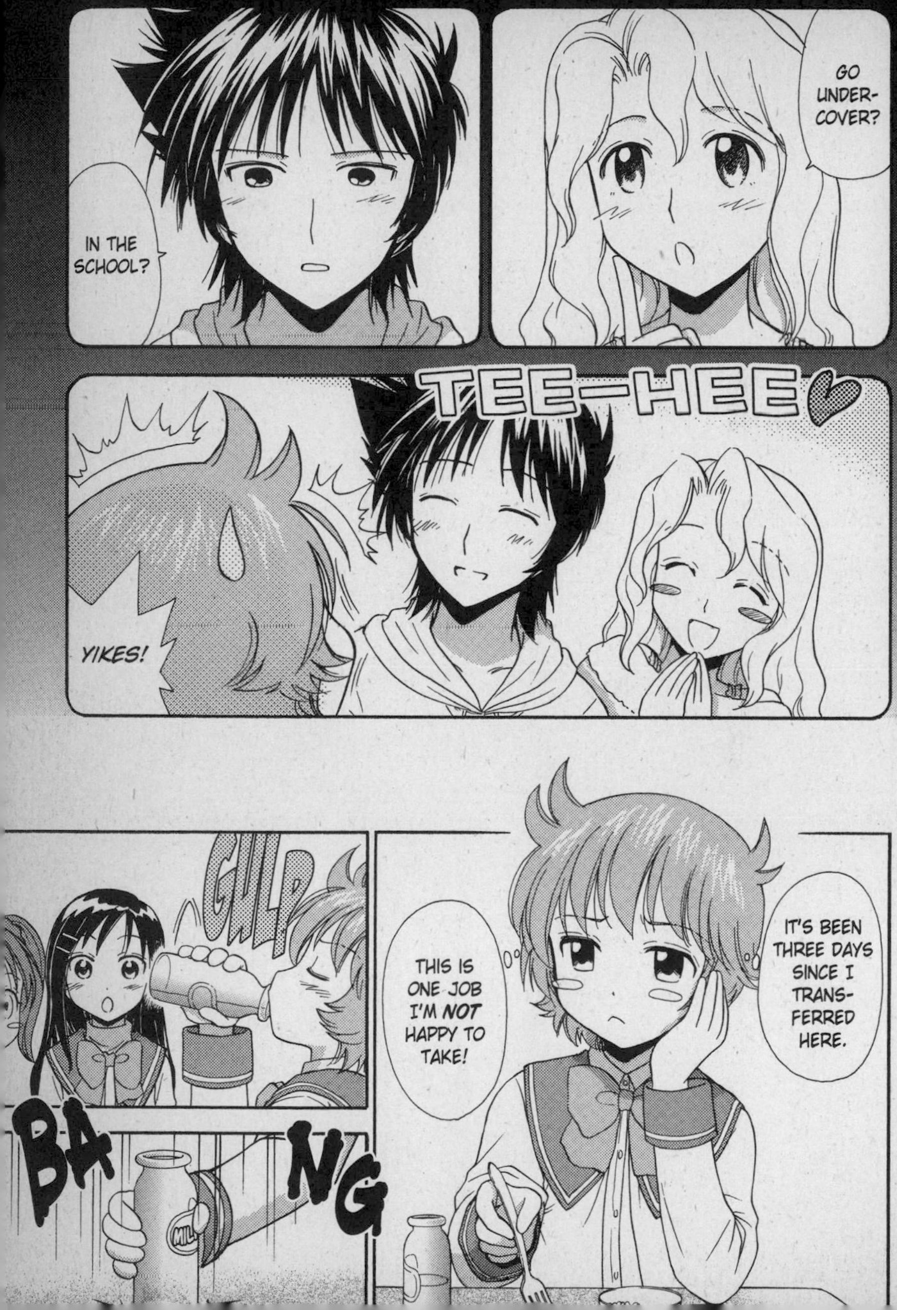

GO UNDER-COVER?
IN THE SCHOOL?
TEE-HEE
YIKES!
IT'S BEEN THREE DAYS SINCE I TRANS-FERRED HERE.
THIS IS ONE JOB I'M ***NOT*** HAPPY TO TAKE!
GULP
BANG

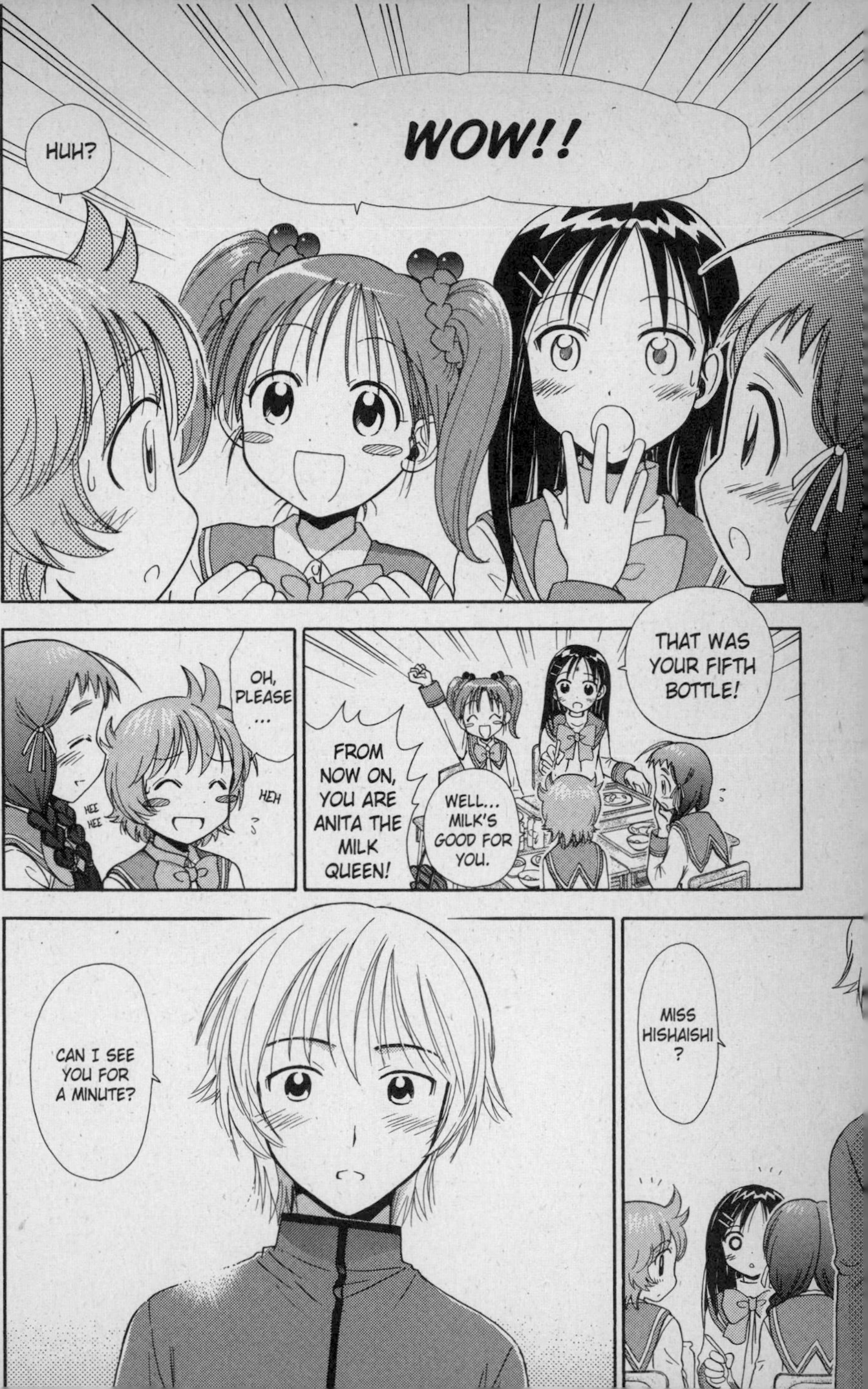
WOW!!
HUH?
THAT WAS YOUR FIFTH BOTTLE!
FROM NOW ON, YOU ARE ANITA THE MILK QUEEN!
WELL... MILK'S GOOD FOR YOU.
OH, PLEASE ...
HEH
HEE HEE
MISS HISHAISHI ?
CAN I SEE YOU FOR A MINUTE?

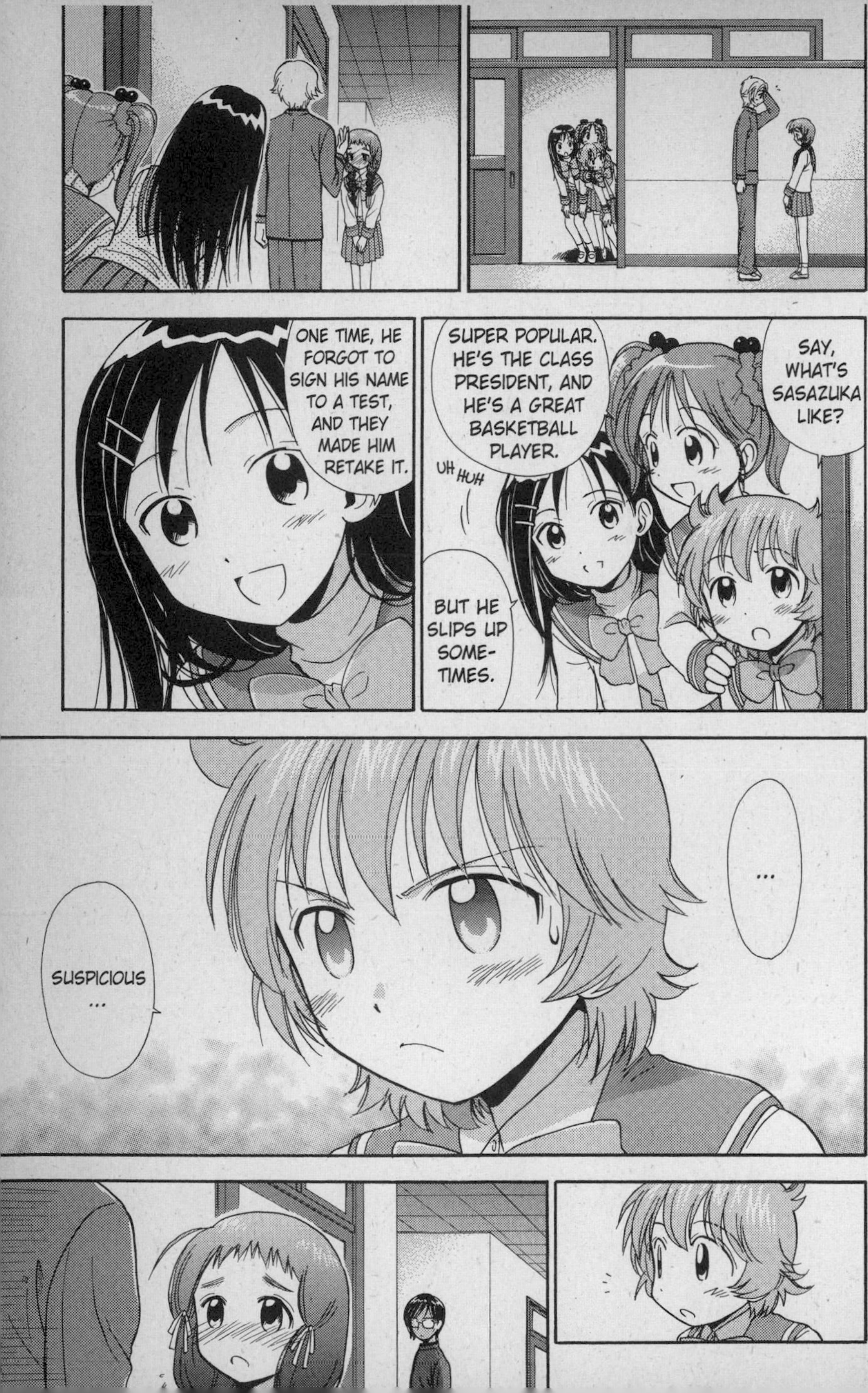
SAY, WHAT'S SASAZUKA LIKE?
SUPER POPULAR. HE'S THE CLASS PRESIDENT, AND HE'S A GREAT BASKETBALL PLAYER.
UH HUH
BUT HE SLIPS UP SOME-TIMES.
ONE TIME, HE FORGOT TO SIGN HIS NAME TO A TEST, AND THEY MADE HIM RETAKE IT.
...
SUSPICIOUS ...

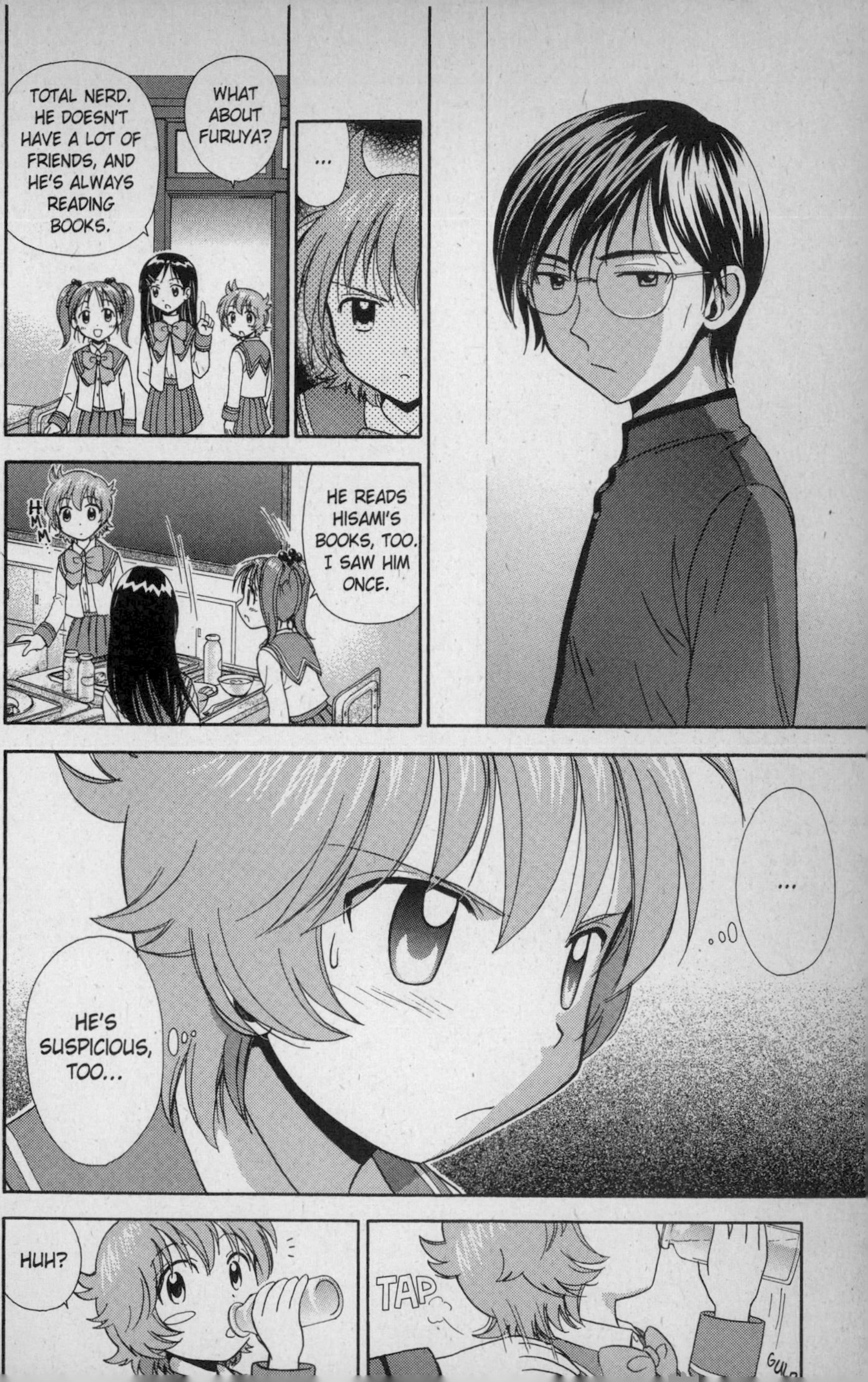
...
WHAT ABOUT FURUYA?
TOTAL NERD. HE DOESN'T HAVE A LOT OF FRIENDS, AND HE'S ALWAYS READING BOOKS.
HE READS HISAMI'S BOOKS, TOO. I SAW HIM ONCE.
HMM
...
HE'S SUSPICIOUS, TOO...
TAP
HUH?

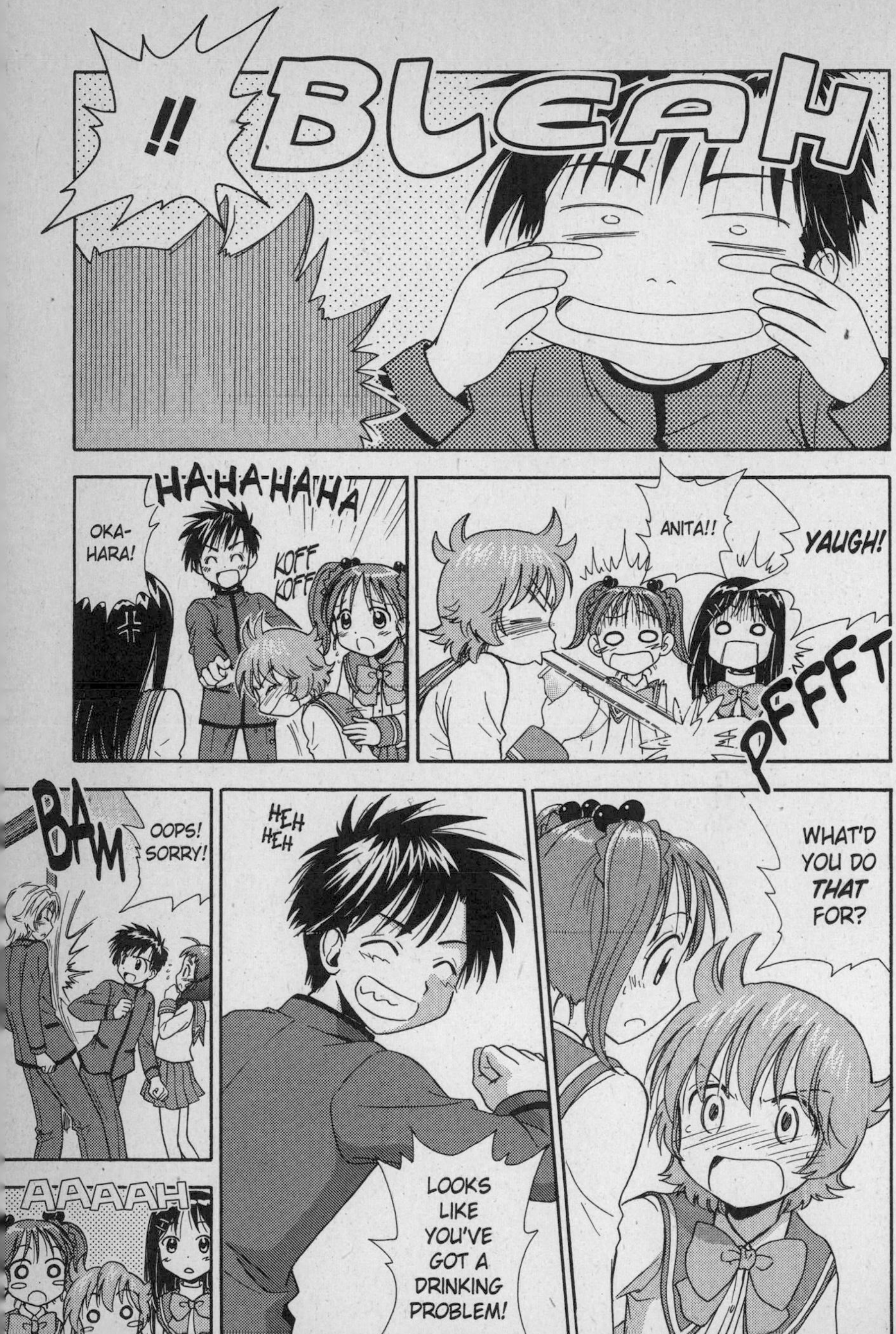
BLEAH
!!
YAUGH!
ANITA!!
PFFFT
HAHAHAHA
KOFF KOFF
OKA-HARA!
WHAT'D YOU DO THAT FOR?
HEH HEH
LOOKS LIKE YOU'VE GOT A DRINKING PROBLEM!
BAM
OOPS! SORRY!
AAAAH

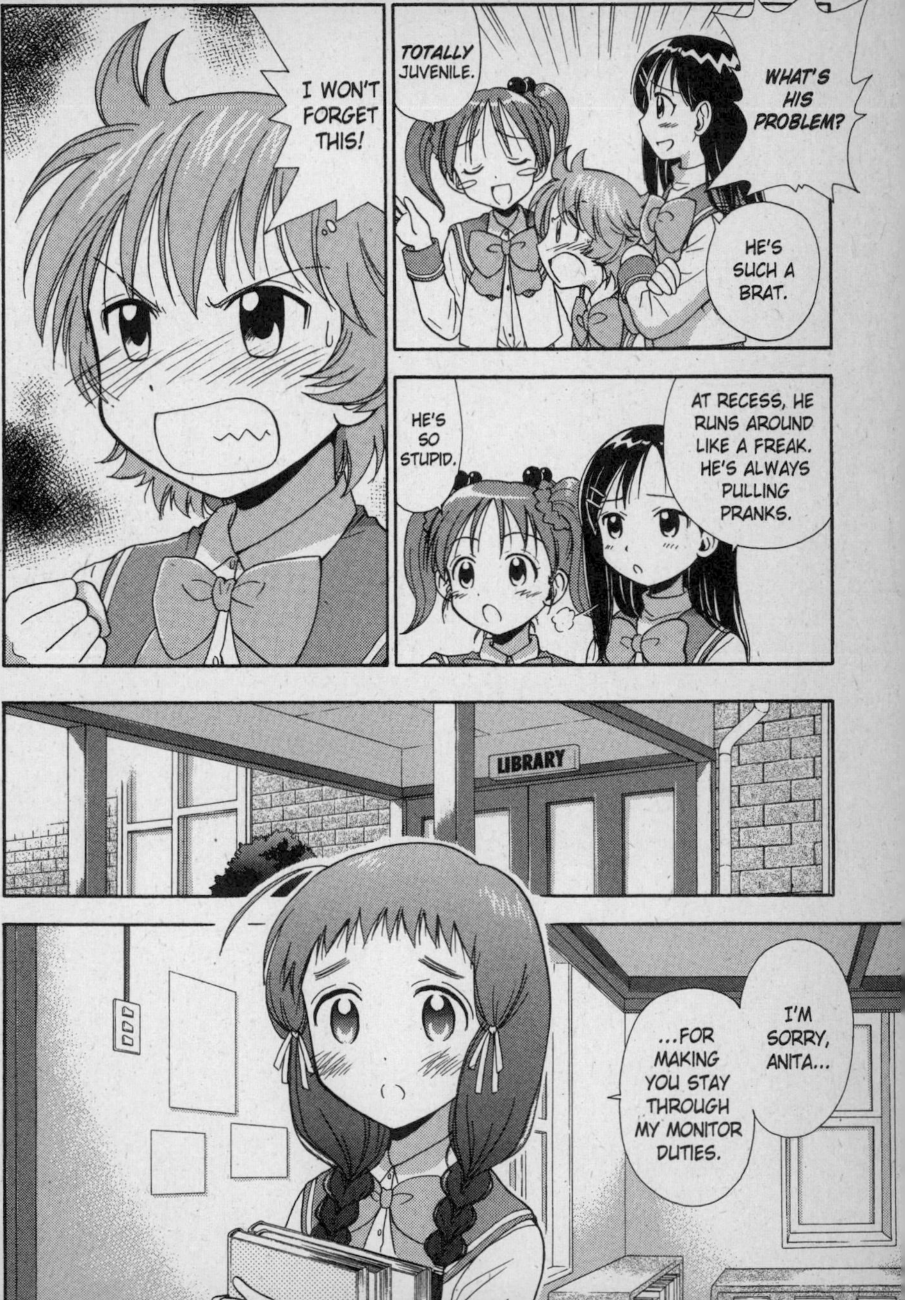
WHAT'S HIS PROBLEM?
TOTALLY JUVENILE.
HE'S SUCH A BRAT.
AT RECESS, HE RUNS AROUND LIKE A FREAK. HE'S ALWAYS PULLING PRANKS.
HE'S SO STUPID.
I WON'T FORGET THIS!
LIBRARY
I'M SORRY, ANITA...
...FOR MAKING YOU STAY THROUGH MY MONITOR DUTIES.

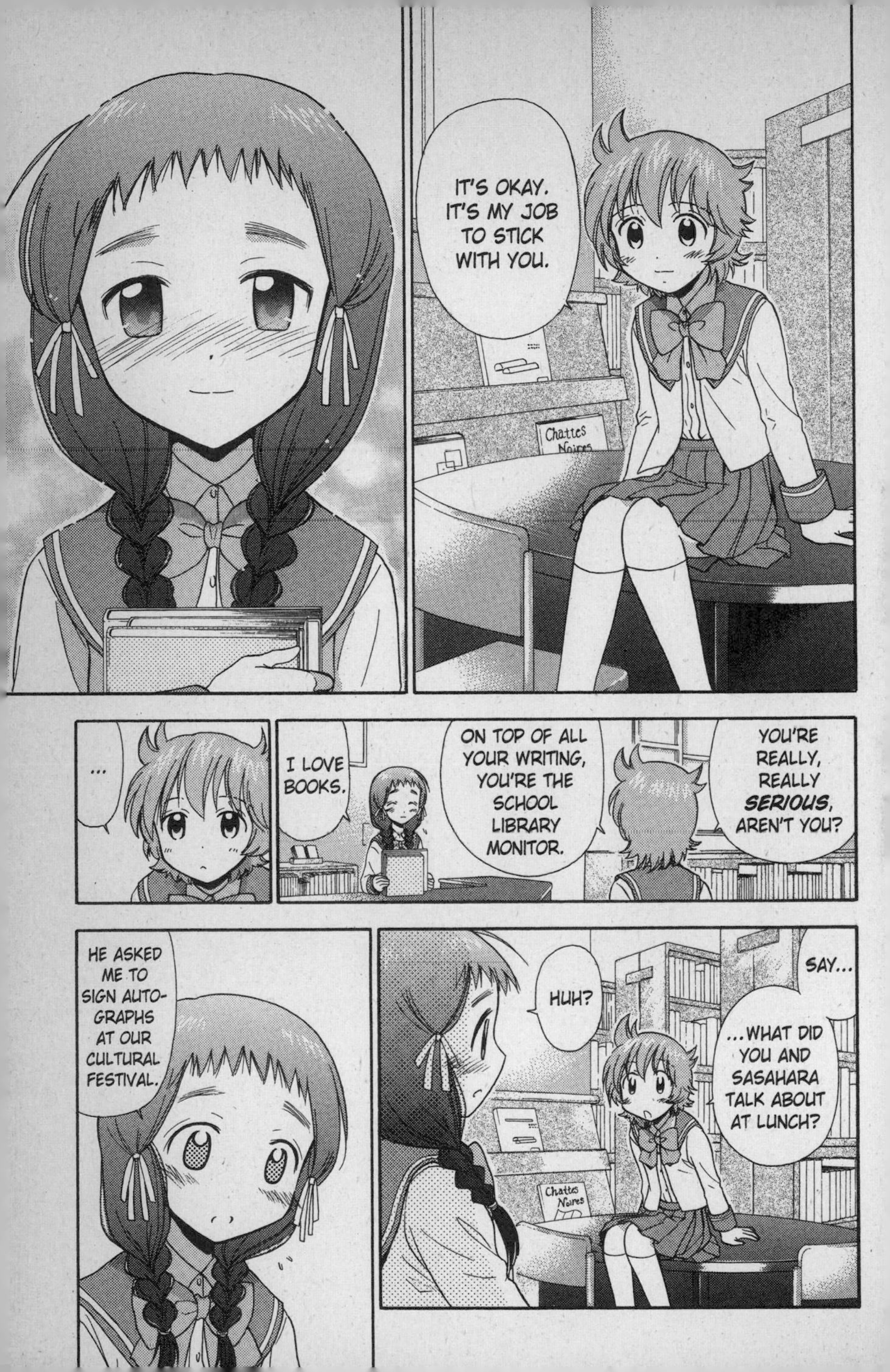
IT'S OKAY. IT'S MY JOB TO STICK WITH YOU.
Chattes Noires
YOU'RE REALLY, REALLY **SERIOUS**, AREN'T YOU?
ON TOP OF ALL YOUR WRITING, YOU'RE THE SCHOOL LIBRARY MONITOR.
I LOVE BOOKS.
...
SAY...
...WHAT DID YOU AND SASAHARA TALK ABOUT AT LUNCH?
HUH?
Chattes Noires
HE ASKED ME TO SIGN AUTO-GRAPHS AT OUR CULTURAL FESTIVAL.

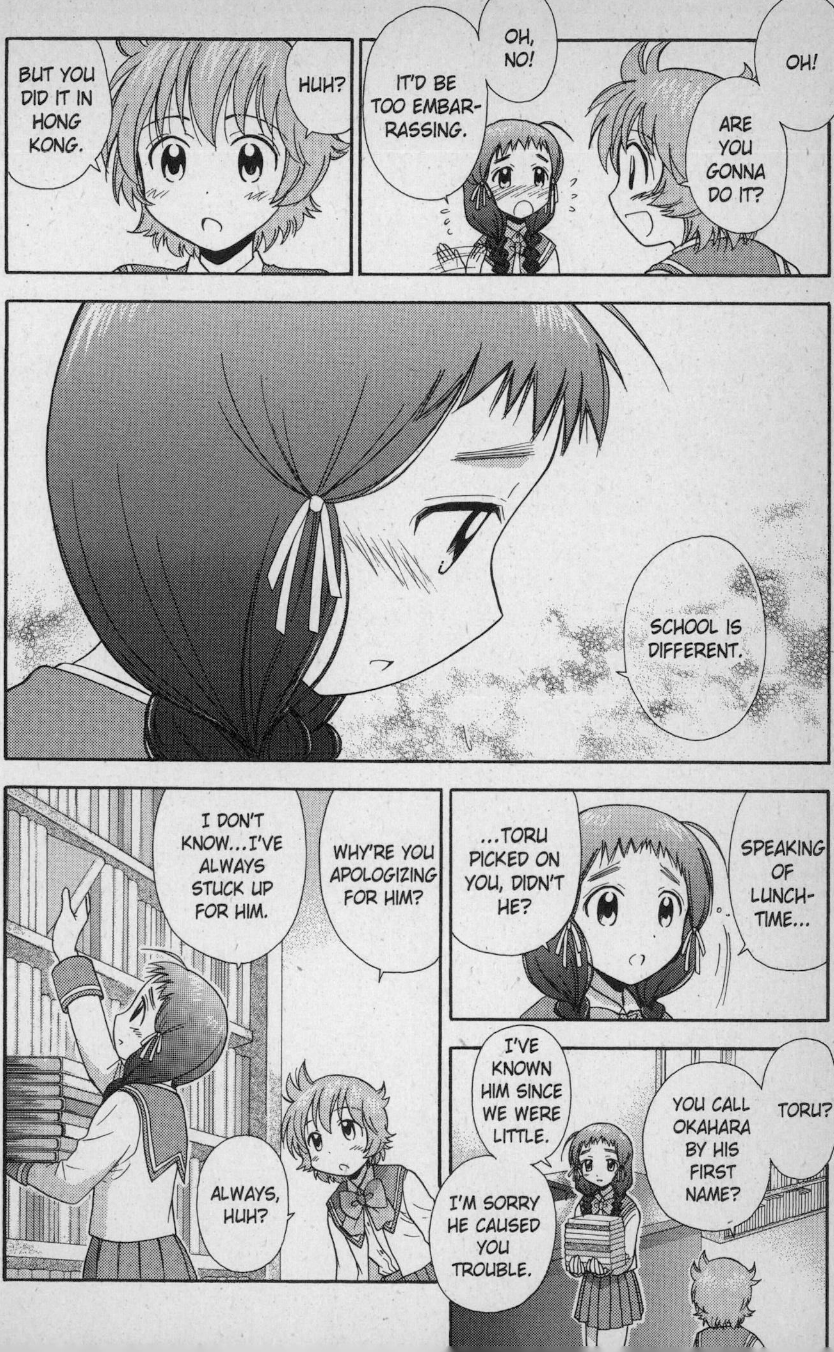
OH!
ARE YOU GONNA DO IT?
OH, NO!
IT'D BE TOO EMBARRASSING.
HUH?
BUT YOU DID IT IN HONG KONG.
SCHOOL IS DIFFERENT.
SPEAKING OF LUNCHTIME...
...TORU PICKED ON YOU, DIDN'T HE?
TORU?
YOU CALL OKAHARA BY HIS FIRST NAME?
I'VE KNOWN HIM SINCE WE WERE LITTLE.
I'M SORRY HE CAUSED YOU TROUBLE.
WHY'RE YOU APOLOGIZING FOR HIM?
I DON'T KNOW...I'VE ALWAYS STUCK UP FOR HIM.
ALWAYS, HUH?

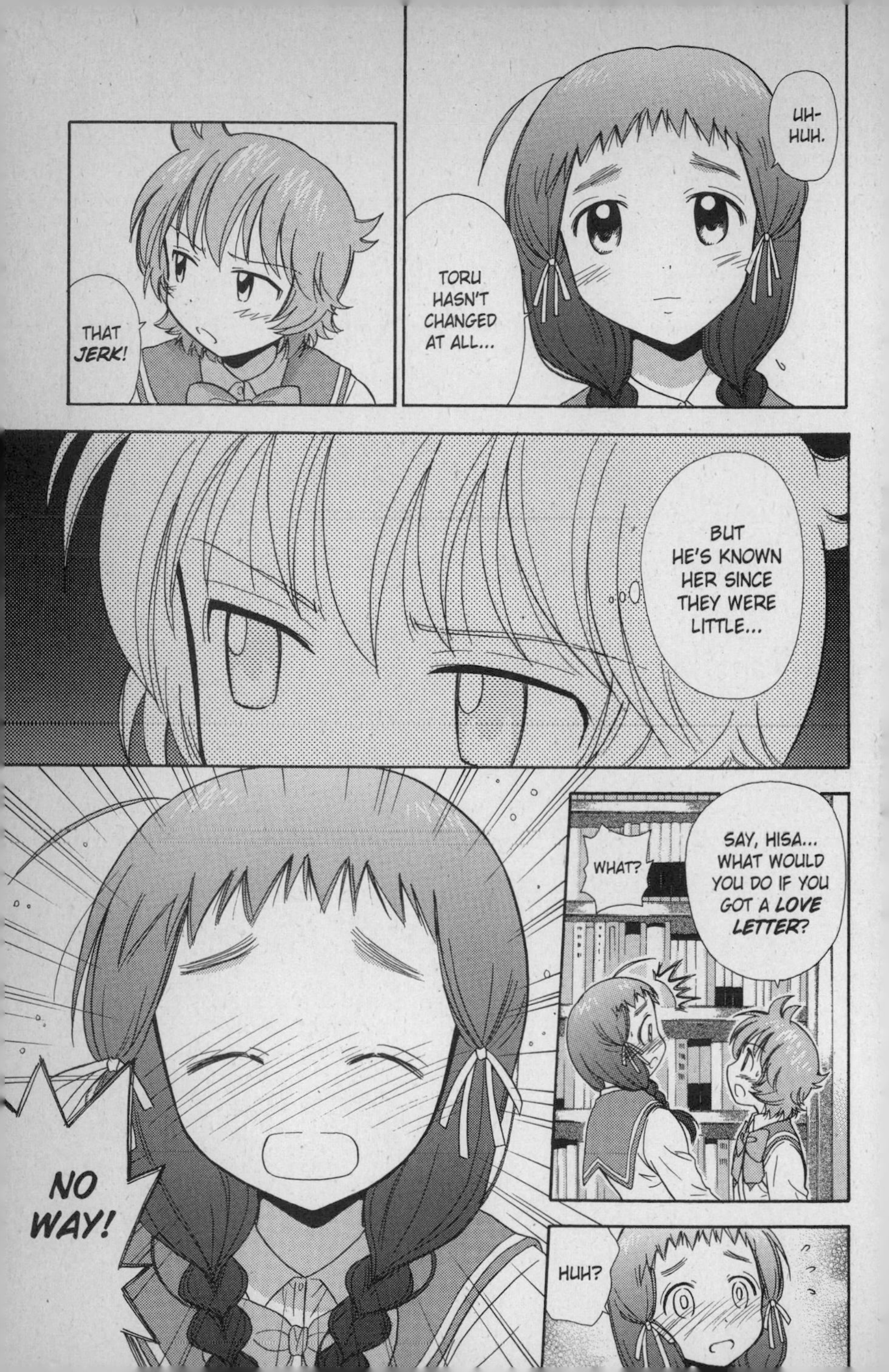
UH-HUH.
TORU HASN'T CHANGED AT ALL...
THAT JERK!
BUT HE'S KNOWN HER SINCE THEY WERE LITTLE...
SAY, HISA... WHAT WOULD YOU DO IF YOU GOT A LOVE LETTER?
WHAT?
HUH?
NO WAY!

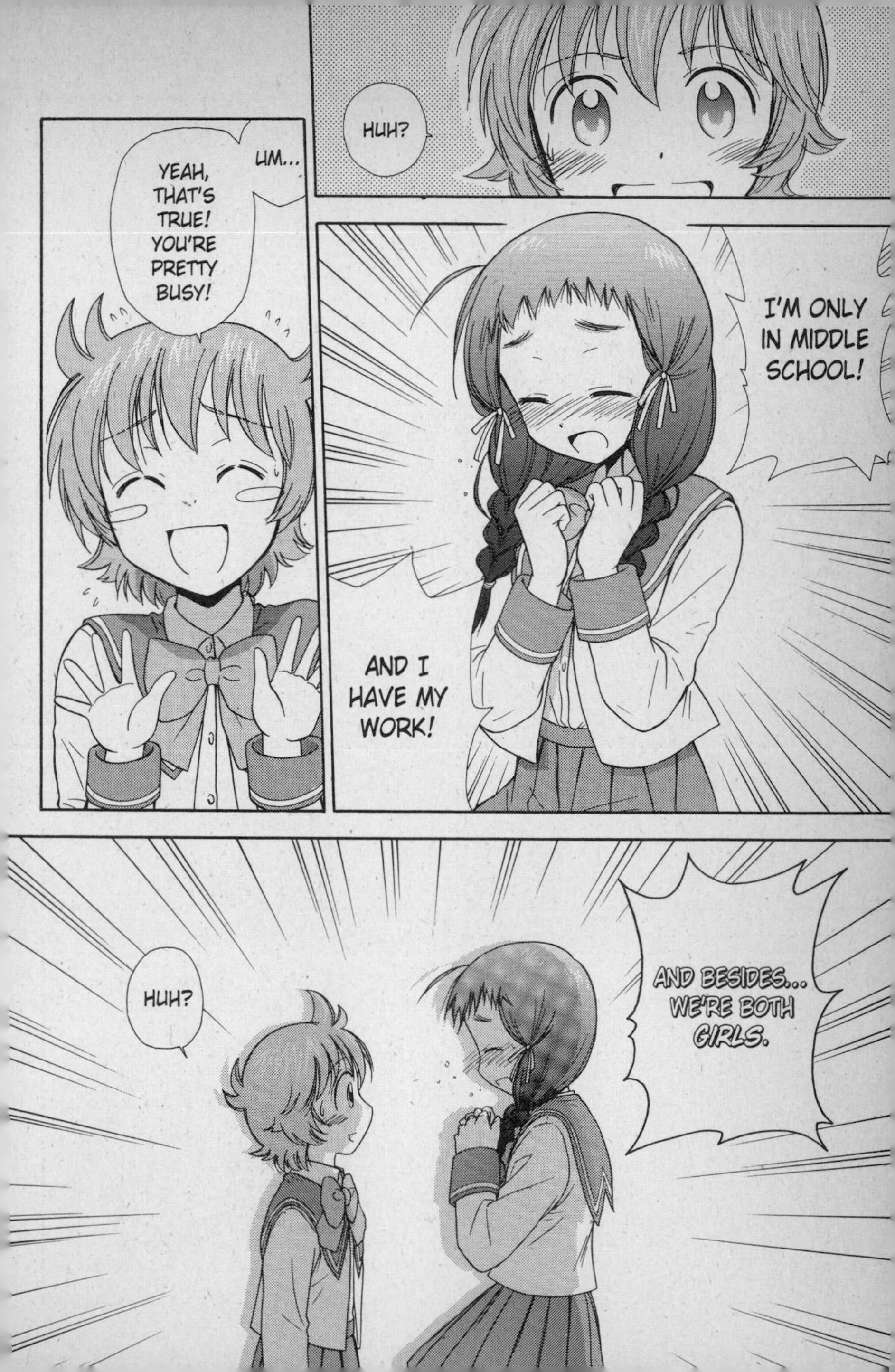
HUH?
I'M ONLY IN MIDDLE SCHOOL!
AND I HAVE MY WORK!
UM...
YEAH, THAT'S TRUE! YOU'RE PRETTY BUSY!
AND BESIDES... WE'RE BOTH GIRLS.
HUH?

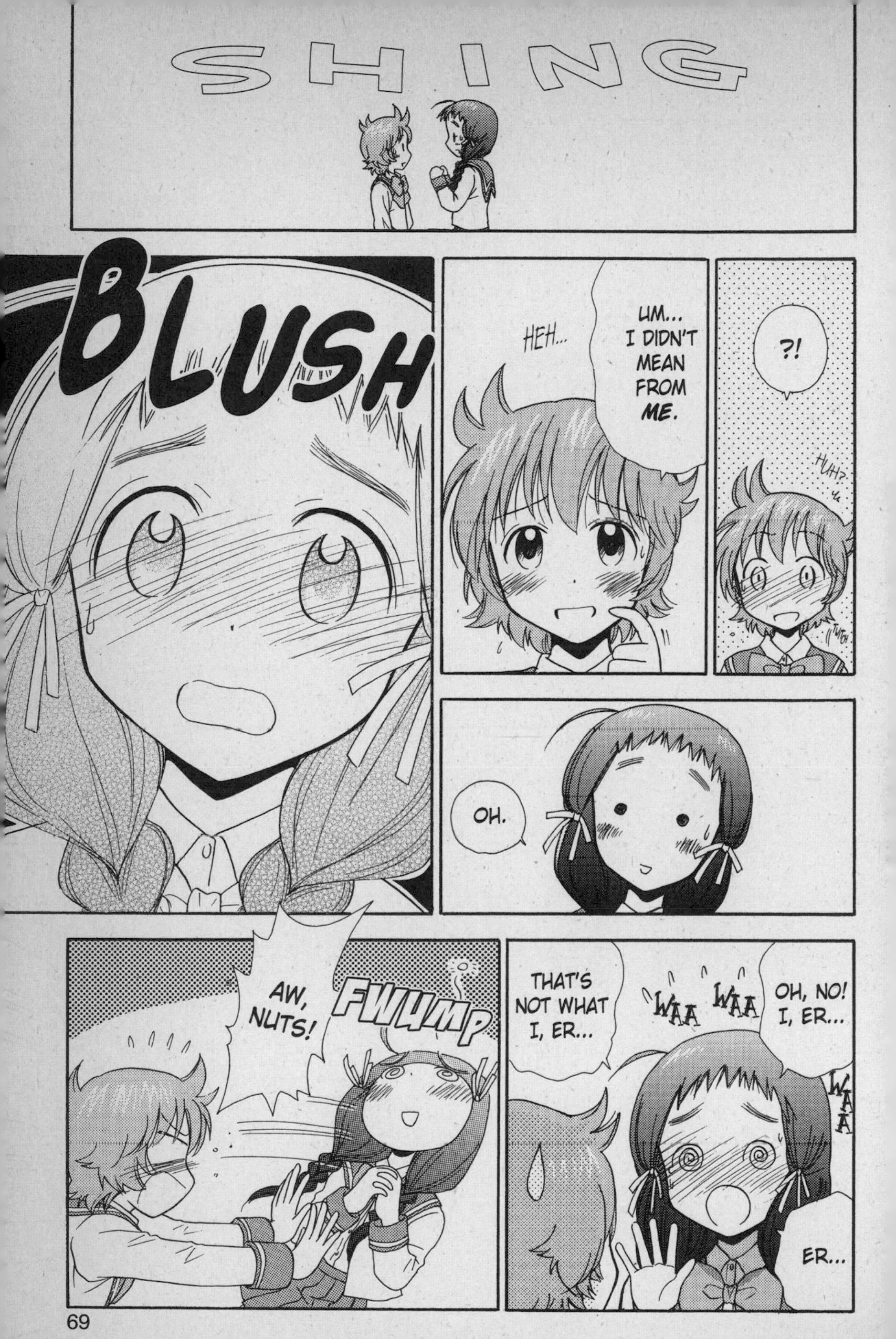
SHING
?!
HUH?
TWITCH
UM... I DIDN'T MEAN FROM *ME*.
HEH...
OH.
BLUSH
OH, NO! I, ER...
WAA
WAA
WAA
THAT'S NOT WHAT I, ER...
ER...
FWUMP
AW, NUTS!

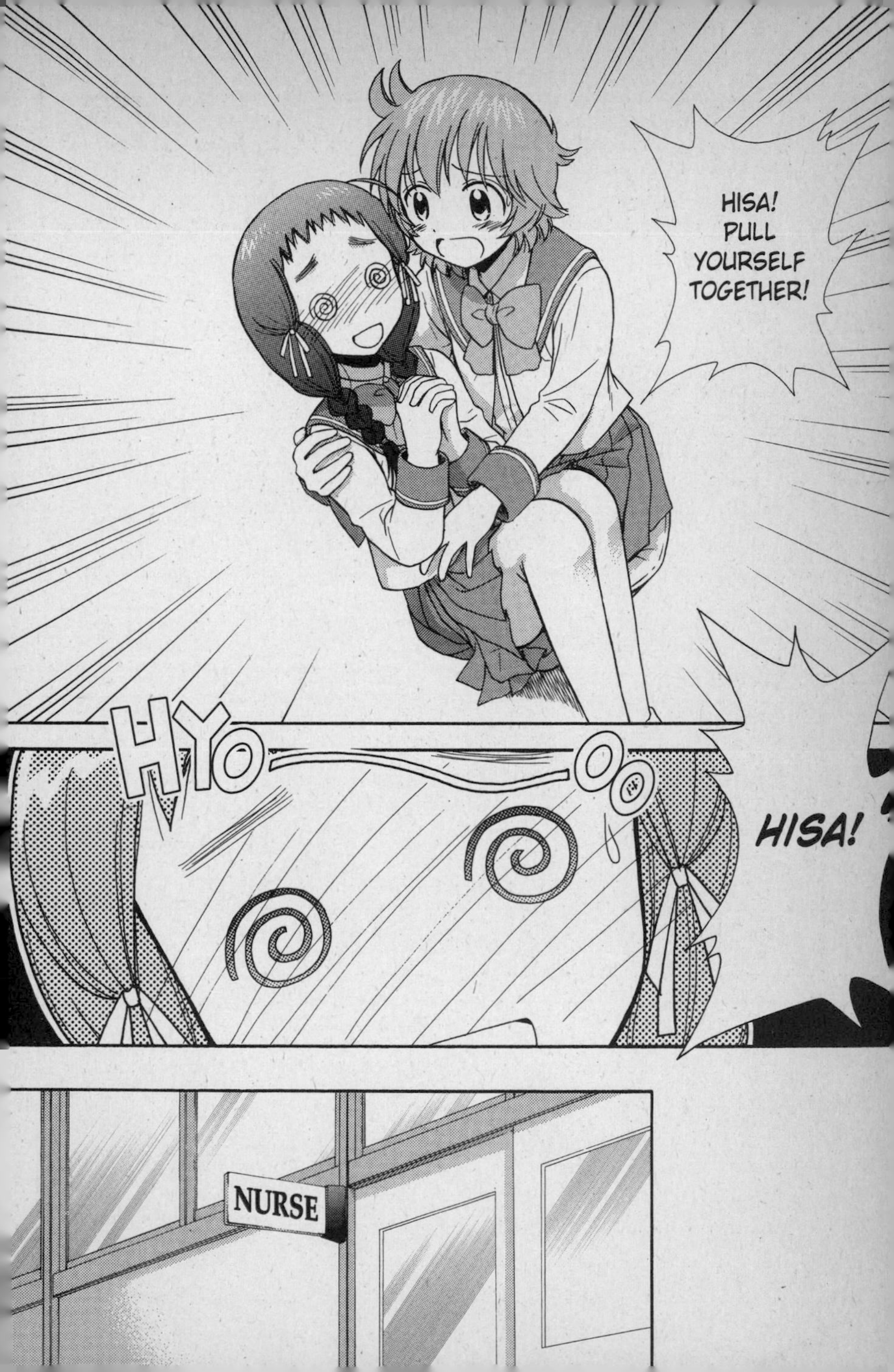
HISA! PULL YOURSELF TOGETHER!
HISA!
HYO—OO
NURSE

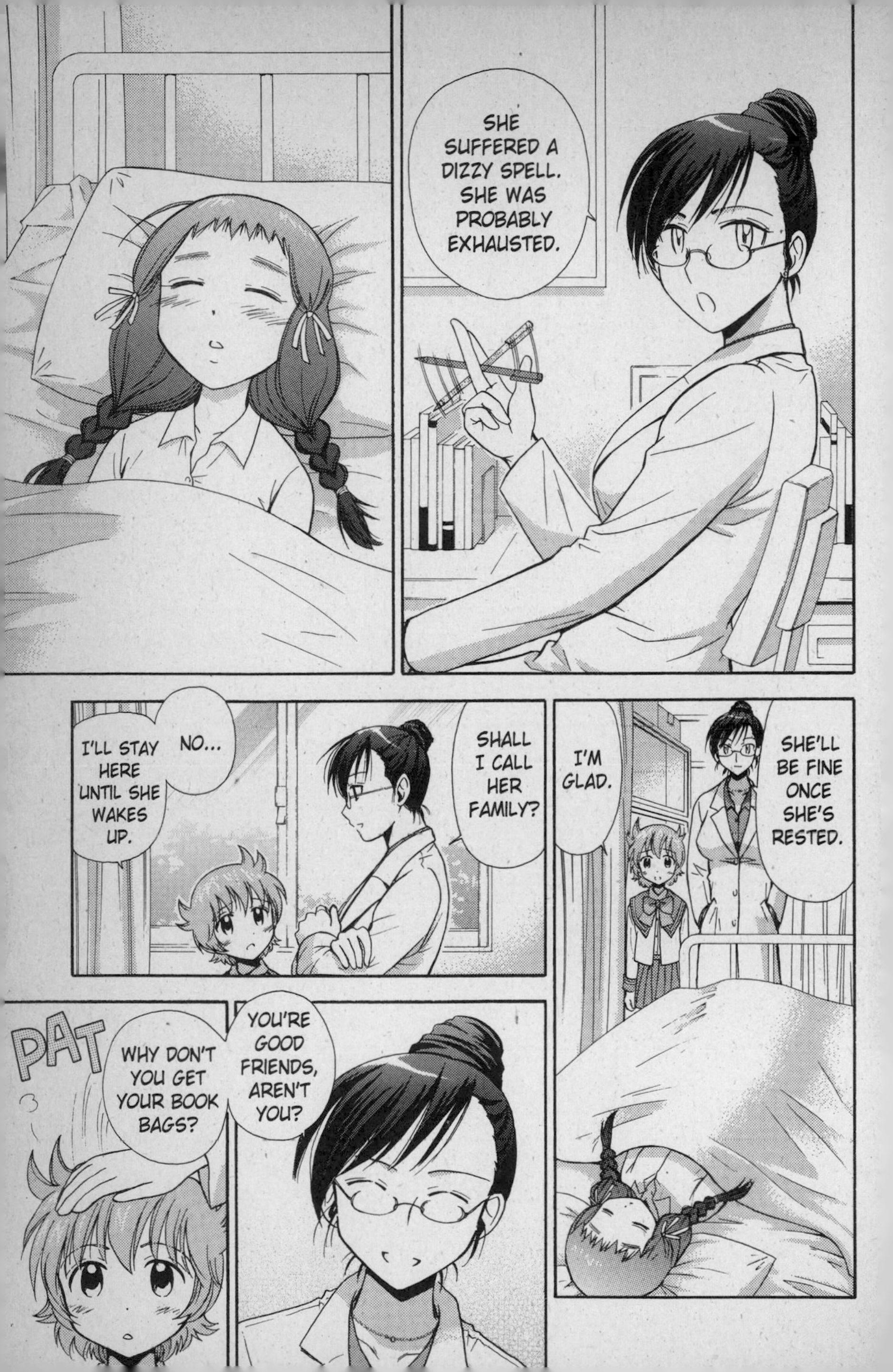
SHE SUFFERED A DIZZY SPELL. SHE WAS PROBABLY EXHAUSTED.
SHE'LL BE FINE ONCE SHE'S RESTED.
I'M GLAD.
SHALL I CALL HER FAMILY?
NO...
I'LL STAY HERE UNTIL SHE WAKES UP.
YOU'RE GOOD FRIENDS, AREN'T YOU?
PAT
WHY DON'T YOU GET YOUR BOOK BAGS?

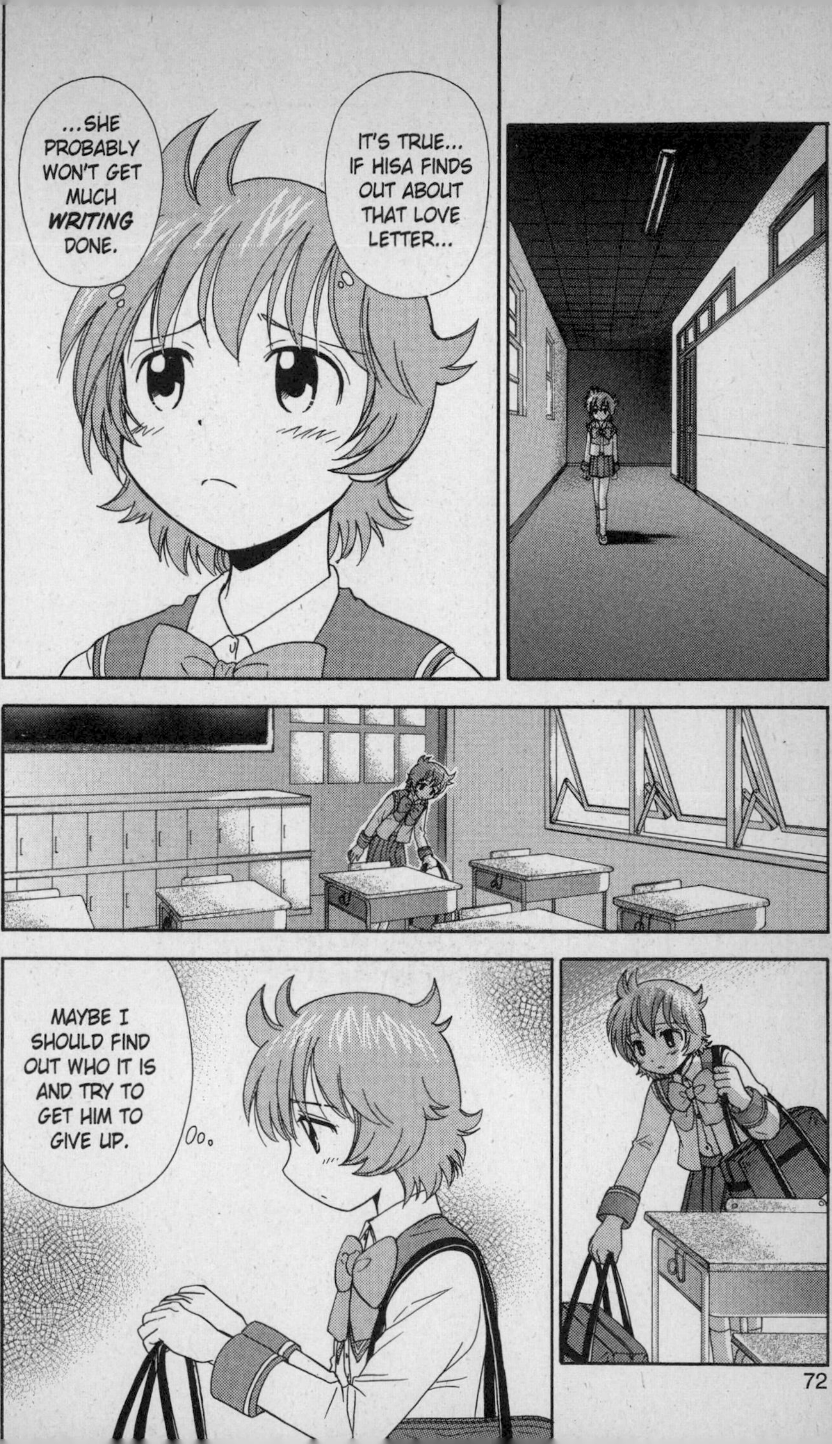
IT'S TRUE... IF HISA FINDS OUT ABOUT THAT LOVE LETTER...
...SHE PROBABLY WON'T GET MUCH *WRITING* DONE.
MAYBE I SHOULD FIND OUT WHO IT IS AND TRY TO GET HIM TO GIVE UP.
Ooo

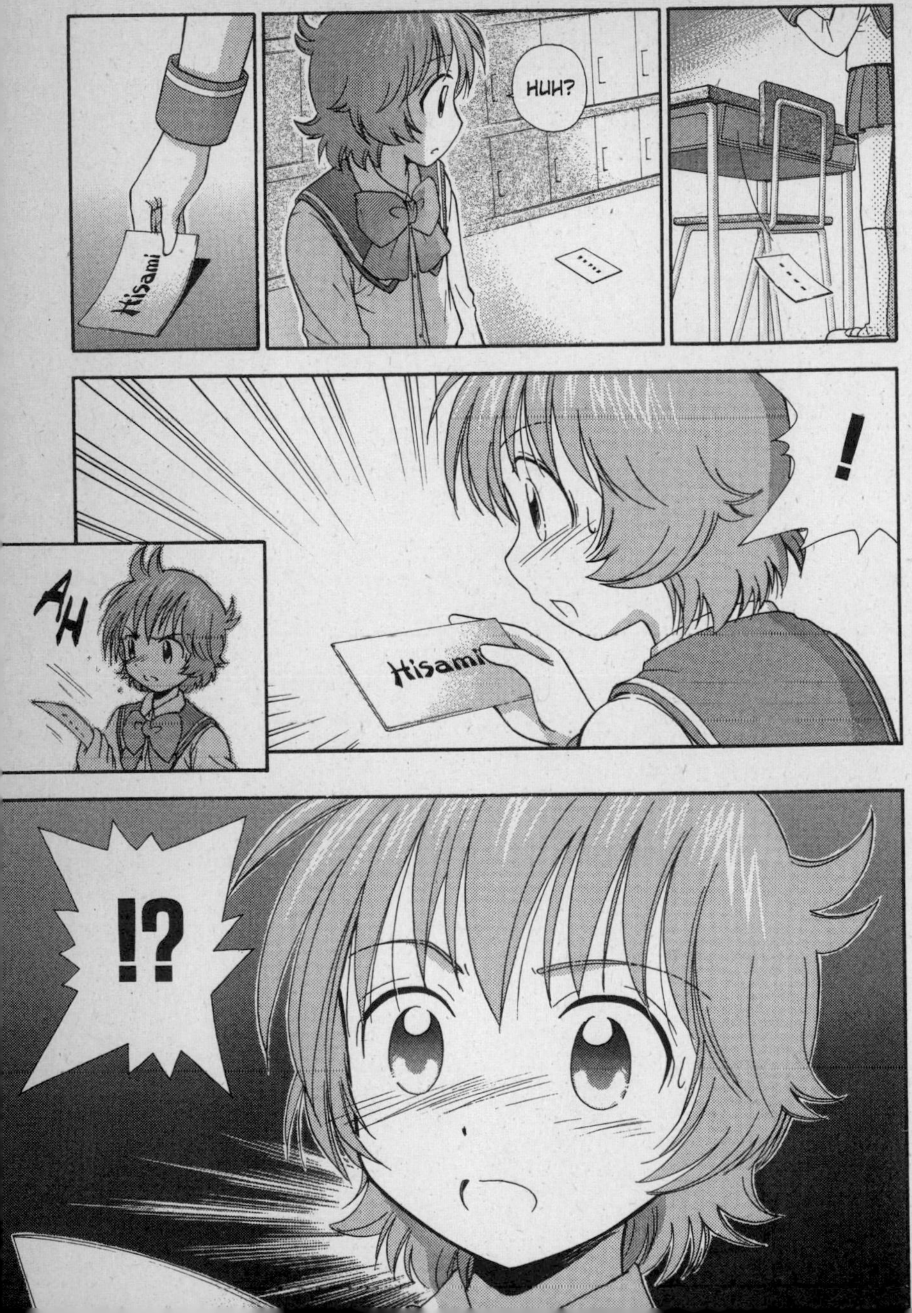
HUH?
Hisami
!
Hisami
AH
!?

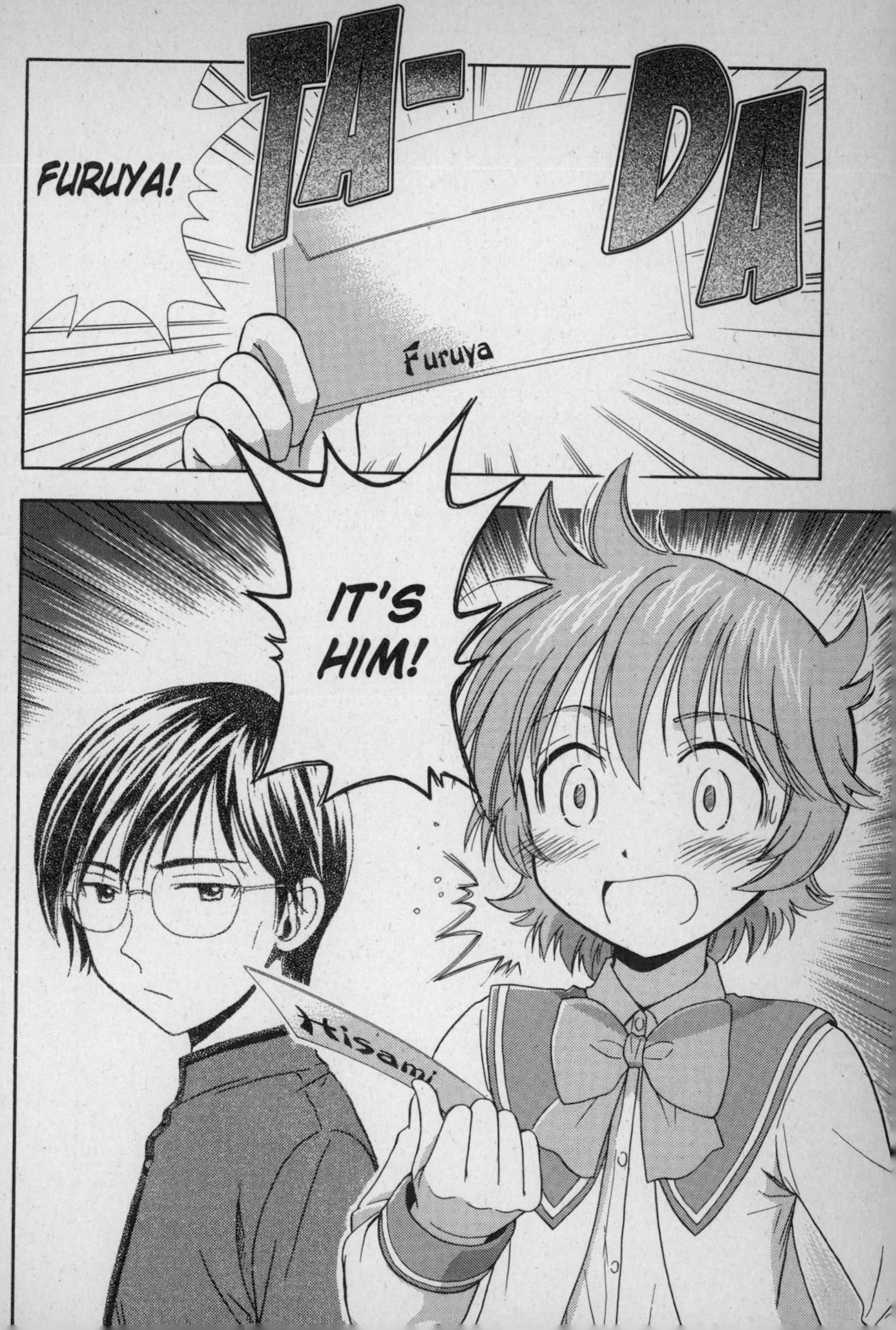
TA-DA
FURUYA!
Furuya
IT'S HIM!

CHAPTER 27

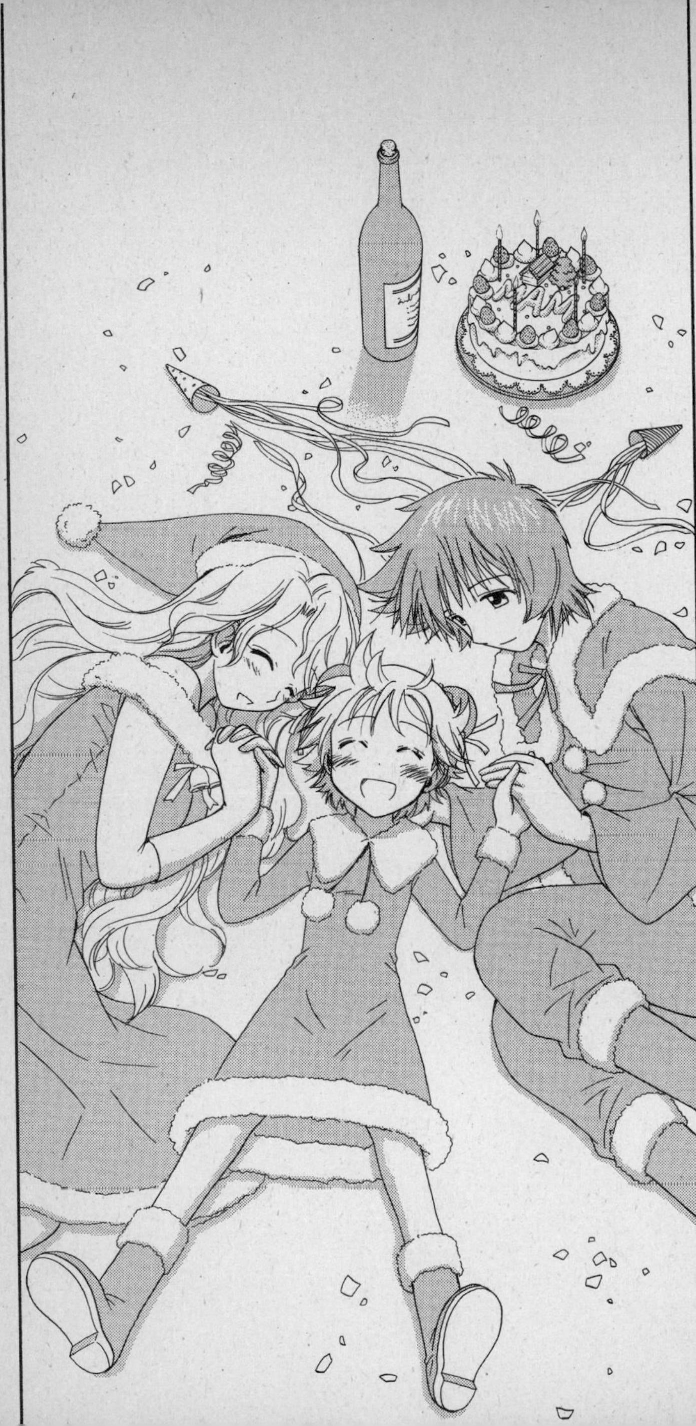

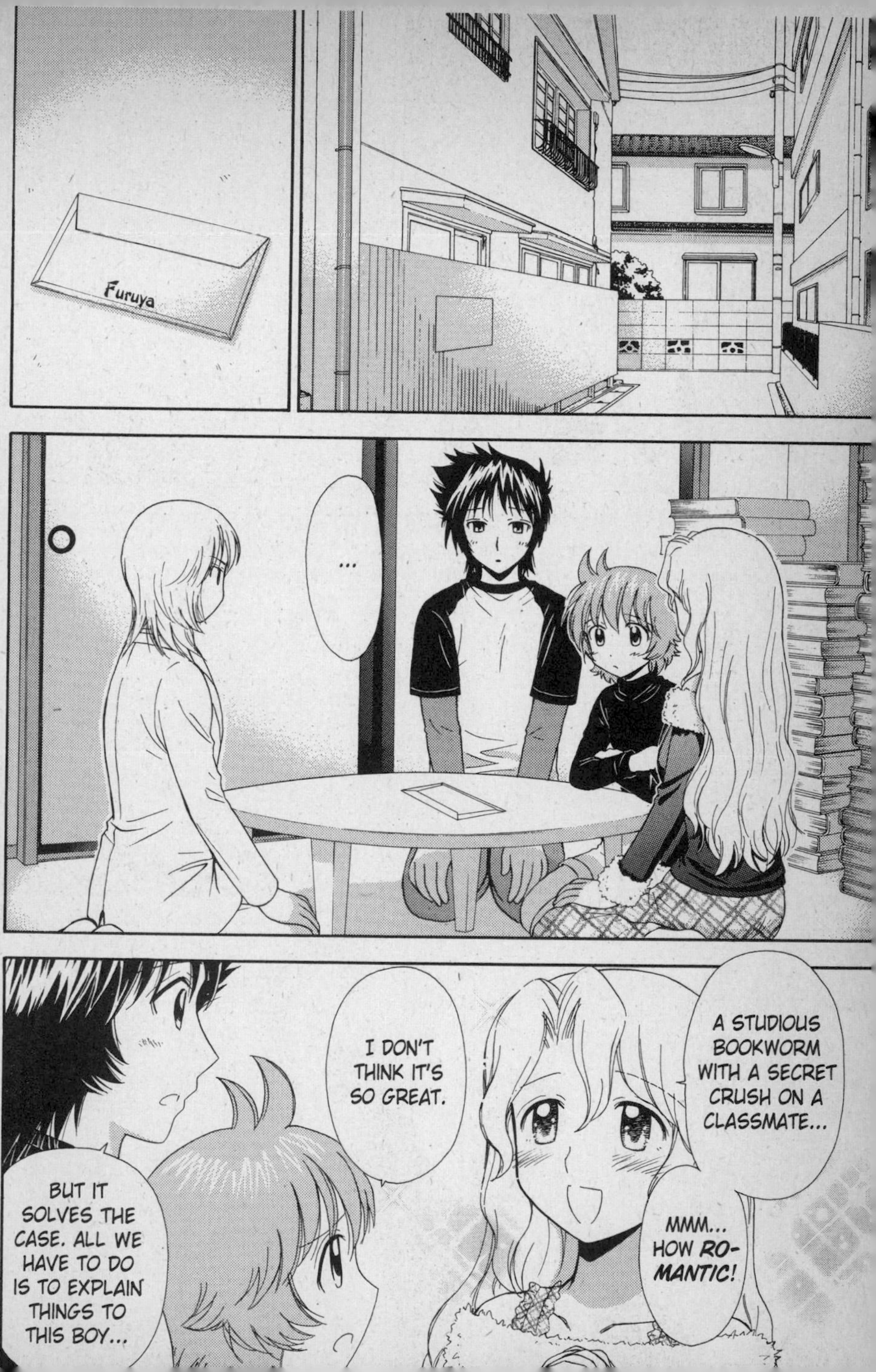
Furuya
...
A STUDIOUS BOOKWORM WITH A SECRET CRUSH ON A CLASSMATE...
I DON'T THINK IT'S SO GREAT.
MMM... HOW ROMANTIC!
BUT IT SOLVES THE CASE. ALL WE HAVE TO DO IS TO EXPLAIN THINGS TO THIS BOY...

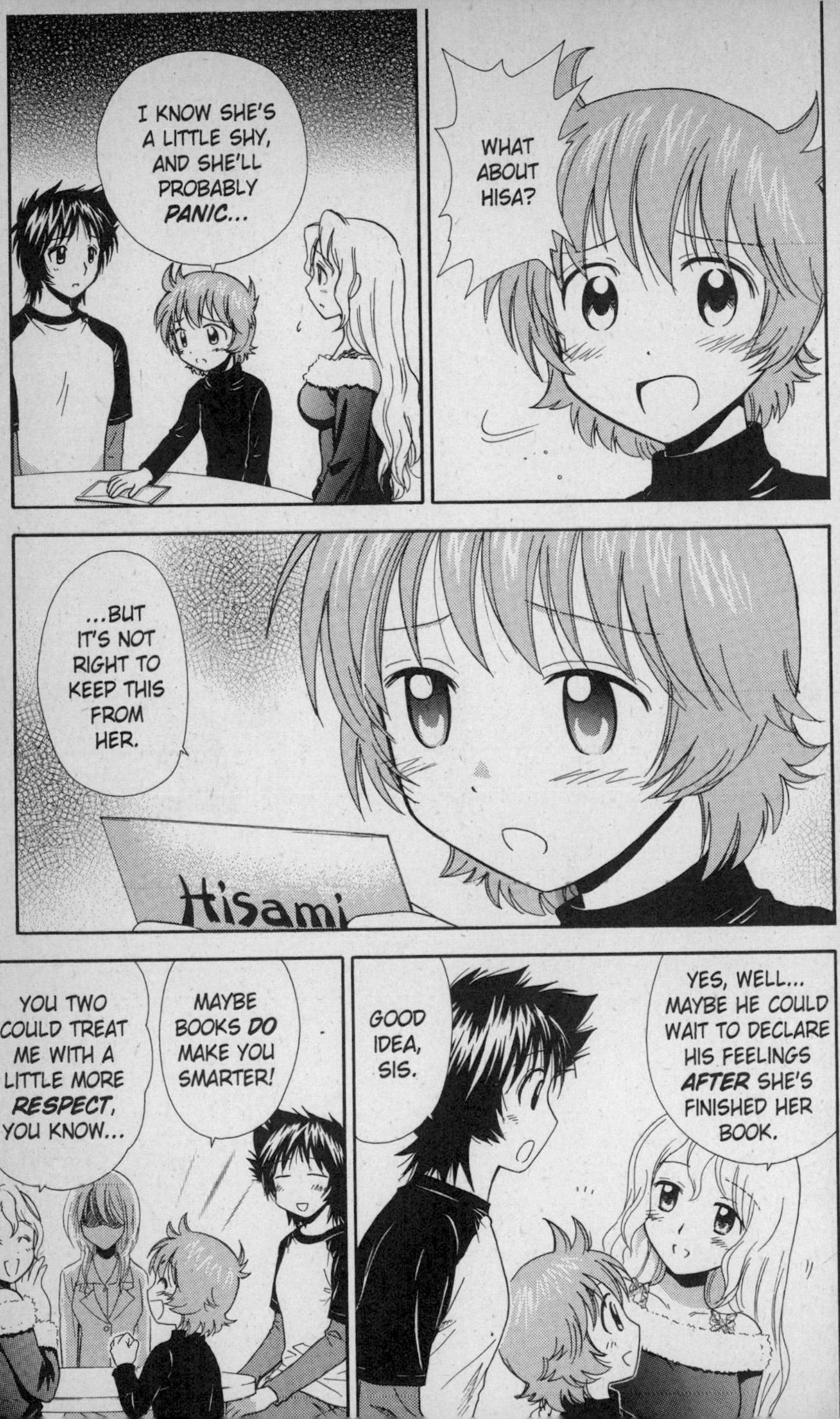
WHAT ABOUT HISA?
I KNOW SHE'S A LITTLE SHY, AND SHE'LL PROBABLY *PANIC*...
...BUT IT'S NOT RIGHT TO KEEP THIS FROM HER.
Hisami
YES, WELL... MAYBE HE COULD WAIT TO DECLARE HIS FEELINGS ***AFTER*** SHE'S FINISHED HER BOOK.
GOOD IDEA, SIS.
MAYBE BOOKS *DO* MAKE YOU SMARTER!
YOU TWO COULD TREAT ME WITH A LITTLE MORE ***RESPECT***, YOU KNOW...

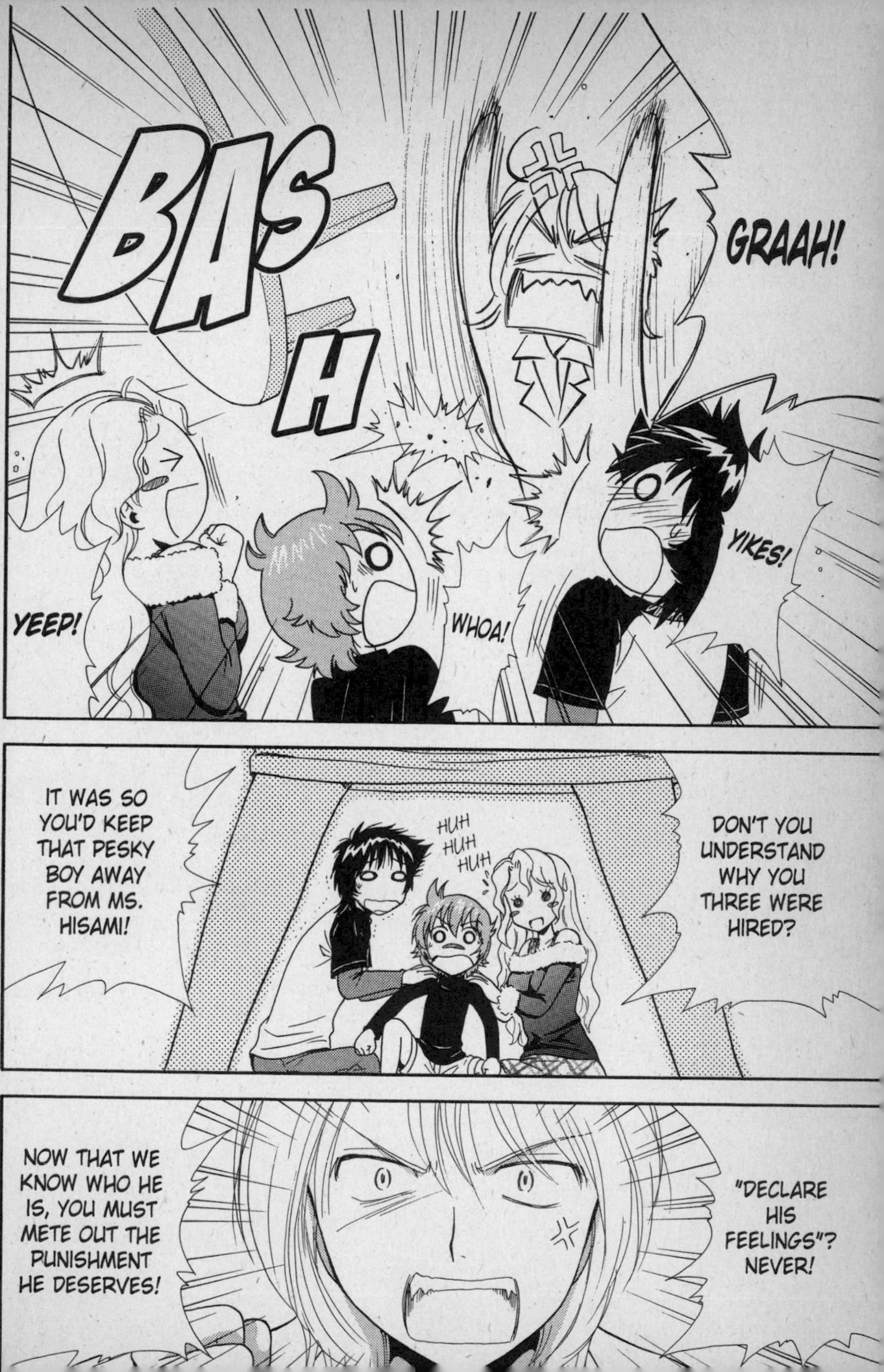
GRAAH!
BASH
YIKES!
WHOA!
YEEP!
DON'T YOU UNDERSTAND WHY YOU THREE WERE HIRED?
HUH HUH HUH
IT WAS SO YOU'D KEEP THAT PESKY BOY AWAY FROM MS. HISAMI!
"DECLARE HIS FEELINGS"? NEVER!
NOW THAT WE KNOW WHO HE IS, YOU MUST METE OUT THE PUNISHMENT HE DESERVES!

LIKE WHAT?

THE PUNISH-MENT...

...HE DE-SERVES?

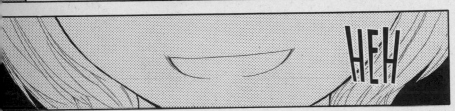

HEH

WHEW

FLIK

SHF

HELLO. THIS IS MS. ISHII.

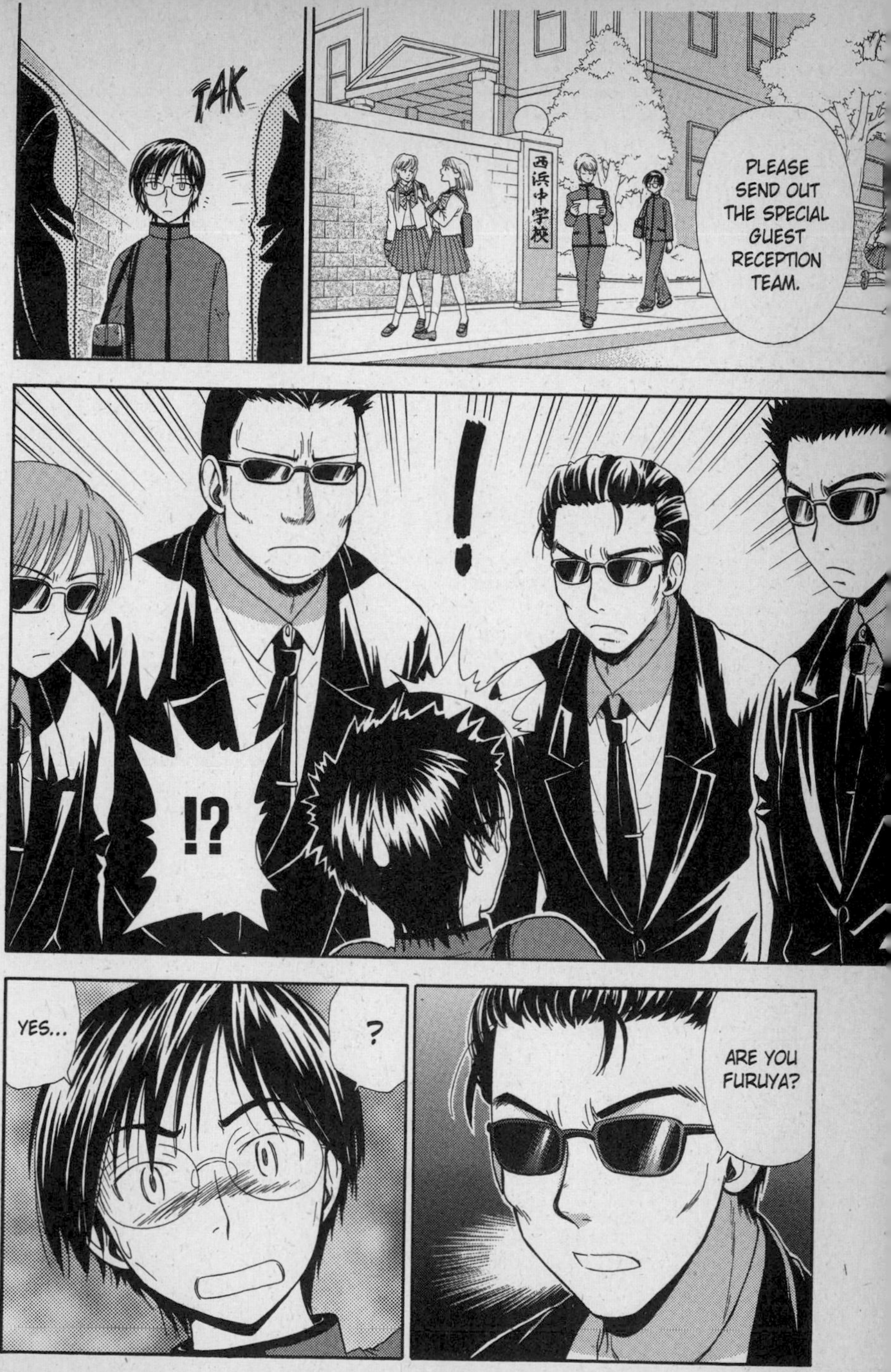

西浜中学校
PLEASE SEND OUT THE SPECIAL GUEST RECEPTION TEAM.
TAK
!
!?
ARE YOU FURUYA?
?
YES...

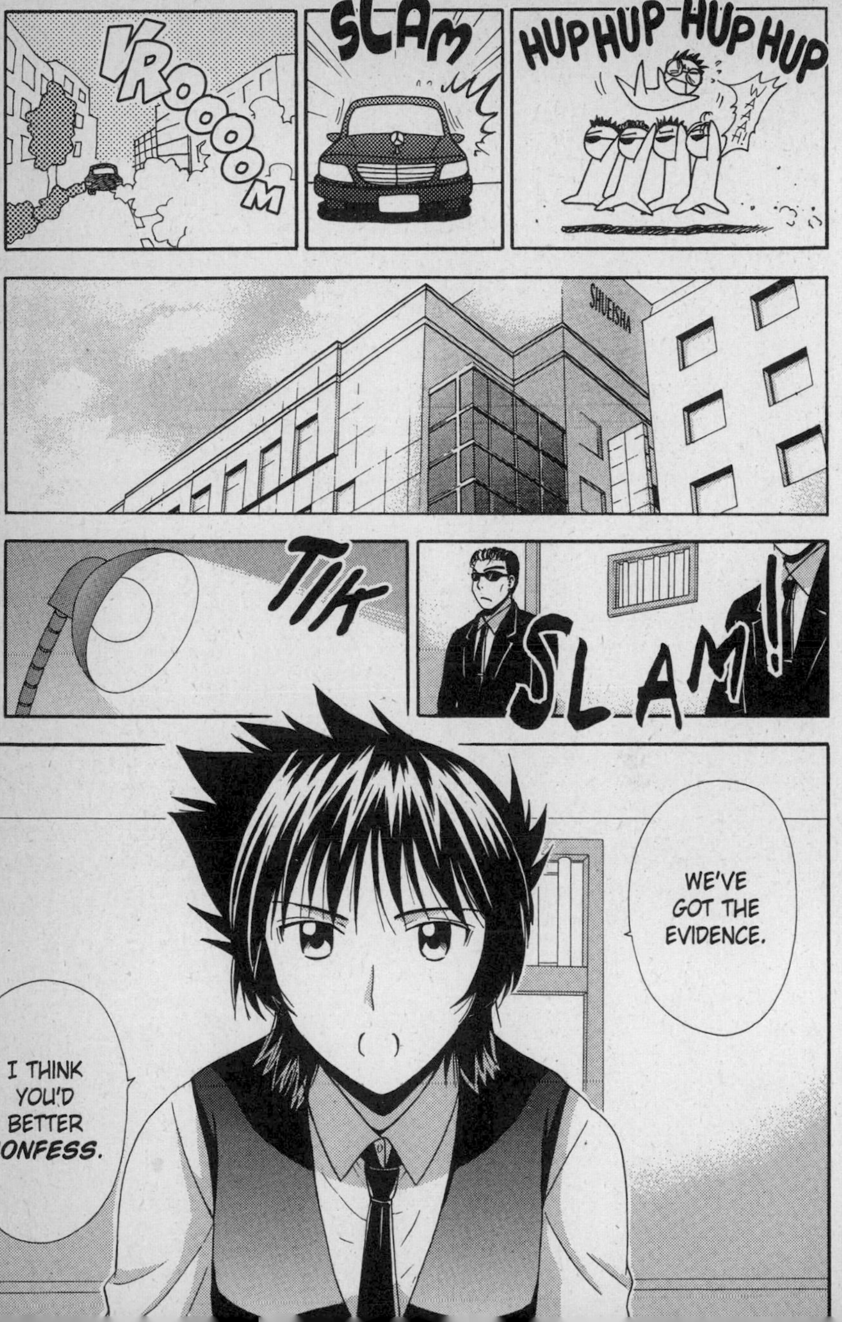
HUP HUP HUP HUP
WAAAH!
SLAM
VROOOOM
SHUEISHA
SLAM!
TIK
WE'VE GOT THE EVIDENCE.
I THINK YOU'D BETTER CONFESS.

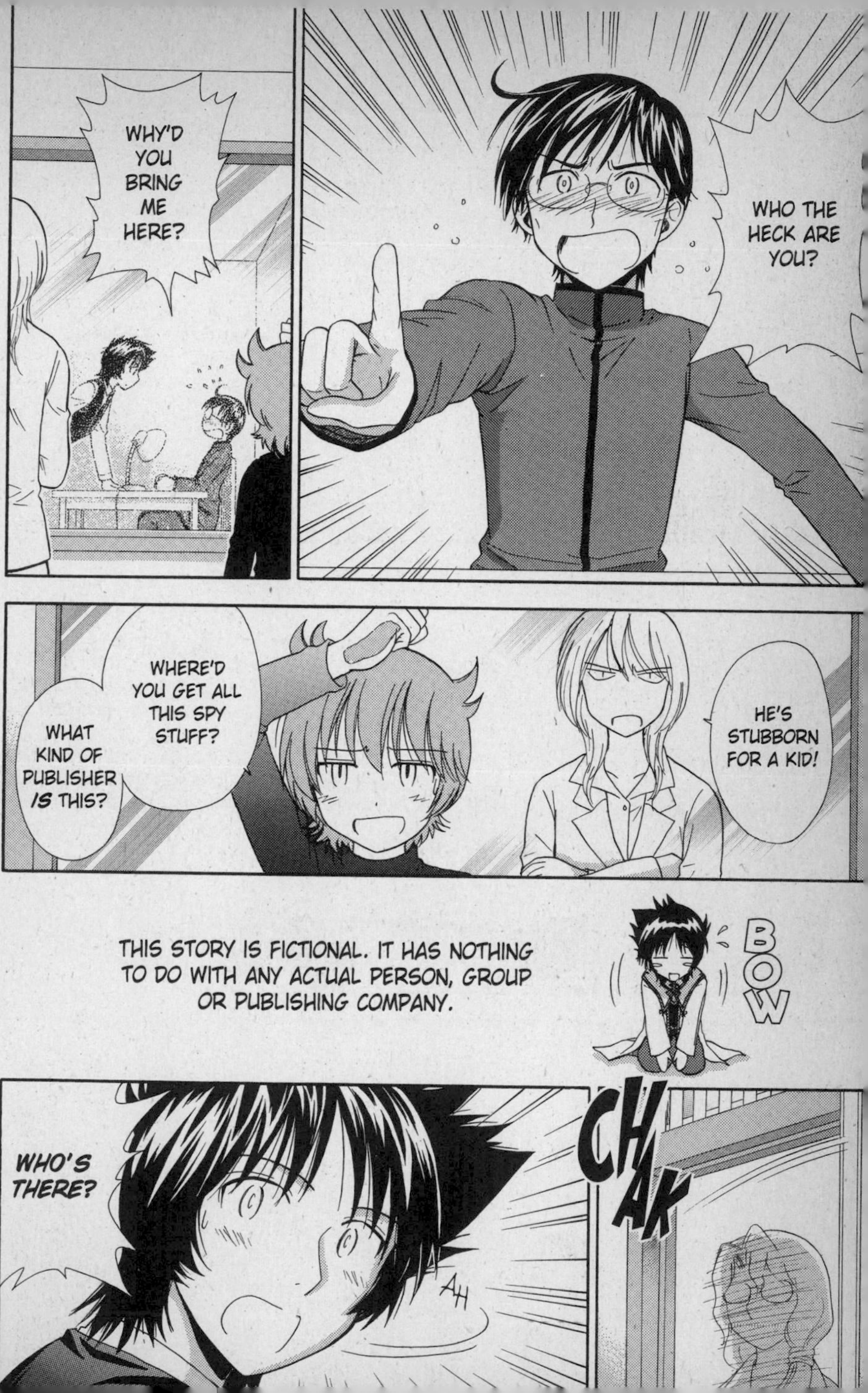
WHO THE HECK ARE YOU?
WHY'D YOU BRING ME HERE?
HE'S STUBBORN FOR A KID!
WHERE'D YOU GET ALL THIS SPY STUFF?
WHAT KIND OF PUBLISHER *IS* THIS?
BOW
THIS STORY IS FICTIONAL. IT HAS NOTHING TO DO WITH ANY ACTUAL PERSON, GROUP OR PUBLISHING COMPANY.
CHAK
AH
WHO'S THERE?

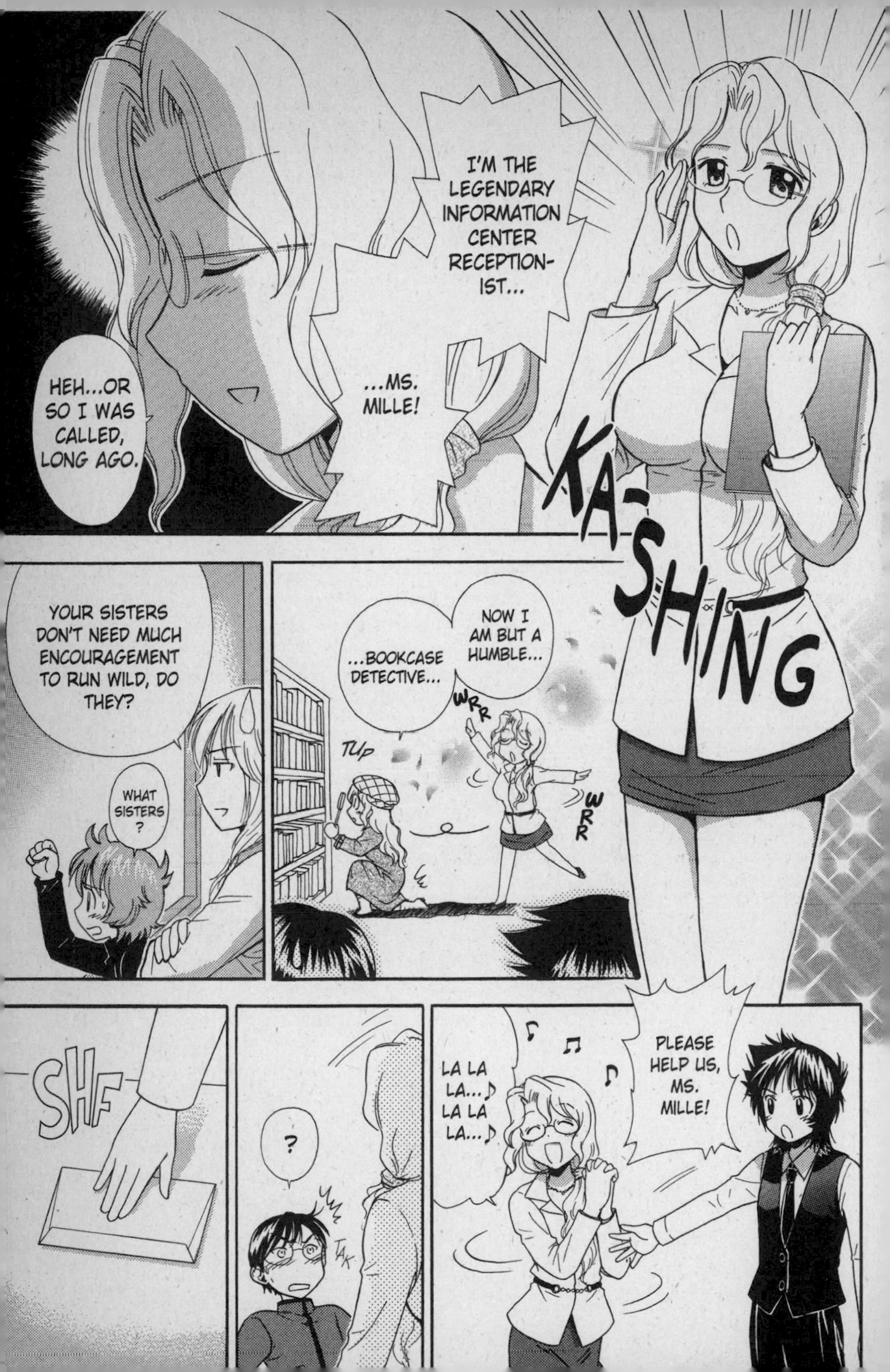
I'M THE LEGENDARY INFORMATION CENTER RECEPTION-IST...
...MS. MILLE!
KA-SHING
HEH...OR SO I WAS CALLED, LONG AGO.
NOW I AM BUT A HUMBLE...
...BOOKCASE DETECTIVE...
WRR
WRR
TUP
YOUR SISTERS DON'T NEED MUCH ENCOURAGEMENT TO RUN WILD, DO THEY?
WHAT SISTERS?
PLEASE HELP US, MS. MILLE!
LA LA LA...♪ LA LA LA...♪
?
TAK
SHF

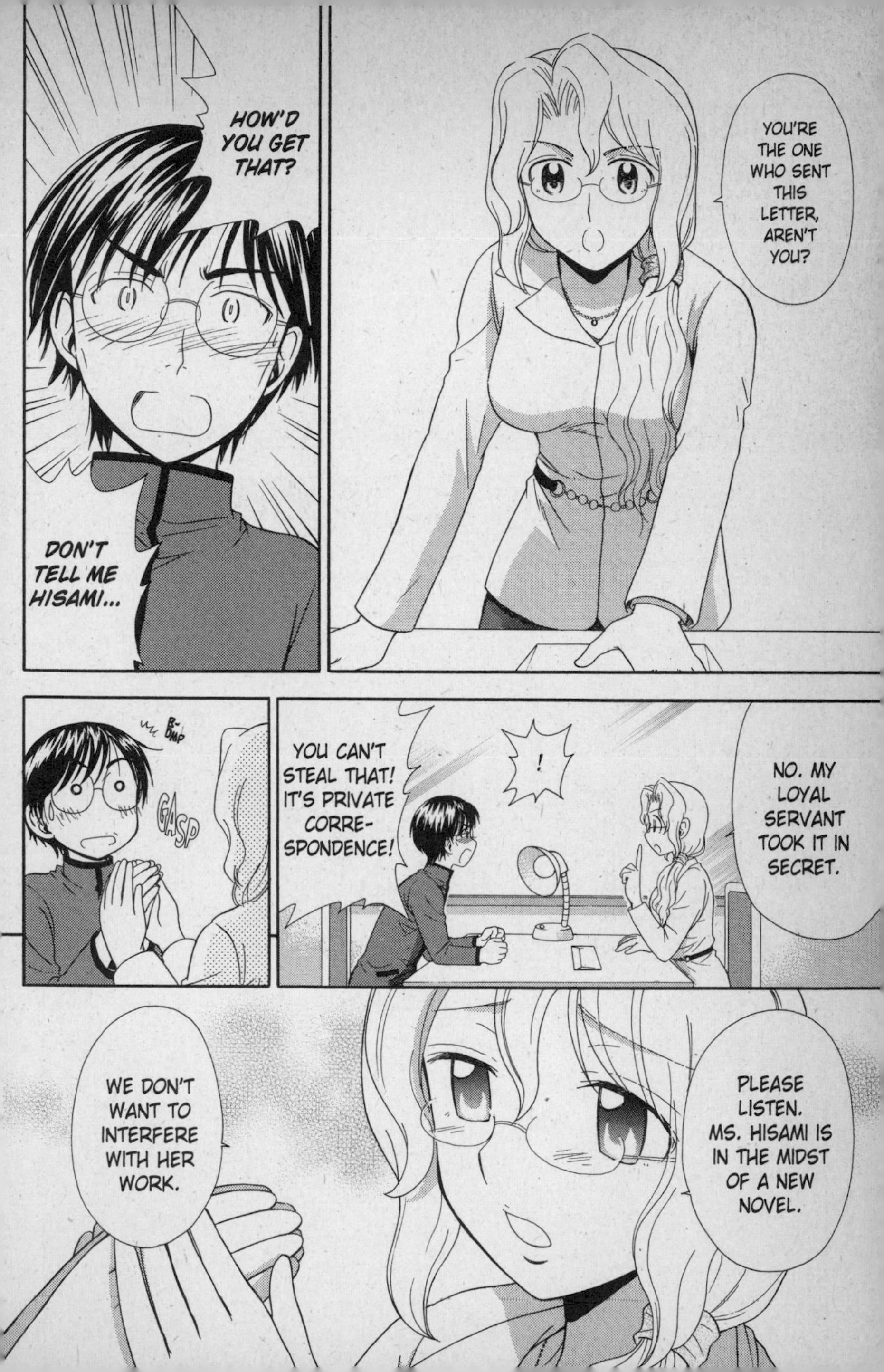
YOU'RE THE ONE WHO SENT THIS LETTER, AREN'T YOU?
HOW'D YOU GET THAT?
DON'T TELL ME HISAMI...
NO. MY LOYAL SERVANT TOOK IT IN SECRET.
!
YOU CAN'T STEAL THAT! IT'S PRIVATE CORRE-SPONDENCE!
B-DMP
GASP
PLEASE LISTEN. MS. HISAMI IS IN THE MIDST OF A NEW NOVEL.
WE DON'T WANT TO INTERFERE WITH HER WORK.

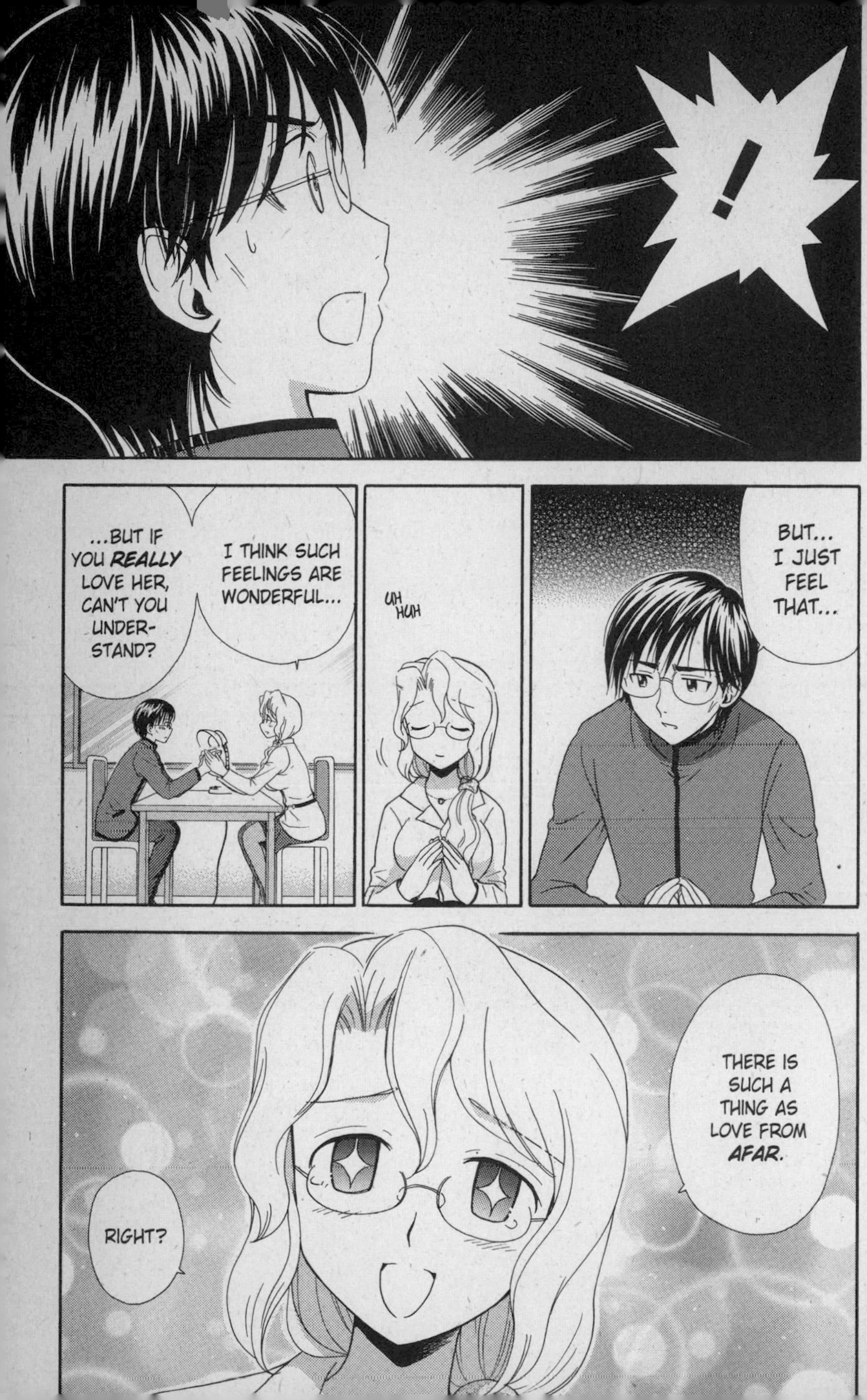
!
BUT... I JUST FEEL THAT...
UH HUH
I THINK SUCH FEELINGS ARE WONDERFUL...
...BUT IF YOU *REALLY* LOVE HER, CAN'T YOU UNDER-STAND?
THERE IS SUCH A THING AS LOVE FROM *AFAR*.
RIGHT?

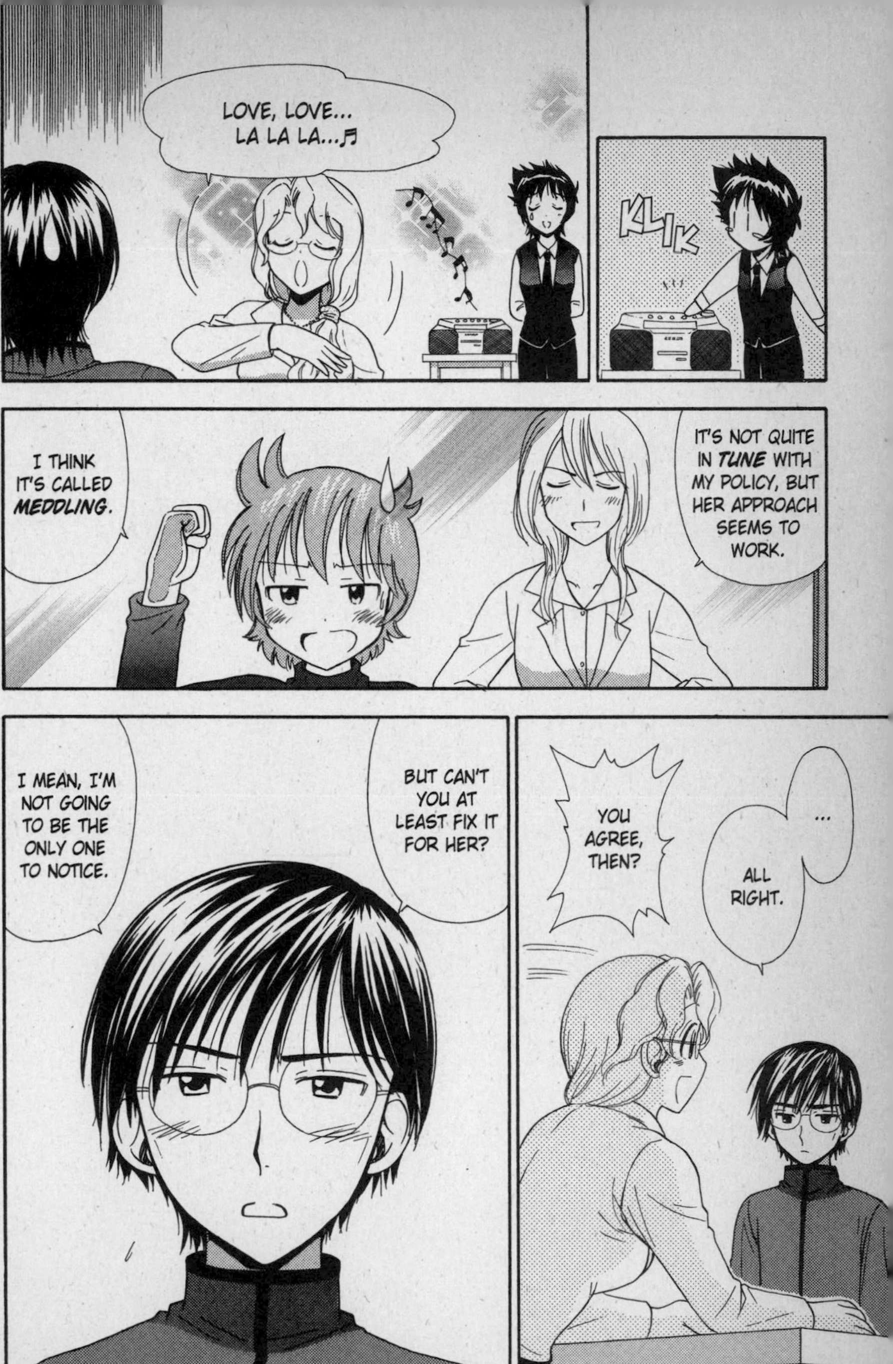
KLIK
LOVE, LOVE... LA LA LA...♬
IT'S NOT QUITE IN TUNE WITH MY POLICY, BUT HER APPROACH SEEMS TO WORK.
I THINK IT'S CALLED MEDDLING.
YOU AGREE, THEN?
... ALL RIGHT.
BUT CAN'T YOU AT LEAST FIX IT FOR HER?
I MEAN, I'M NOT GOING TO BE THE ONLY ONE TO NOTICE.

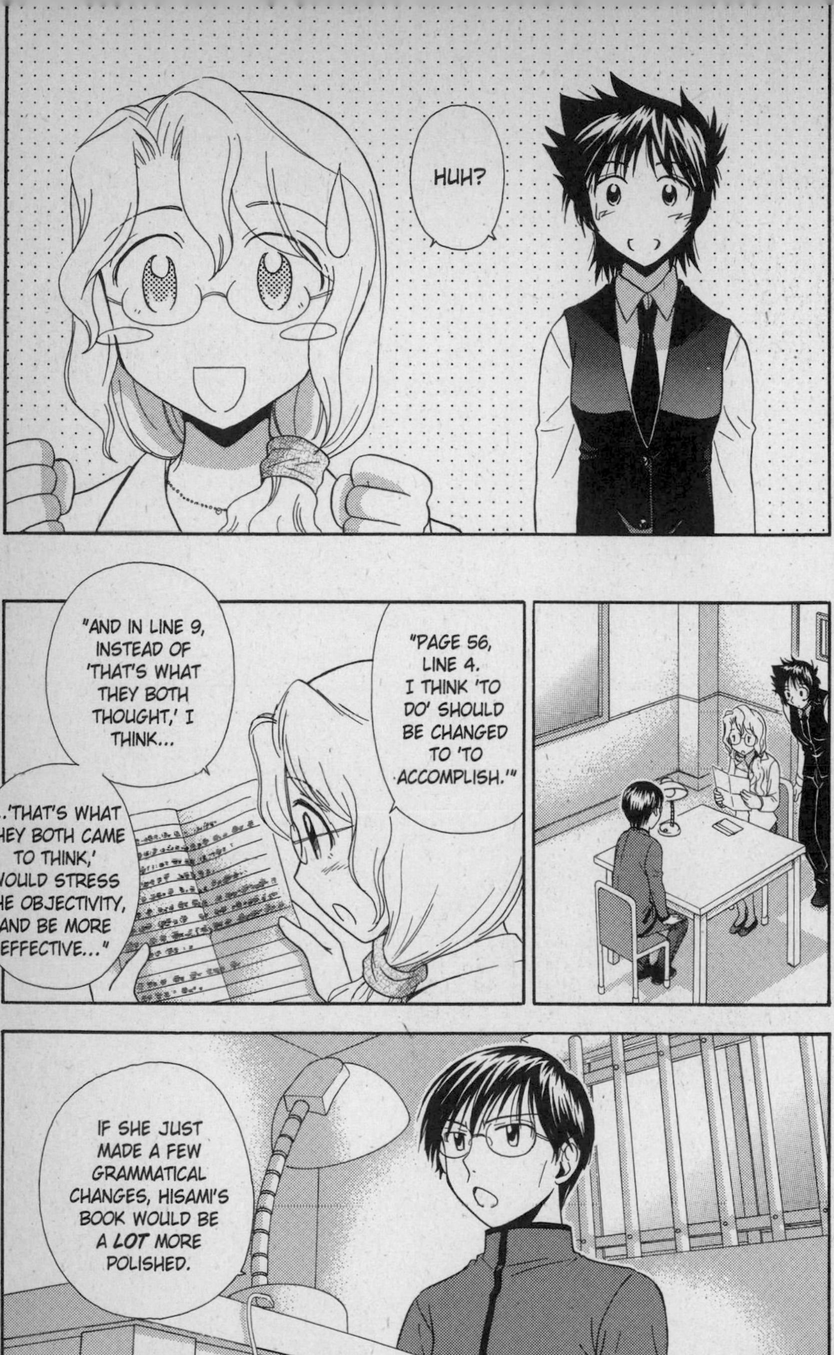
HUH?
"PAGE 56, LINE 4. I THINK 'TO DO' SHOULD BE CHANGED TO 'TO ACCOMPLISH.'"
"AND IN LINE 9, INSTEAD OF 'THAT'S WHAT THEY BOTH THOUGHT,' I THINK...
...'THAT'S WHAT THEY BOTH CAME TO THINK,' WOULD STRESS THE OBJECTIVITY, AND BE MORE EFFECTIVE..."
IF SHE JUST MADE A FEW GRAMMATICAL CHANGES, HISAMI'S BOOK WOULD BE A *LOT* MORE POLISHED.

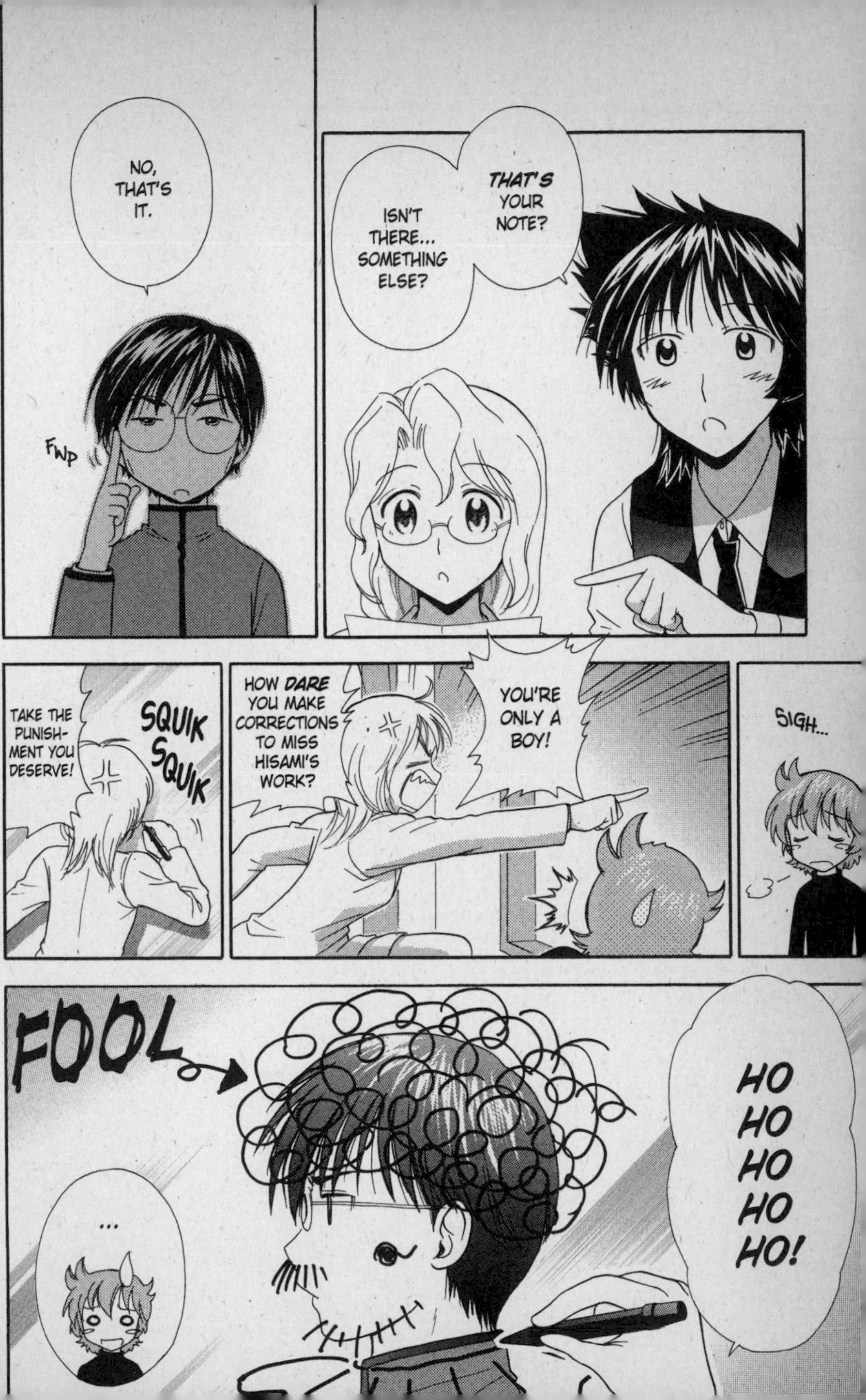
THAT'S YOUR NOTE?
ISN'T THERE... SOMETHING ELSE?
NO, THAT'S IT.
FWP
SIGH...
YOU'RE ONLY A BOY!
HOW DARE YOU MAKE CORRECTIONS TO MISS HISAMI'S WORK?
SQUIK SQUIK
TAKE THE PUNISH-MENT YOU DESERVE!
HO HO HO HO HO HO!
FOOL
...

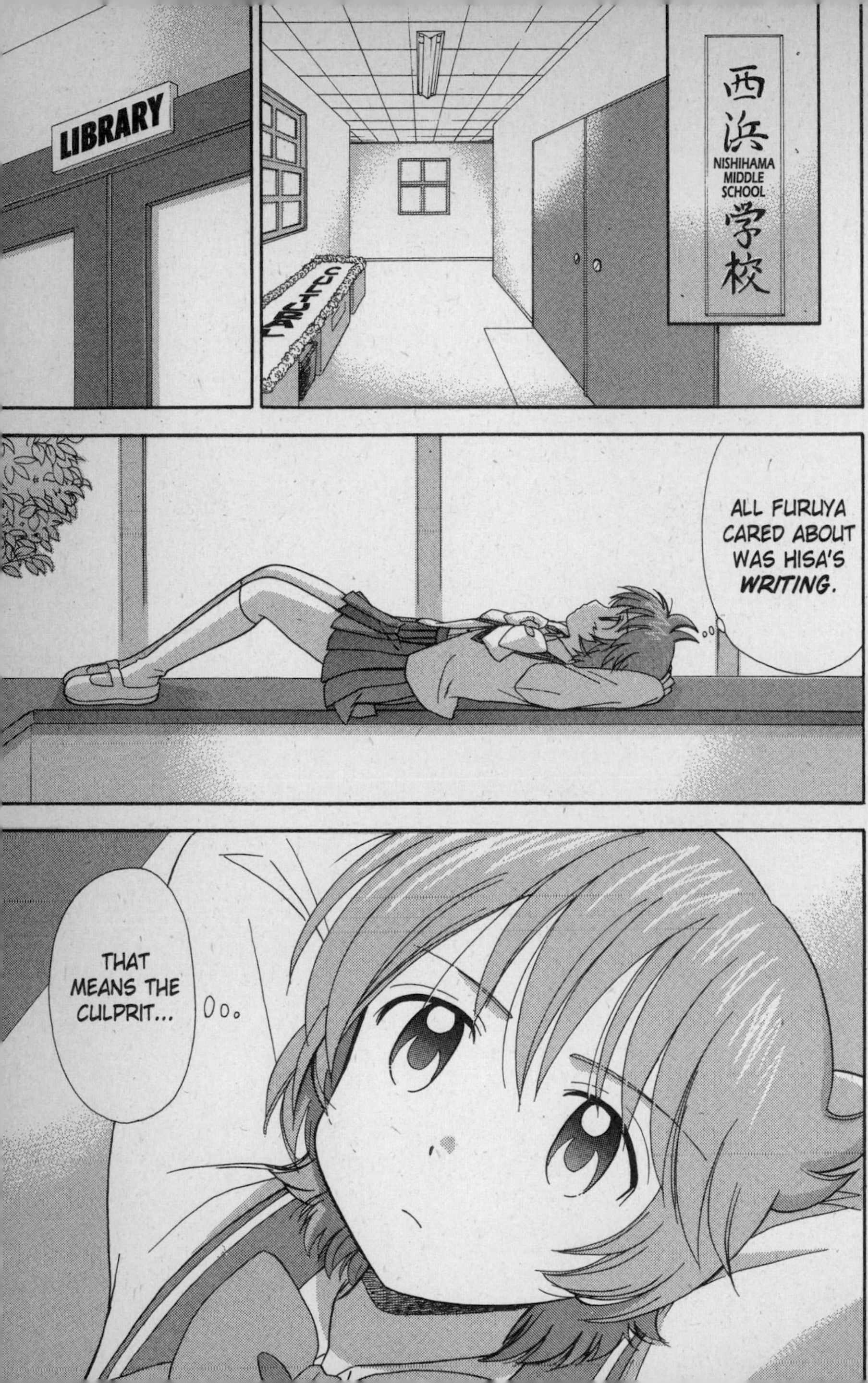
西浜
NISHIHAMA MIDDLE SCHOOL
学校
LIBRARY
ALL FURUYA CARED ABOUT WAS HISA'S *WRITING*.
THAT MEANS THE CULPRIT...

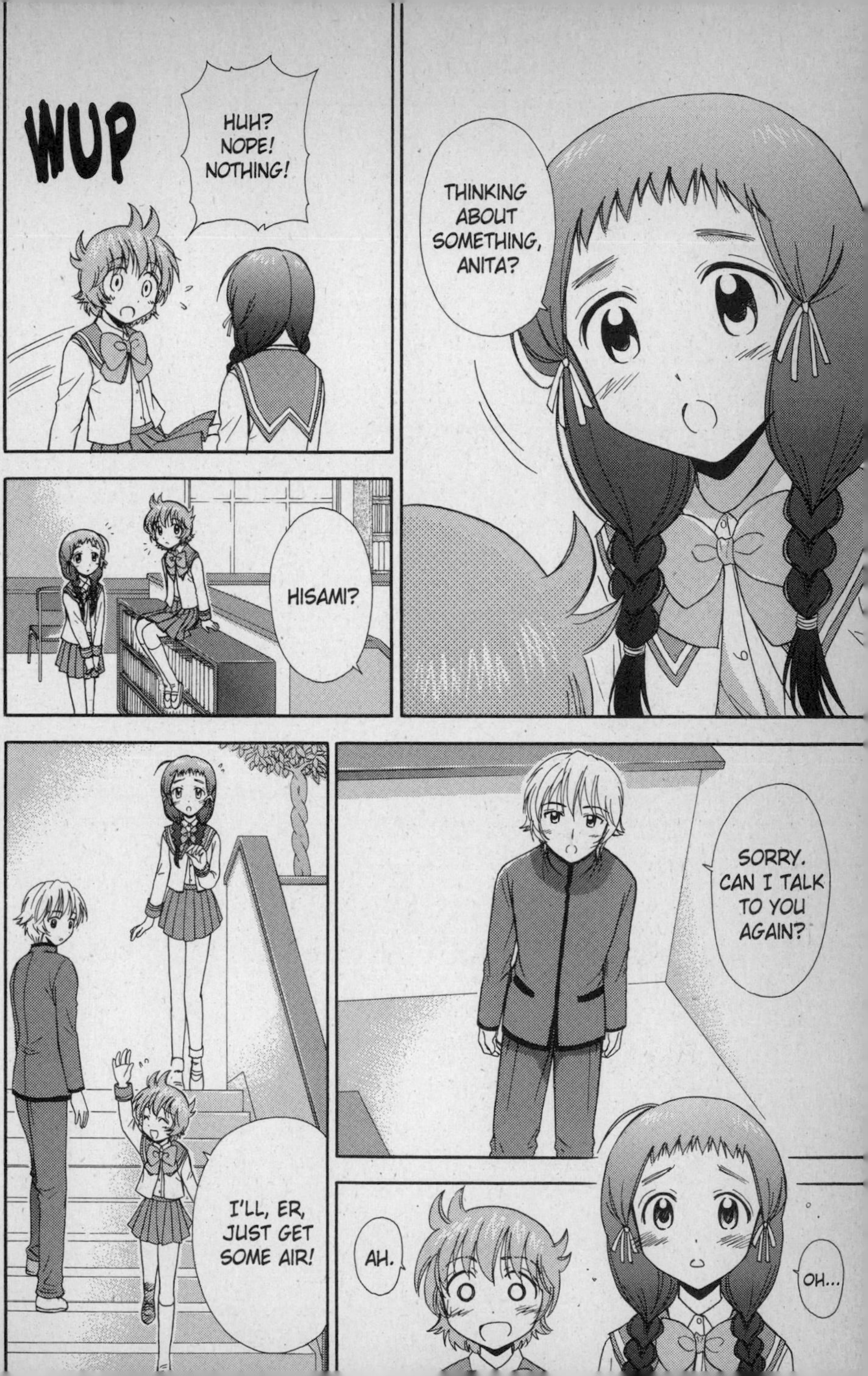
THINKING ABOUT SOMETHING, ANITA?
WUP
HUH? NOPE! NOTHING!
HISAMI?
SORRY. CAN I TALK TO YOU AGAIN?
OH...
AH.
I'LL, ER, JUST GET SOME AIR!

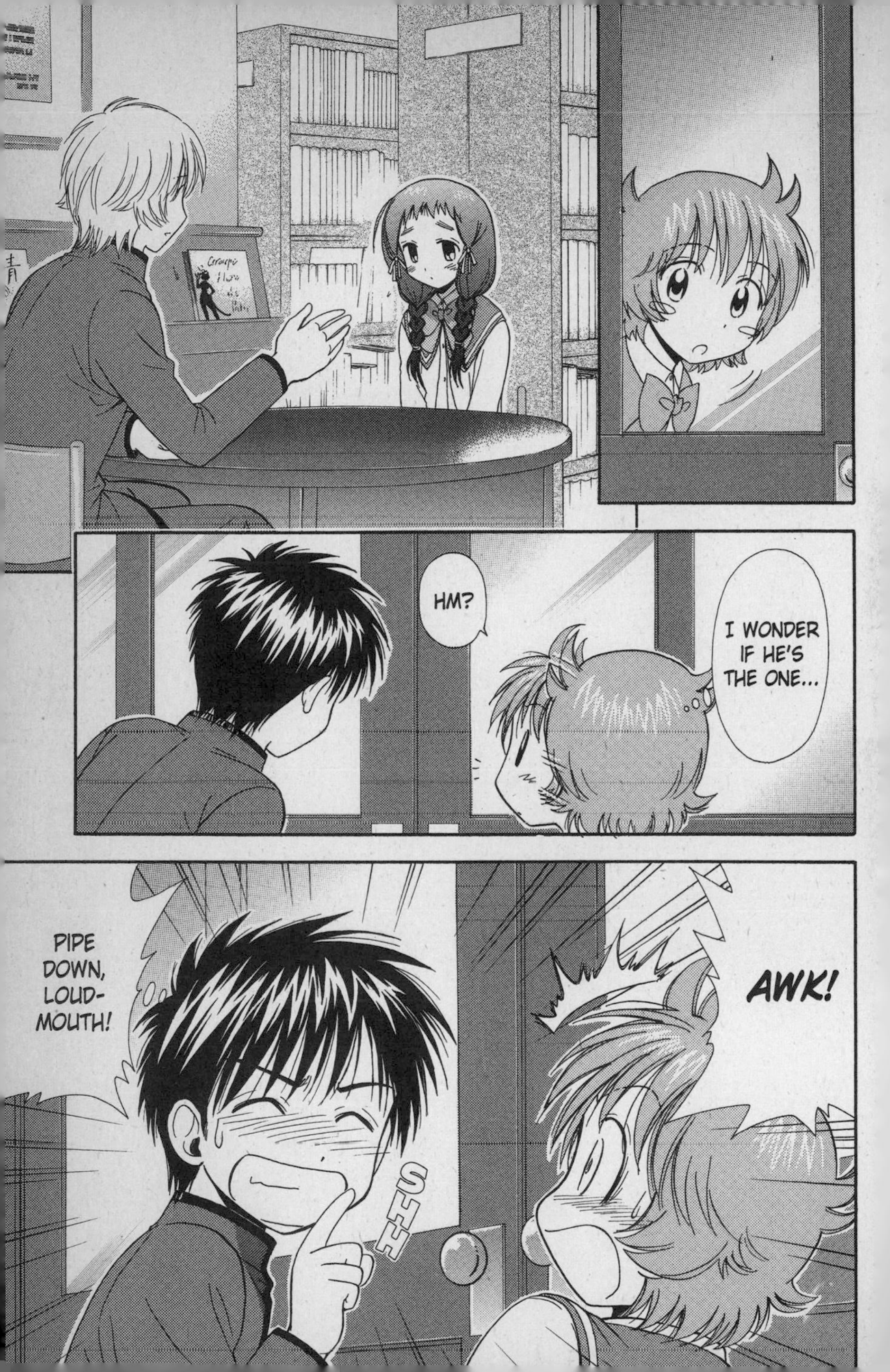
I WONDER IF HE'S THE ONE...
HM?
AWK!
PIPE DOWN, LOUD-MOUTH!
SHHH

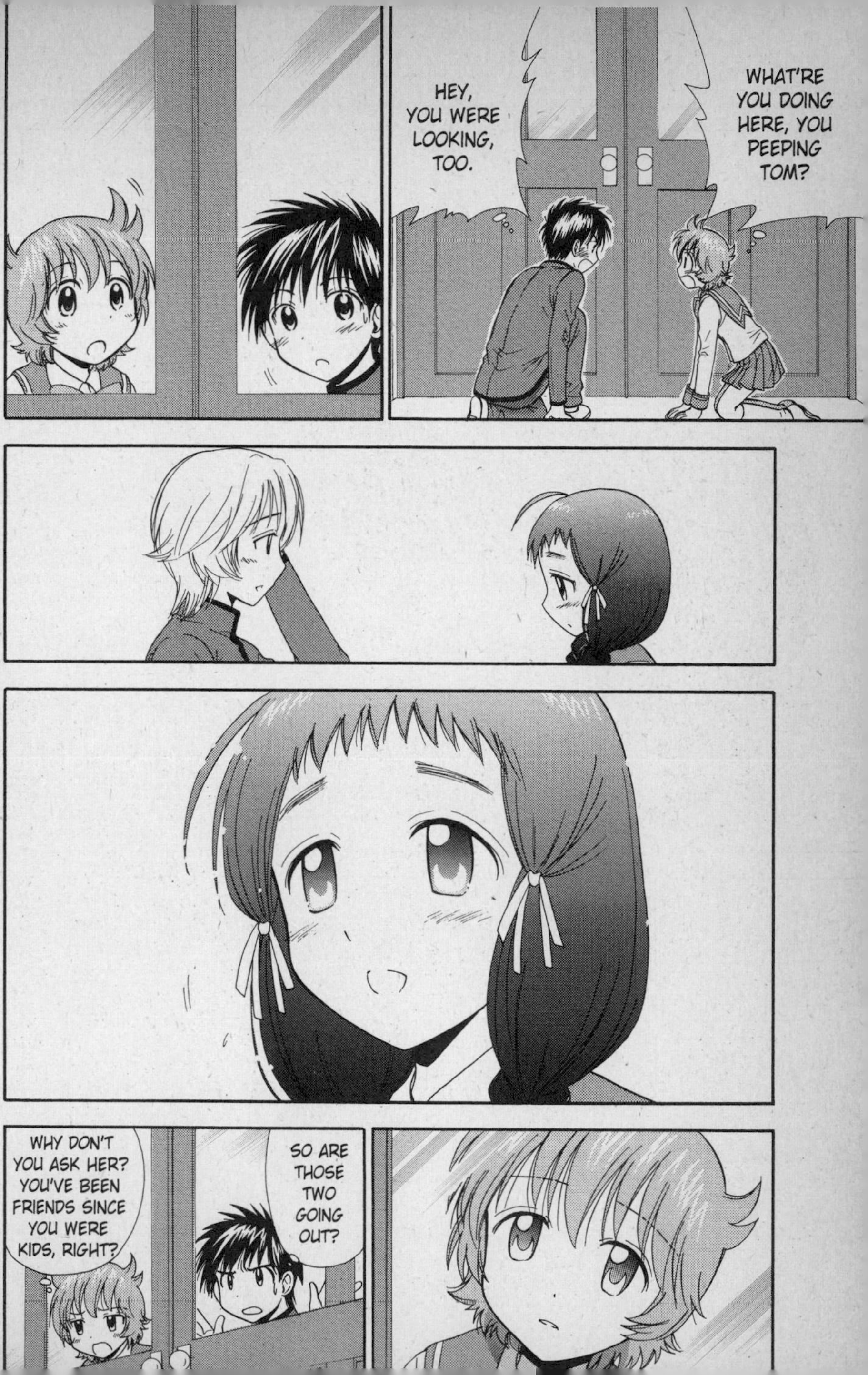
WHAT'RE YOU DOING HERE, YOU PEEPING TOM?
HEY, YOU WERE LOOKING, TOO.
SO ARE THOSE TWO GOING OUT?
WHY DON'T YOU ASK HER? YOU'VE BEEN FRIENDS SINCE YOU WERE KIDS, RIGHT?

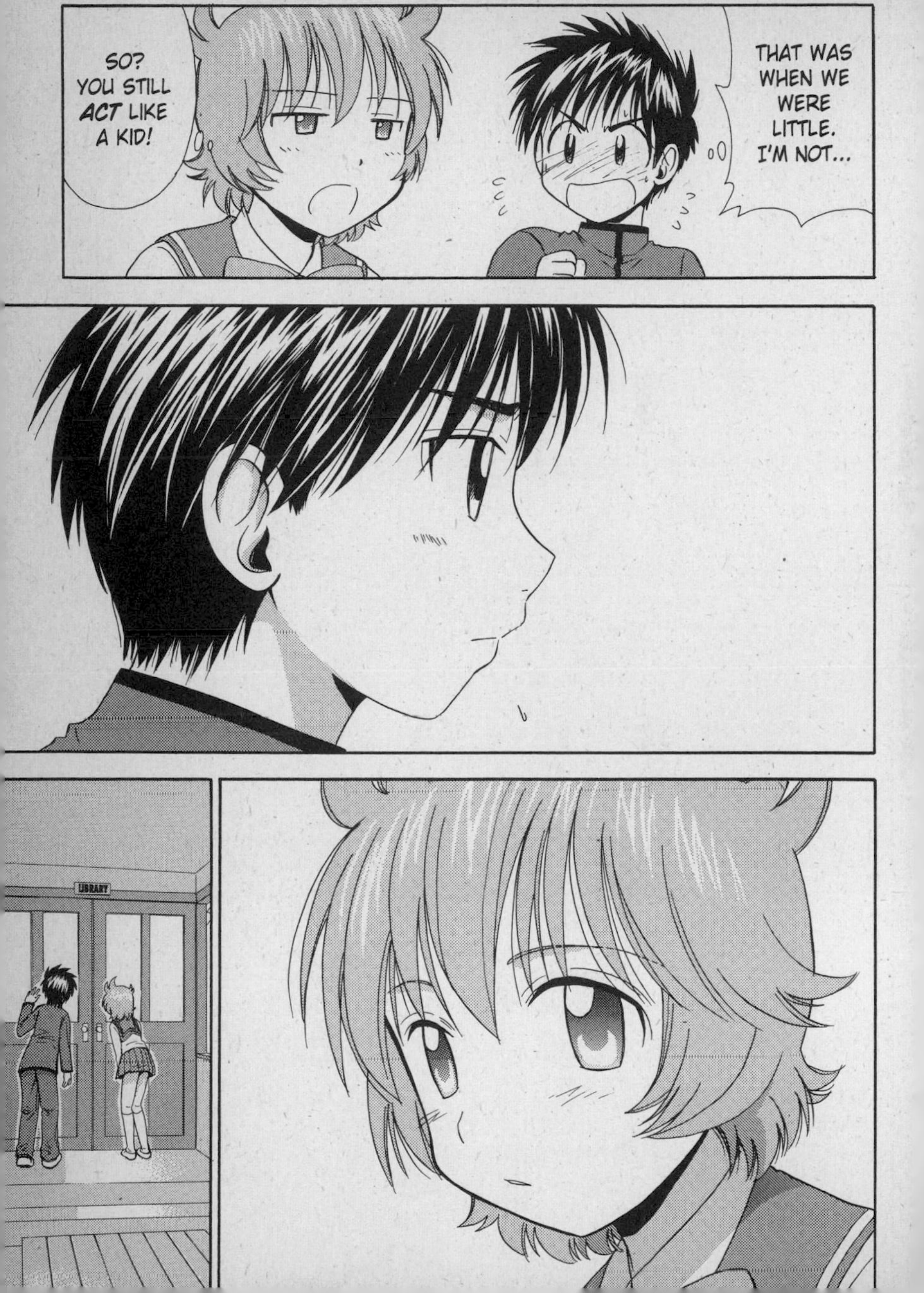
THAT WAS WHEN WE WERE LITTLE. I'M NOT...
SO? YOU STILL *ACT* LIKE A KID!
LIBRARY

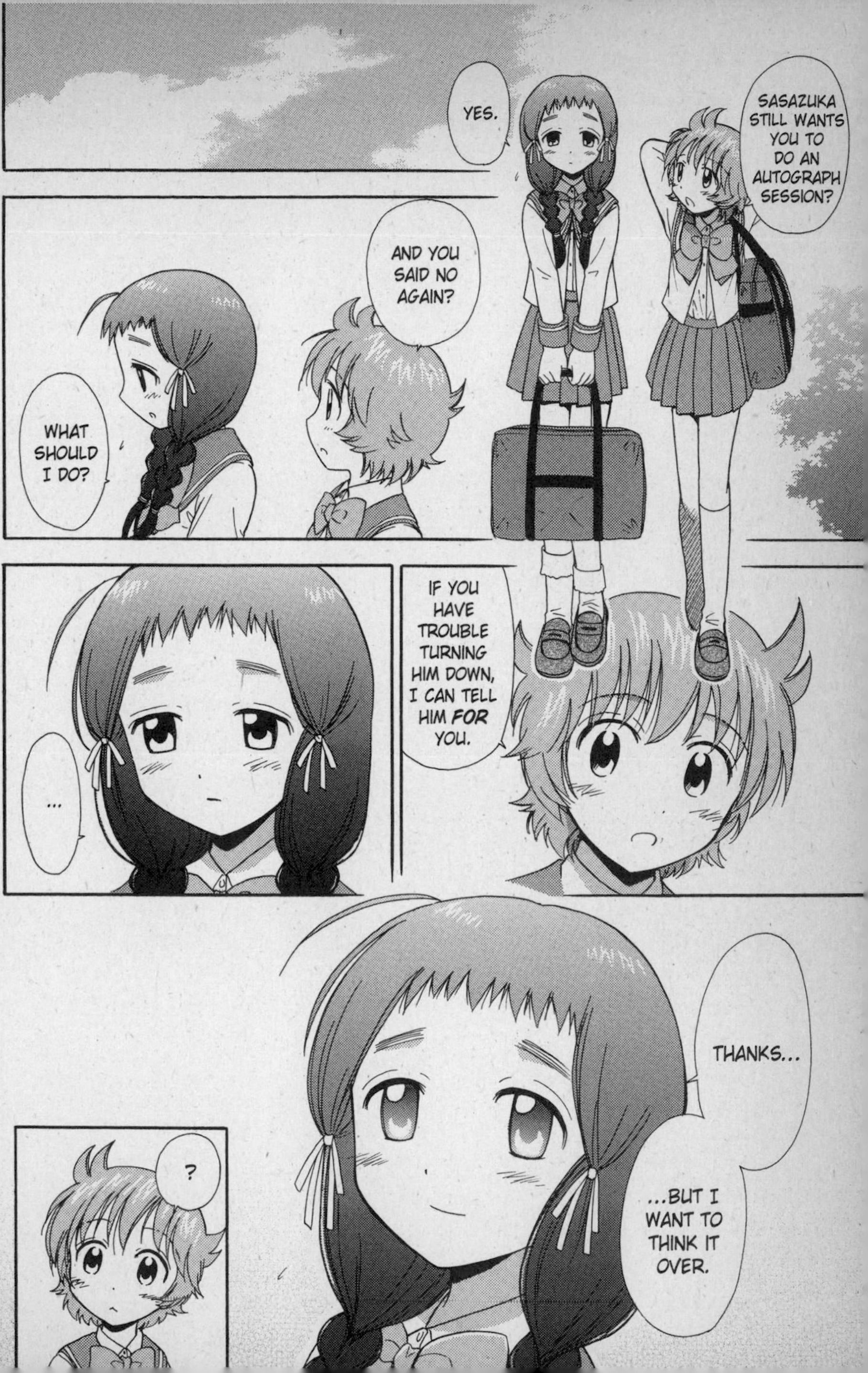
SASAZUKA STILL WANTS YOU TO DO AN AUTOGRAPH SESSION?
YES.
AND YOU SAID NO AGAIN?
WHAT SHOULD I DO?
IF YOU HAVE TROUBLE TURNING HIM DOWN, I CAN TELL HIM *FOR* YOU.
...
THANKS...
...BUT I WANT TO THINK IT OVER.
?

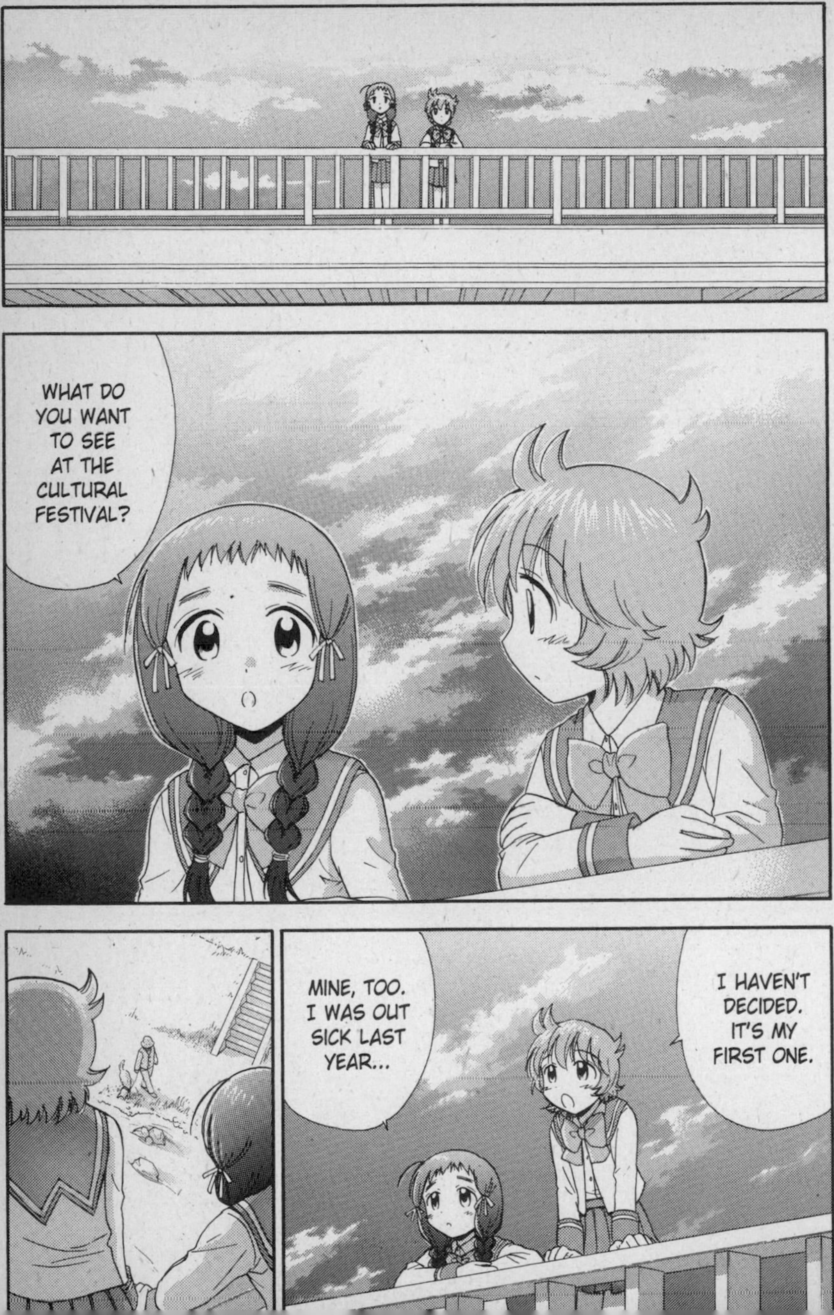
WHAT DO YOU WANT TO SEE AT THE CULTURAL FESTIVAL?
I HAVEN'T DECIDED. IT'S MY FIRST ONE.
MINE, TOO. I WAS OUT SICK LAST YEAR...

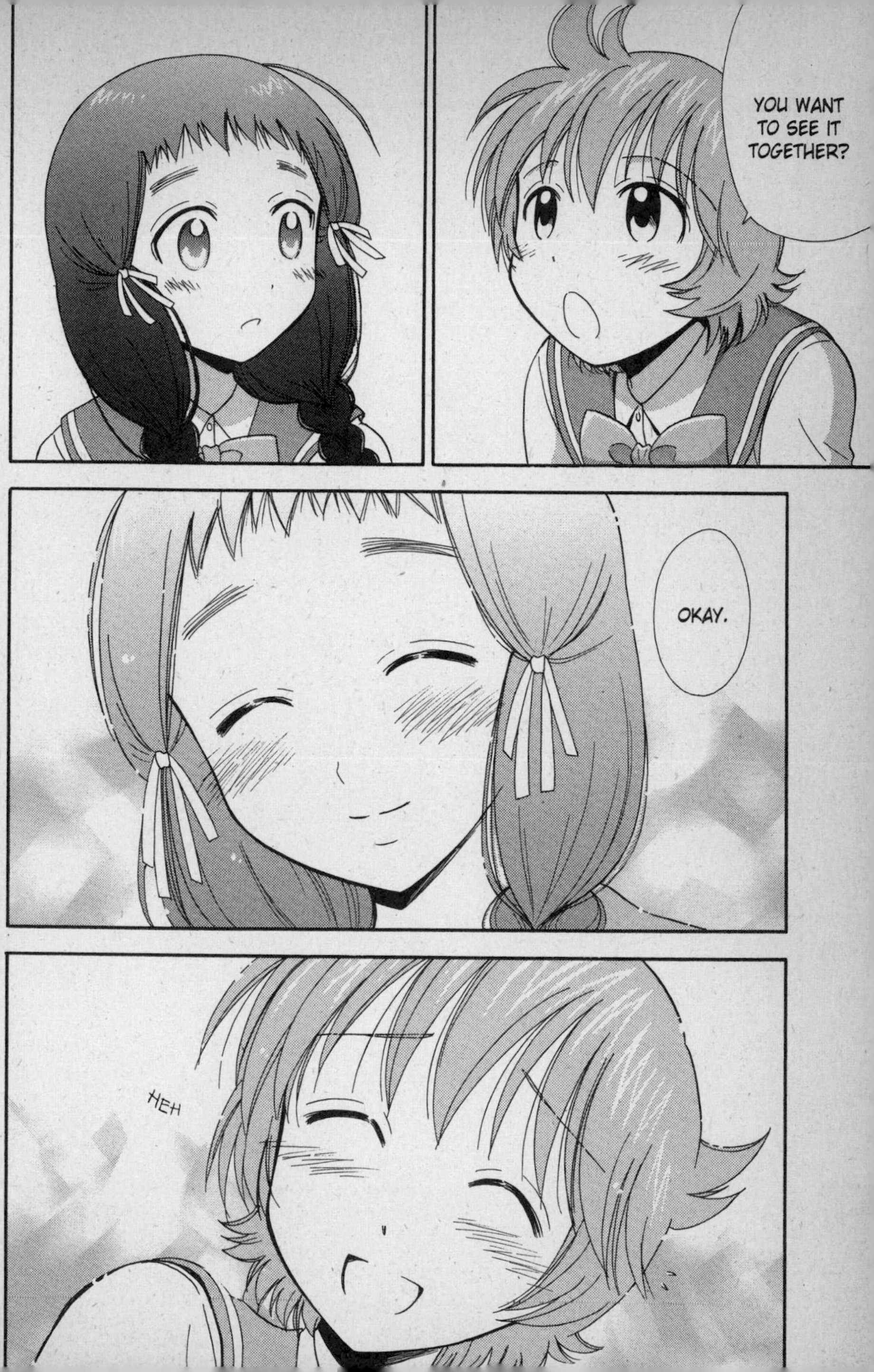
YOU WANT TO SEE IT TOGETHER?
OKAY.
HEH

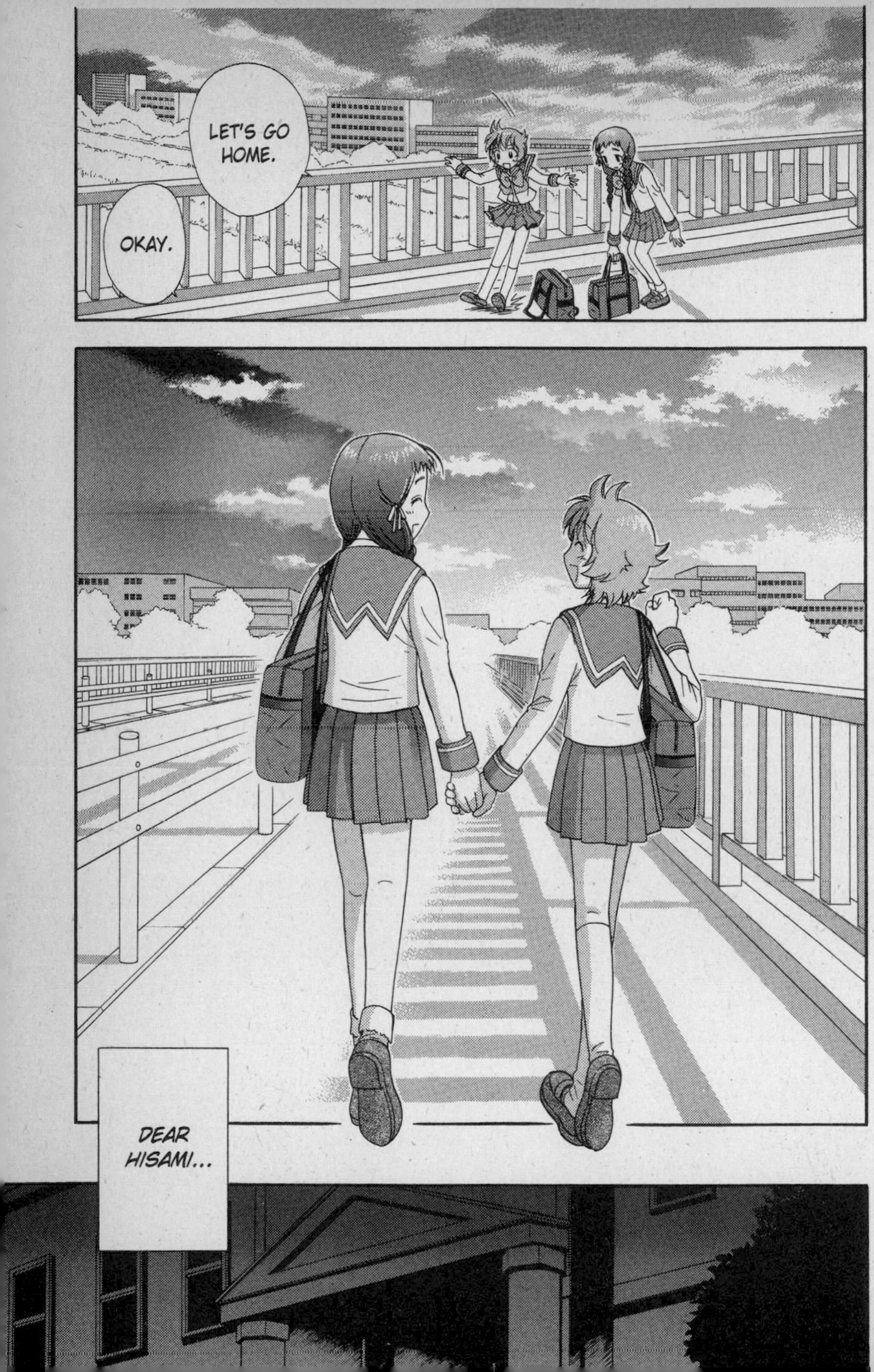
LET'S GO HOME.
OKAY.
DEAR HISAMI...

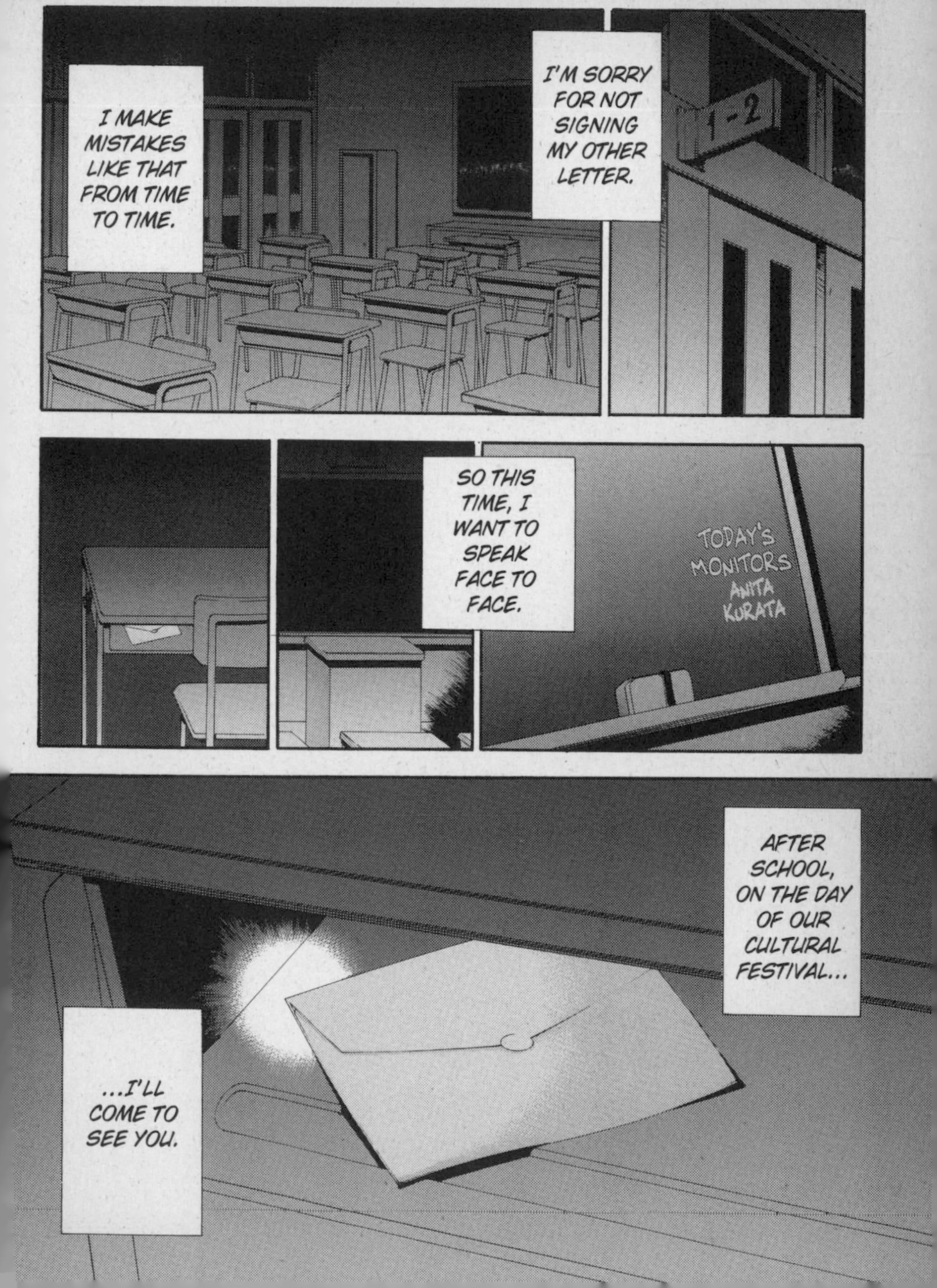
I'M SORRY FOR NOT SIGNING MY OTHER LETTER.
1-2
I MAKE MISTAKES LIKE THAT FROM TIME TO TIME.
TODAY'S MONITORS
ANITA
KURATA
SO THIS TIME, I WANT TO SPEAK FACE TO FACE.
AFTER SCHOOL, ON THE DAY OF OUR CULTURAL FESTIVAL...
...I'LL COME TO SEE YOU.

CHAPTER 28

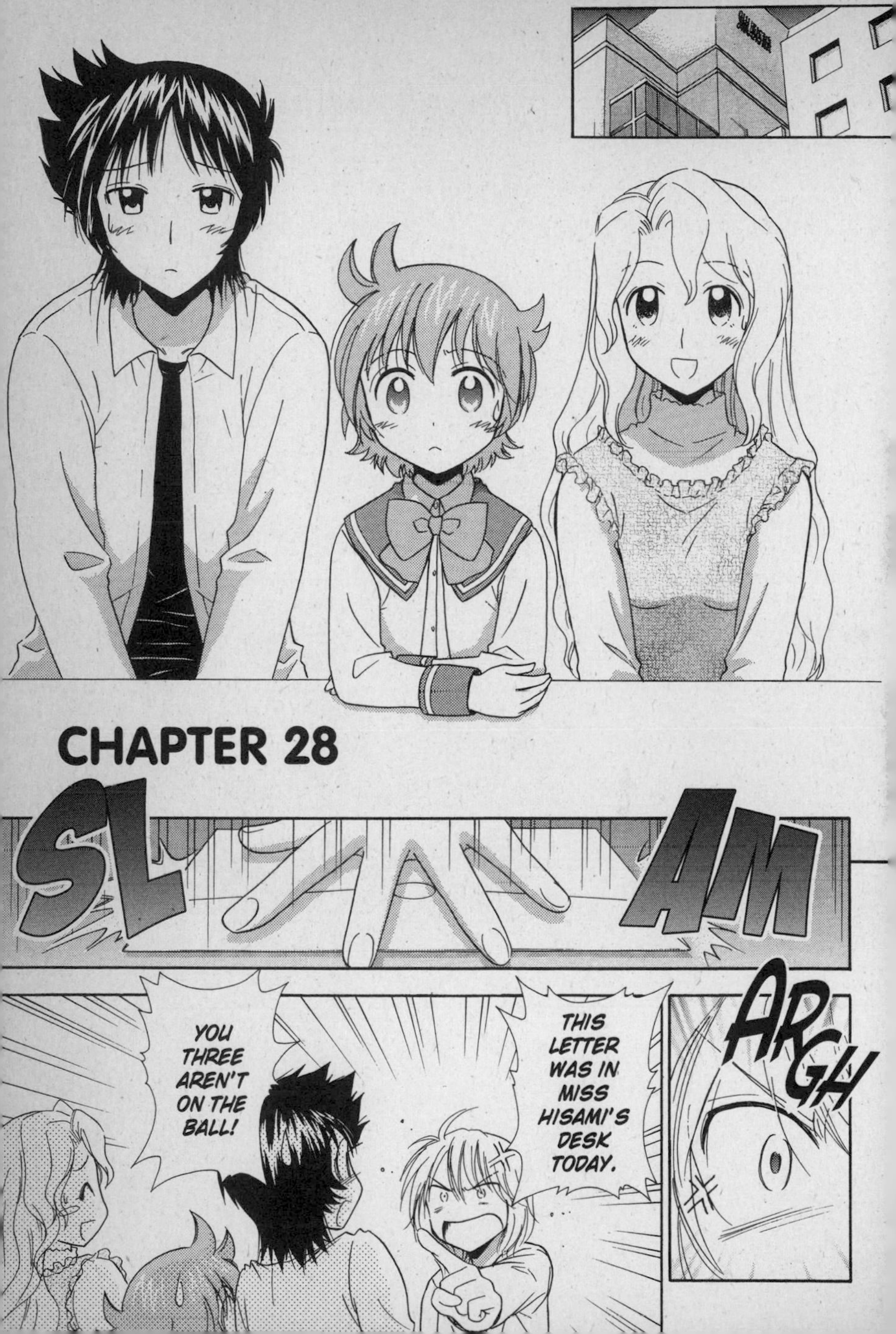
SLAM
ARGH
THIS LETTER WAS IN MISS HISAMI'S DESK TODAY.
YOU THREE AREN'T ON THE BALL!

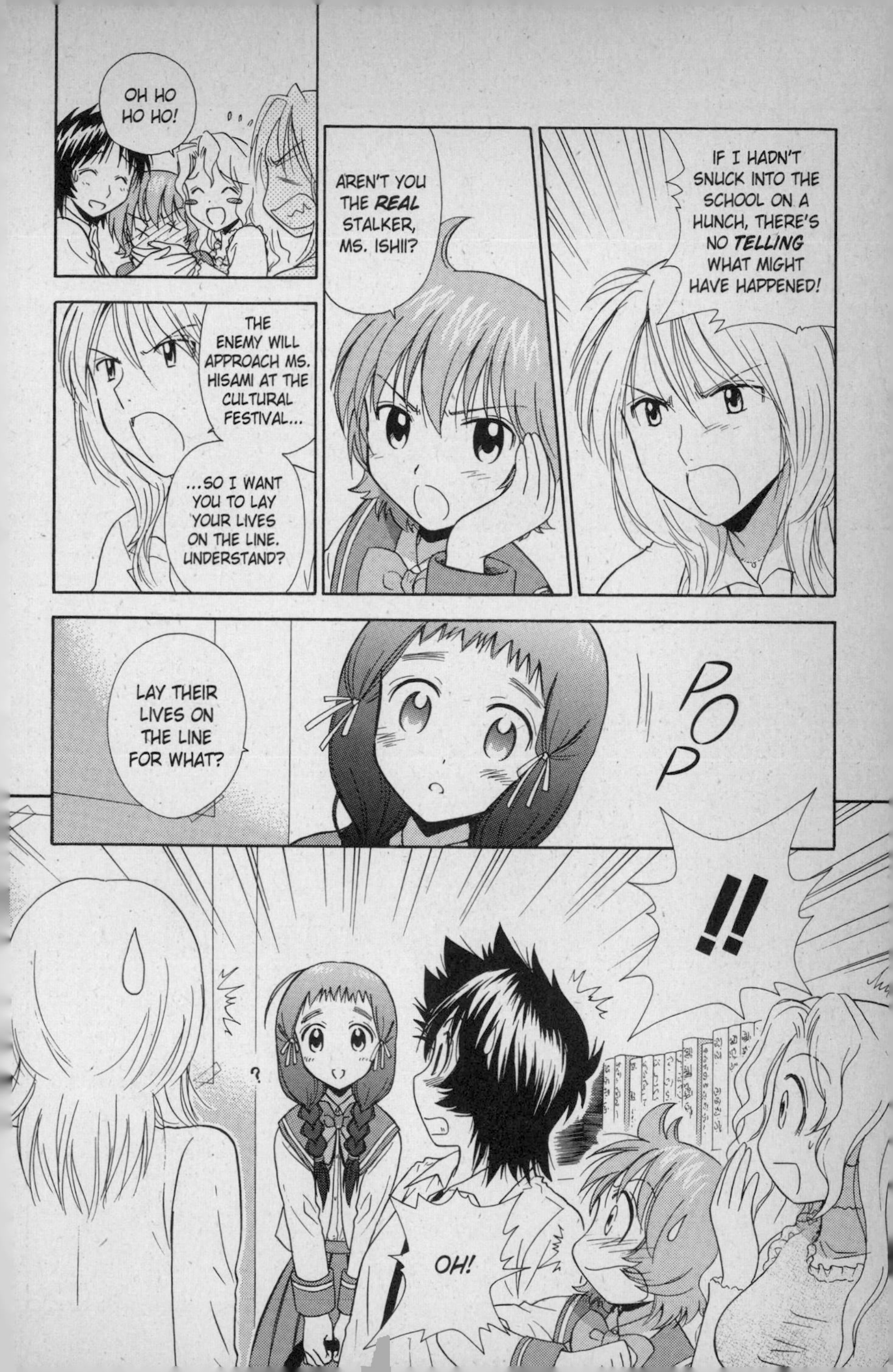
IF I HADN'T SNUCK INTO THE SCHOOL ON A HUNCH, THERE'S NO *TELLING* WHAT MIGHT HAVE HAPPENED!
AREN'T YOU THE *REAL* STALKER, MS. ISHII?
OH HO HO HO!
THE ENEMY WILL APPROACH MS. HISAMI AT THE CULTURAL FESTIVAL...
...SO I WANT YOU TO LAY YOUR LIVES ON THE LINE. UNDERSTAND?
POP
LAY THEIR LIVES ON THE LINE FOR WHAT?
!!
?
OH!

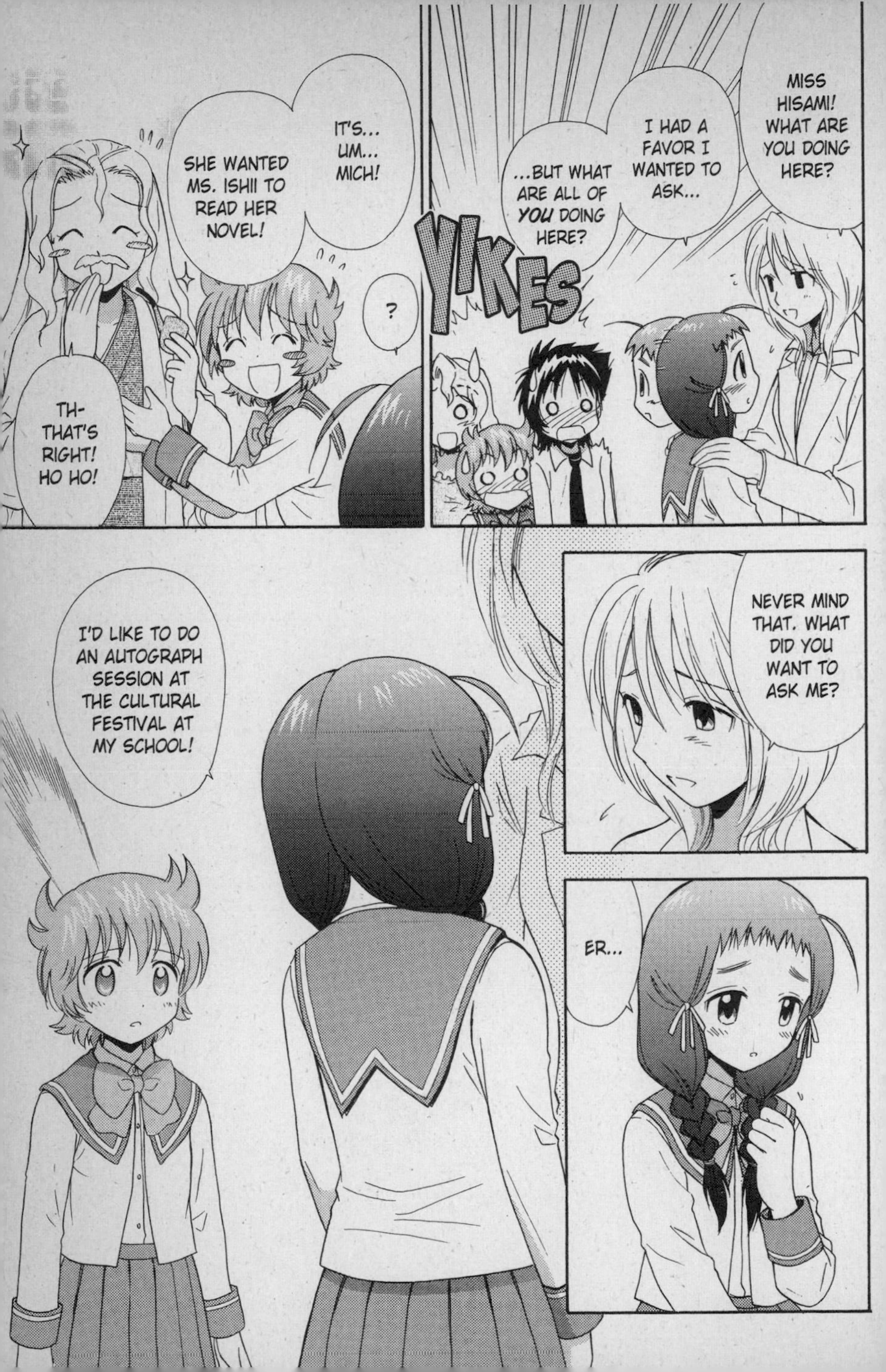
MISS HISAMI! WHAT ARE YOU DOING HERE?
I HAD A FAVOR I WANTED TO ASK...
...BUT WHAT ARE ALL OF *YOU* DOING HERE?
YIKES
IT'S... UM... MICH!
SHE WANTED MS. ISHII TO READ HER NOVEL!
?
TH- THAT'S RIGHT! HO HO!
NEVER MIND THAT. WHAT DID YOU WANT TO ASK ME?
ER...
I'D LIKE TO DO AN AUTOGRAPH SESSION AT THE CULTURAL FESTIVAL AT MY SCHOOL!

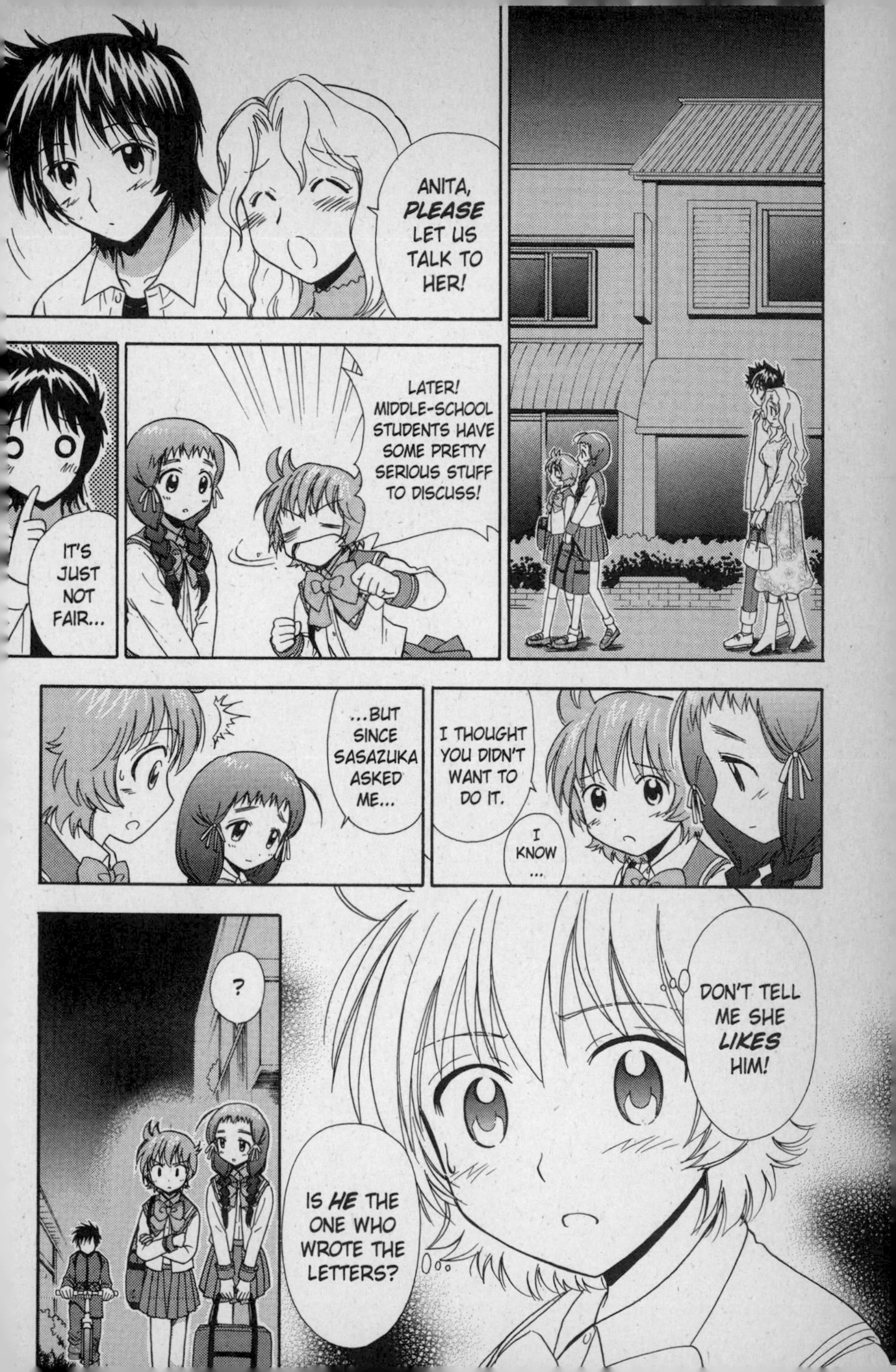
ANITA, PLEASE LET US TALK TO HER!
LATER! MIDDLE-SCHOOL STUDENTS HAVE SOME PRETTY SERIOUS STUFF TO DISCUSS!
IT'S JUST NOT FAIR...
I THOUGHT YOU DIDN'T WANT TO DO IT.
I KNOW ...
...BUT SINCE SASAZUKA ASKED ME...
DON'T TELL ME SHE LIKES HIM!
IS HE THE ONE WHO WROTE THE LETTERS?
?

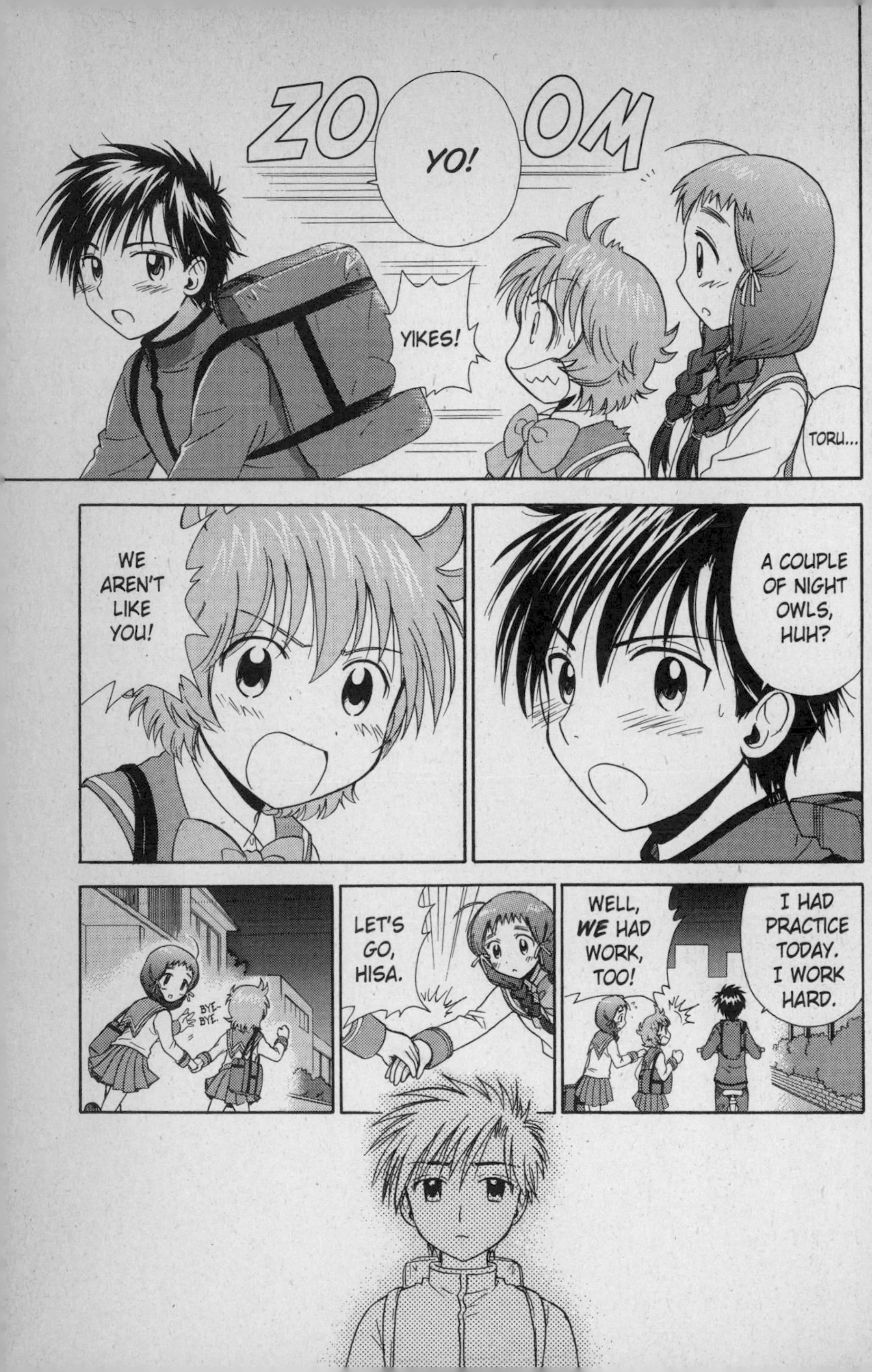
ZOOOM
YO!
YIKES!
TORU...
A COUPLE OF NIGHT OWLS, HUH?
WE AREN'T LIKE YOU!
I HAD PRACTICE TODAY. I WORK HARD.
WELL, WE HAD WORK, TOO!
LET'S GO, HISA.
BYE-BYE.

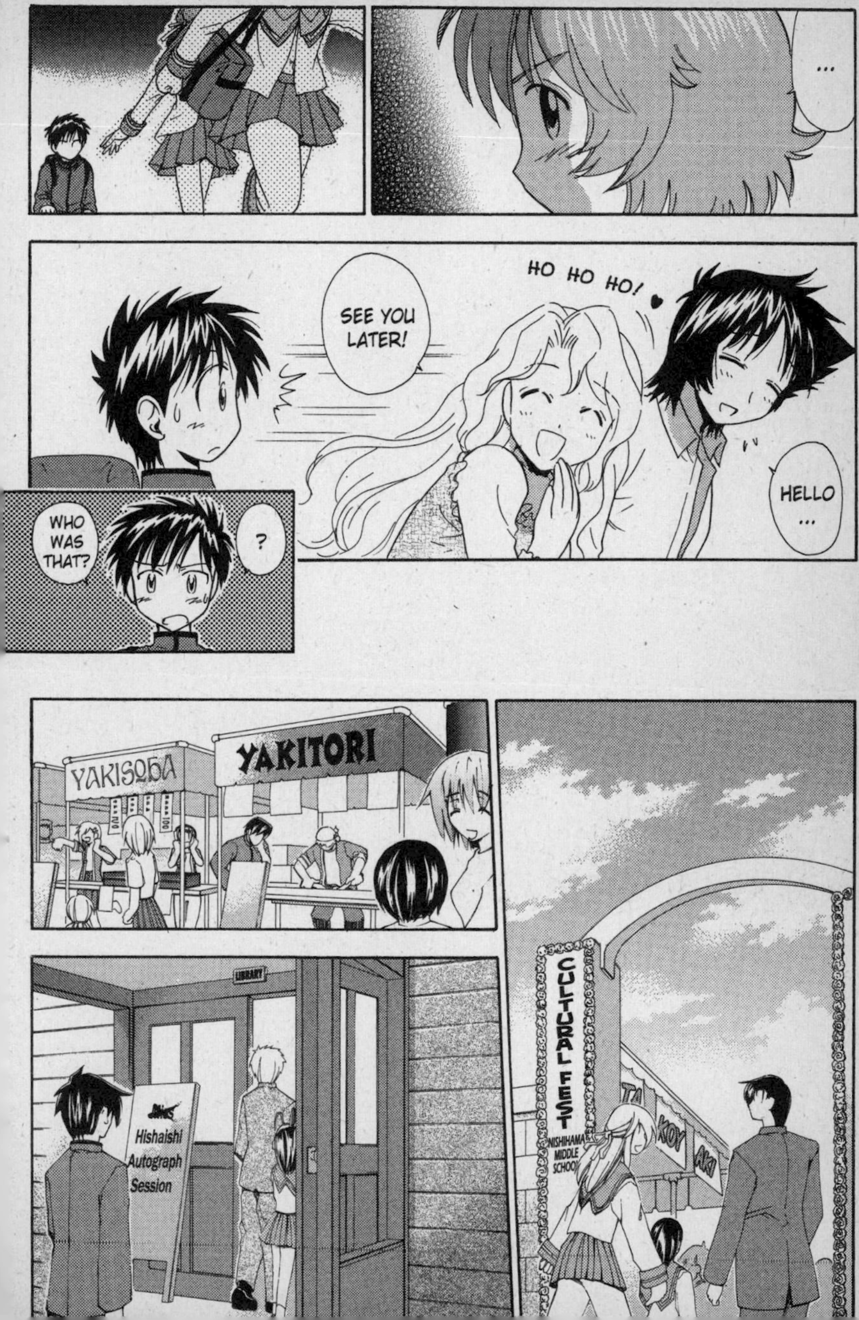
...
HO HO HO!
SEE YOU LATER!
HELLO ...
?
WHO WAS THAT?
CULTURAL FEST
NISHIHAMA MIDDLE SCHOOL
TA KOY AKI
YAKITORI
YAKISOBA
LIBRARY
Hishaishi Autograph Session

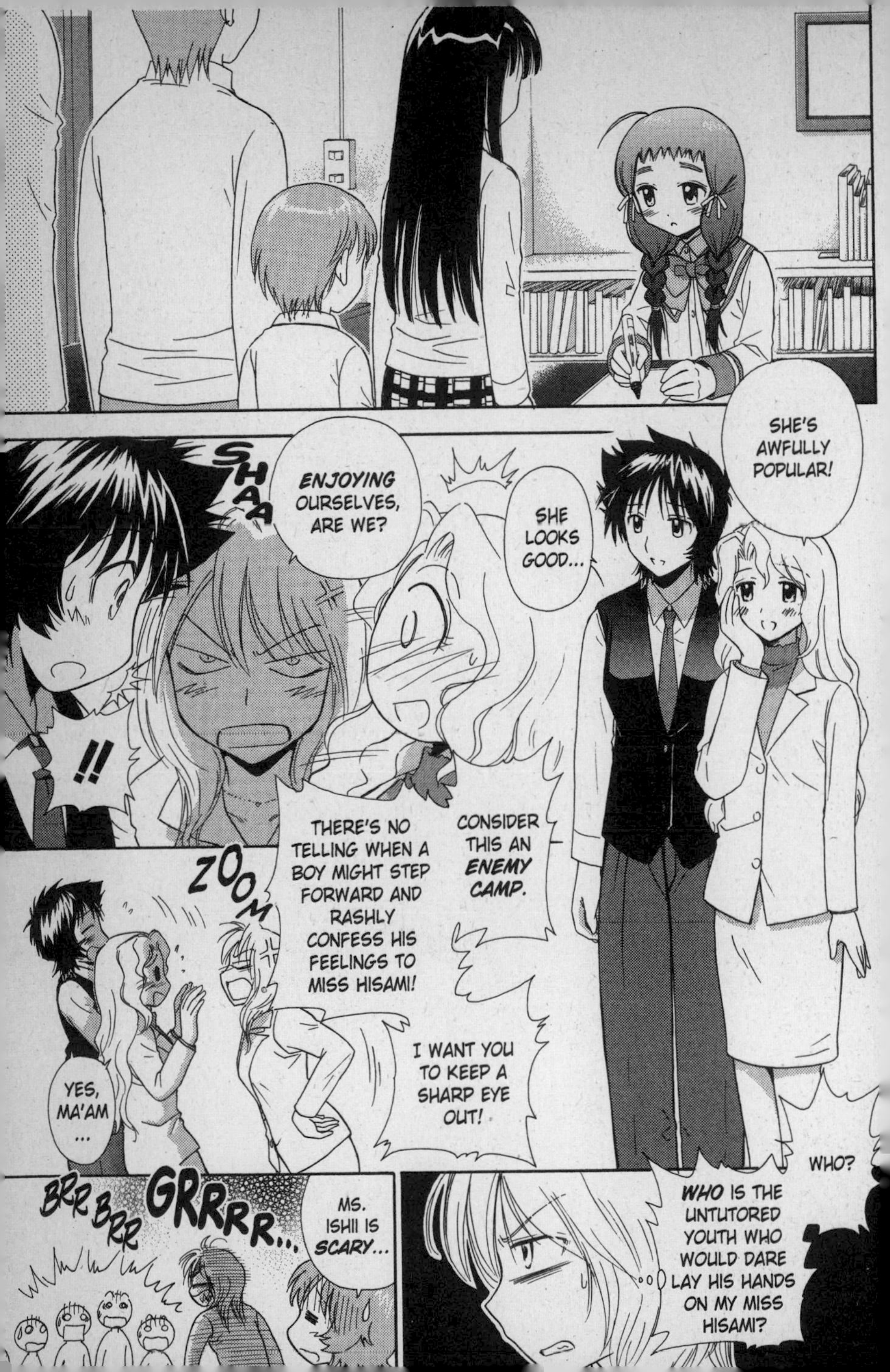
SHE'S AWFULLY POPULAR!
SHE LOOKS GOOD...
SHAAA
ENJOYING OURSELVES, ARE WE?
!!
CONSIDER THIS AN ENEMY CAMP.
THERE'S NO TELLING WHEN A BOY MIGHT STEP FORWARD AND RASHLY CONFESS HIS FEELINGS TO MISS HISAMI!
ZOOM
I WANT YOU TO KEEP A SHARP EYE OUT!
YES, MA'AM ...
WHO?
WHO IS THE UNTUTORED YOUTH WHO WOULD DARE LAY HIS HANDS ON MY MISS HISAMI?
MS. ISHII IS SCARY...
GRRRRR...
BRR BRR

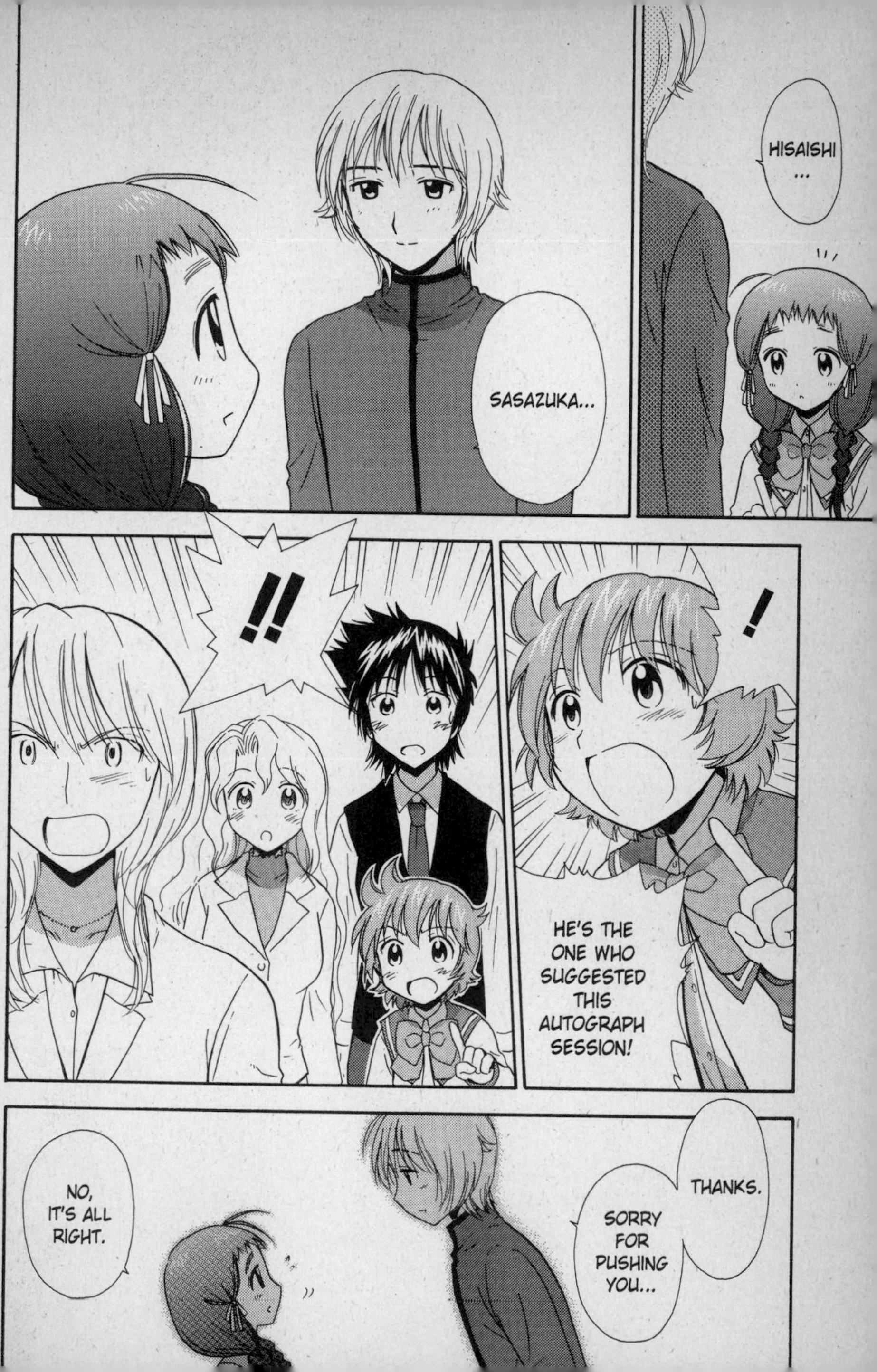
HISAISHI ...
SASAZUKA...
!
HE'S THE ONE WHO SUGGESTED THIS AUTOGRAPH SESSION!
!!
THANKS.
SORRY FOR PUSHING YOU...
NO, IT'S ALL RIGHT.

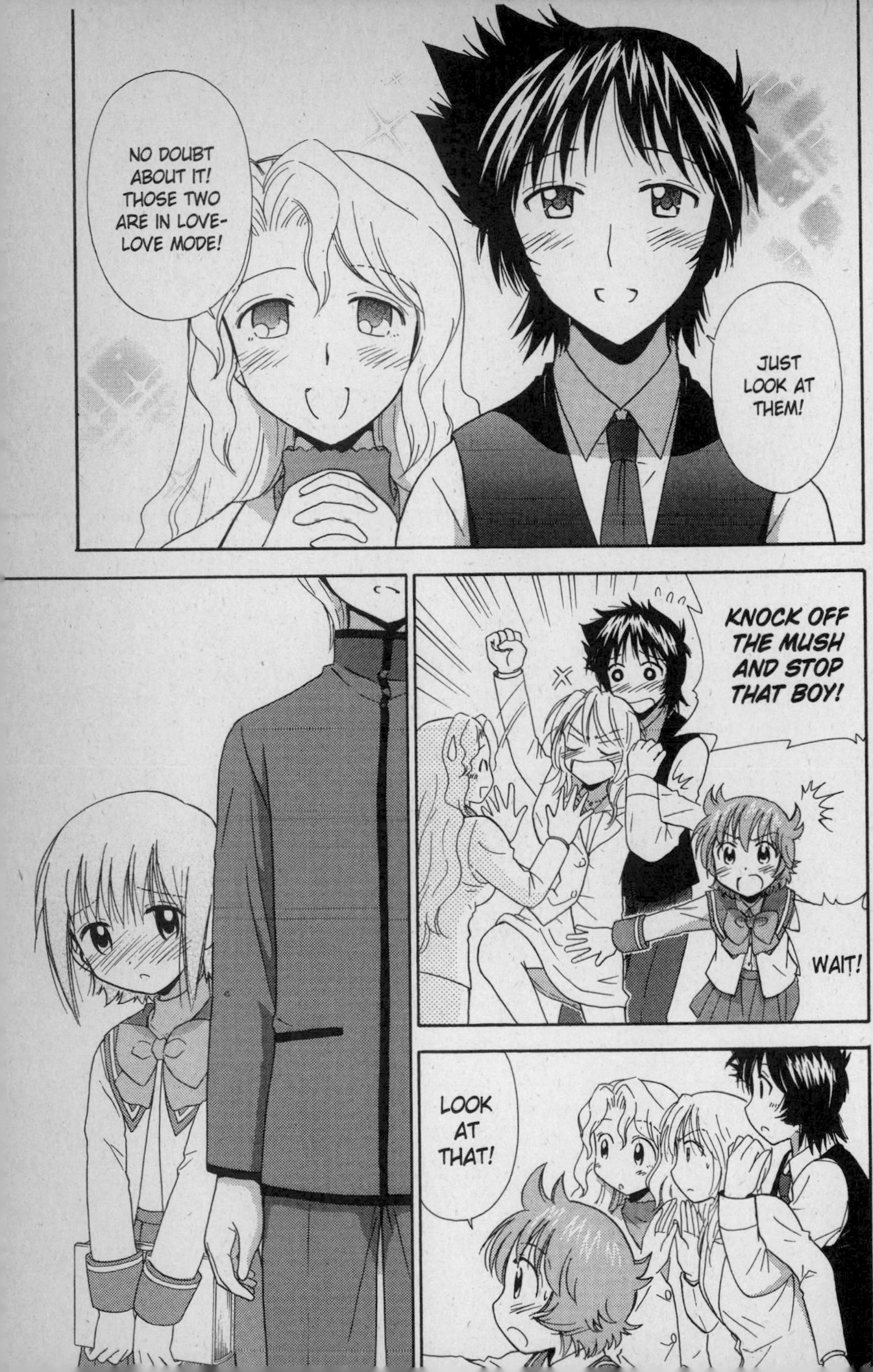
JUST LOOK AT THEM!
NO DOUBT ABOUT IT! THOSE TWO ARE IN LOVE-LOVE MODE!
KNOCK OFF THE MUSH AND STOP THAT BOY!
WAIT!
LOOK AT THAT!

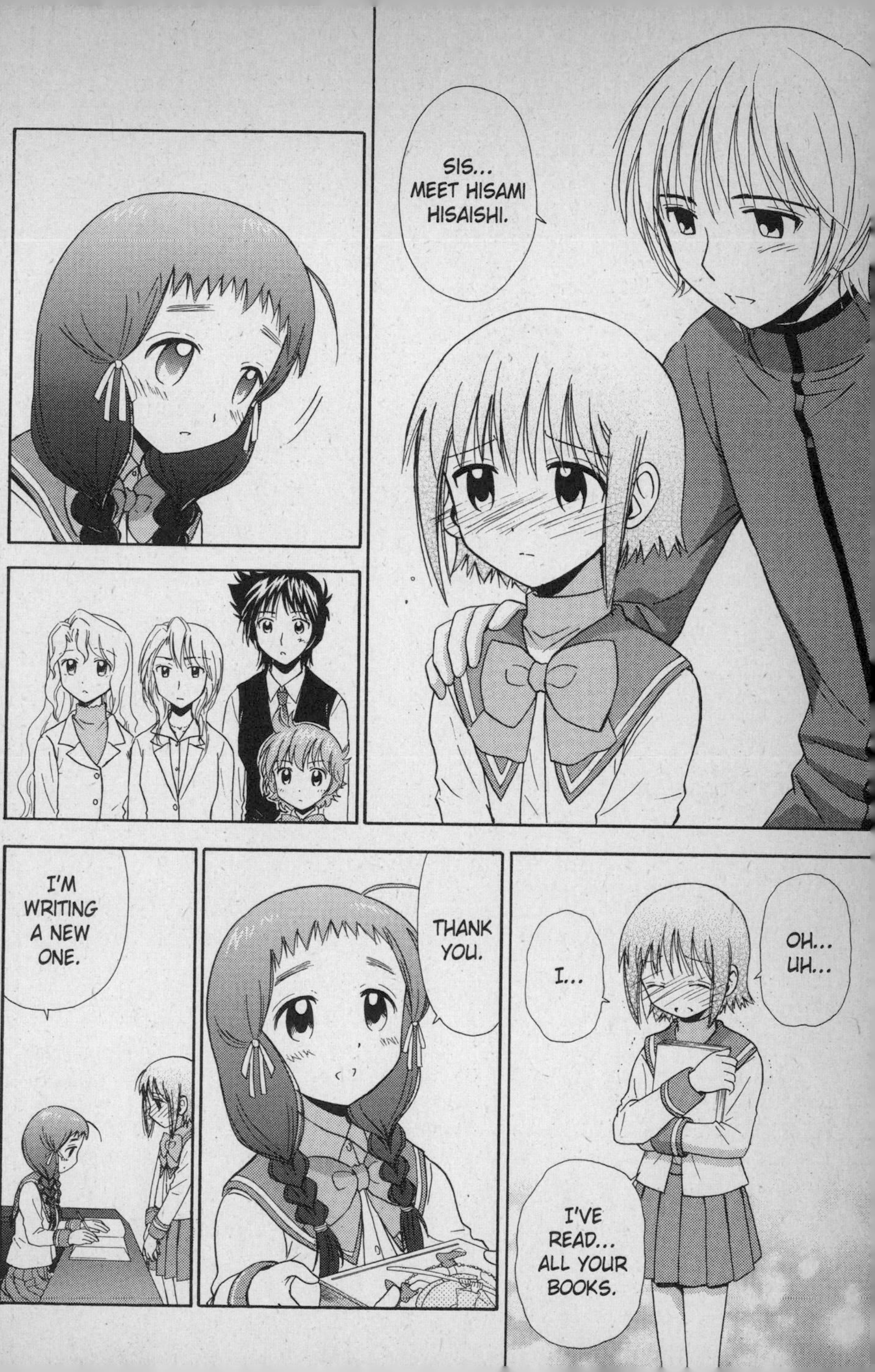
SIS... MEET HISAMI HISAISHI.
OH... UH...
I...
I'VE READ... ALL YOUR BOOKS.
THANK YOU.
I'M WRITING A NEW ONE.

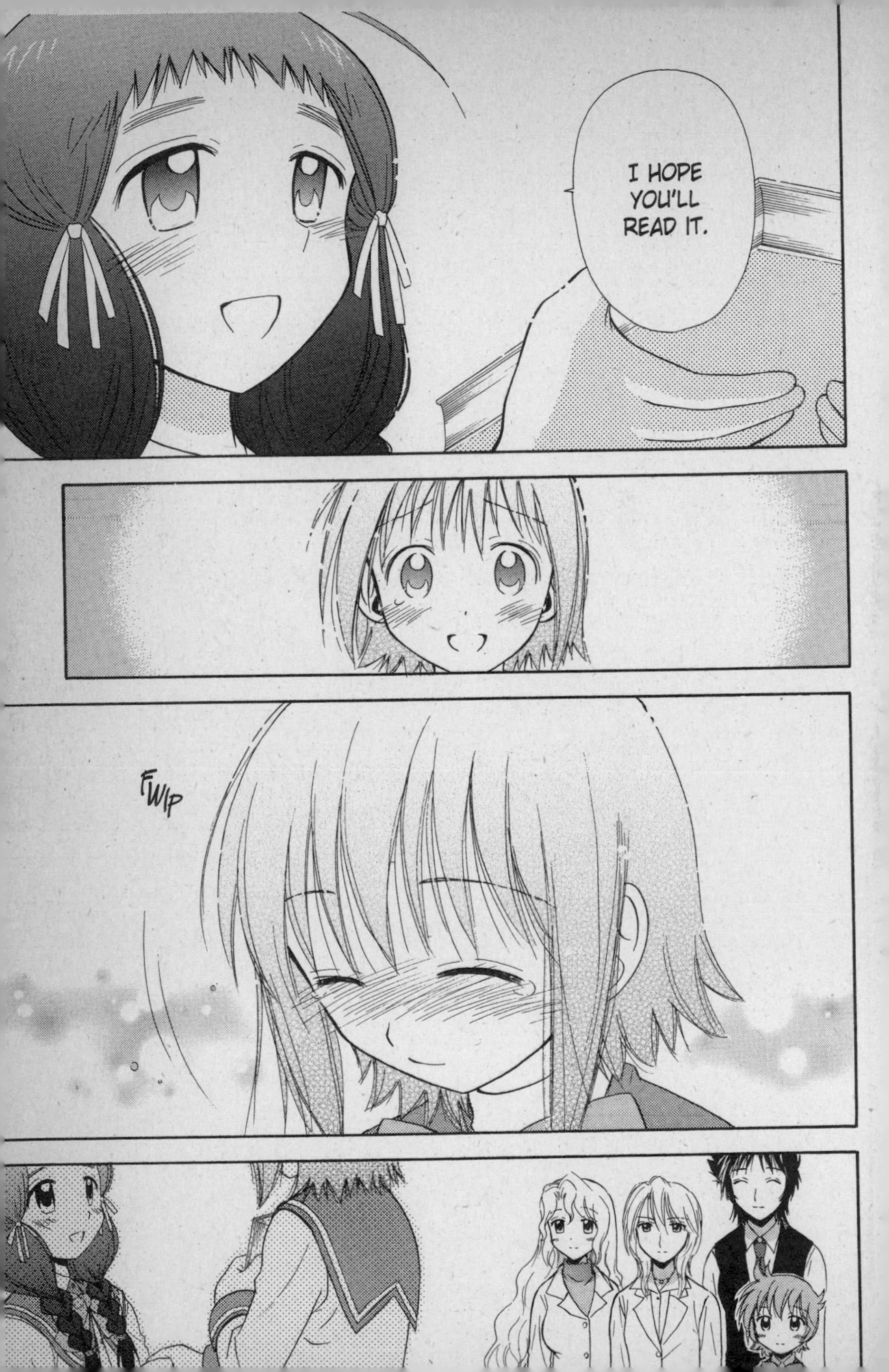
I HOPE YOU'LL READ IT.
FWIP

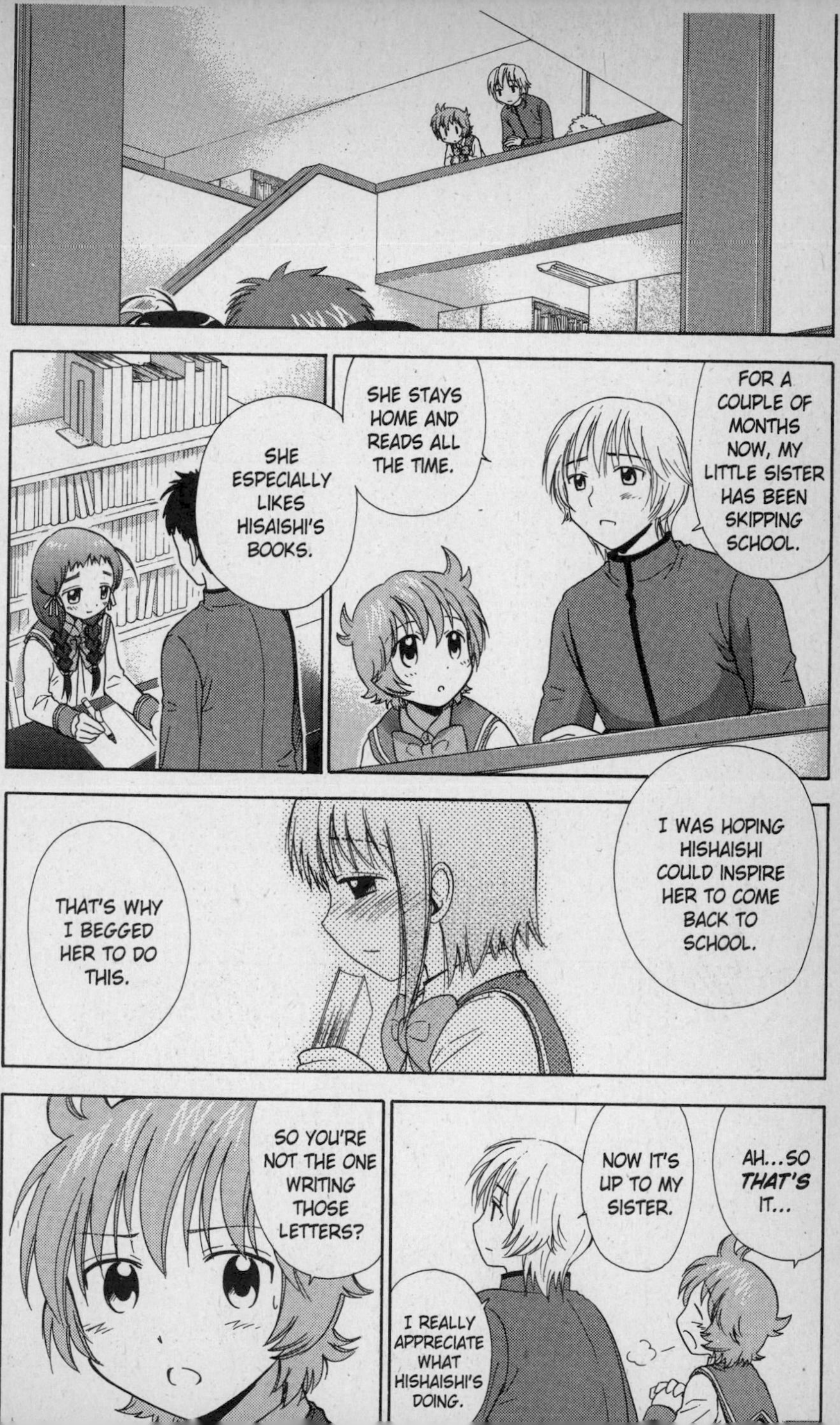
FOR A COUPLE OF MONTHS NOW, MY LITTLE SISTER HAS BEEN SKIPPING SCHOOL.
SHE STAYS HOME AND READS ALL THE TIME.
SHE ESPECIALLY LIKES HISAISHI'S BOOKS.
I WAS HOPING HISHAISHI COULD INSPIRE HER TO COME BACK TO SCHOOL.
THAT'S WHY I BEGGED HER TO DO THIS.
AH...SO *THAT'S* IT...
NOW IT'S UP TO MY SISTER.
I REALLY APPRECIATE WHAT HISHAISHI'S DOING.
SO YOU'RE NOT THE ONE WRITING THOSE LETTERS?

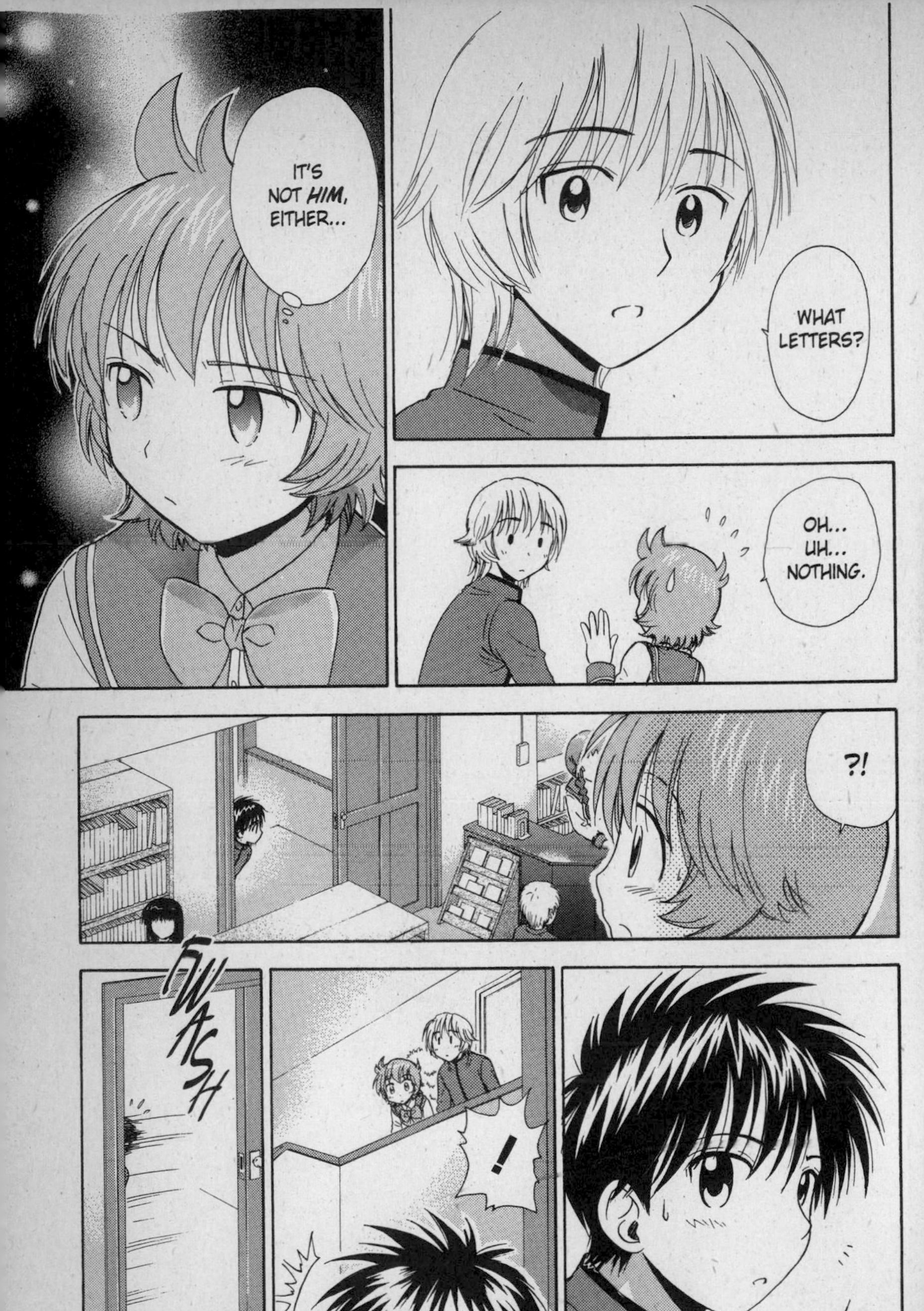
WHAT LETTERS?
OH... UH... NOTHING.
IT'S NOT *HIM*, EITHER...
?!
!
FWASH

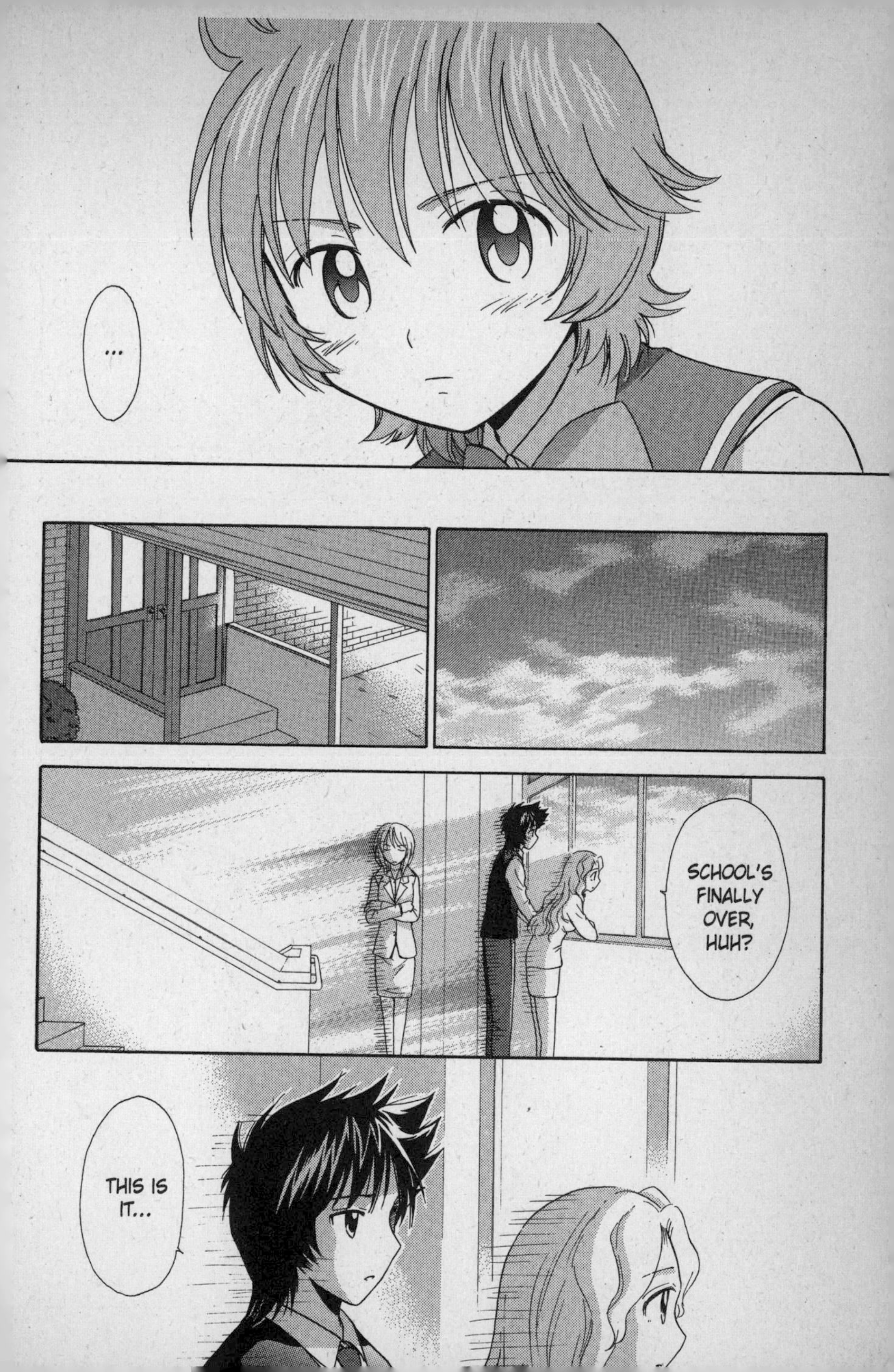
...
SCHOOL'S FINALLY OVER, HUH?
THIS IS IT...

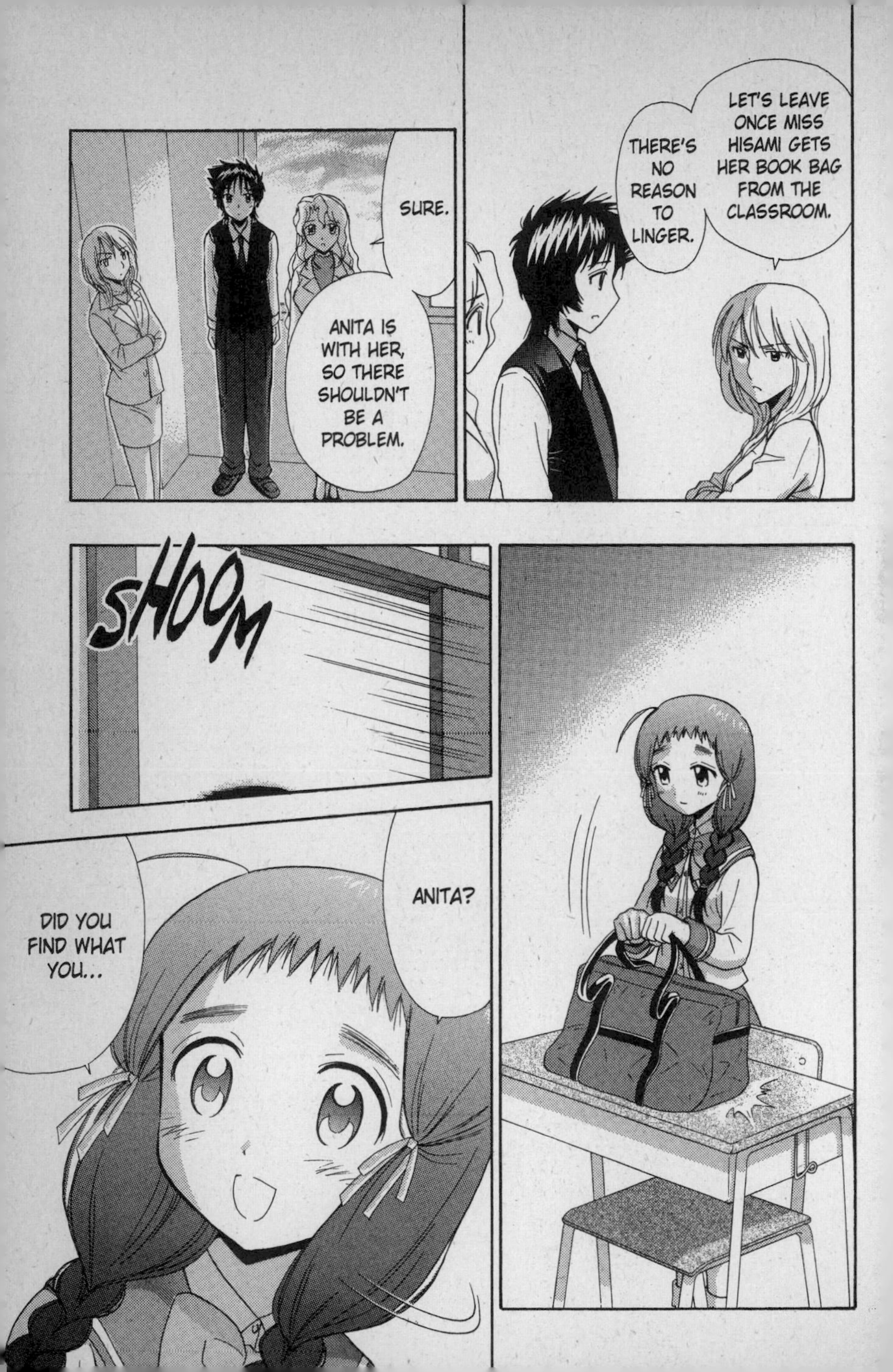
LET'S LEAVE ONCE MISS HISAMI GETS HER BOOK BAG FROM THE CLASSROOM.
THERE'S NO REASON TO LINGER.
SURE.
ANITA IS WITH HER, SO THERE SHOULDN'T BE A PROBLEM.
SHOOM
ANITA?
DID YOU FIND WHAT YOU...

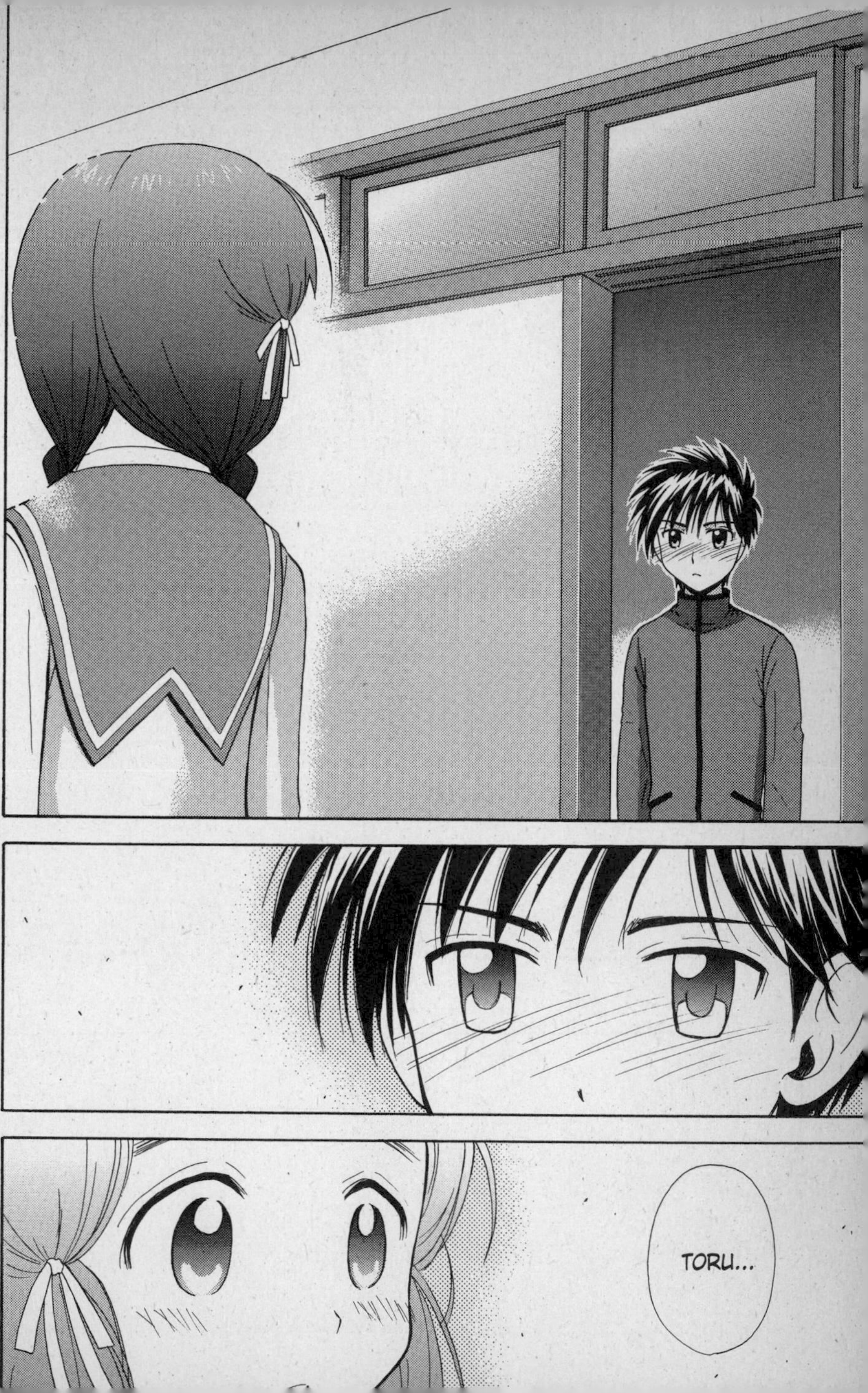
TORU...

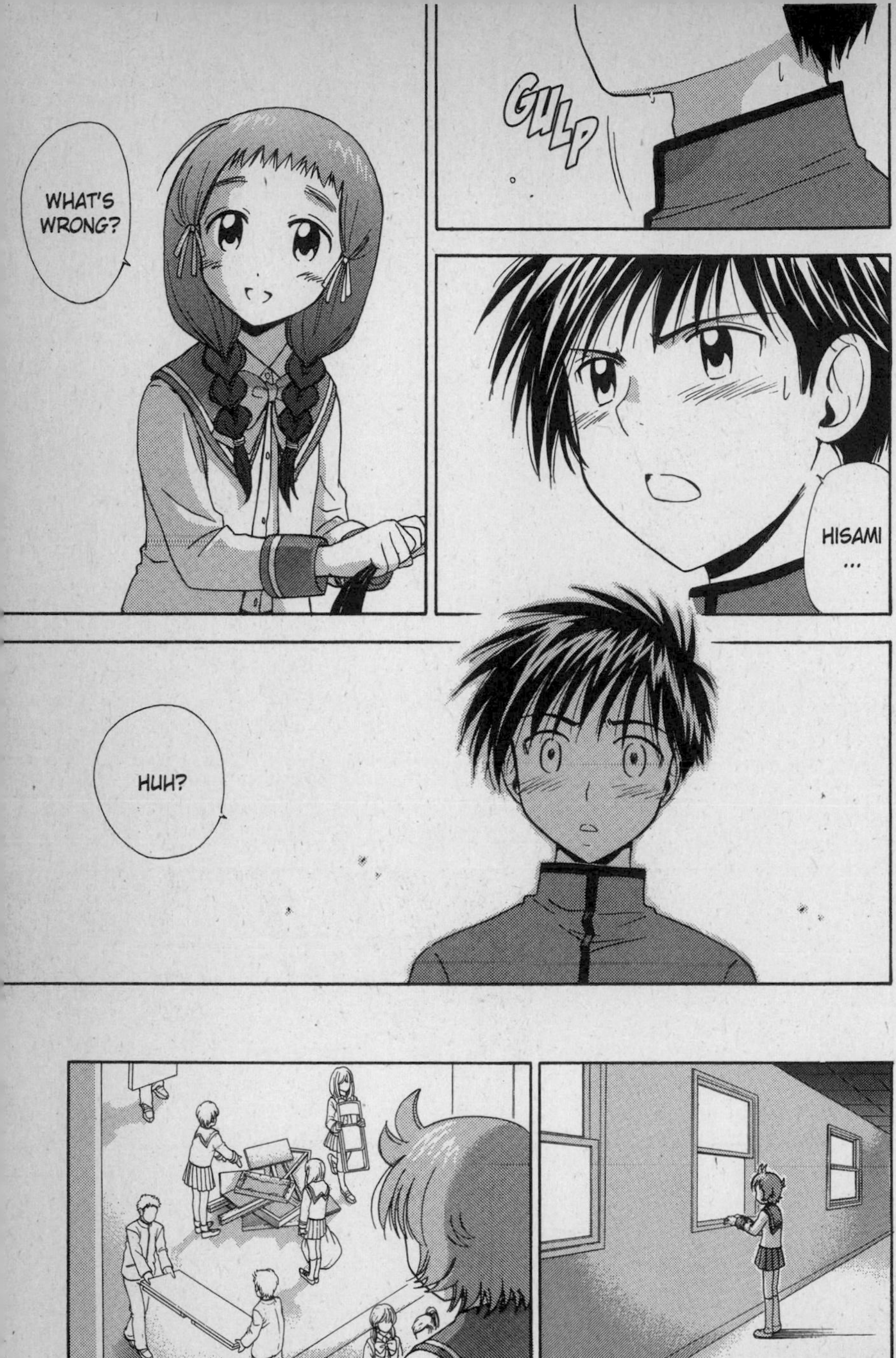
GULP
HISAMI ...
WHAT'S WRONG?
HUH?

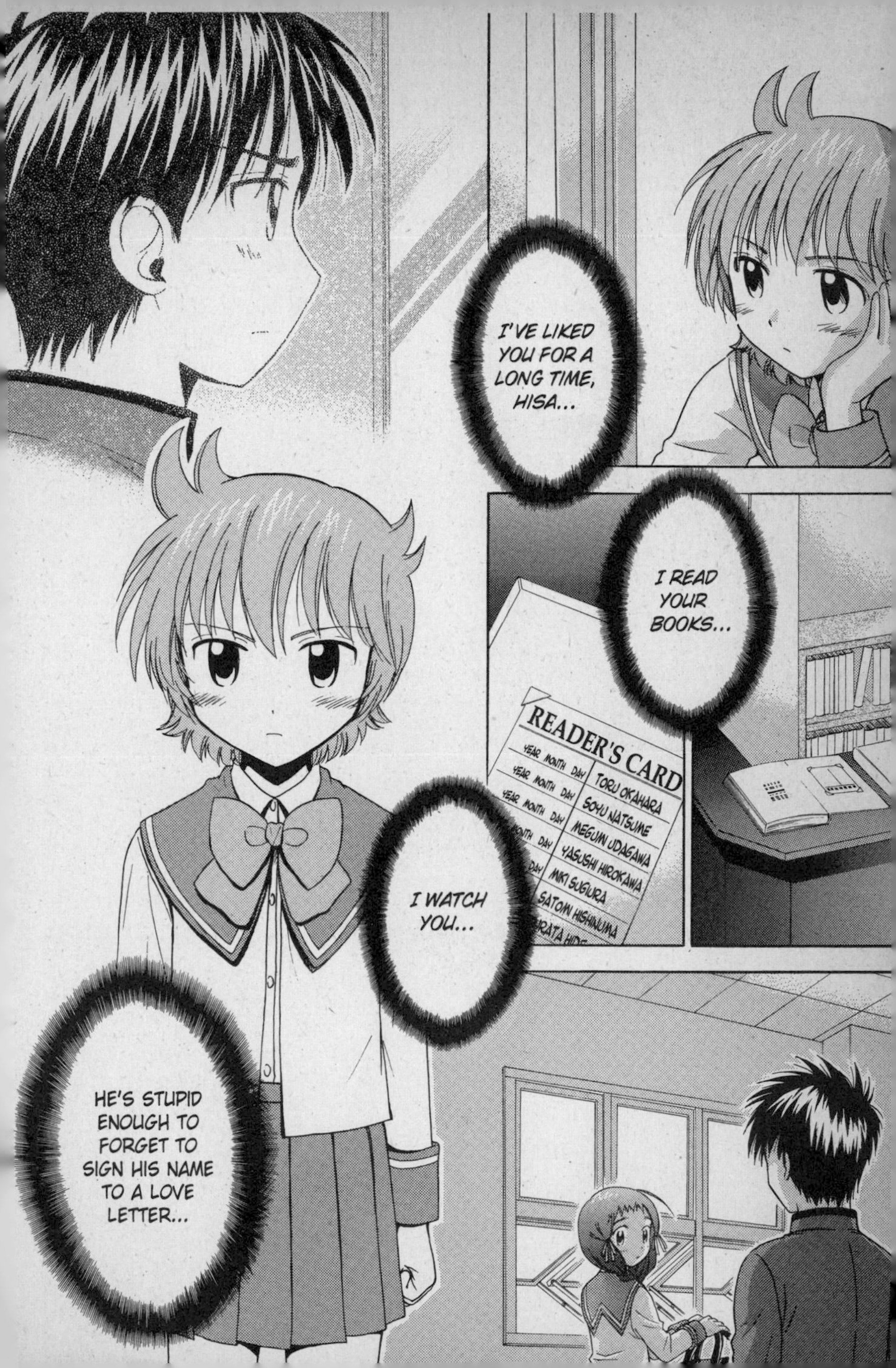
I'VE LIKED YOU FOR A LONG TIME, HISA...
I READ YOUR BOOKS...
READER'S CARD
YEAR MONTH DAY TORU OKAHARA
YEAR MONTH DAY SOYU NATSUME
YEAR MONTH DAY MEGUMI UDAGAWA
YASUSHI HIROKAWA
MIKI SUGURA
SATOMI HISHINUMA
I WATCH YOU...
HE'S STUPID ENOUGH TO FORGET TO SIGN HIS NAME TO A LOVE LETTER...

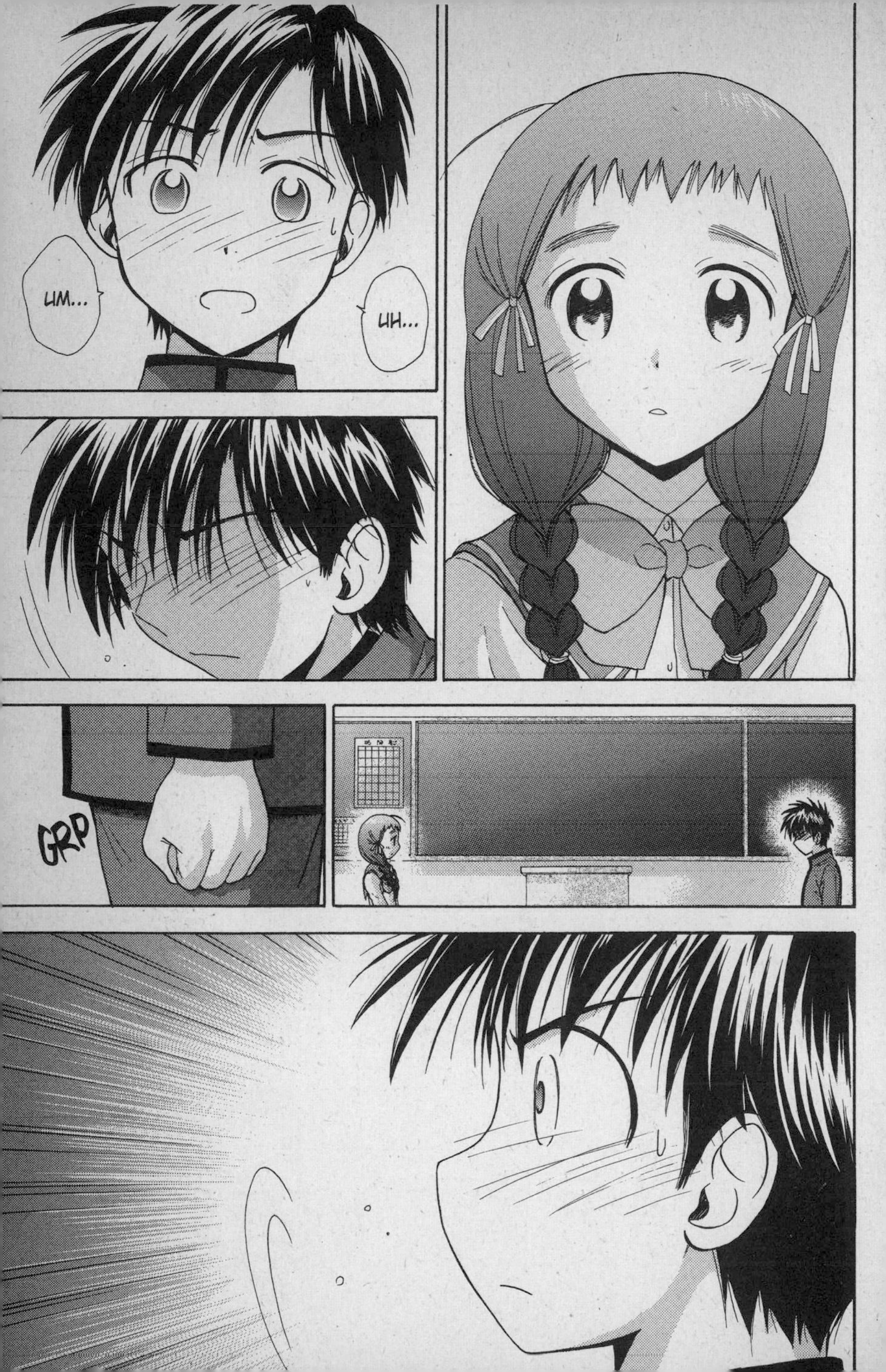
UH...
UM...
GRP

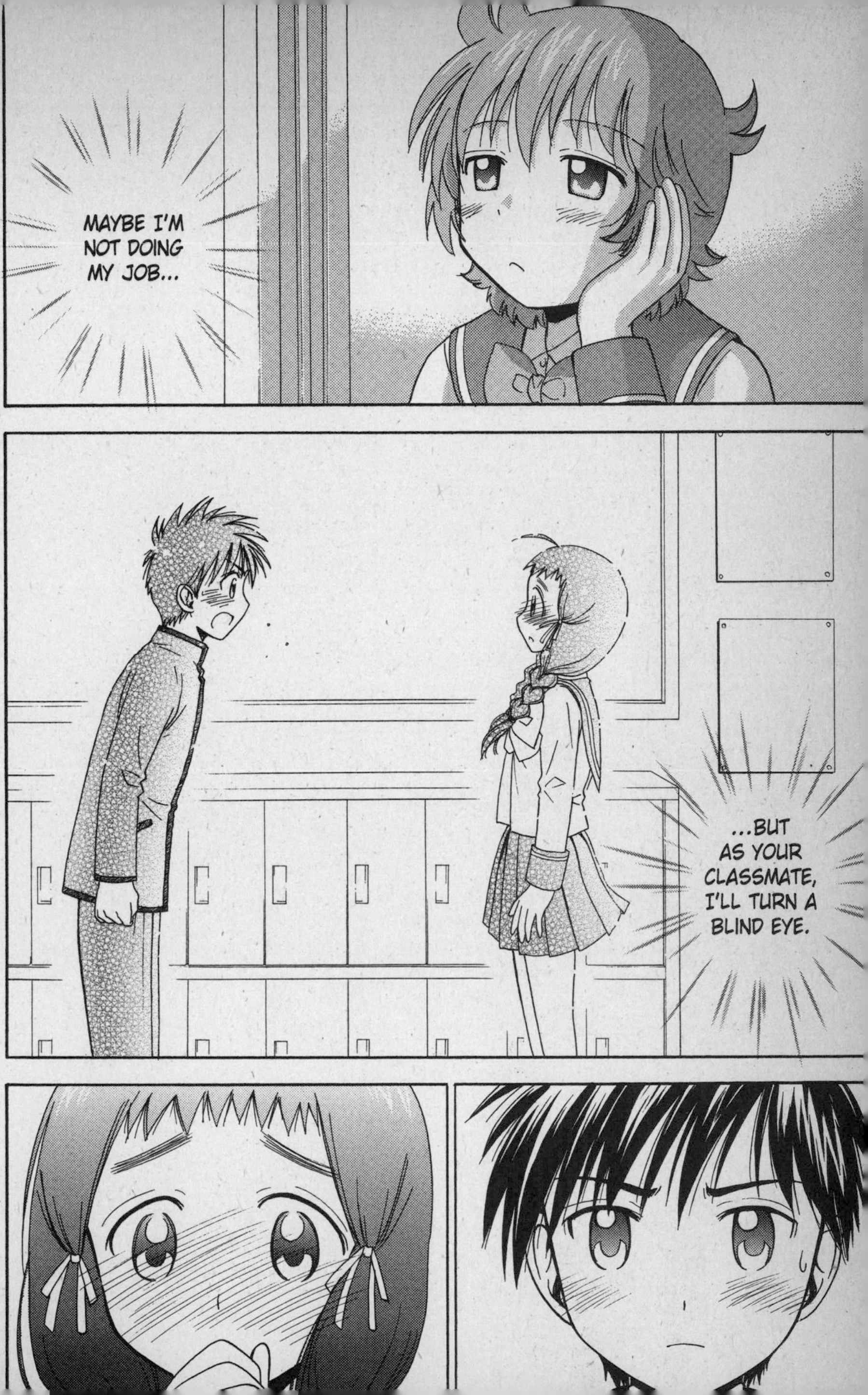
MAYBE I'M NOT DOING MY JOB...
...BUT AS YOUR CLASSMATE, I'LL TURN A BLIND EYE.

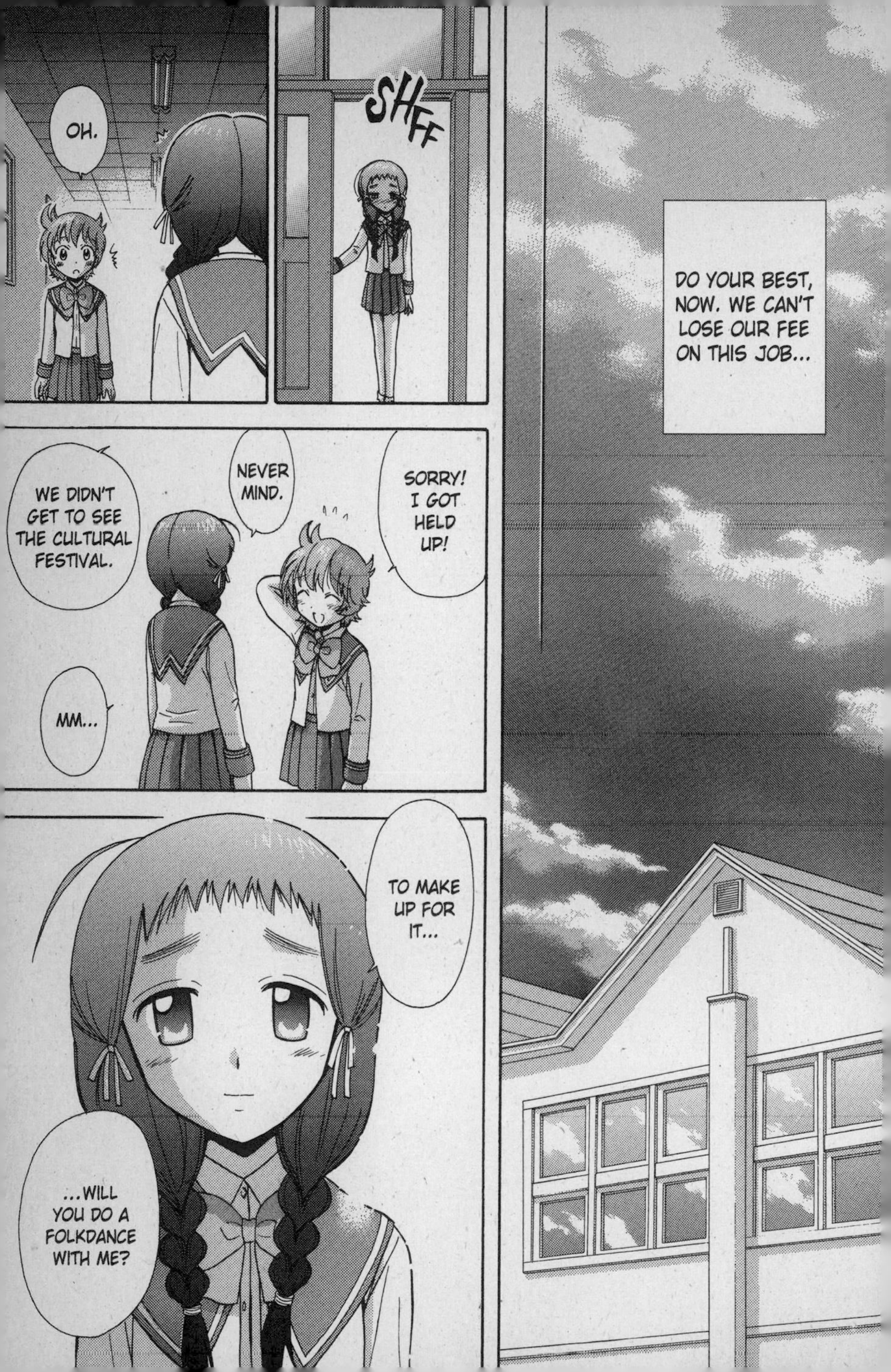
DO YOUR BEST, NOW. WE CAN'T LOSE OUR FEE ON THIS JOB...
SHFF
OH.
SORRY! I GOT HELD UP!
NEVER MIND.
WE DIDN'T GET TO SEE THE CULTURAL FESTIVAL.
MM...
TO MAKE UP FOR IT...
...WILL YOU DO A FOLKDANCE WITH ME?

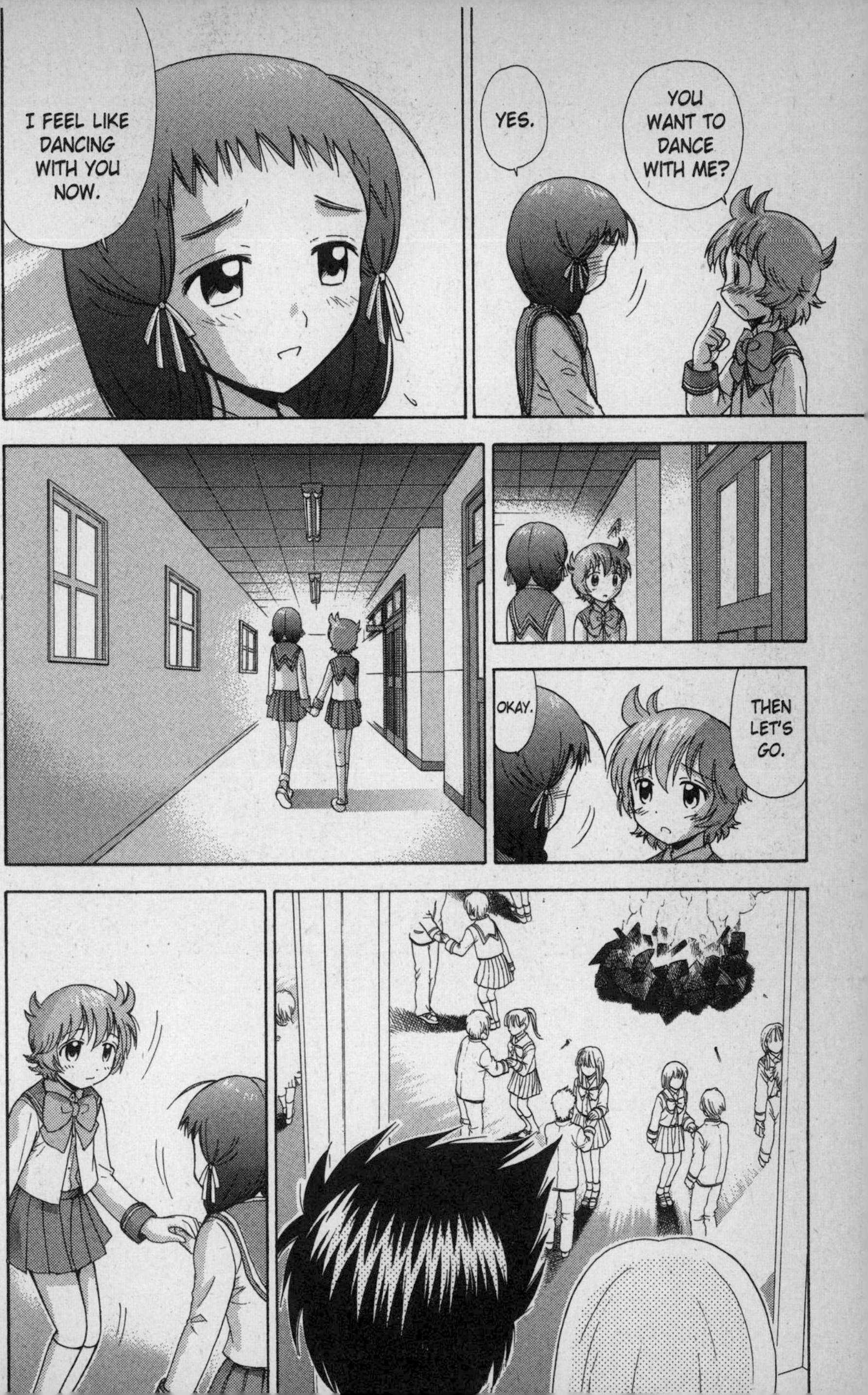
YOU WANT TO DANCE WITH ME?
YES.
I FEEL LIKE DANCING WITH YOU NOW.
THEN LET'S GO.
OKAY.

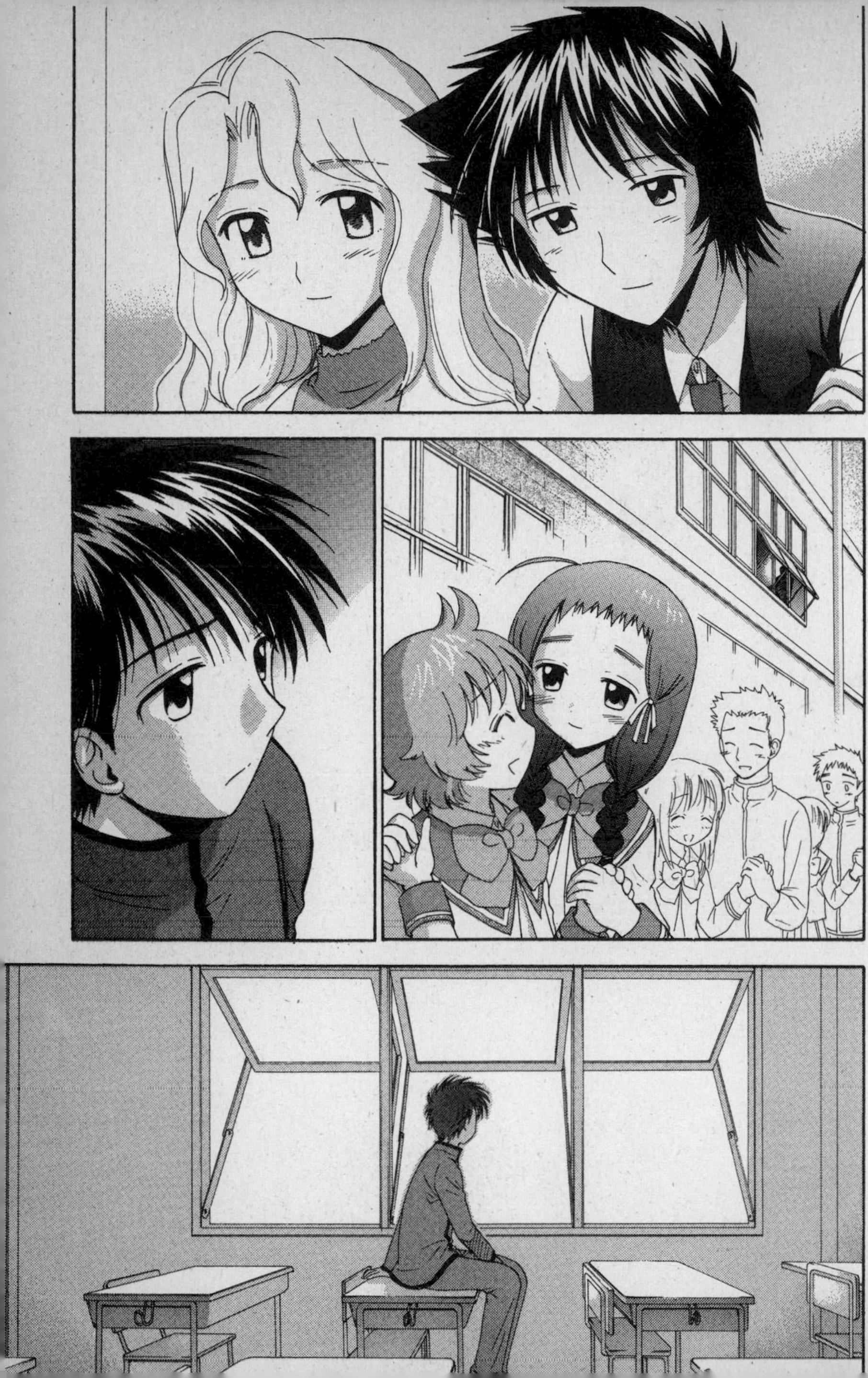

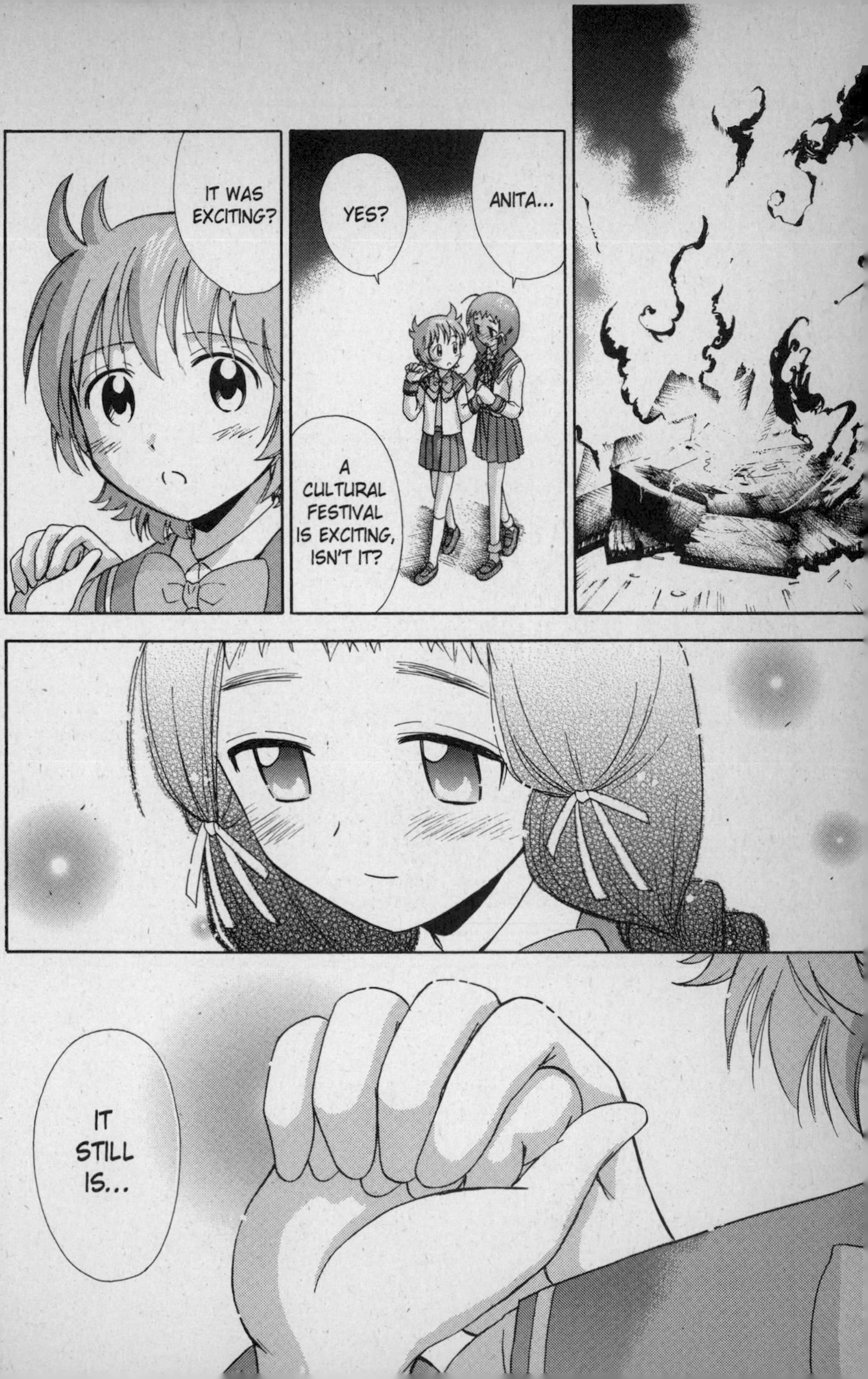
ANITA...
YES?
A CULTURAL FESTIVAL IS EXCITING, ISN'T IT?
IT WAS EXCITING?
IT STILL IS...

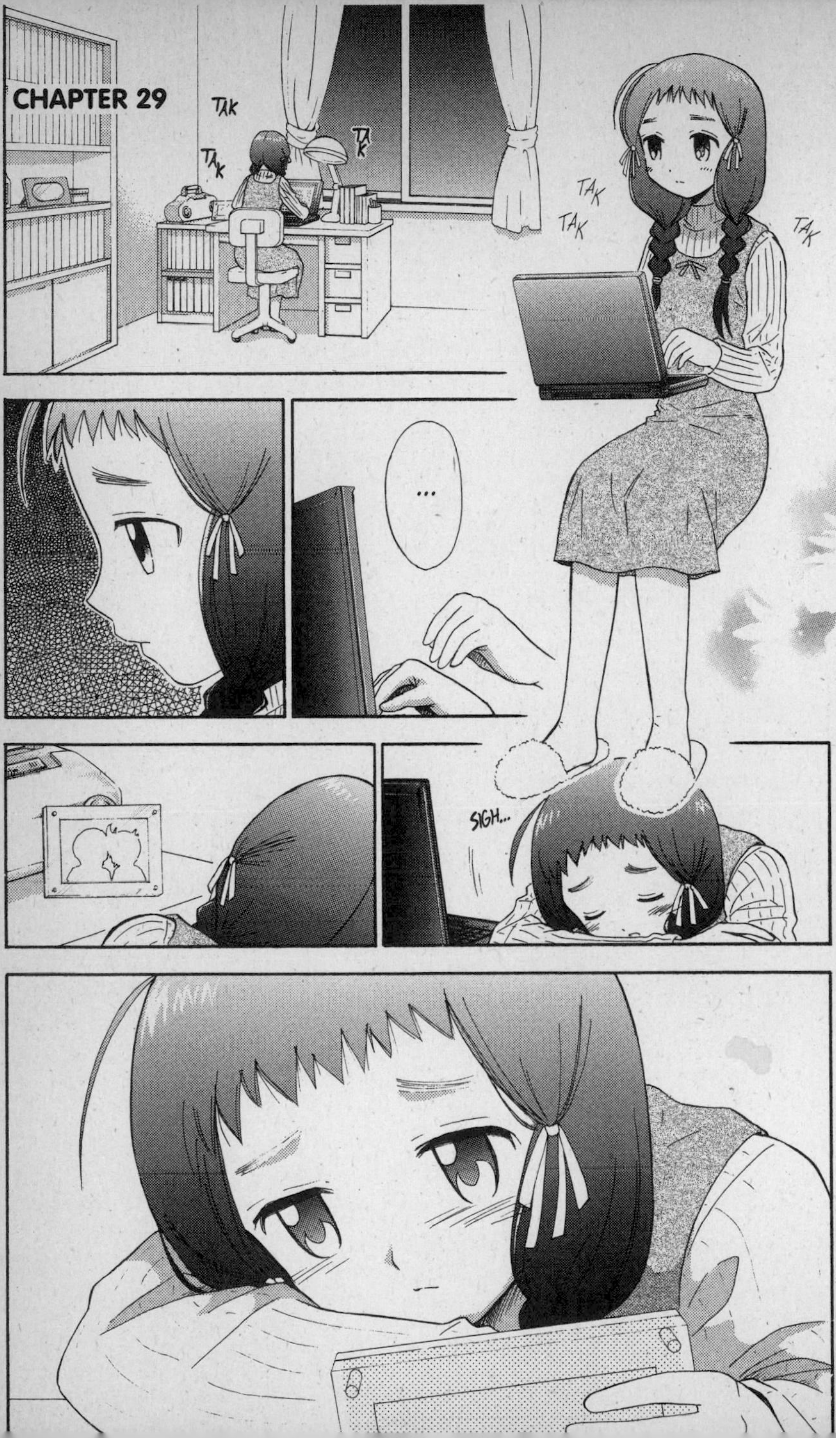
CHAPTER 29
TAK
TAK
TAK
TAK
TAK
TAK
...
SIGH...

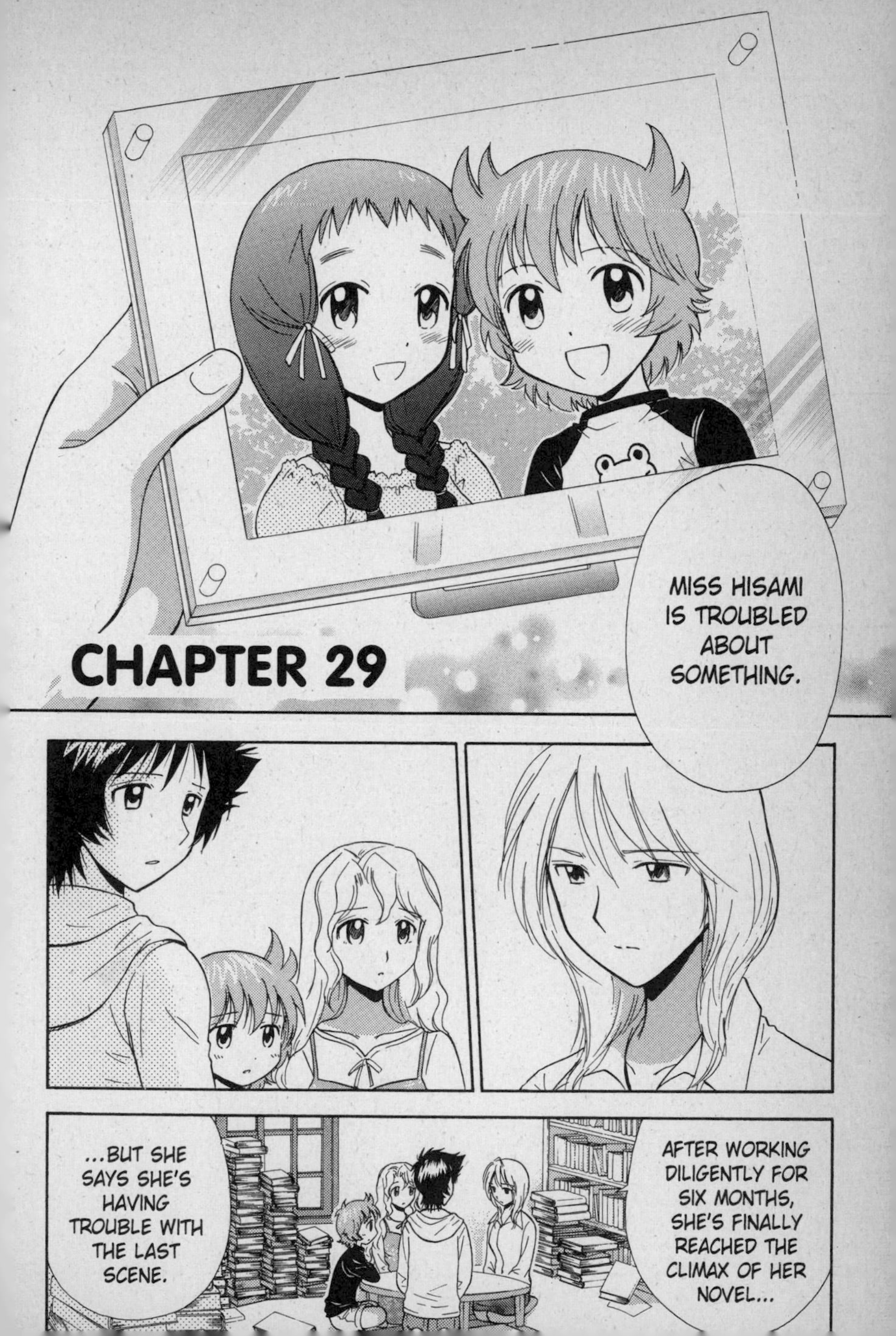
CHAPTER 29
MISS HISAMI IS TROUBLED ABOUT SOMETHING.
AFTER WORKING DILIGENTLY FOR SIX MONTHS, SHE'S FINALLY REACHED THE CLIMAX OF HER NOVEL...
...BUT SHE SAYS SHE'S HAVING TROUBLE WITH THE LAST SCENE.

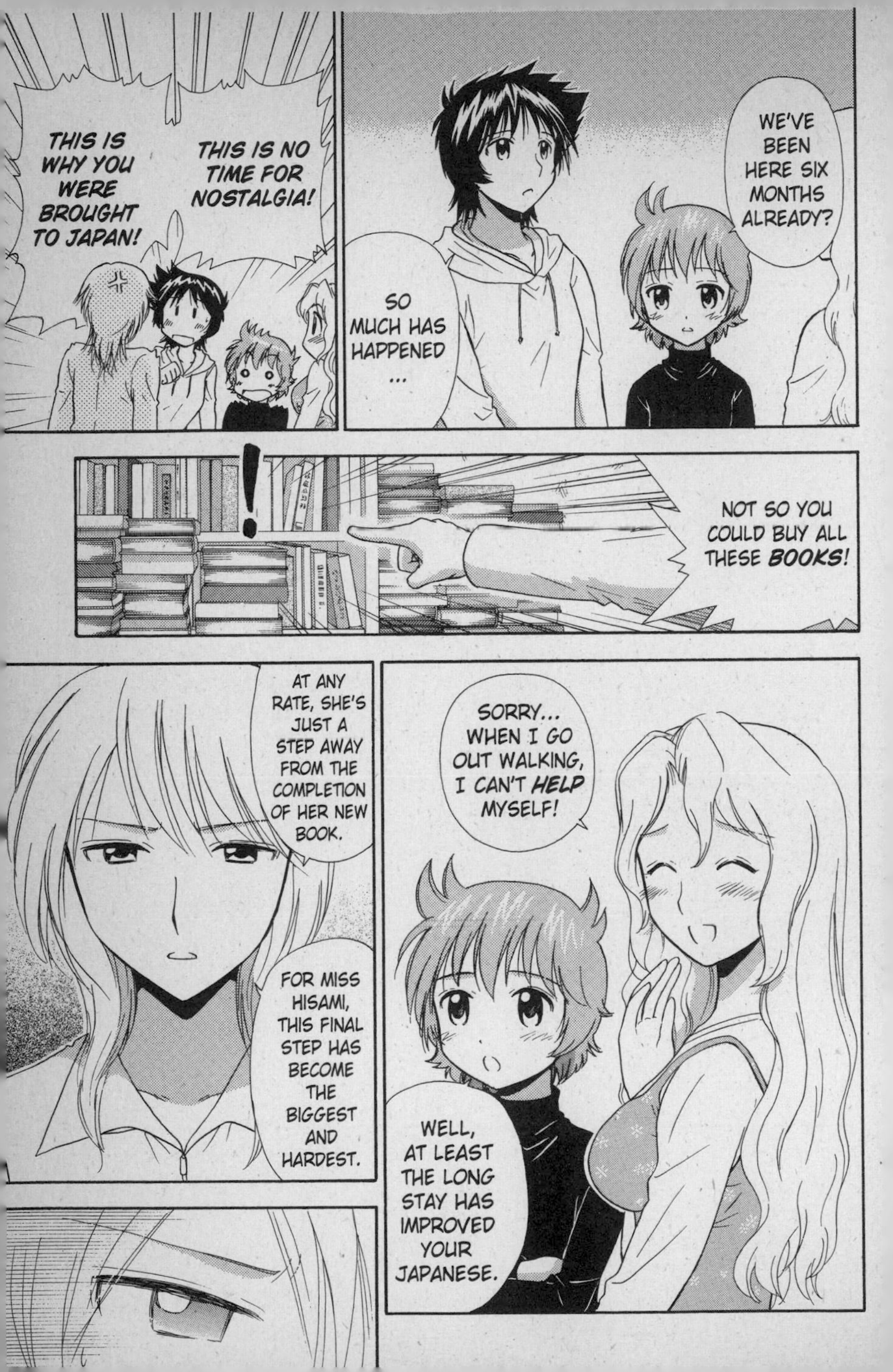

WE'VE BEEN HERE SIX MONTHS ALREADY?
SO MUCH HAS HAPPENED ...
THIS IS NO TIME FOR NOSTALGIA!
THIS IS WHY YOU WERE BROUGHT TO JAPAN!
NOT SO YOU COULD BUY ALL THESE *BOOKS*!
SORRY... WHEN I GO OUT WALKING, I CAN'T *HELP* MYSELF!
WELL, AT LEAST THE LONG STAY HAS IMPROVED YOUR JAPANESE.
AT ANY RATE, SHE'S JUST A STEP AWAY FROM THE COMPLETION OF HER NEW BOOK.
FOR MISS HISAMI, THIS FINAL STEP HAS BECOME THE BIGGEST AND HARDEST.

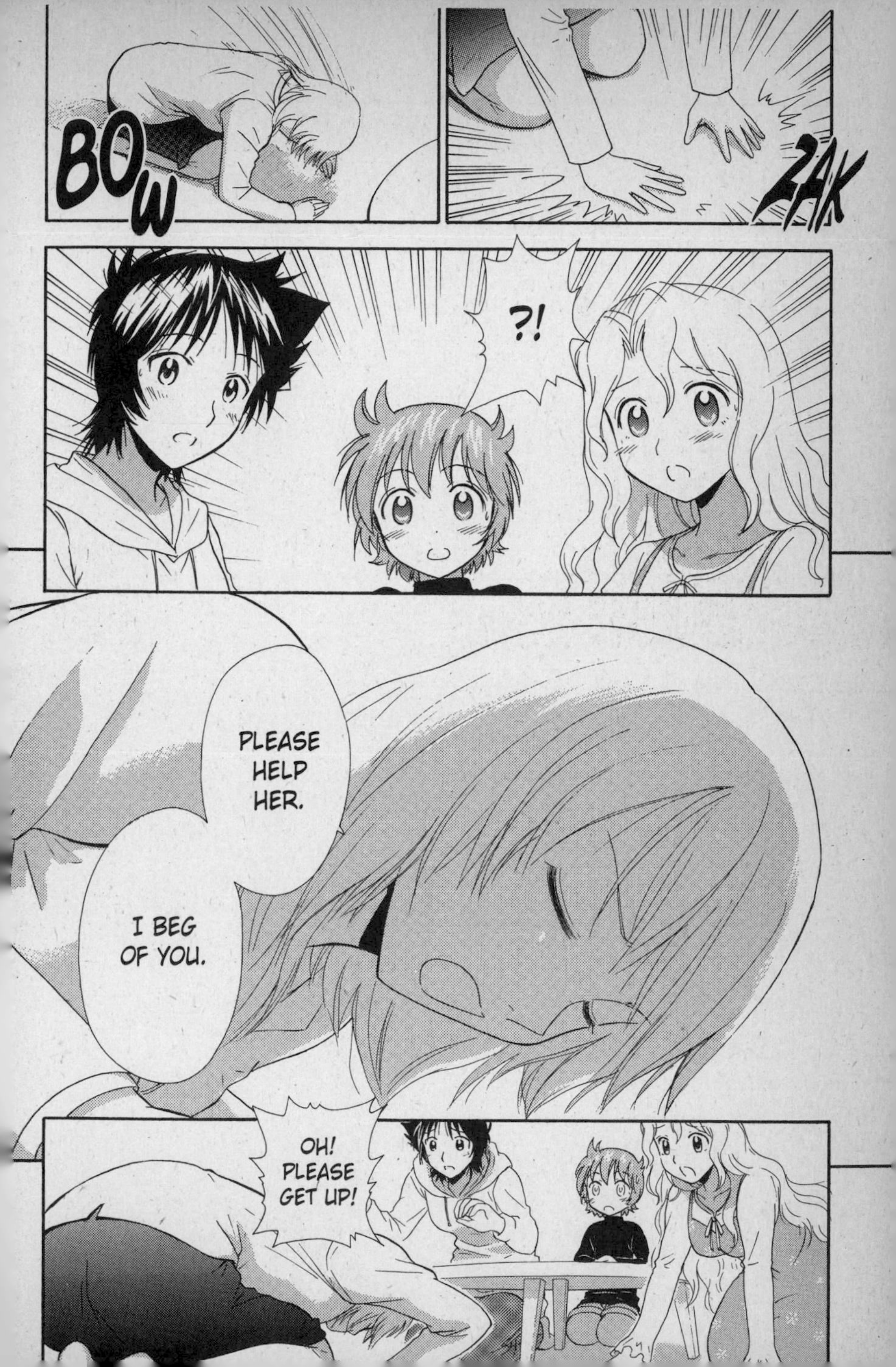
ZAK
BOW
?!
PLEASE HELP HER.
I BEG OF YOU.
OH! PLEASE GET UP!

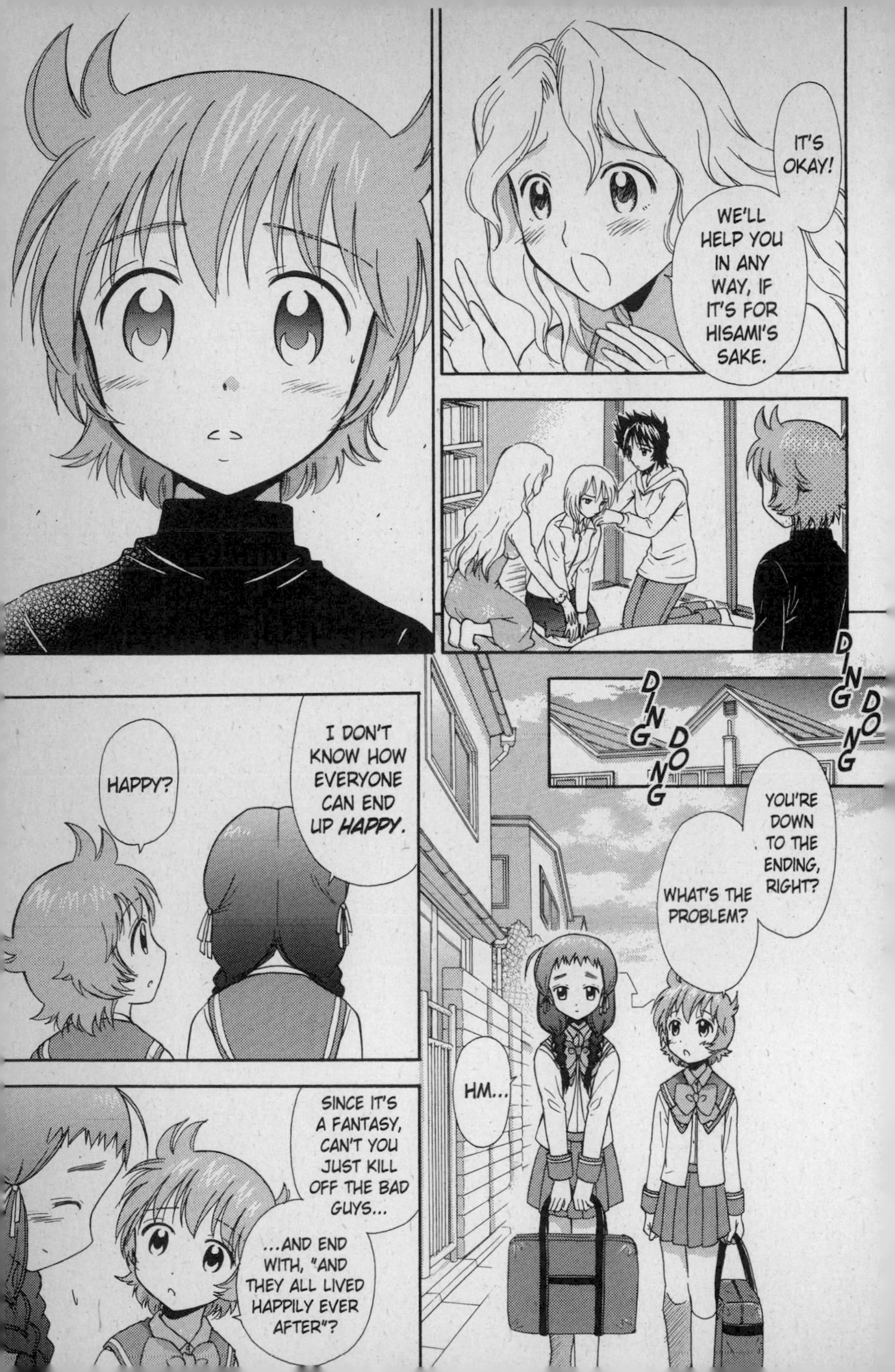
IT'S OKAY!
WE'LL HELP YOU IN ANY WAY, IF IT'S FOR HISAMI'S SAKE.
DING DONG
DING DONG
YOU'RE DOWN TO THE ENDING, RIGHT?
WHAT'S THE PROBLEM?
HM...
I DON'T KNOW HOW EVERYONE CAN END UP *HAPPY*.
HAPPY?
SINCE IT'S A FANTASY, CAN'T YOU JUST KILL OFF THE BAD GUYS...
...AND END WITH, "AND THEY ALL LIVED HAPPILY EVER AFTER"?

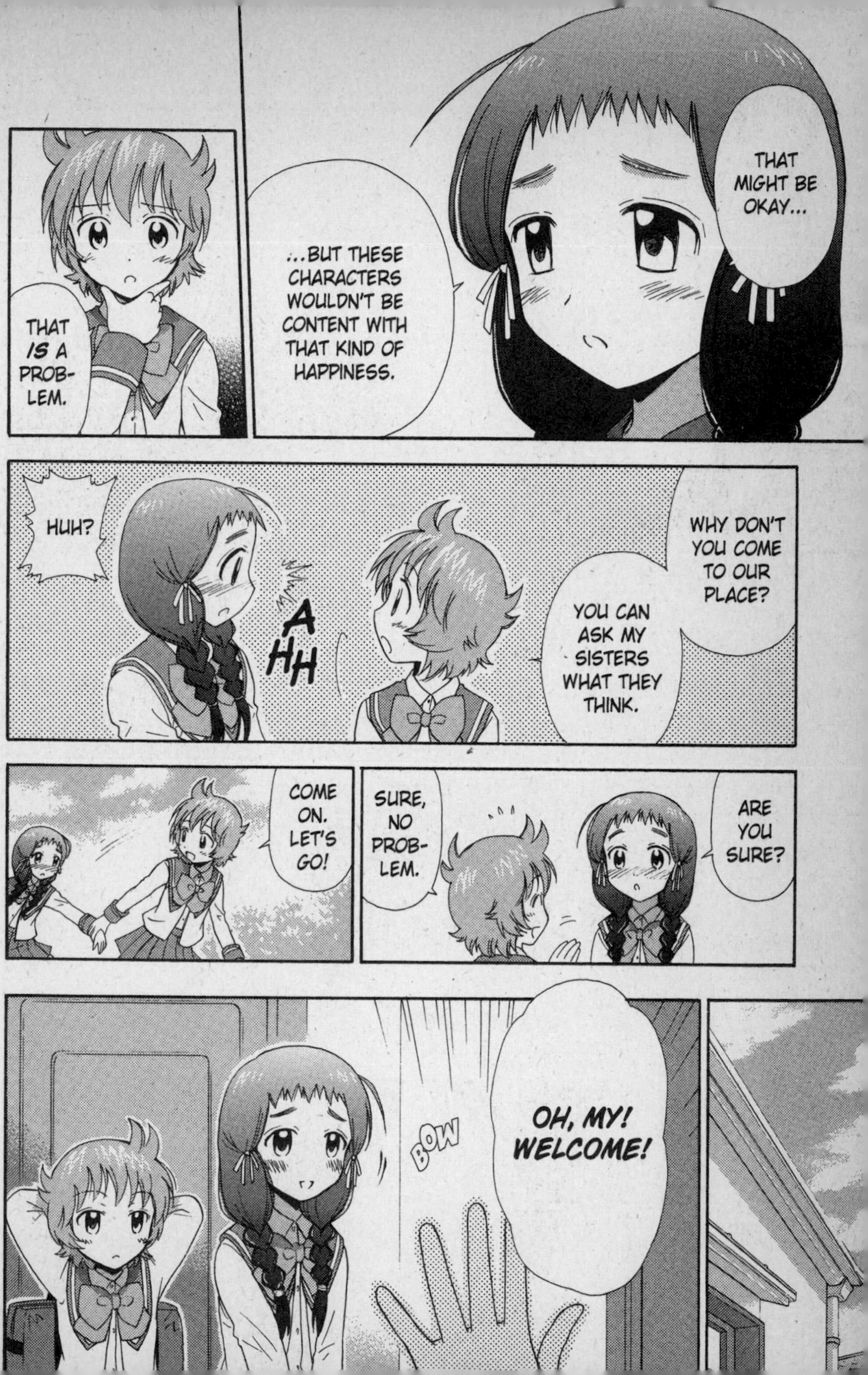
THAT MIGHT BE OKAY...
...BUT THESE CHARACTERS WOULDN'T BE CONTENT WITH THAT KIND OF HAPPINESS.
THAT *IS* A PROB-LEM.
WHY DON'T YOU COME TO OUR PLACE?
YOU CAN ASK MY SISTERS WHAT THEY THINK.
AHH
HUH?
ARE YOU SURE?
SURE, NO PROB-LEM.
COME ON. LET'S GO!
OH, MY! WELCOME!
BOW

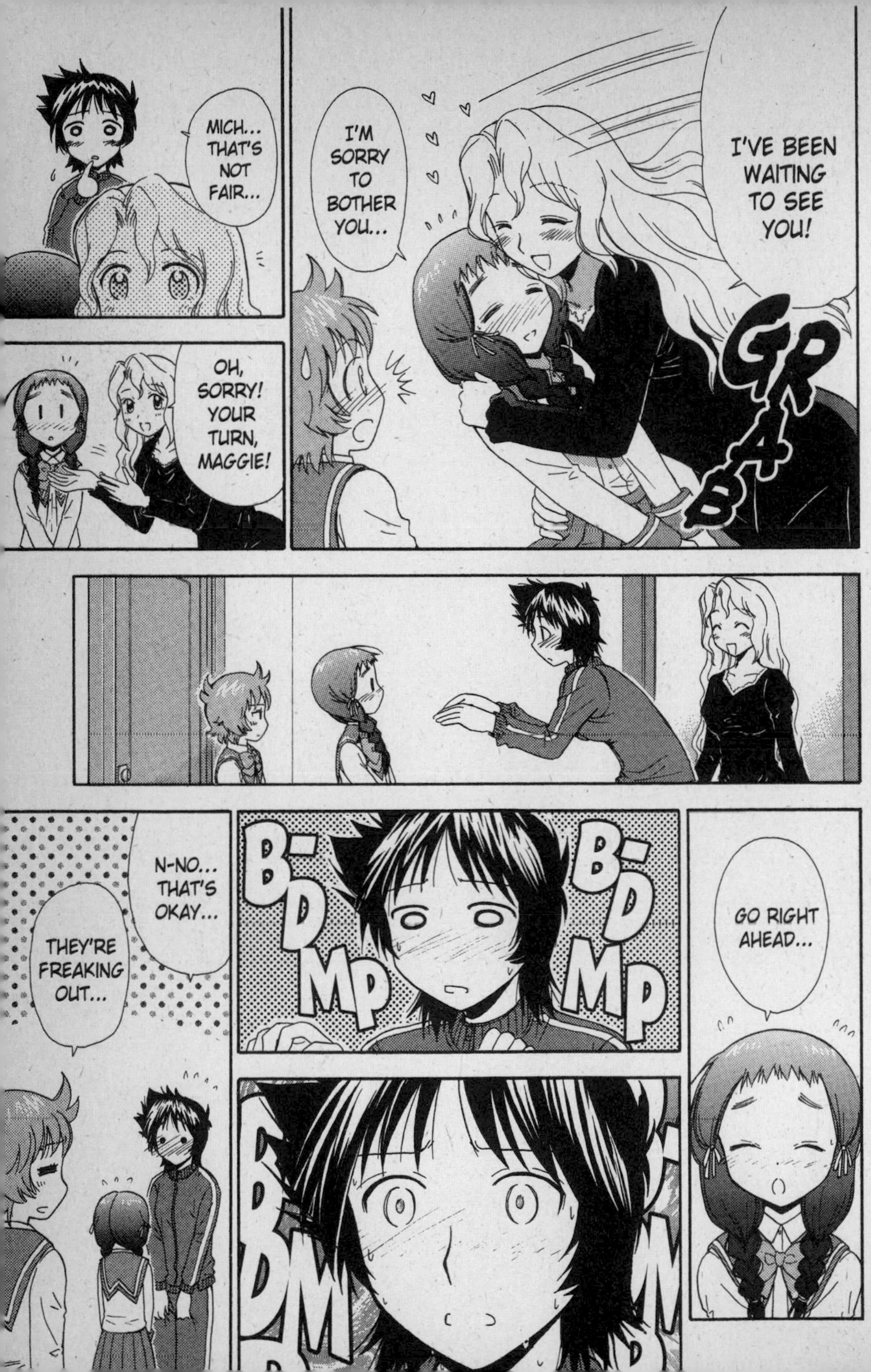
I'VE BEEN WAITING TO SEE YOU!
GRAB
I'M SORRY TO BOTHER YOU...
MICH... THAT'S NOT FAIR...
OH, SORRY! YOUR TURN, MAGGIE!
GO RIGHT AHEAD...
B-DMP
B-DMP
N-NO... THAT'S OKAY...
THEY'RE FREAKING OUT...

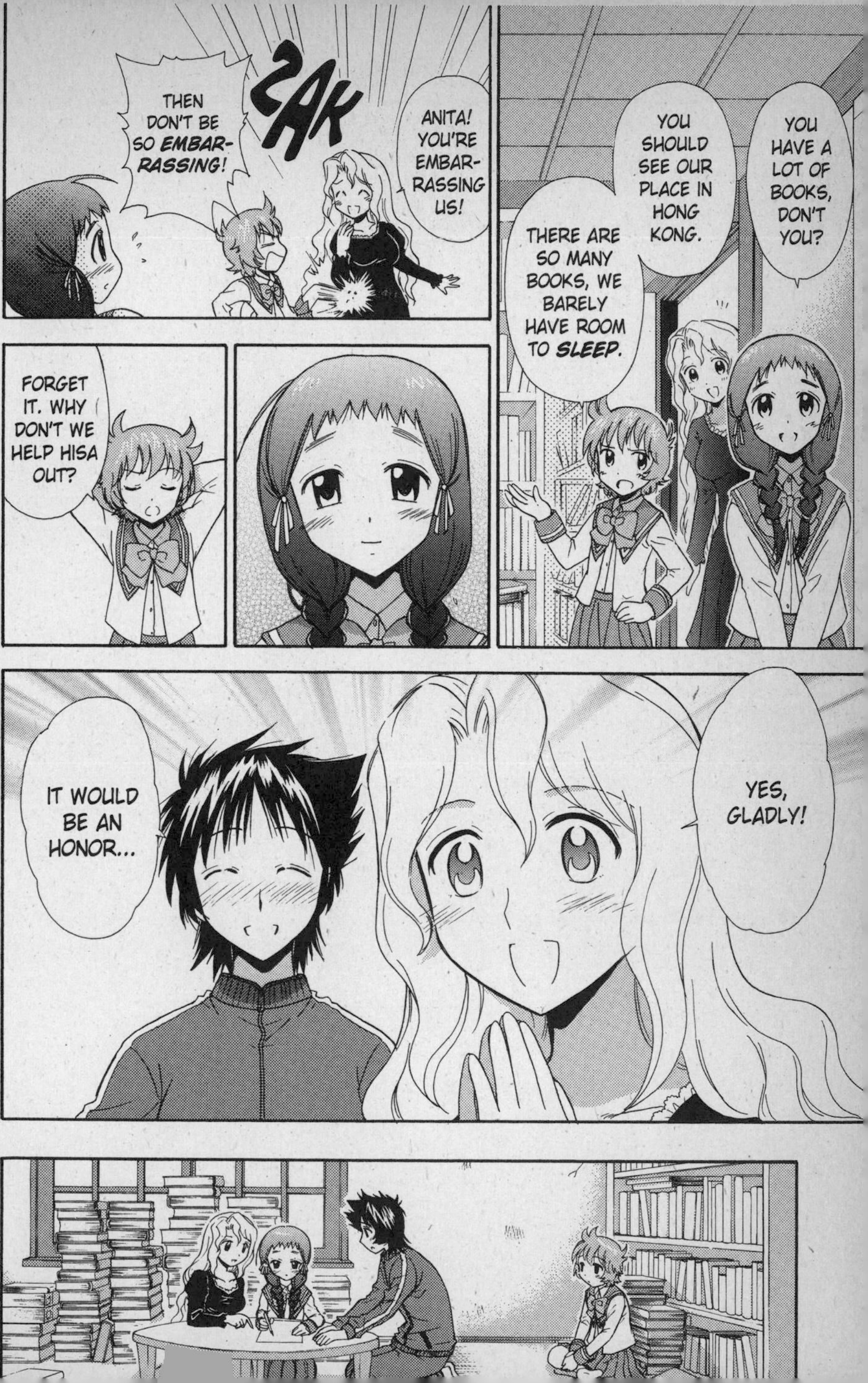
YOU HAVE A LOT OF BOOKS, DON'T YOU?
YOU SHOULD SEE OUR PLACE IN HONG KONG.
THERE ARE SO MANY BOOKS, WE BARELY HAVE ROOM TO SLEEP.
ANITA! YOU'RE EMBAR-RASSING US!
ZAK
THEN DON'T BE SO EMBAR-RASSING!
FORGET IT. WHY DON'T WE HELP HISA OUT?
YES, GLADLY!
IT WOULD BE AN HONOR...

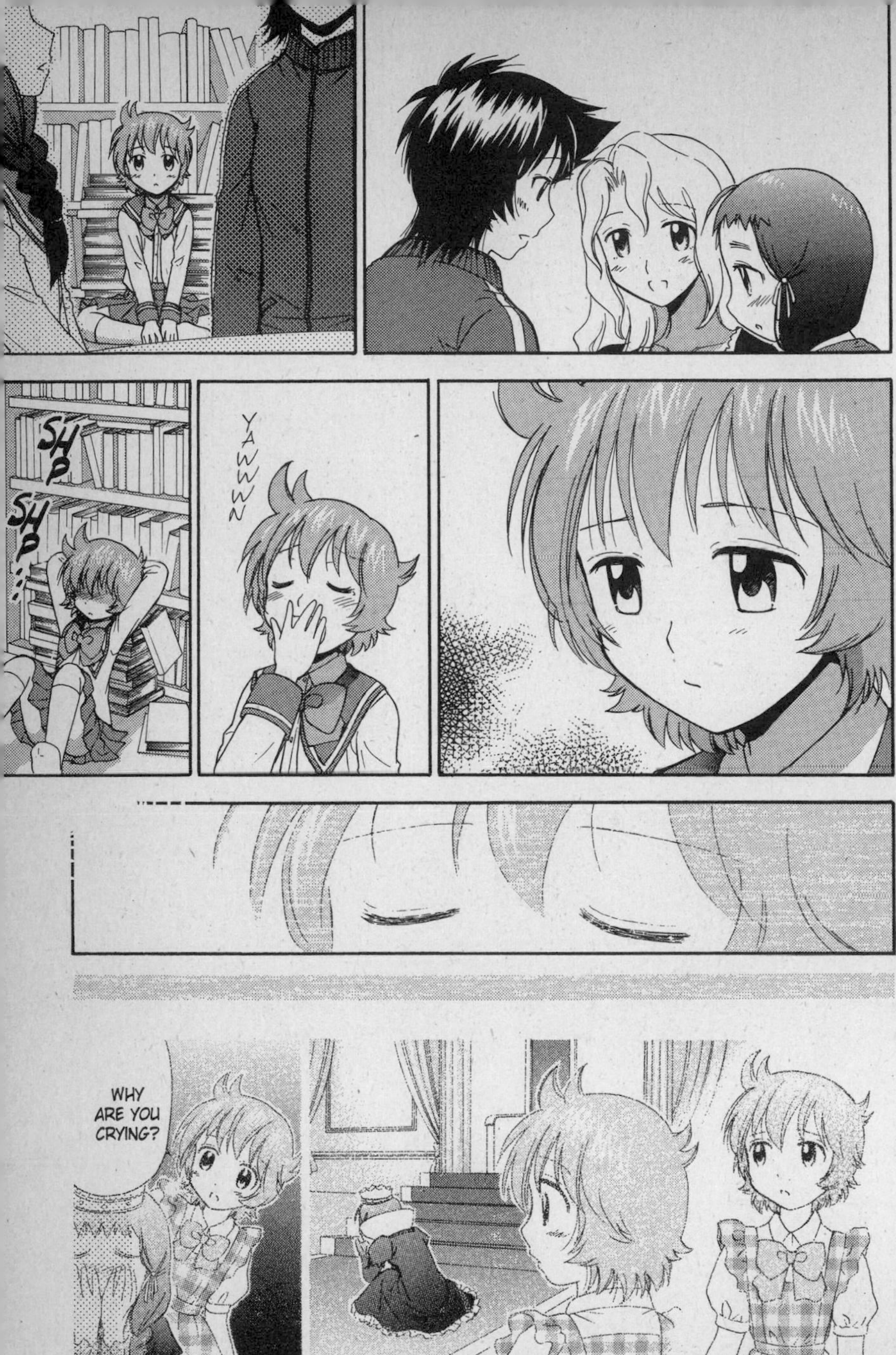
YAWWWN
SHP SHP...
WHY ARE YOU CRYING?

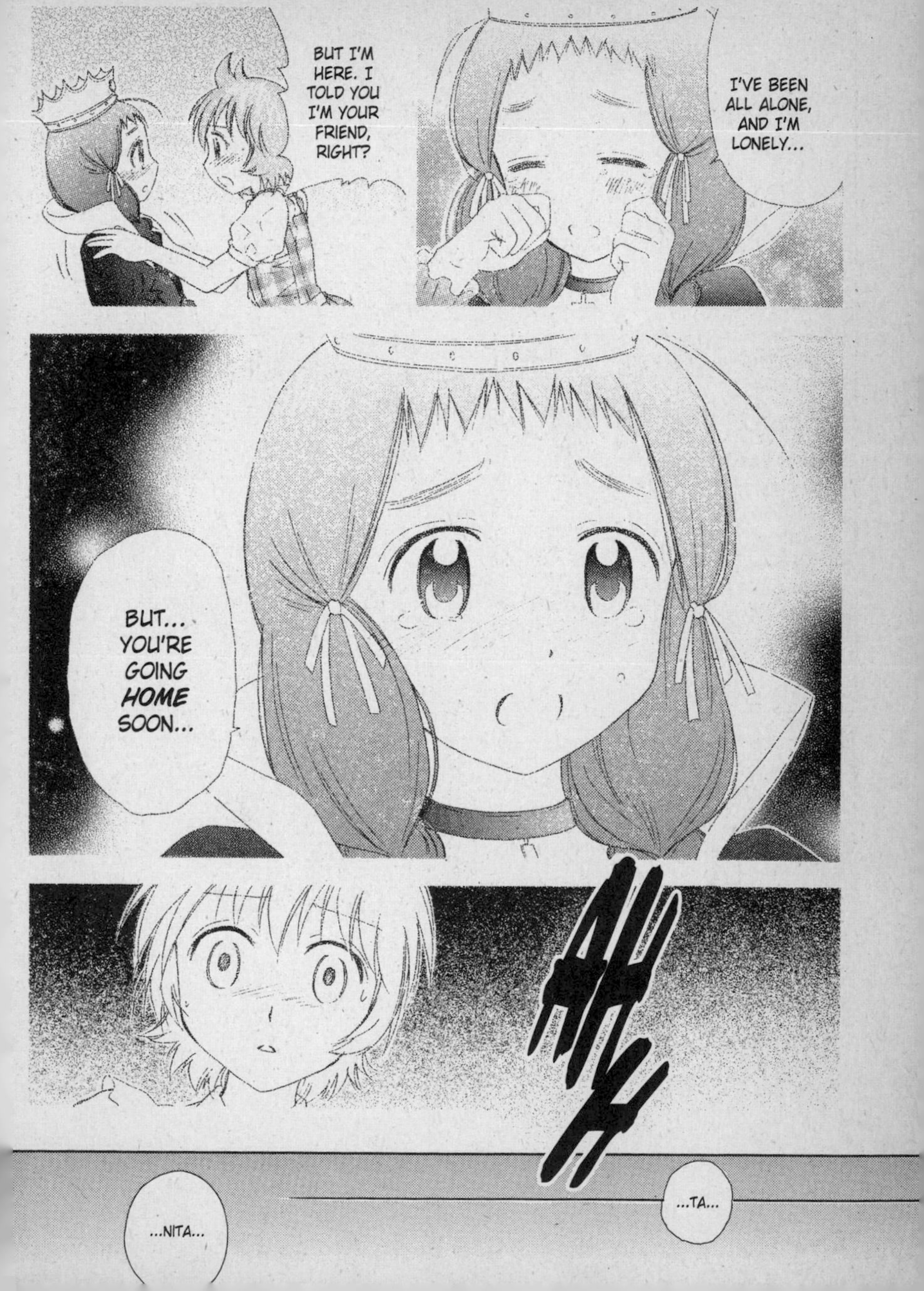
I'VE BEEN ALL ALONE, AND I'M LONELY...
BUT I'M HERE. I TOLD YOU I'M YOUR FRIEND, RIGHT?
BUT... YOU'RE GOING *HOME* SOON...
AHH
...TA...
...NITA...

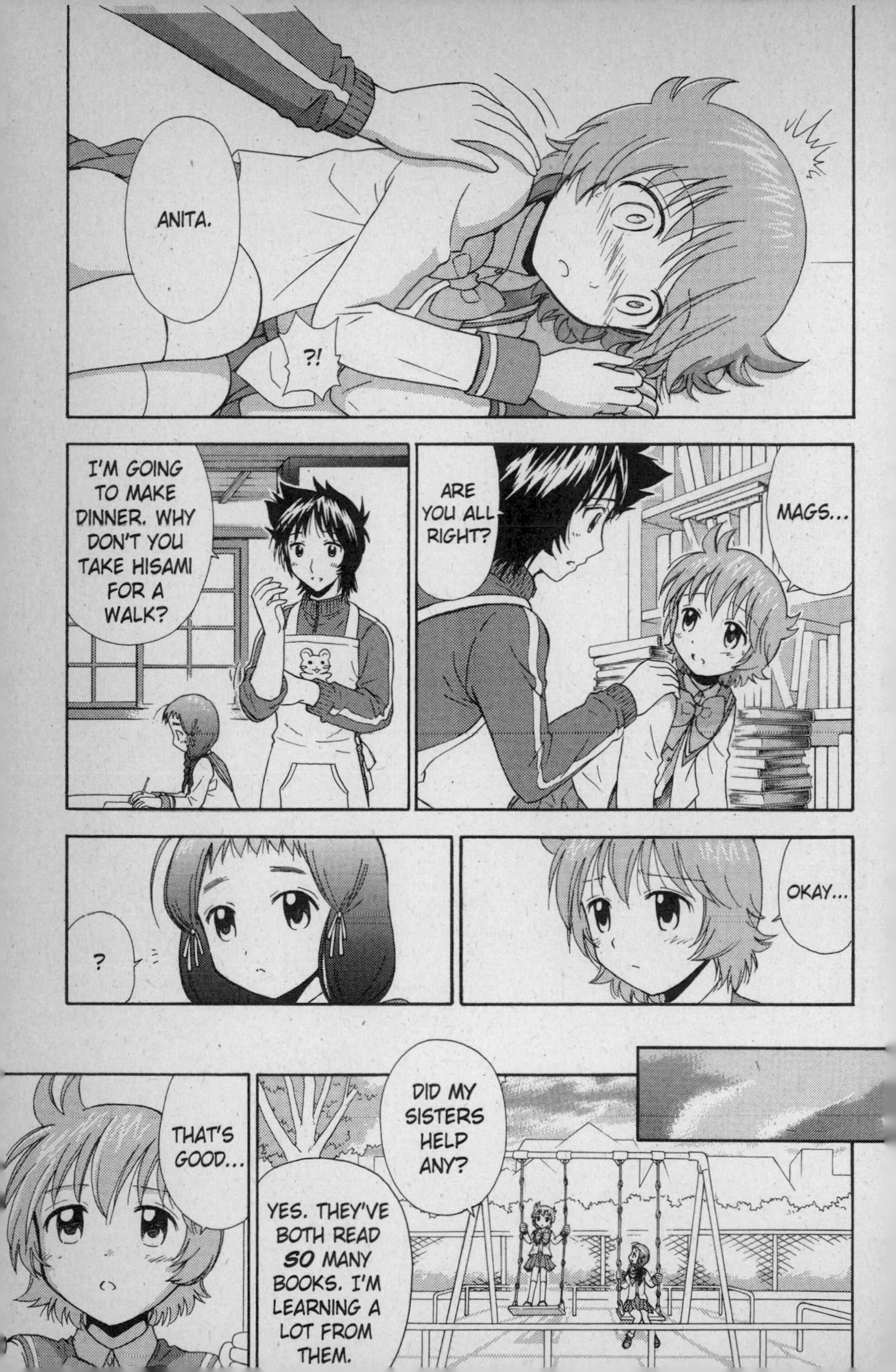
ANITA.
?!
MAGS...
ARE YOU ALL RIGHT?
I'M GOING TO MAKE DINNER. WHY DON'T YOU TAKE HISAMI FOR A WALK?
OKAY...
?
DID MY SISTERS HELP ANY?
YES. THEY'VE BOTH READ *SO* MANY BOOKS. I'M LEARNING A LOT FROM THEM.
THAT'S GOOD...

ISN'T IT BEAUTIFUL?

MM...

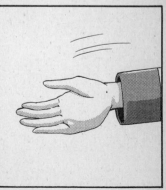

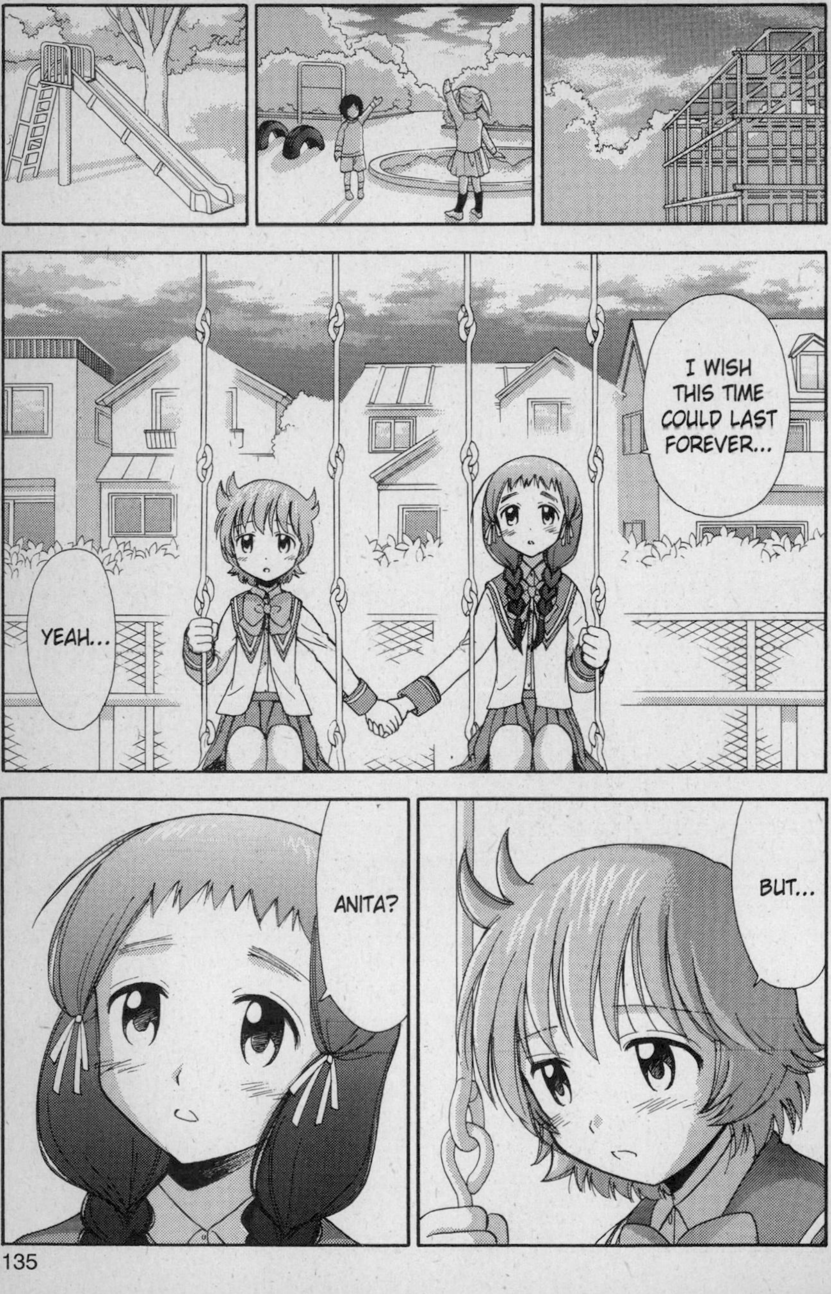
I WISH THIS TIME COULD LAST FOREVER...
YEAH...
BUT...
ANITA?

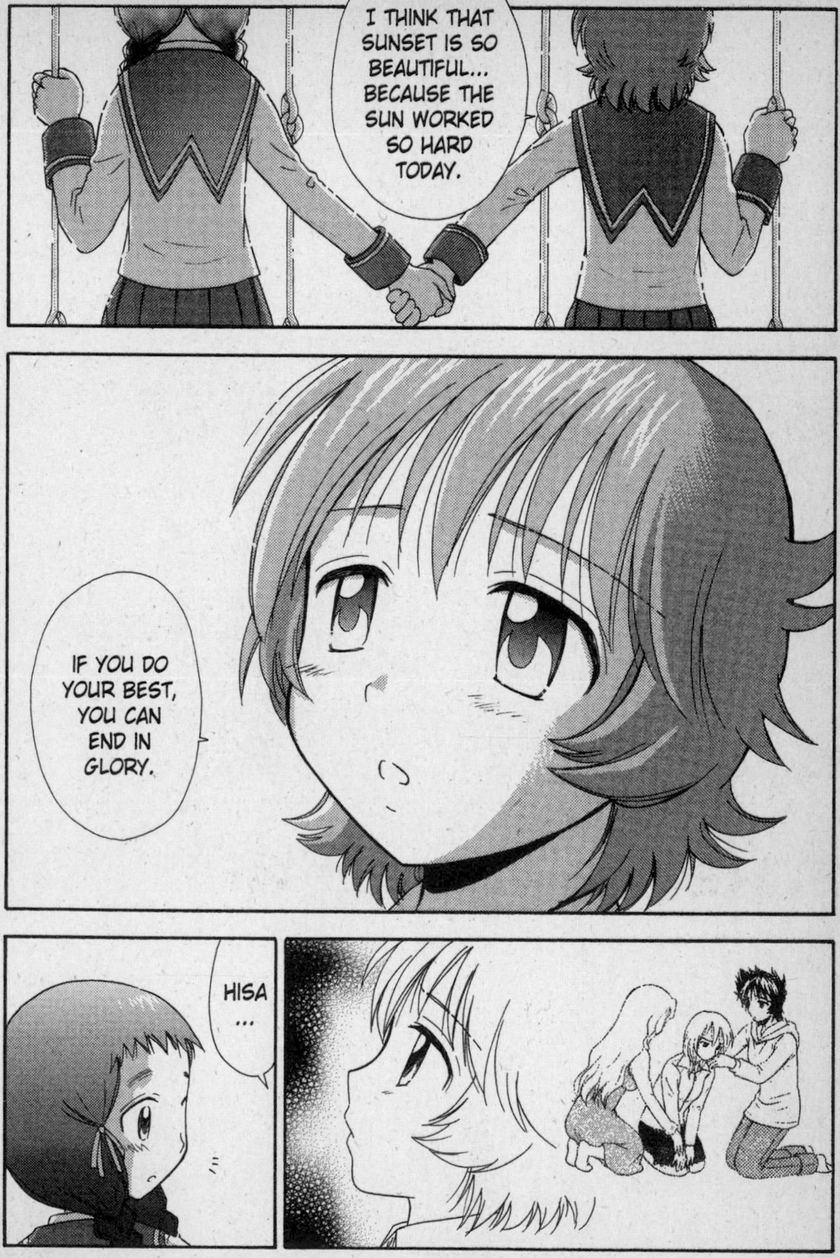
I THINK THAT SUNSET IS SO BEAUTIFUL... BECAUSE THE SUN WORKED SO HARD TODAY.
IF YOU DO YOUR BEST, YOU CAN END IN GLORY.
HISA ...

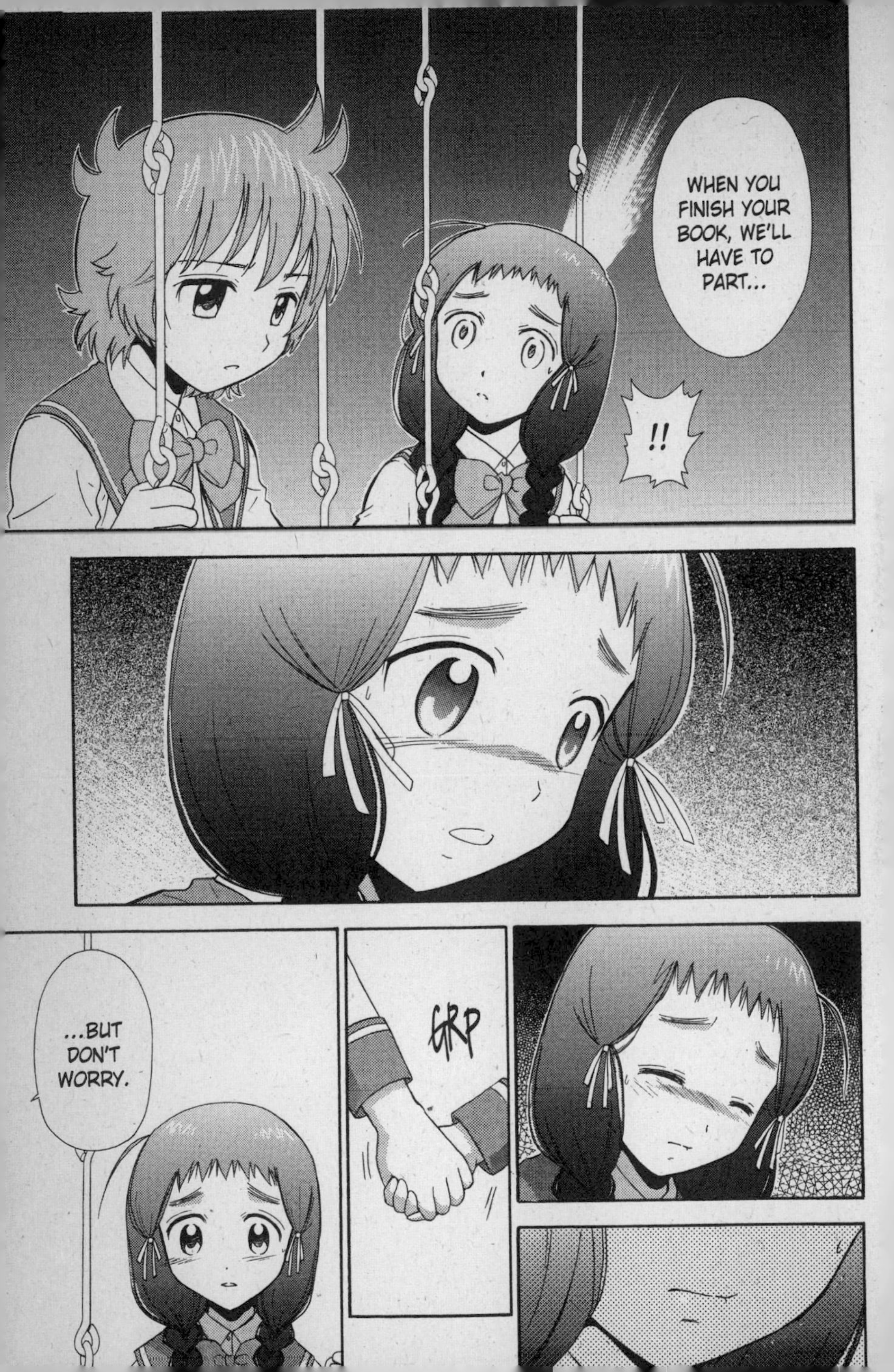
WHEN YOU FINISH YOUR BOOK, WE'LL HAVE TO PART...
!!
GRP
...BUT DON'T WORRY.

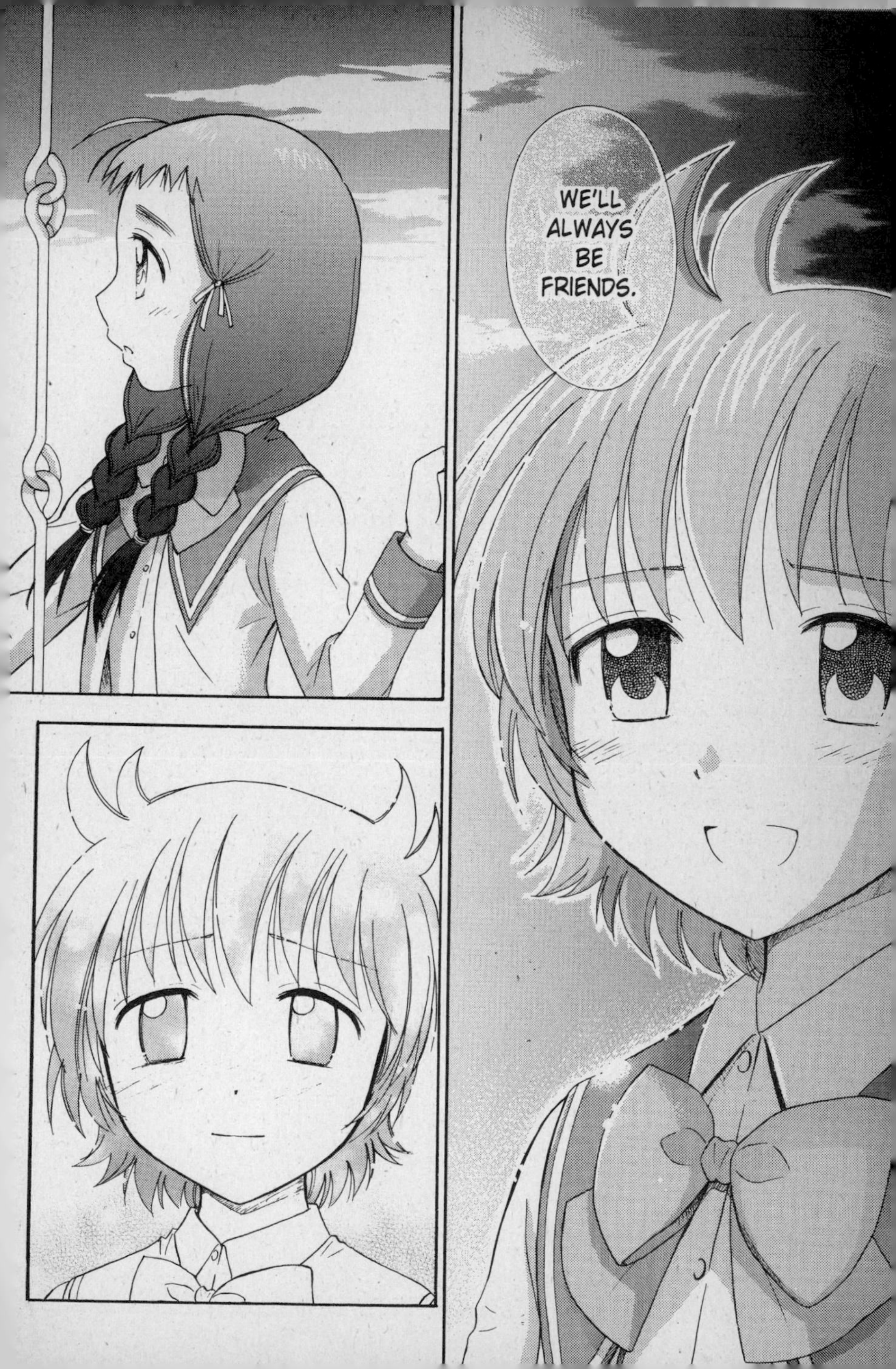
WE'LL ALWAYS BE FRIENDS.

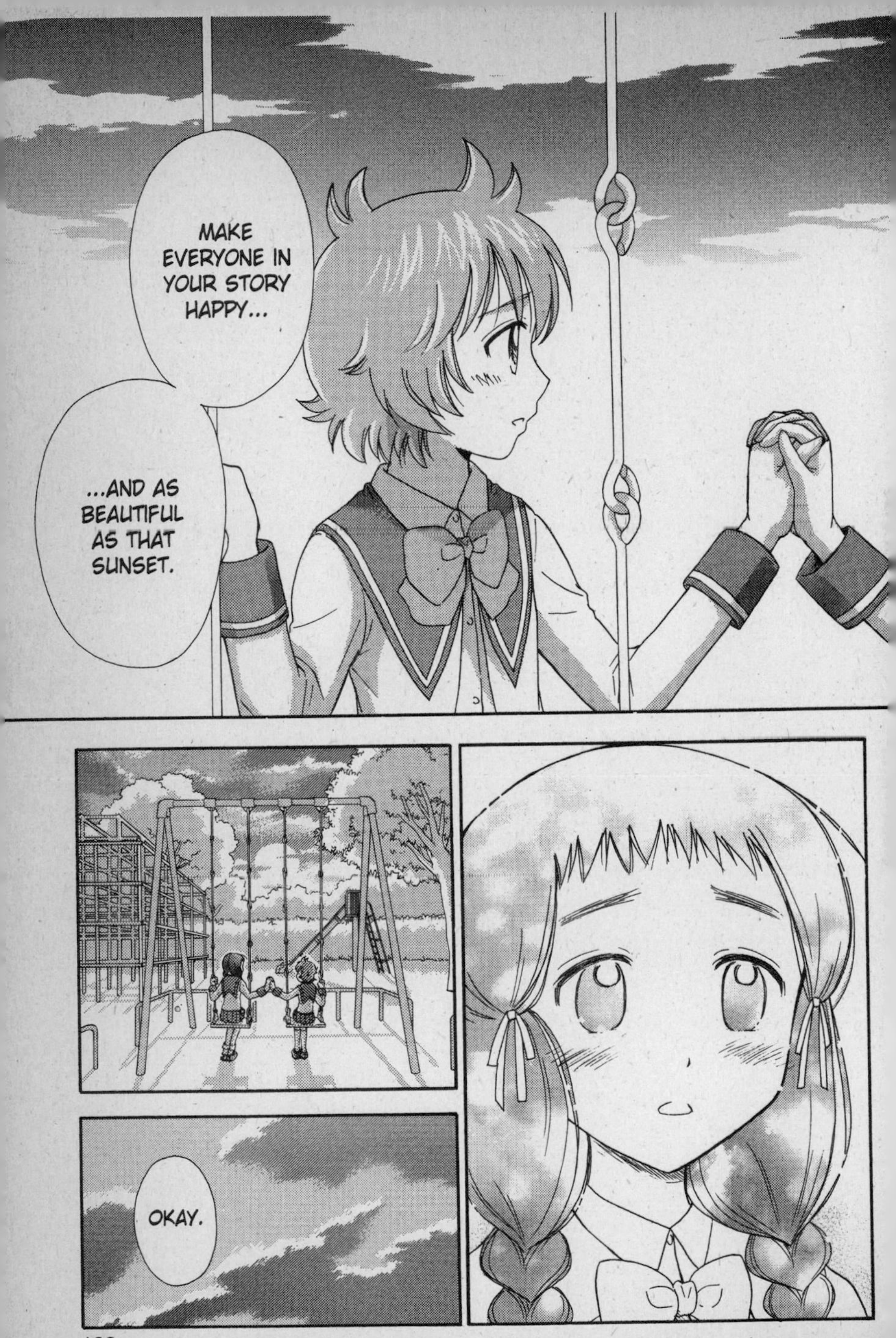
MAKE EVERYONE IN YOUR STORY HAPPY...
...AND AS BEAUTIFUL AS THAT SUNSET.
OKAY.

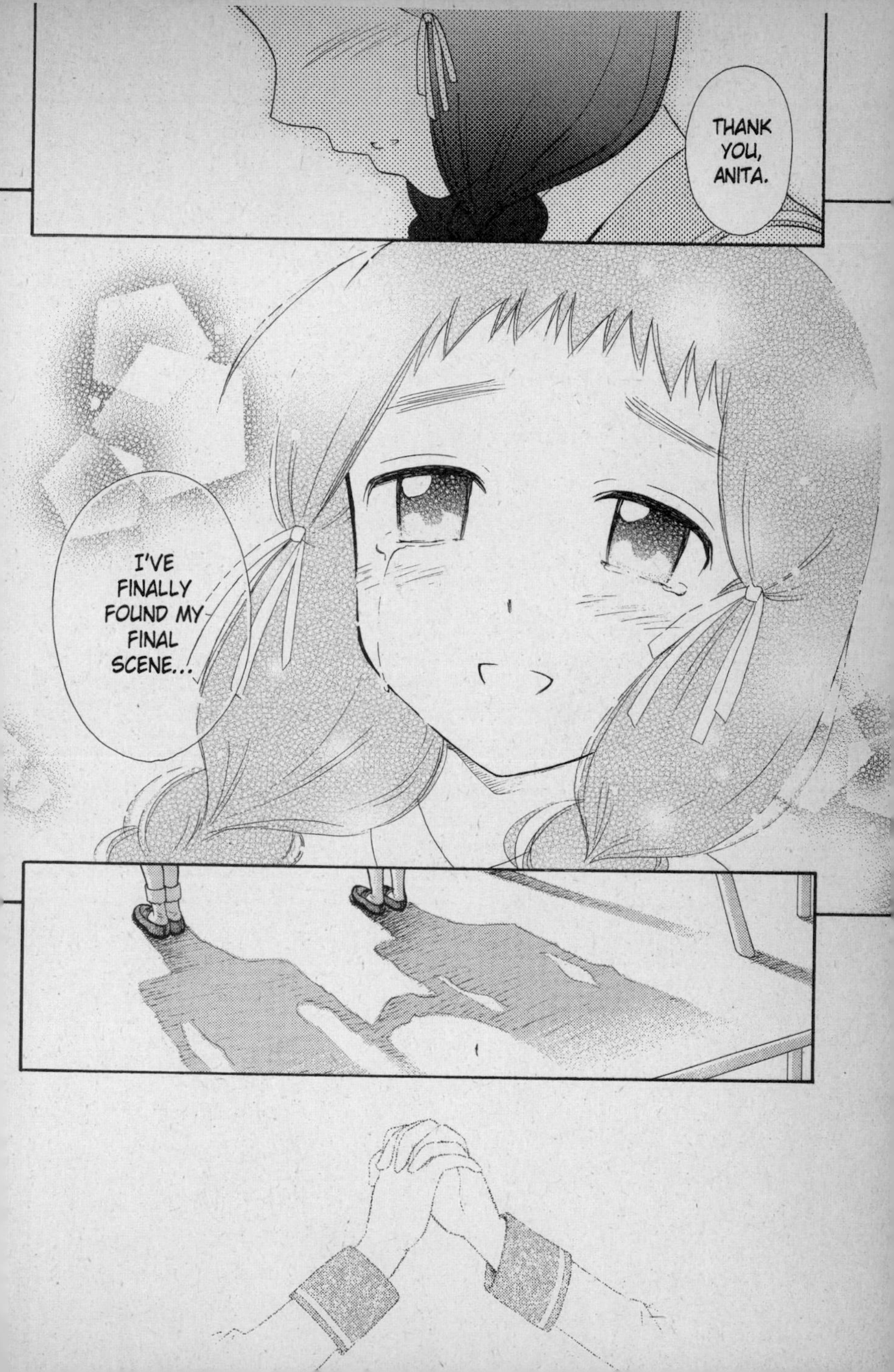
THANK YOU, ANITA.
I'VE FINALLY FOUND MY FINAL SCENE...

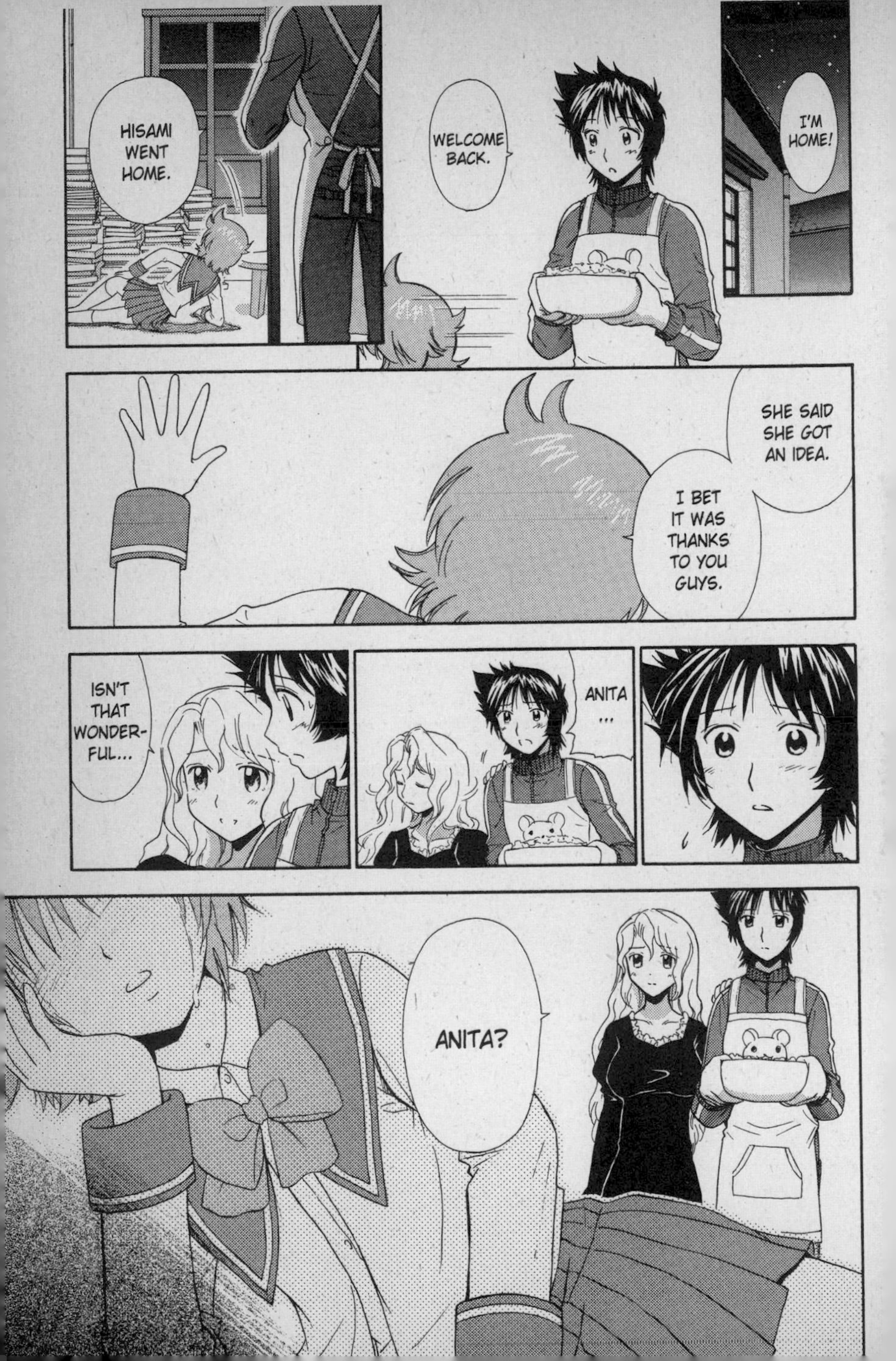
I'M HOME!
WELCOME BACK.
HISAMI WENT HOME.
SHE SAID SHE GOT AN IDEA.
I BET IT WAS THANKS TO YOU GUYS.
ANITA ...
ISN'T THAT WONDER-FUL...
ANITA?

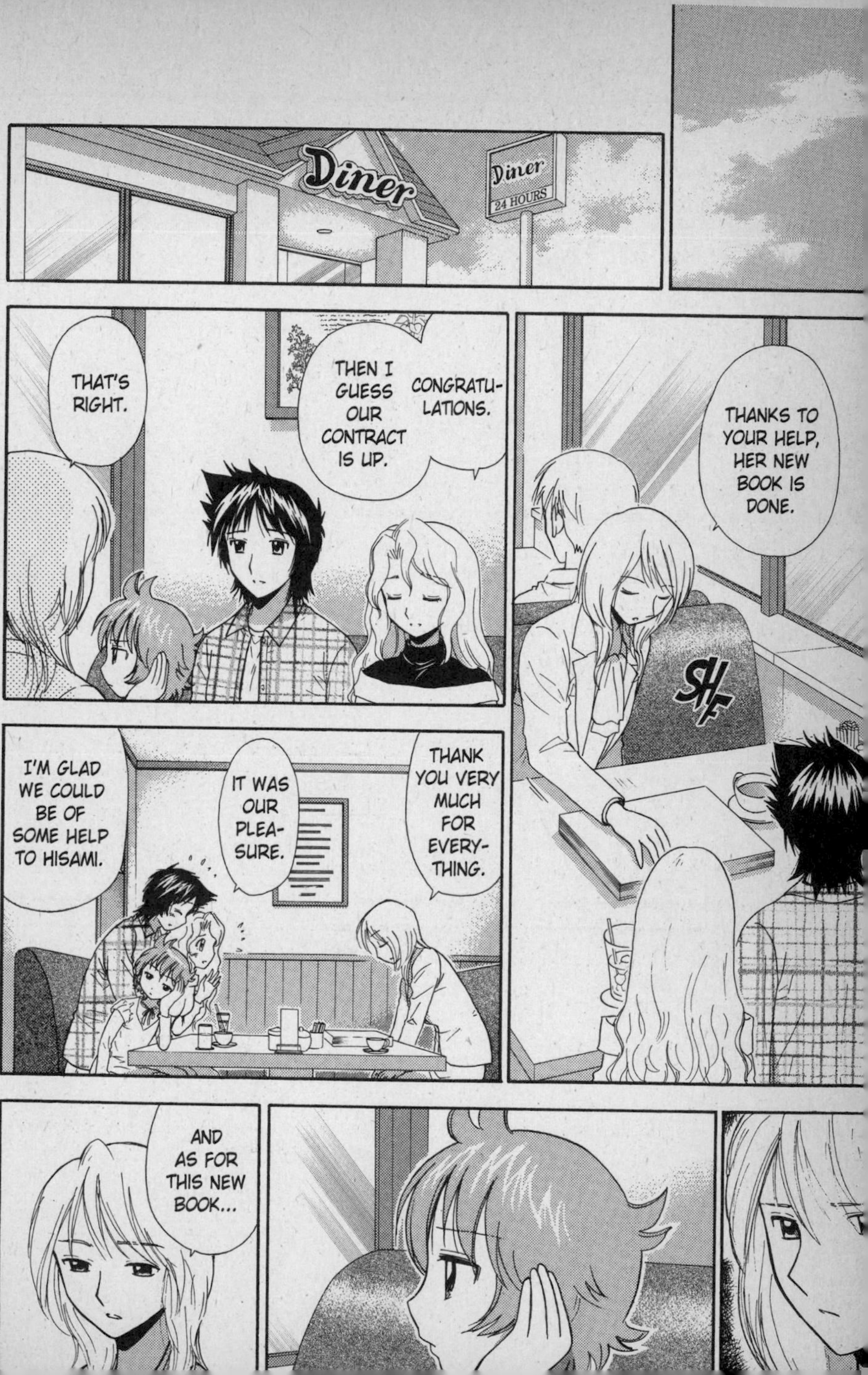
Diner
Diner
24 HOURS
THANKS TO YOUR HELP, HER NEW BOOK IS DONE.
SHF
THEN I GUESS OUR CONTRACT IS UP.
CONGRATULATIONS.
THAT'S RIGHT.
THANK YOU VERY MUCH FOR EVERYTHING.
IT WAS OUR PLEASURE.
I'M GLAD WE COULD BE OF SOME HELP TO HISAMI.
AND AS FOR THIS NEW BOOK...

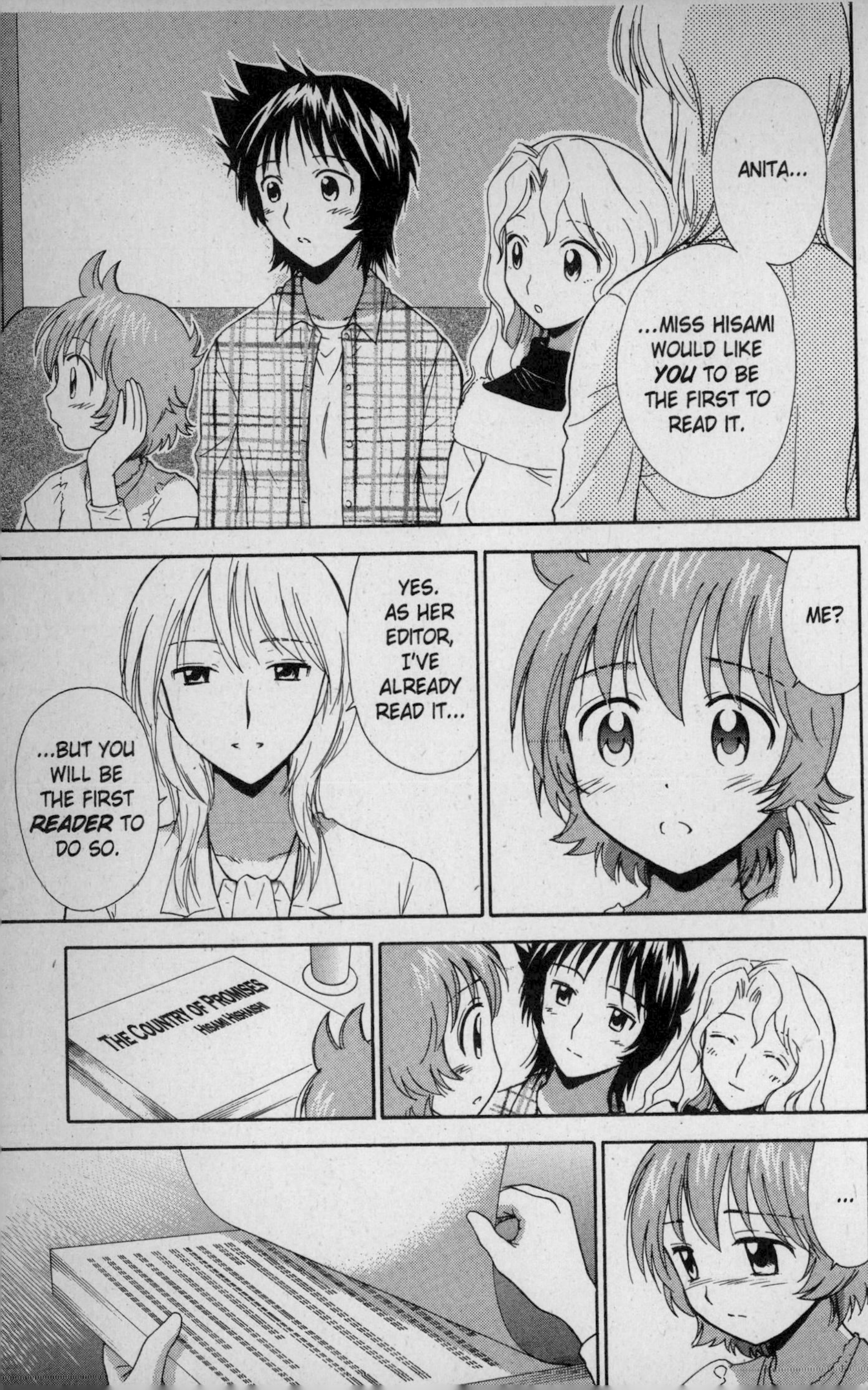
ANITA...
...MISS HISAMI WOULD LIKE YOU TO BE THE FIRST TO READ IT.
ME?
YES. AS HER EDITOR, I'VE ALREADY READ IT...
...BUT YOU WILL BE THE FIRST READER TO DO SO.
THE COUNTRY OF PROMISES
Hisami Hishashi
...

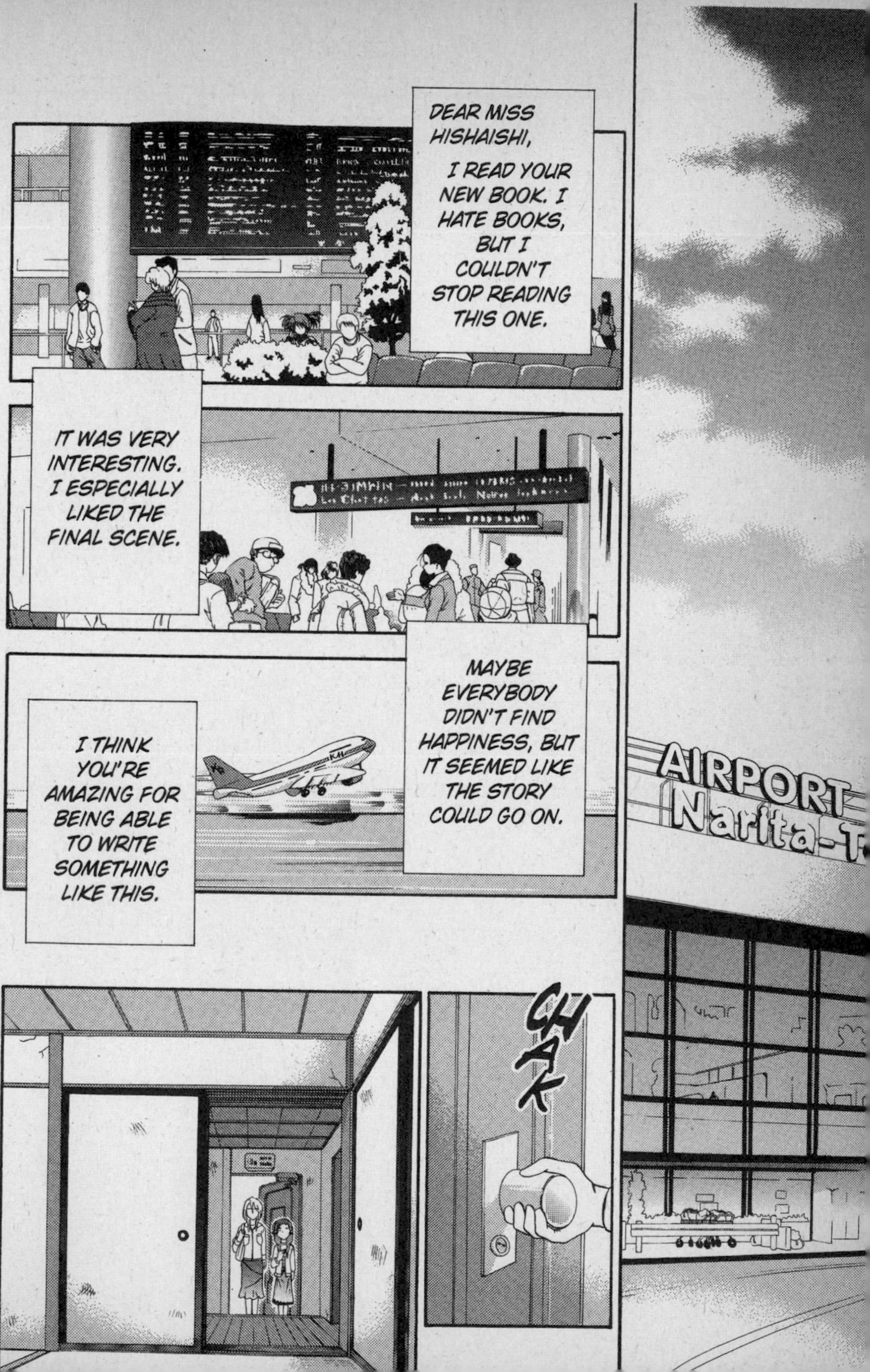
AIRPORT
Narita-T
DEAR MISS HISHAISHI,
I READ YOUR NEW BOOK. I HATE BOOKS, BUT I COULDN'T STOP READING THIS ONE.
IT WAS VERY INTERESTING. I ESPECIALLY LIKED THE FINAL SCENE.
MAYBE EVERYBODY DIDN'T FIND HAPPINESS, BUT IT SEEMED LIKE THE STORY COULD GO ON.
I THINK YOU'RE AMAZING FOR BEING ABLE TO WRITE SOMETHING LIKE THIS.
CHAK

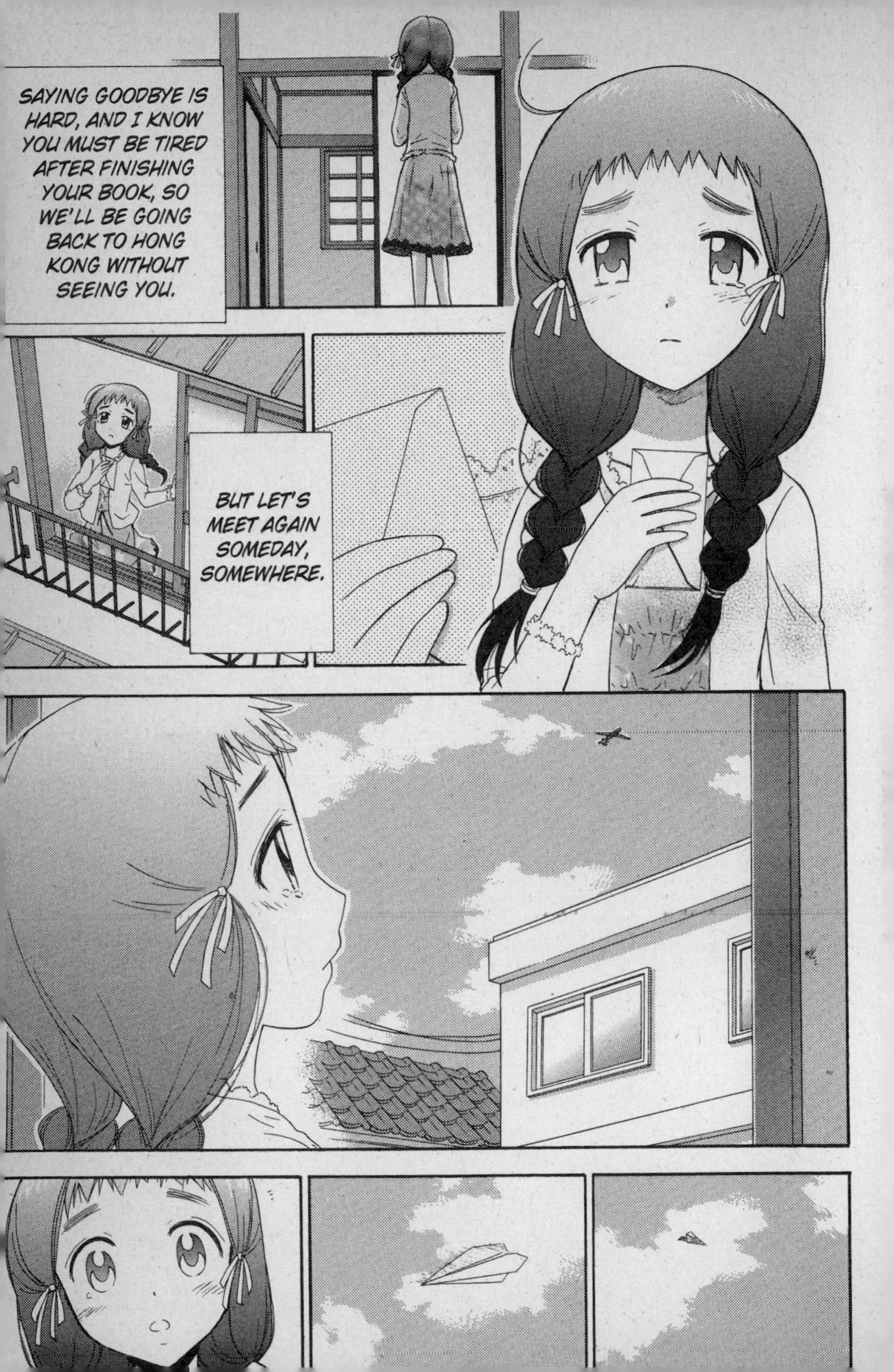
SAYING GOODBYE IS HARD, AND I KNOW YOU MUST BE TIRED AFTER FINISHING YOUR BOOK, SO WE'LL BE GOING BACK TO HONG KONG WITHOUT SEEING YOU.
BUT LET'S MEET AGAIN SOMEDAY, SOMEWHERE.

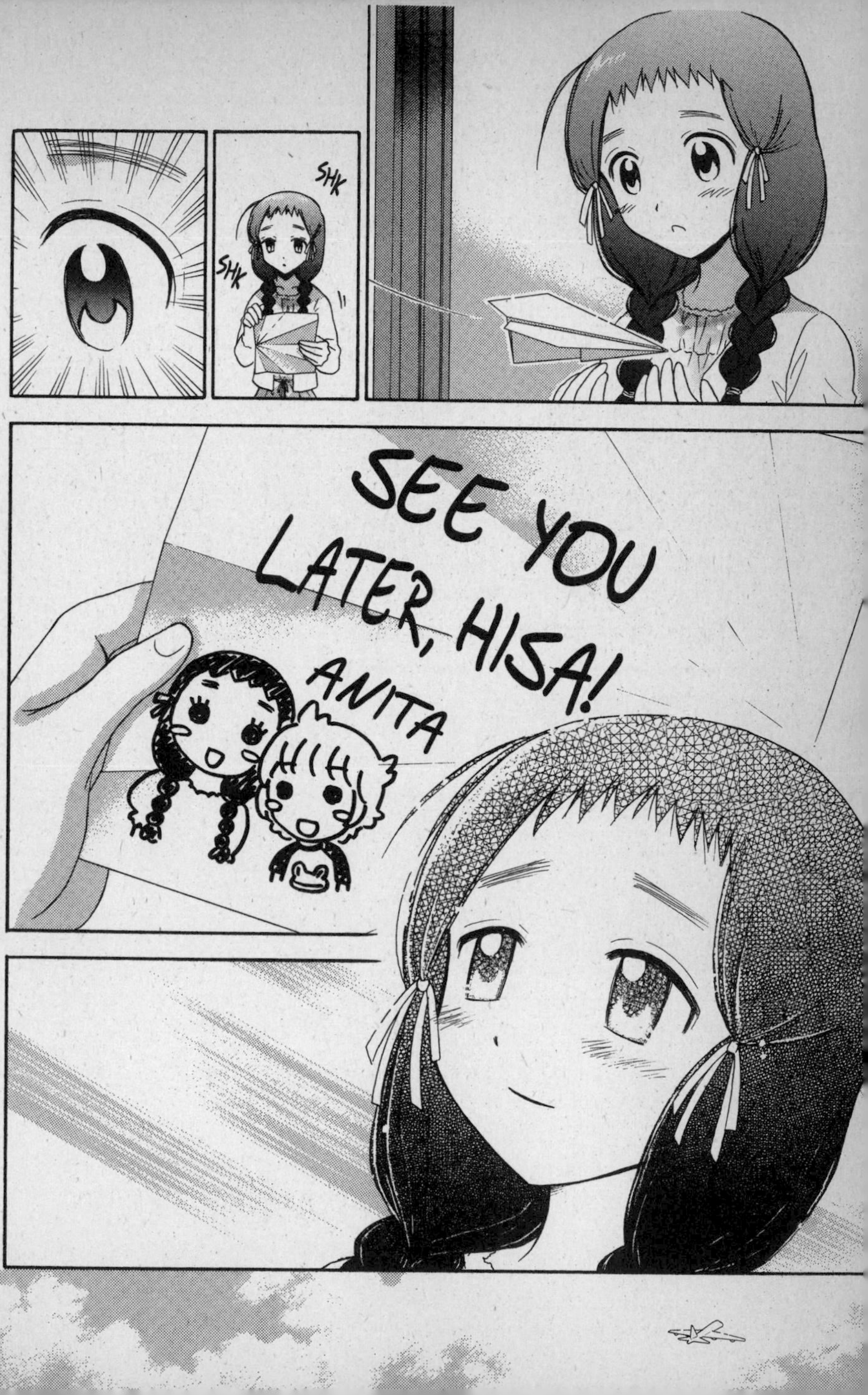
SHK
SHK
SEE YOU LATER, HISA!
ANITA

CHAPTER 30

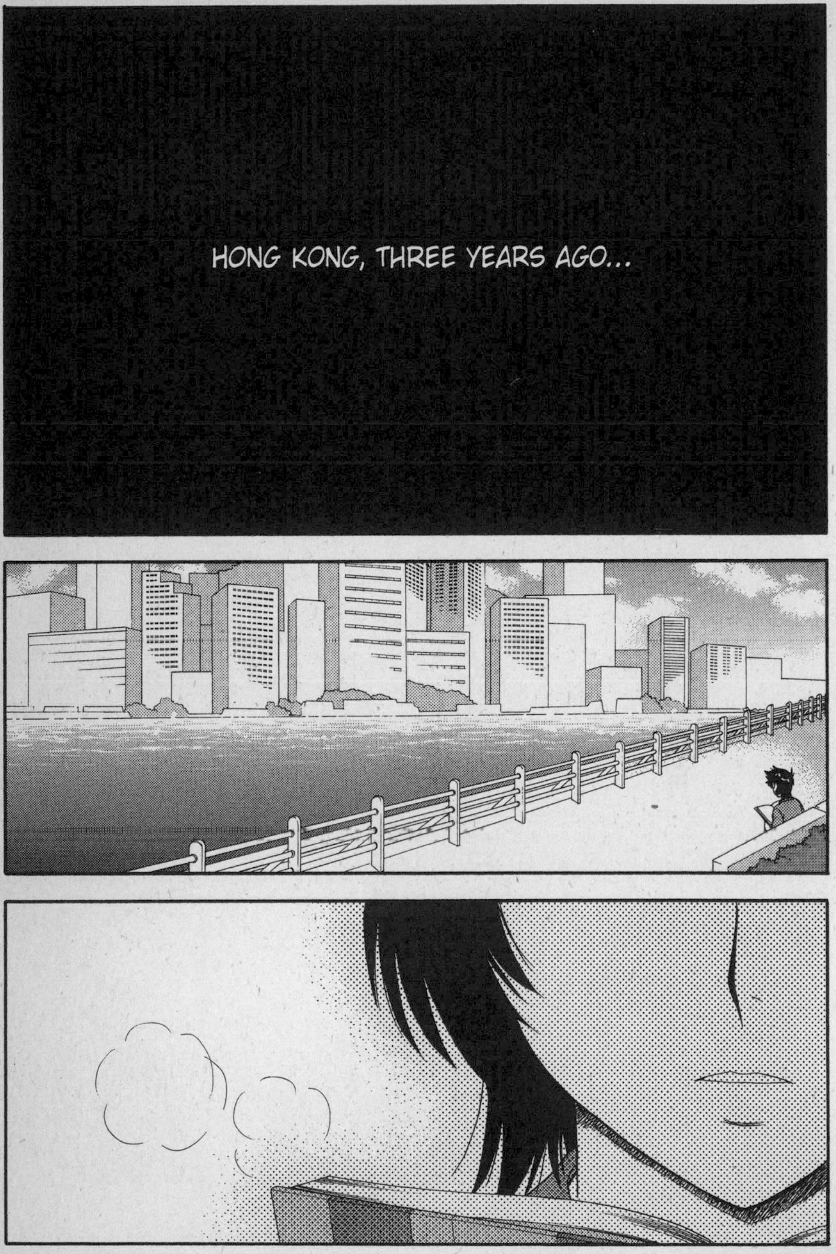
HONG KONG, THREE YEARS AGO...

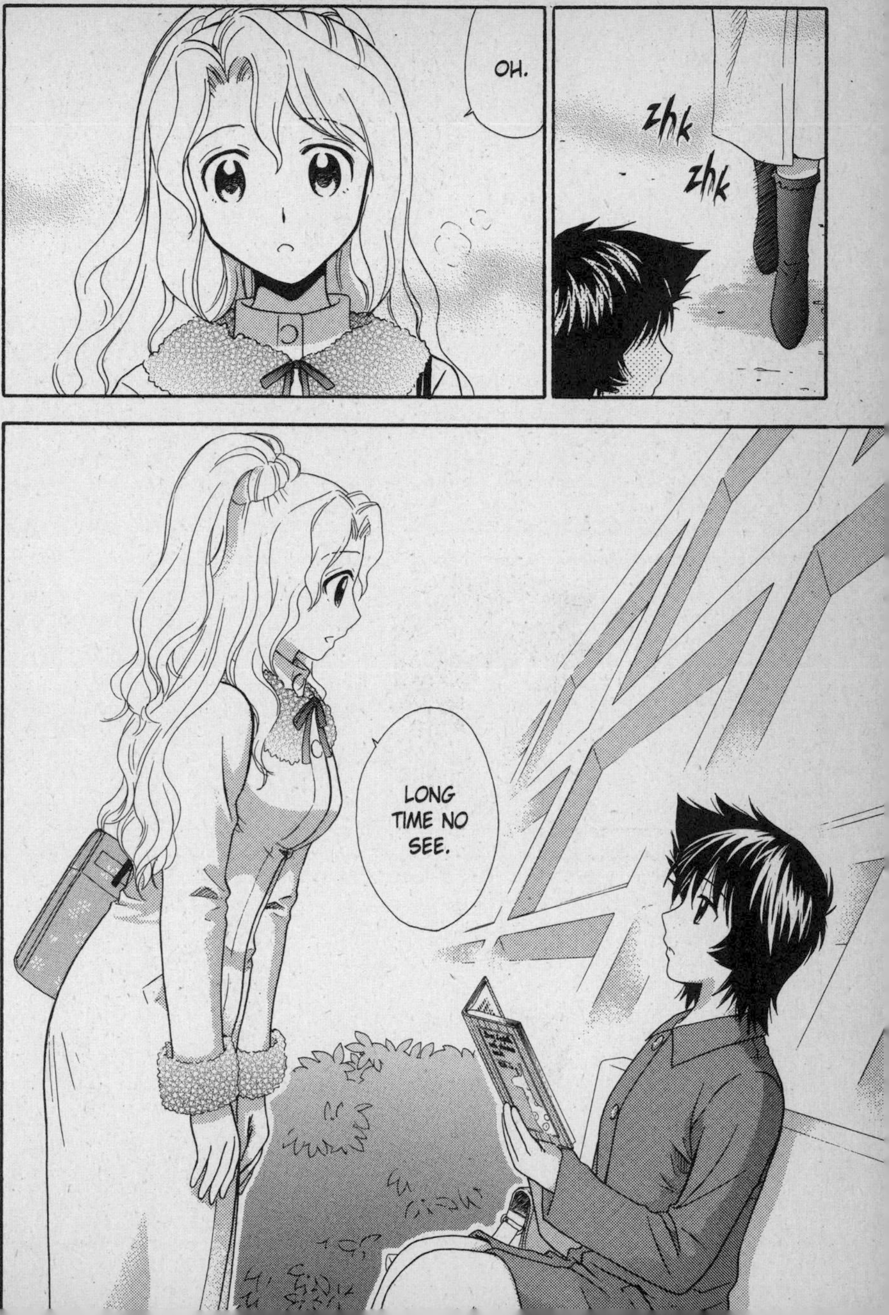
zhk
zhk
OH.
LONG TIME NO SEE.

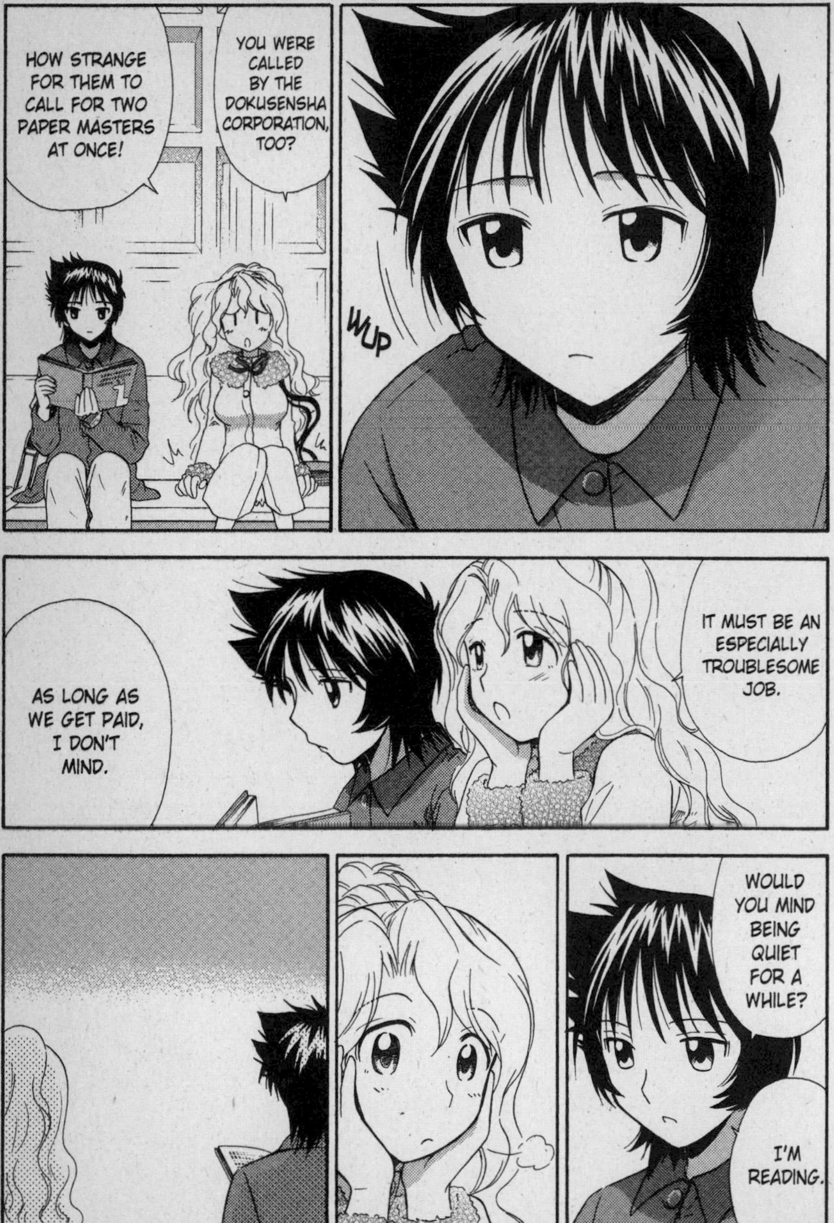
WUP
YOU WERE CALLED BY THE DOKUSENSHA CORPORATION, TOO?
HOW STRANGE FOR THEM TO CALL FOR TWO PAPER MASTERS AT ONCE!
IT MUST BE AN ESPECIALLY TROUBLESOME JOB.
AS LONG AS WE GET PAID, I DON'T MIND.
WOULD YOU MIND BEING QUIET FOR A WHILE?
I'M READING.

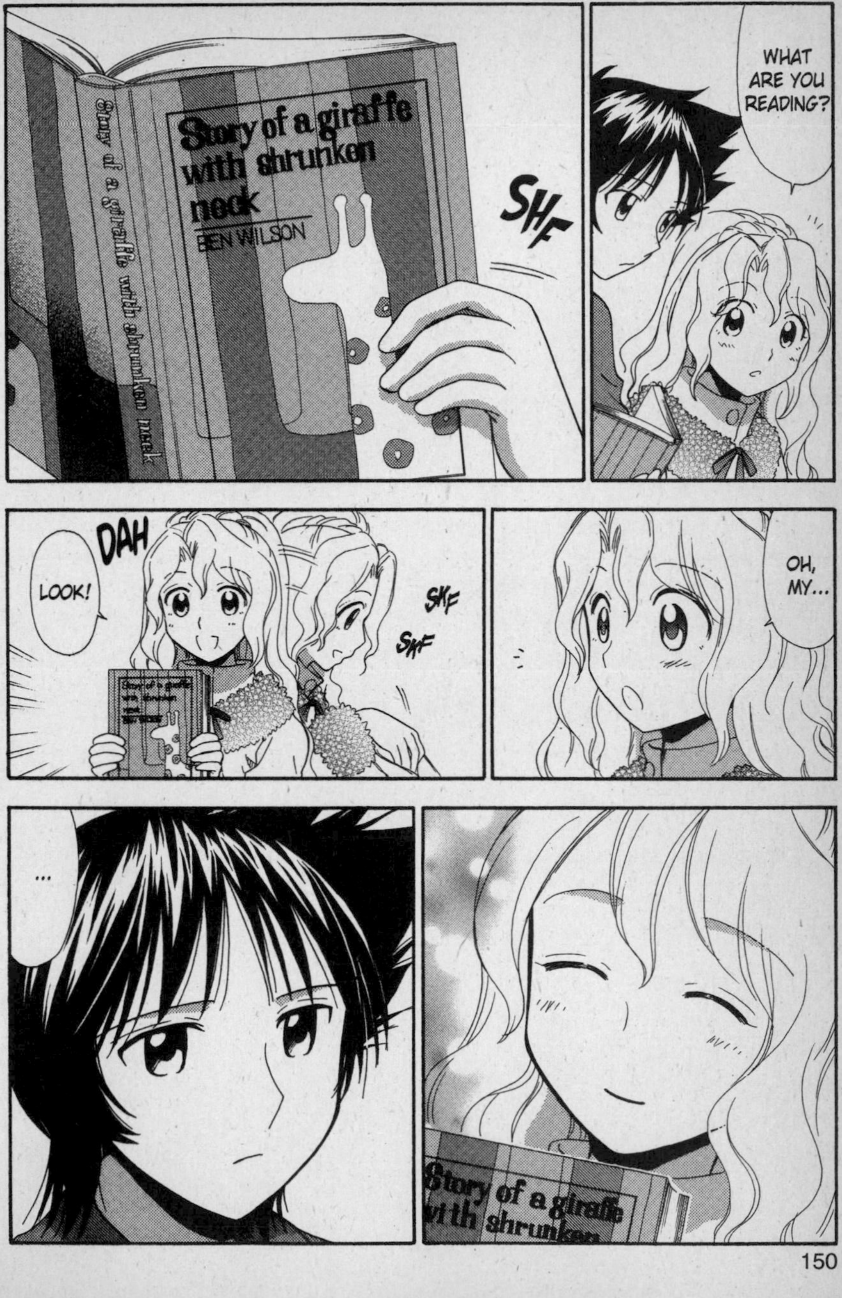
WHAT ARE YOU READING?
Story of a giraffe with shrunken neck
BEN WILSON
Story of a giraffe with shrunken neck
SHF
OH, MY...
DAH
LOOK!
SKF
SKF
Story of a giraffe with shrunken
...

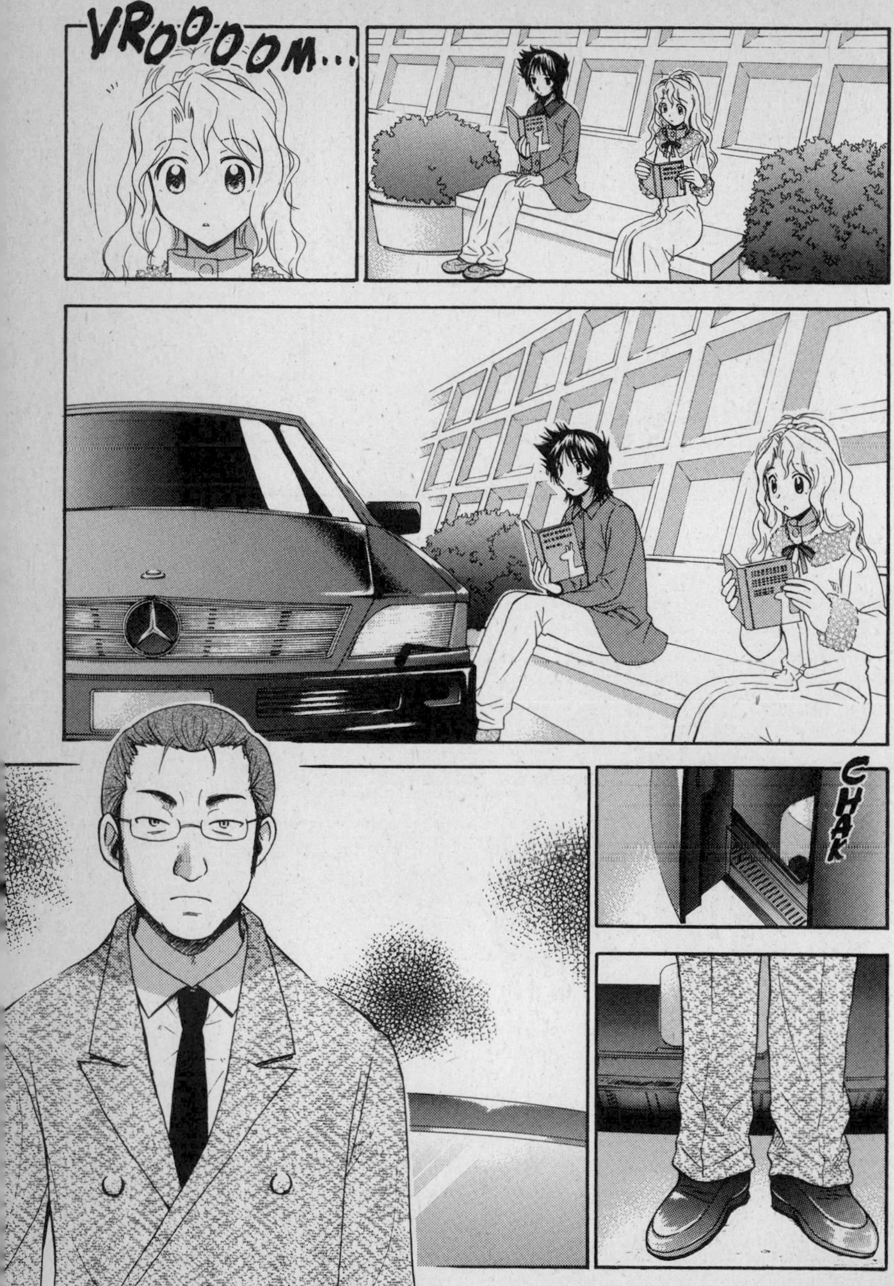
VROOOOM...
CHAK

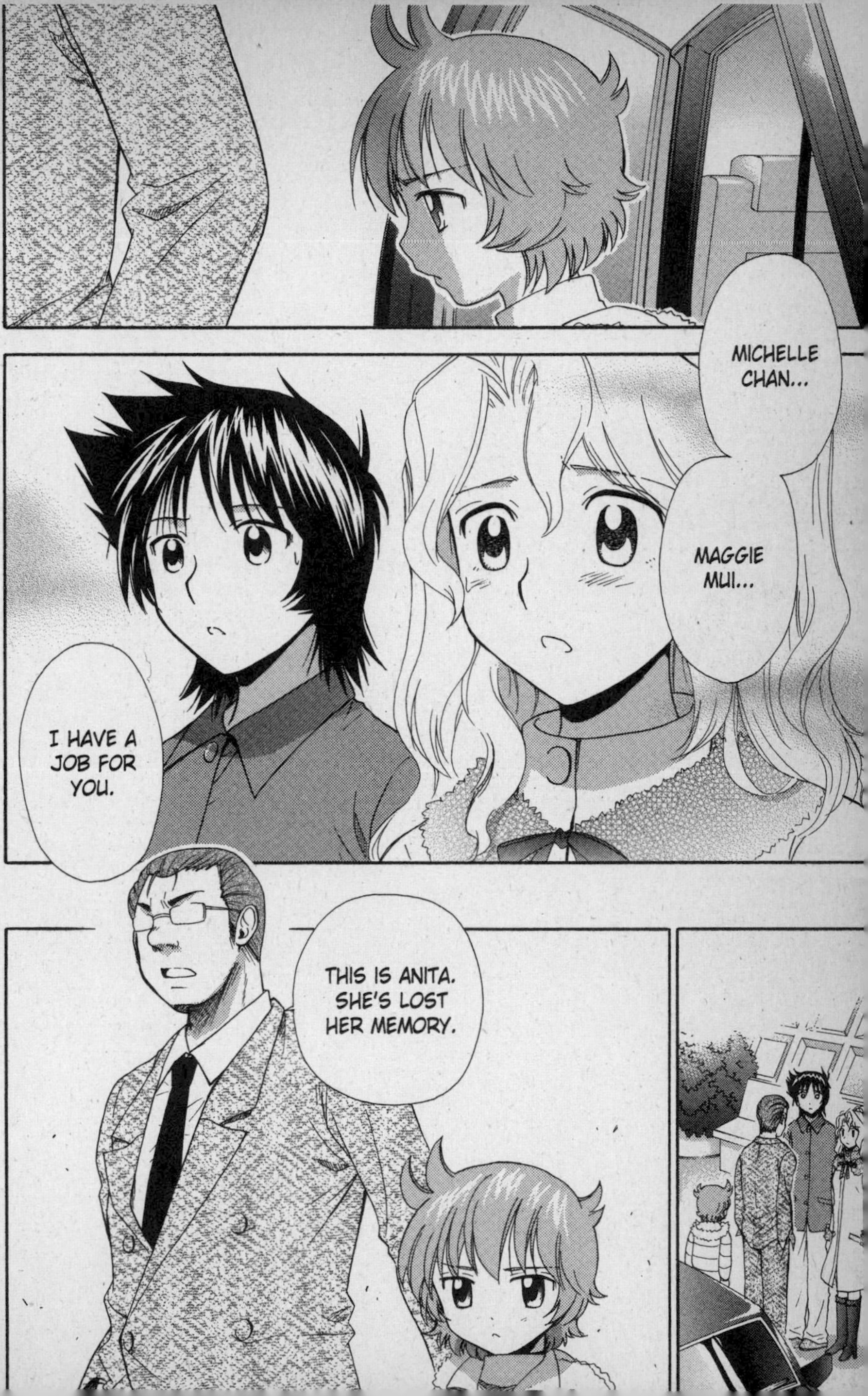
MICHELLE CHAN...
MAGGIE MUI...
I HAVE A JOB FOR YOU.
THIS IS ANITA. SHE'S LOST HER MEMORY.

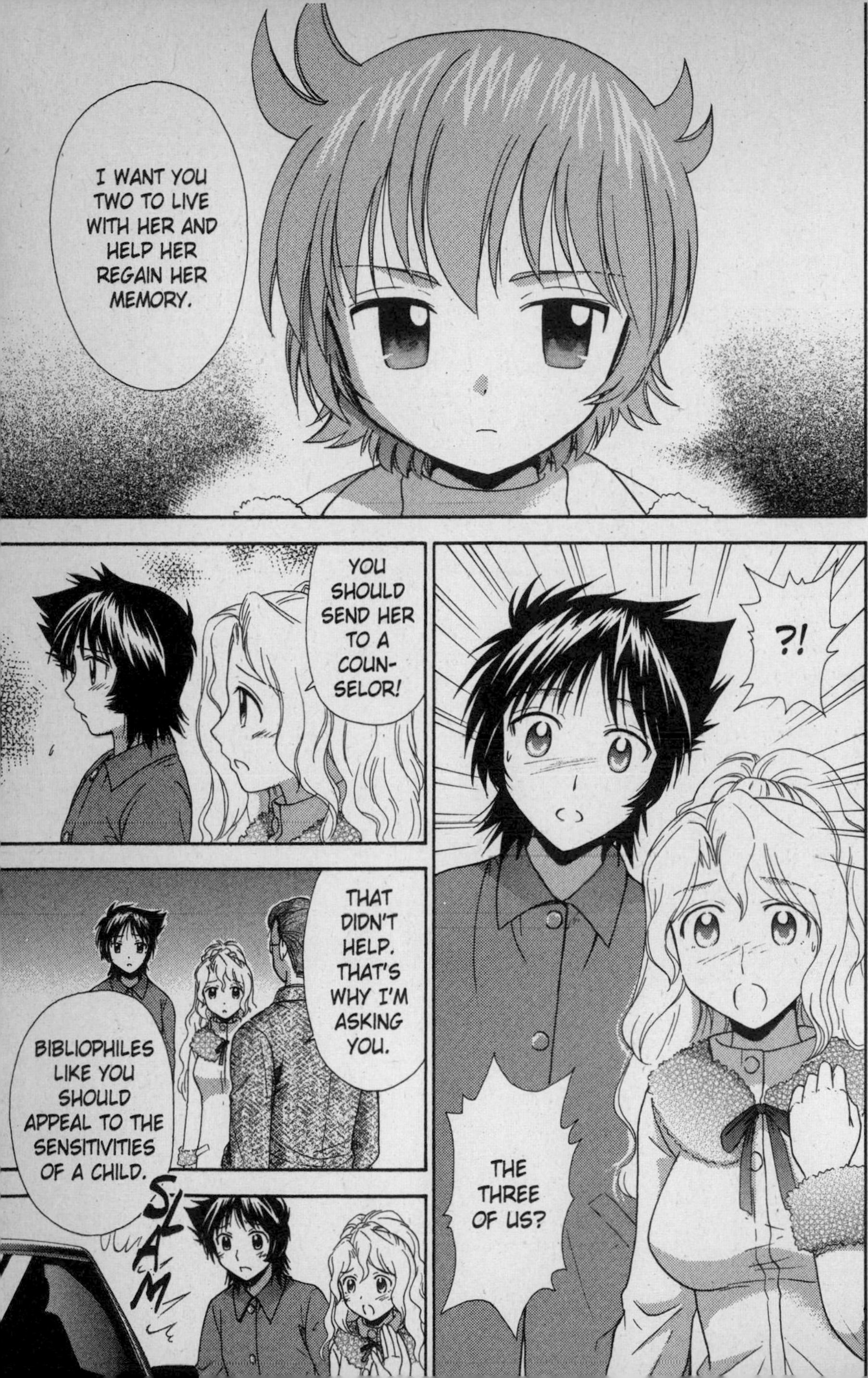
I WANT YOU TWO TO LIVE WITH HER AND HELP HER REGAIN HER MEMORY.
?!
THE THREE OF US?
YOU SHOULD SEND HER TO A COUN-SELOR!
THAT DIDN'T HELP. THAT'S WHY I'M ASKING YOU.
BIBLIOPHILES LIKE YOU SHOULD APPEAL TO THE SENSITIVITIES OF A CHILD.
SLAM

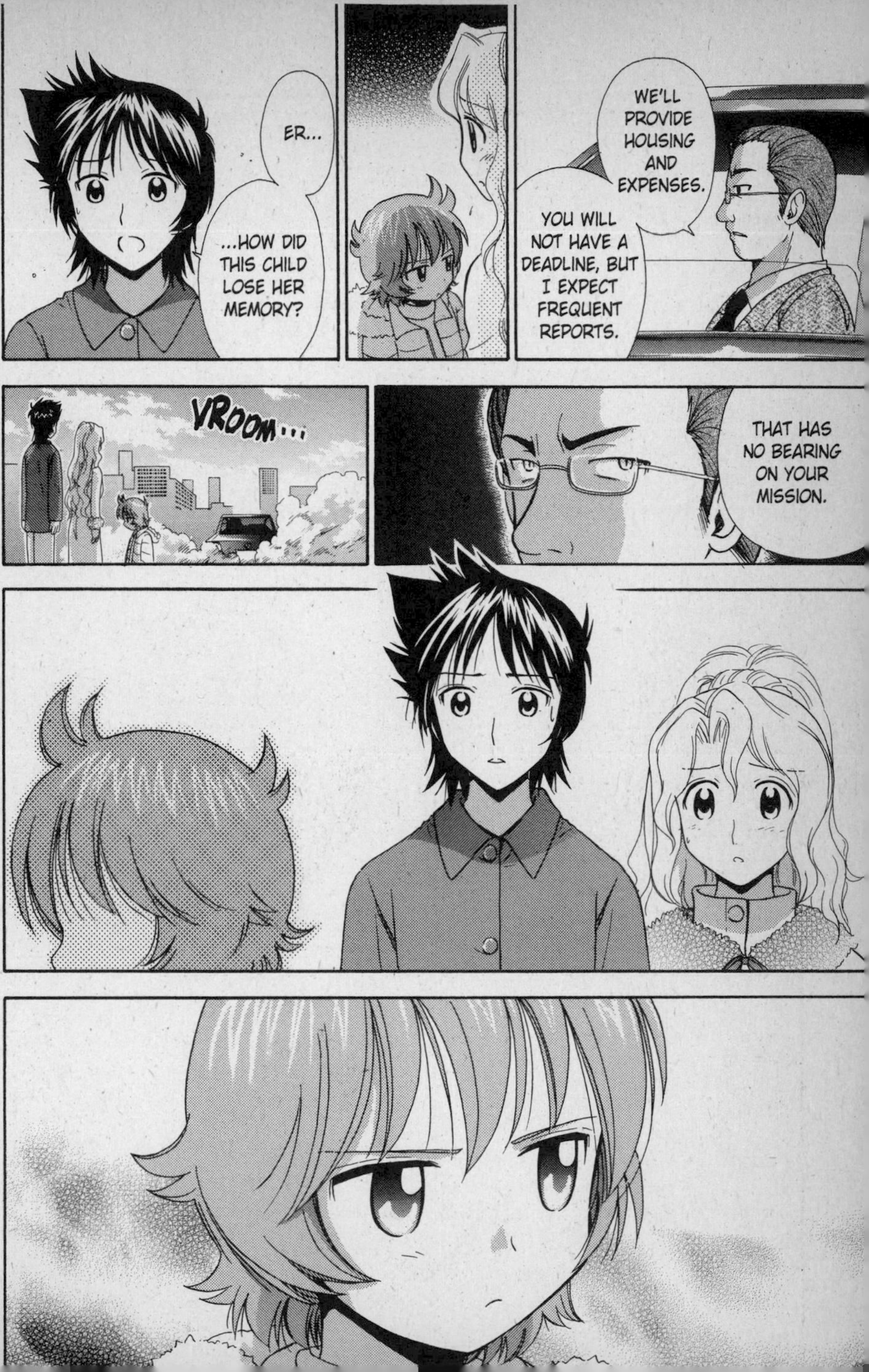
WE'LL PROVIDE HOUSING AND EXPENSES.
YOU WILL NOT HAVE A DEADLINE, BUT I EXPECT FREQUENT REPORTS.
ER...
...HOW DID THIS CHILD LOSE HER MEMORY?
THAT HAS NO BEARING ON YOUR MISSION.
VROOM...

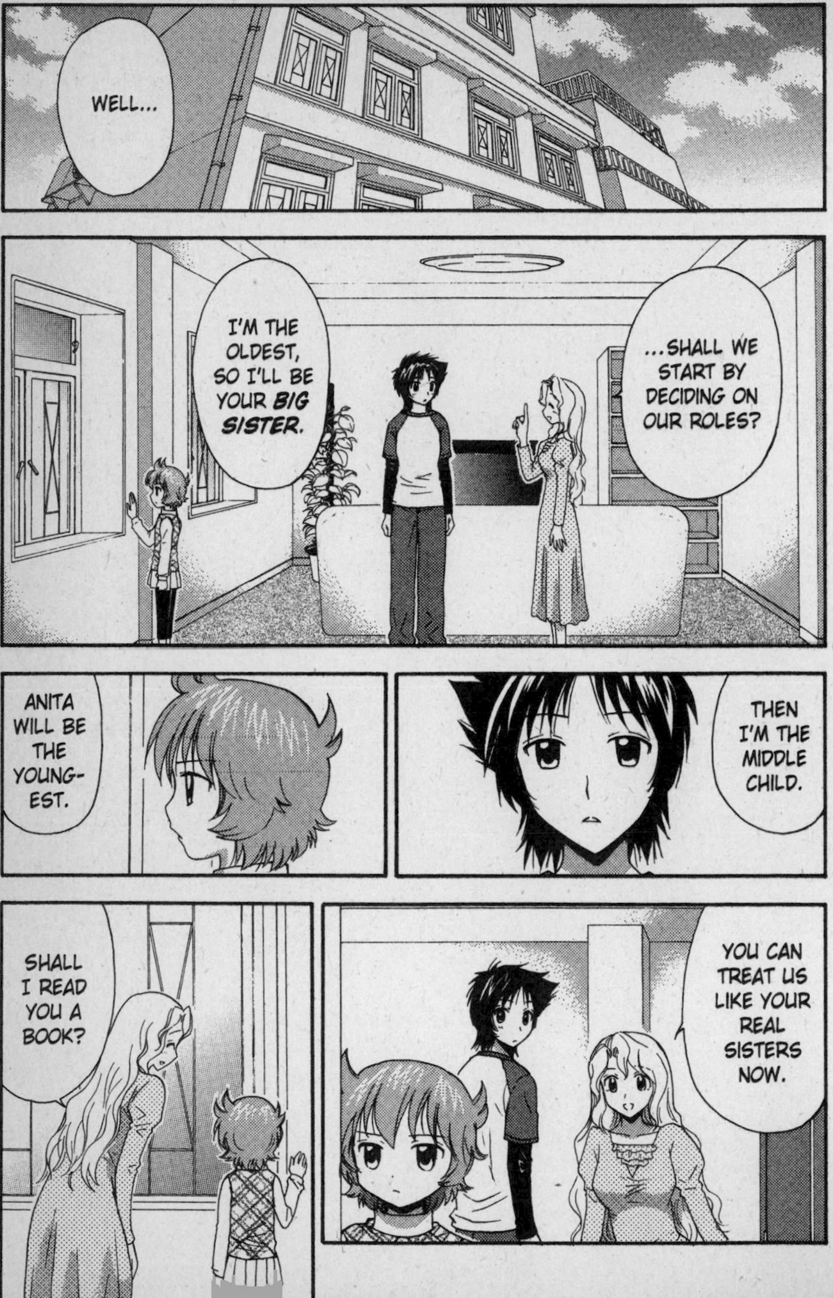
WELL...
...SHALL WE START BY DECIDING ON OUR ROLES?
I'M THE OLDEST, SO I'LL BE YOUR *BIG SISTER*.
THEN I'M THE MIDDLE CHILD.
ANITA WILL BE THE YOUNG-EST.
YOU CAN TREAT US LIKE YOUR REAL SISTERS NOW.
SHALL I READ YOU A BOOK?

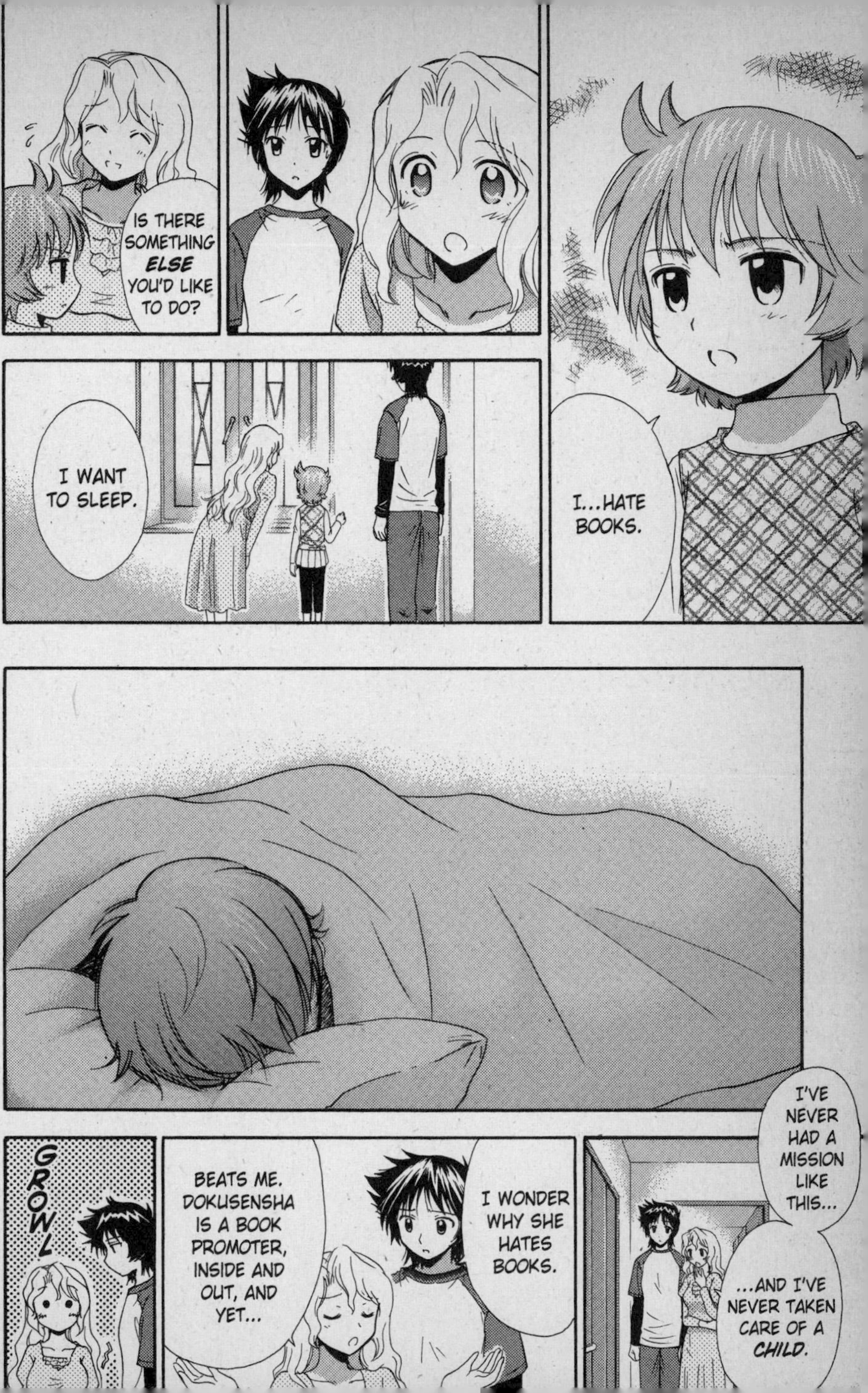
I...HATE BOOKS.
IS THERE SOMETHING ELSE YOU'D LIKE TO DO?
I WANT TO SLEEP.
I'VE NEVER HAD A MISSION LIKE THIS...
...AND I'VE NEVER TAKEN CARE OF A CHILD.
I WONDER WHY SHE HATES BOOKS.
BEATS ME. DOKUSENSHA IS A BOOK PROMOTER, INSIDE AND OUT, AND YET...
GROWL

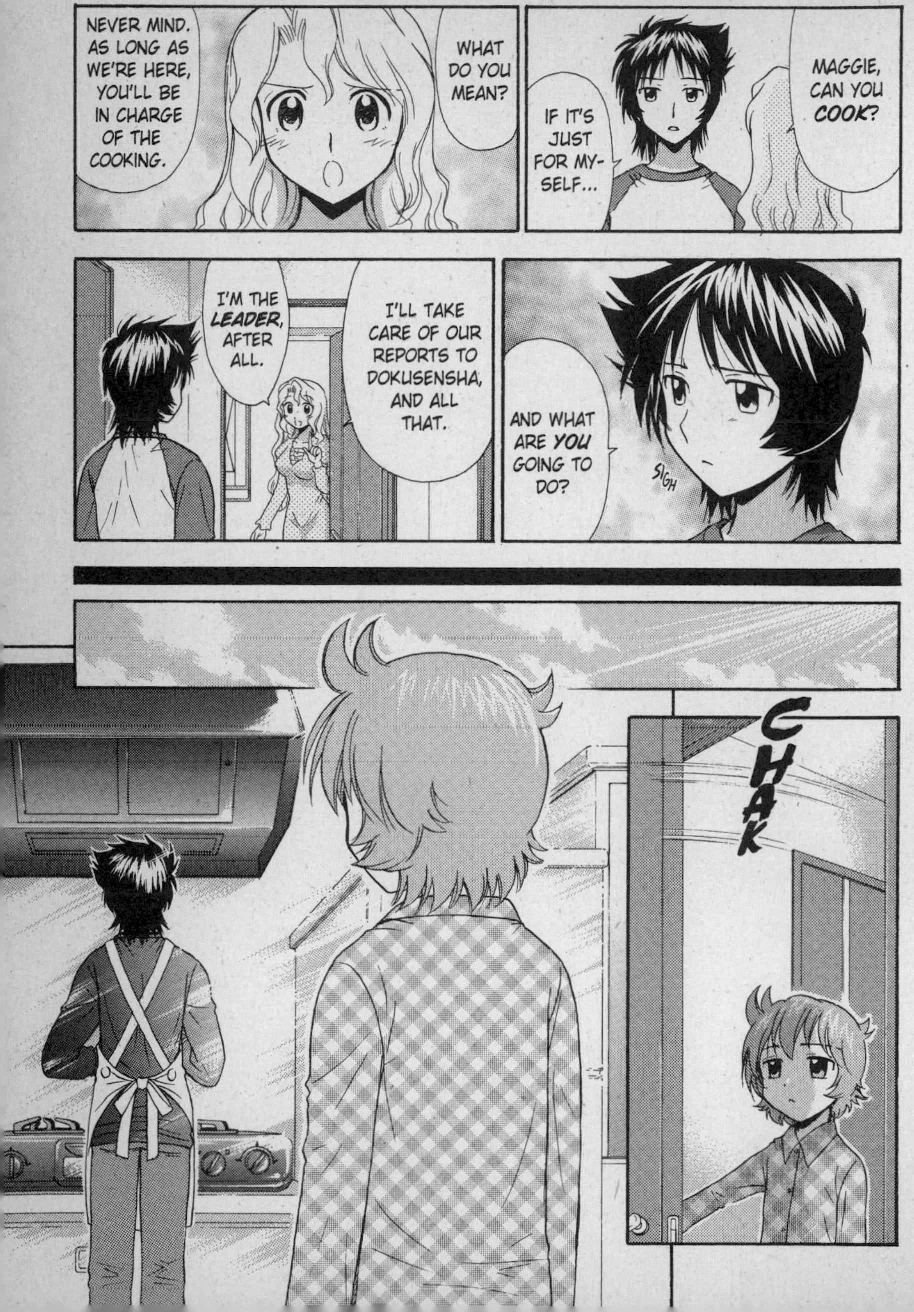
MAGGIE, CAN YOU COOK?
IF IT'S JUST FOR MYSELF...
WHAT DO YOU MEAN?
NEVER MIND. AS LONG AS WE'RE HERE, YOU'LL BE IN CHARGE OF THE COOKING.
AND WHAT ARE YOU GOING TO DO?
SIGH
I'LL TAKE CARE OF OUR REPORTS TO DOKUSENSHA, AND ALL THAT.
I'M THE LEADER, AFTER ALL.
CHAK

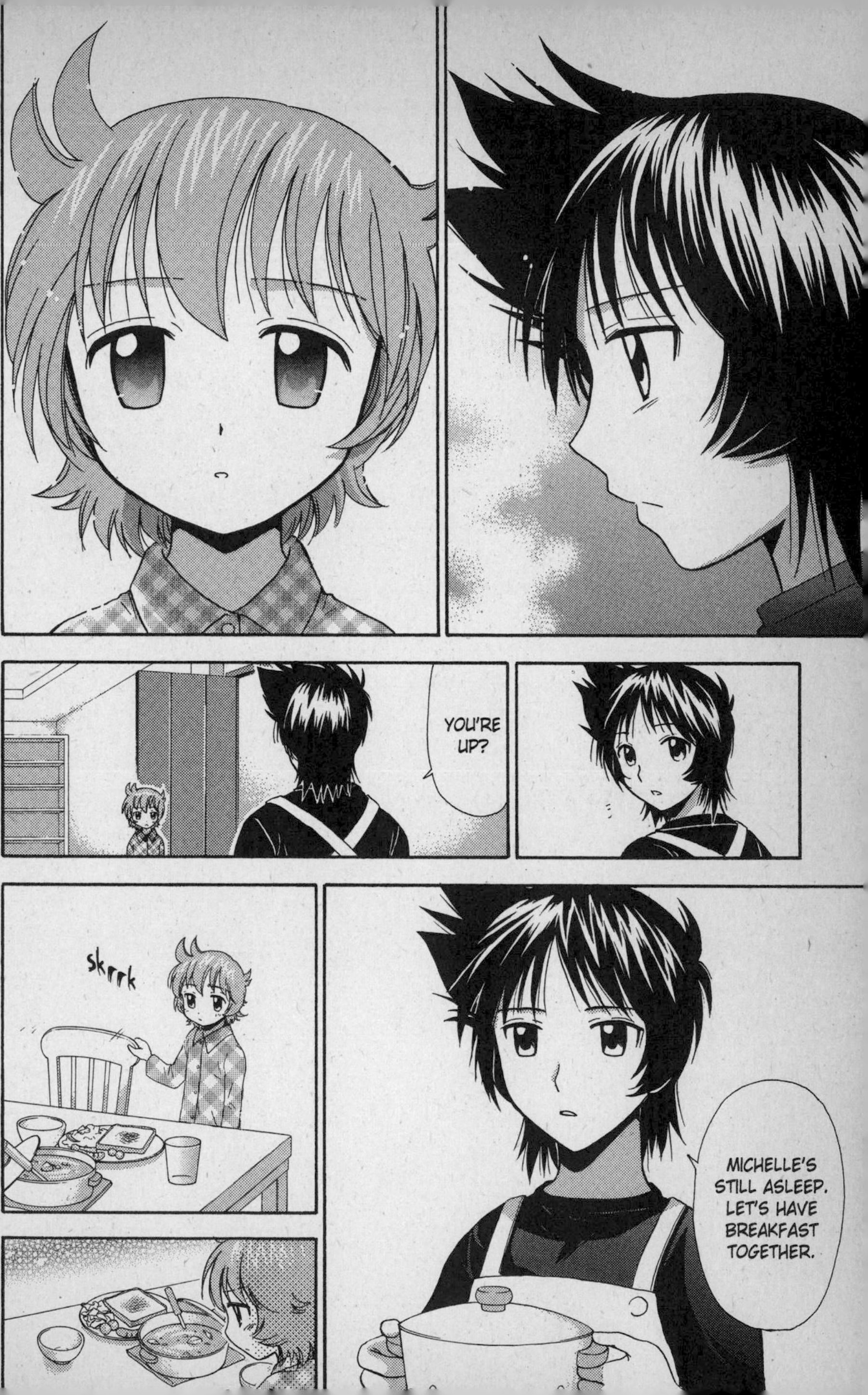
YOU'RE UP?
MICHELLE'S STILL ASLEEP. LET'S HAVE BREAKFAST TOGETHER.
skrrk

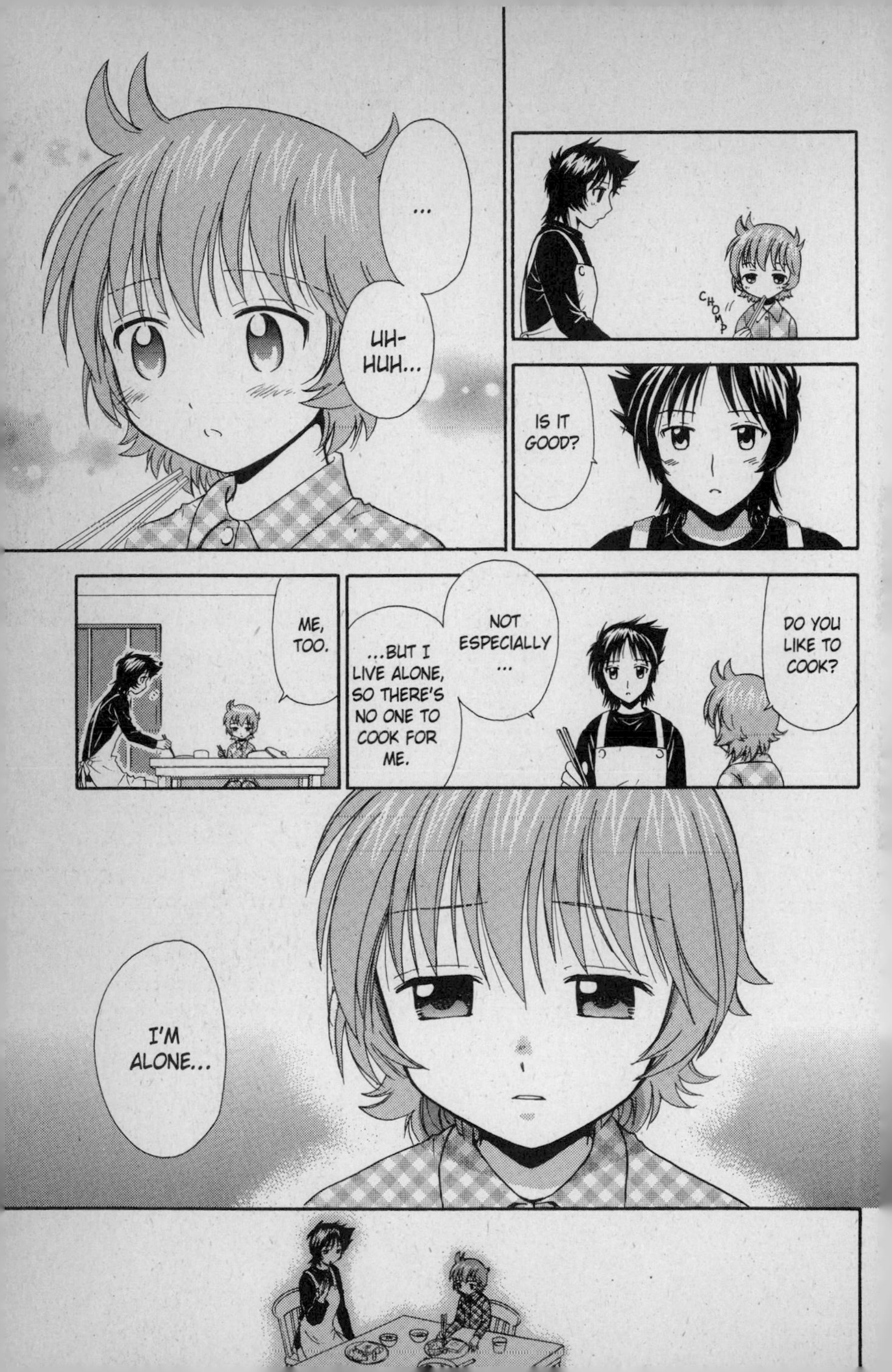
CHOMP
IS IT GOOD?
...
UH-HUH...
DO YOU LIKE TO COOK?
NOT ESPECIALLY...
...BUT I LIVE ALONE, SO THERE'S NO ONE TO COOK FOR ME.
ME, TOO.
I'M ALONE...

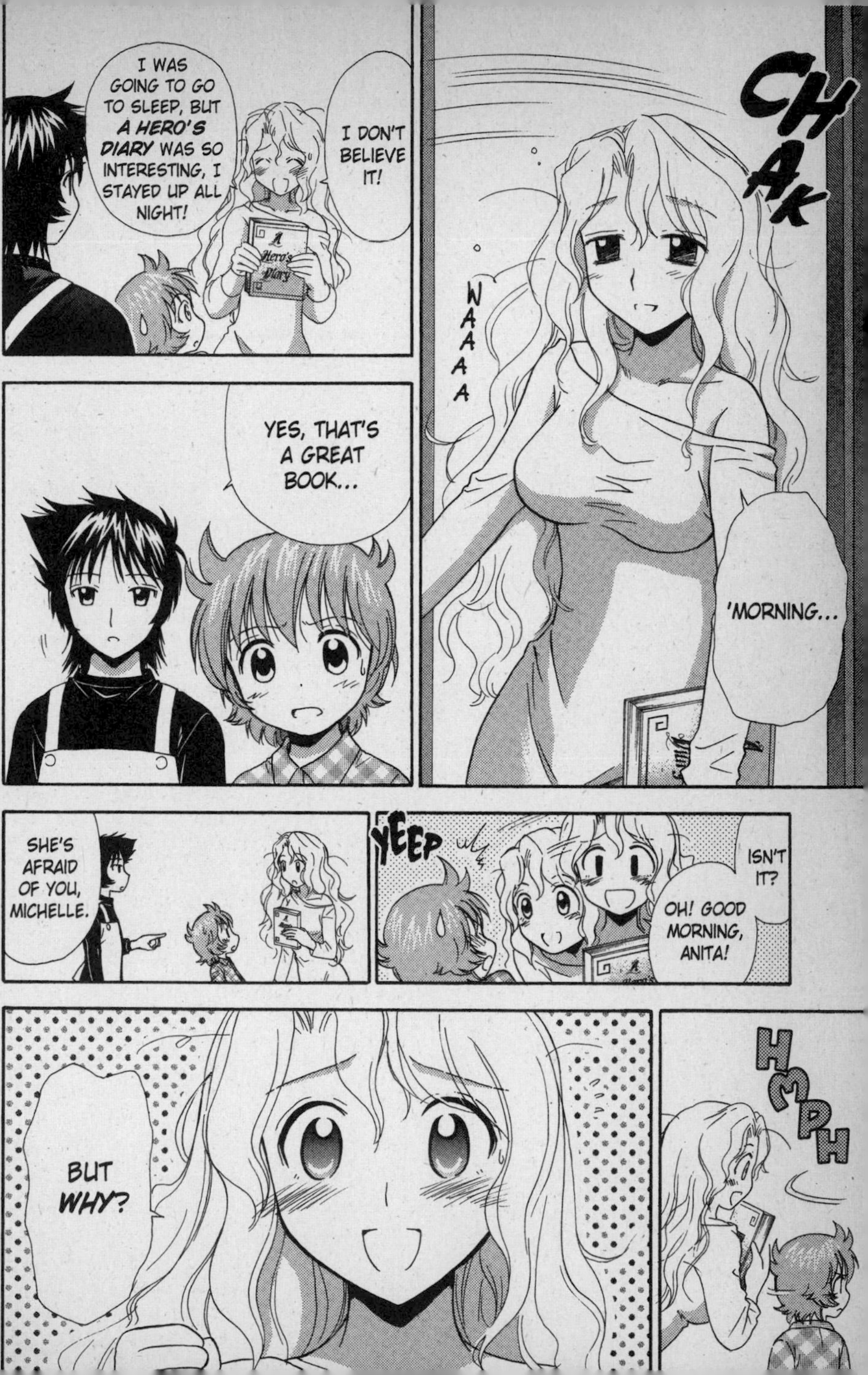
CHAK
WAAAA
'MORNING...
I DON'T BELIEVE IT!
I WAS GOING TO GO TO SLEEP, BUT *A HERO'S DIARY* WAS SO INTERESTING, I STAYED UP ALL NIGHT!
A Hero's Diary
YES, THAT'S A GREAT BOOK...
ISN'T IT?
OH! GOOD MORNING, ANITA!
YEEP
SHE'S AFRAID OF YOU, MICHELLE.
HMPH
BUT *WHY*?

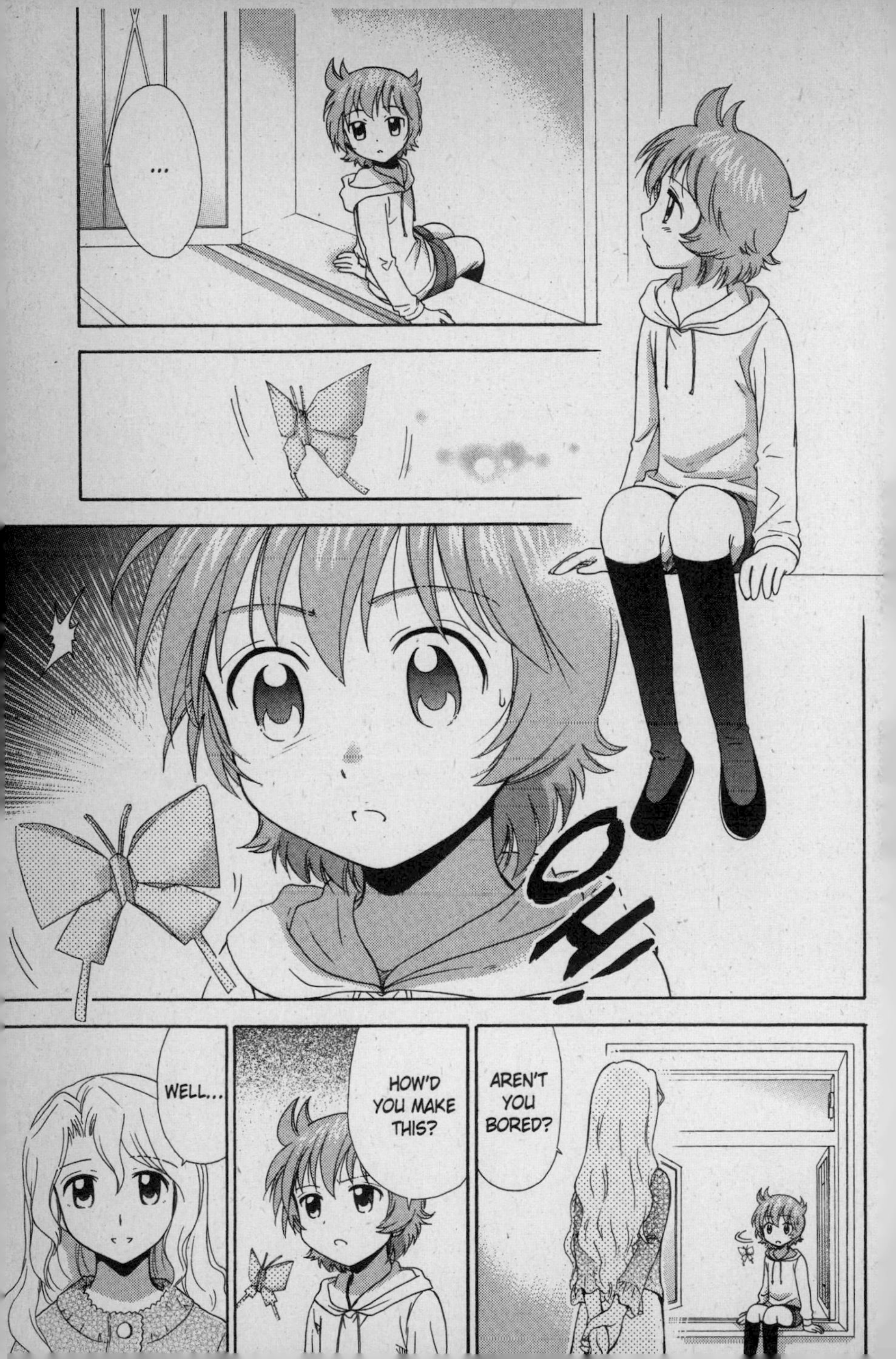
...
OH!
AREN'T YOU BORED?
HOW'D YOU MAKE THIS?
WELL...

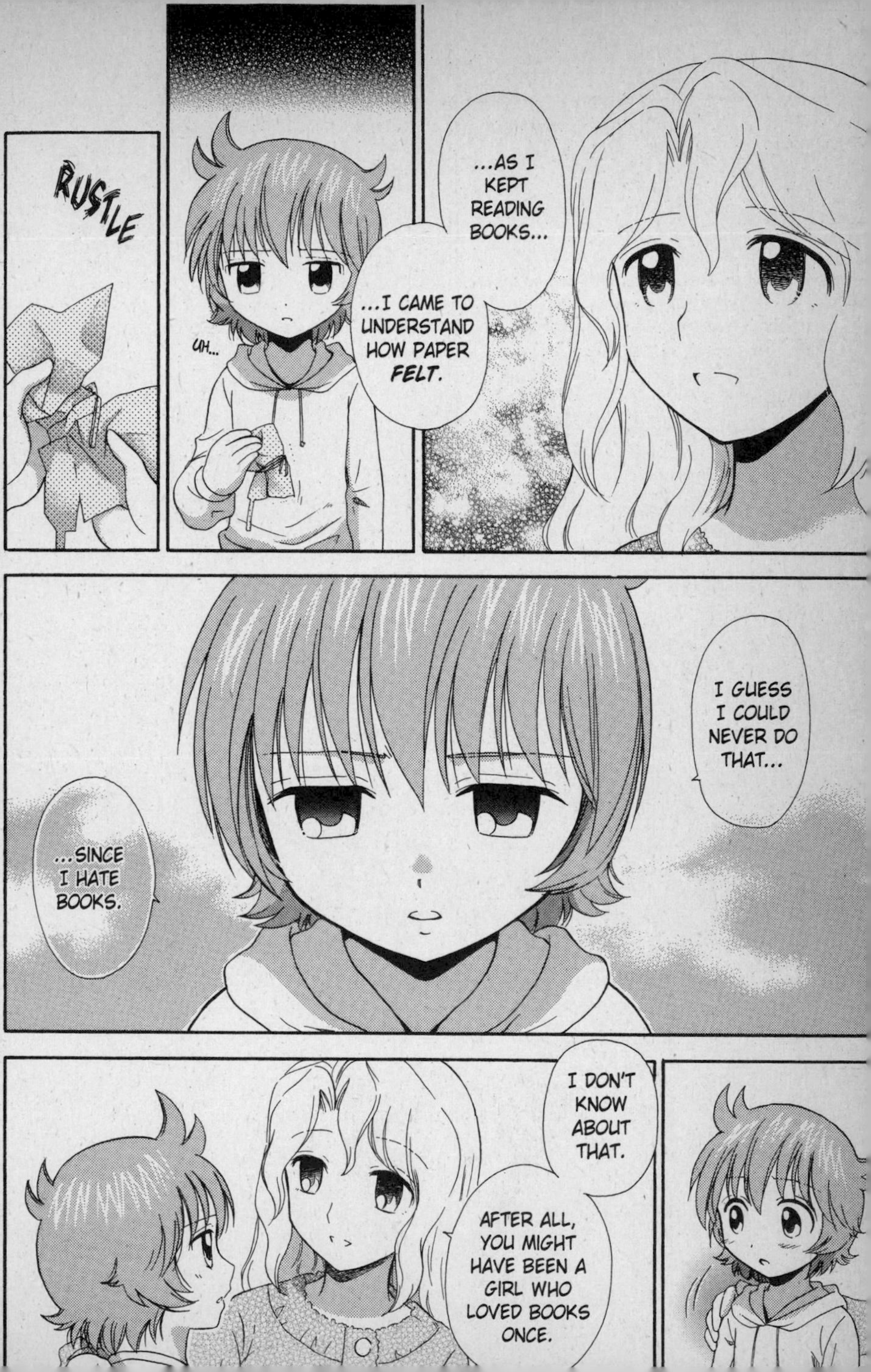
...AS I KEPT READING BOOKS...
...I CAME TO UNDERSTAND HOW PAPER FELT.
UH...
RUSTLE
I GUESS I COULD NEVER DO THAT...
...SINCE I HATE BOOKS.
I DON'T KNOW ABOUT THAT.
AFTER ALL, YOU MIGHT HAVE BEEN A GIRL WHO LOVED BOOKS ONCE.

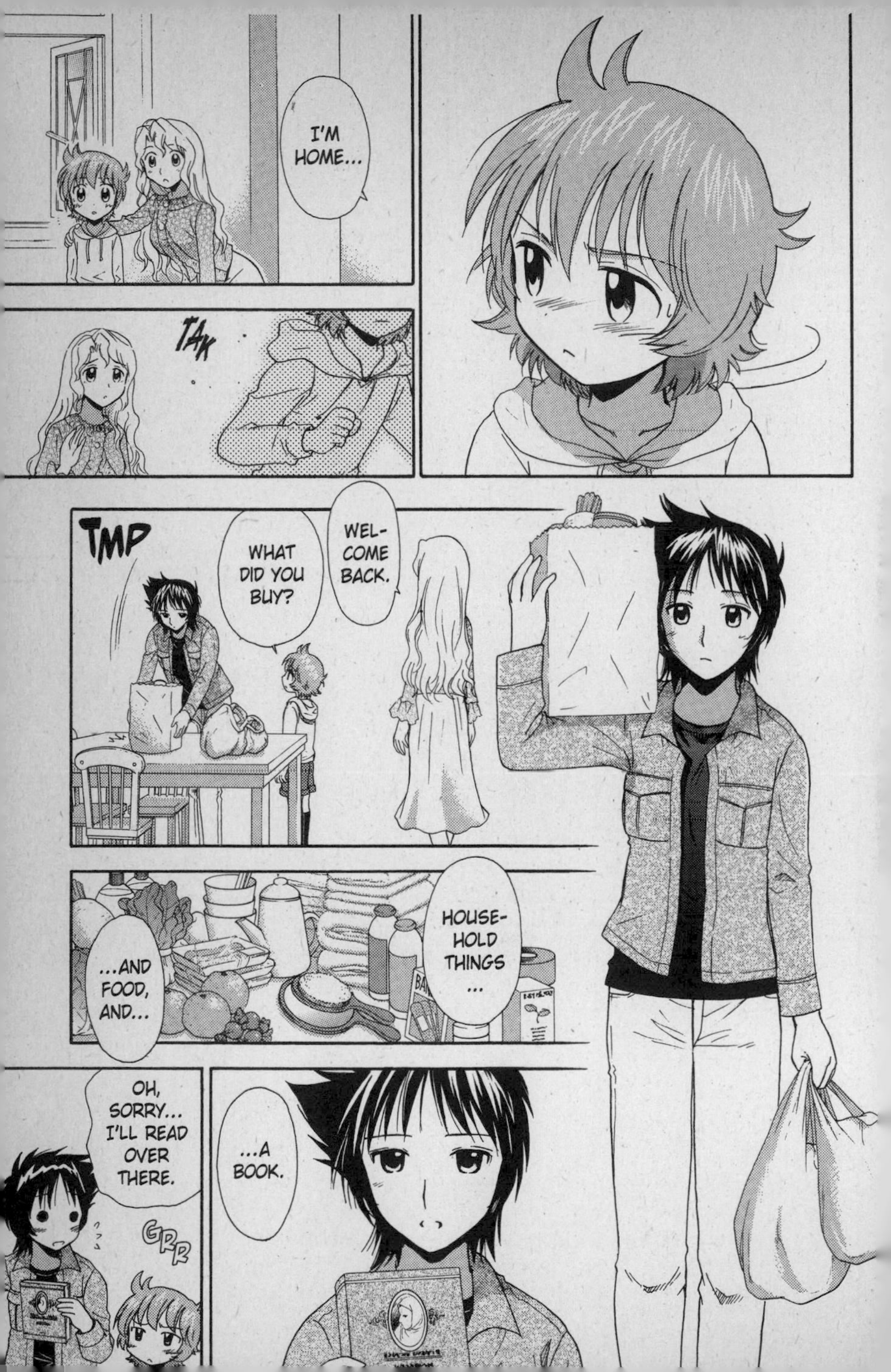
I'M HOME...
TAK
WEL-COME BACK.
WHAT DID YOU BUY?
TMP
HOUSE-HOLD THINGS ...
...AND FOOD, AND...
...A BOOK.
OH, SORRY... I'LL READ OVER THERE.
GRR

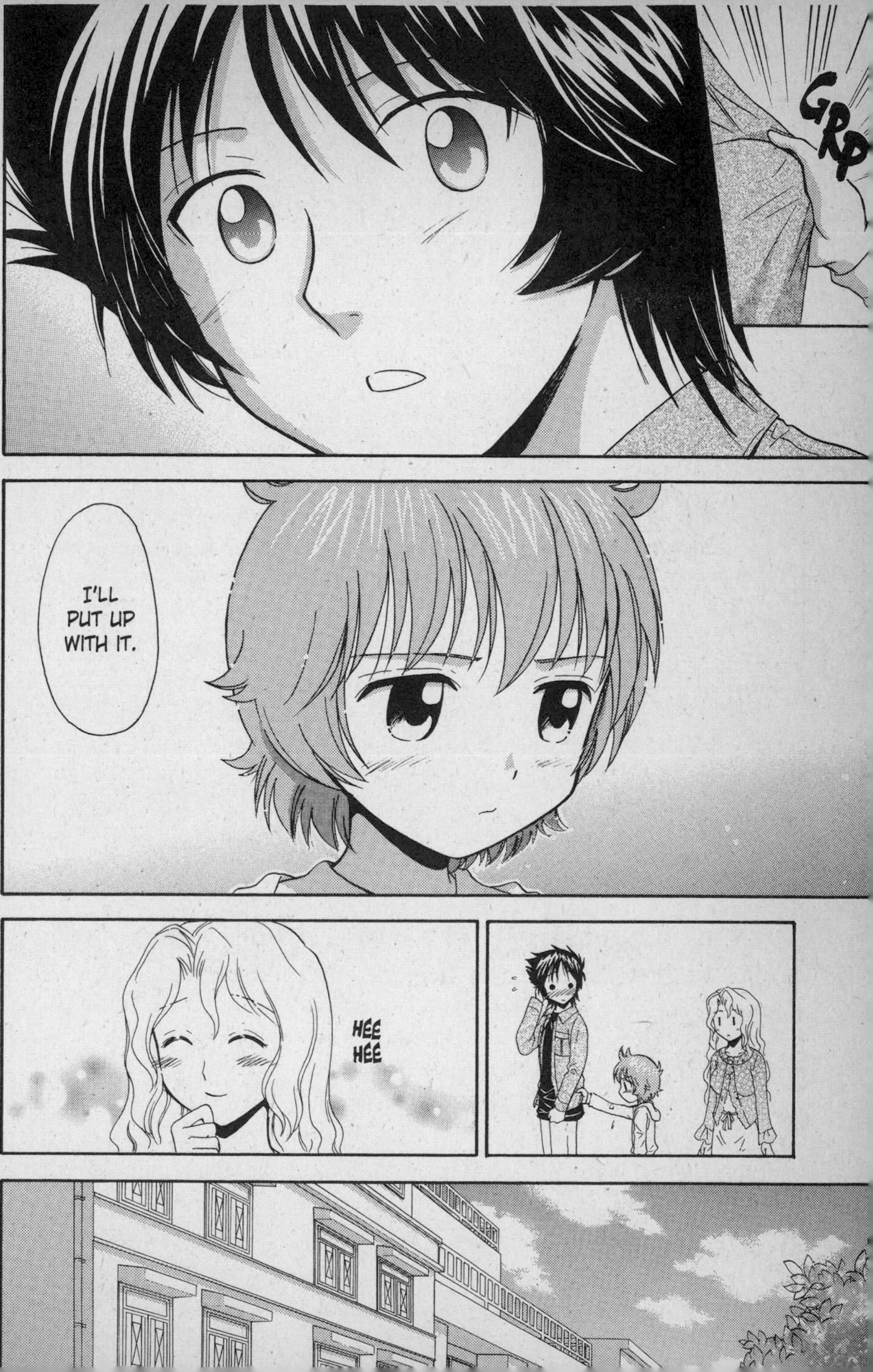
GRP
I'LL PUT UP WITH IT.
HEE HEE

CHAK
TUP
POOF

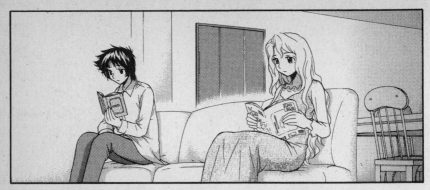

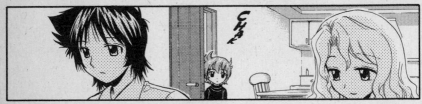

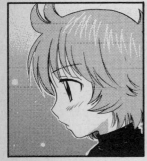

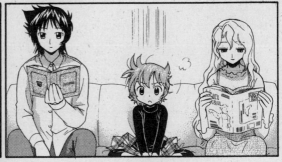

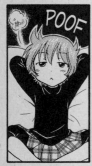

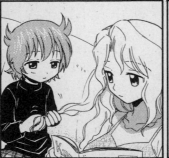

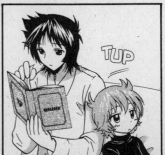

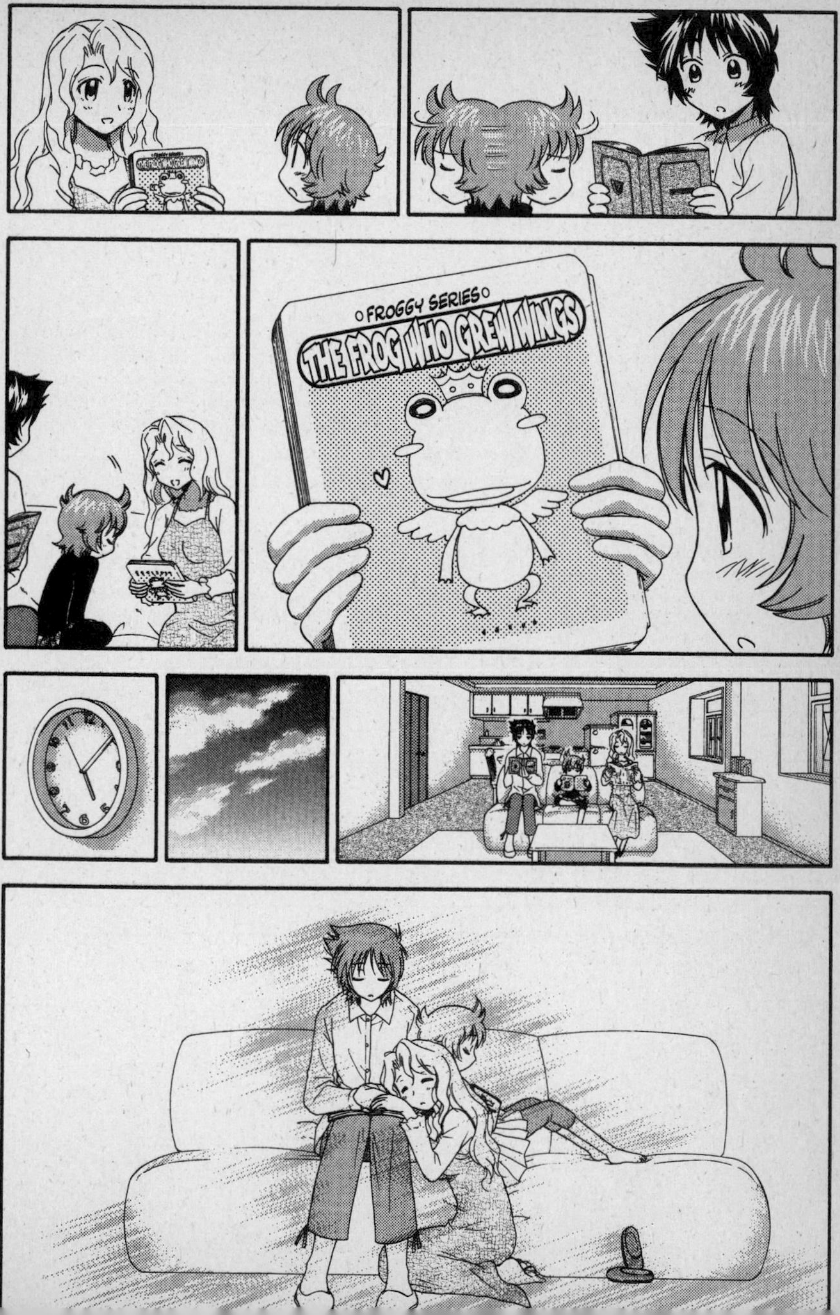

FROGGY SERIES
THE FROG WHO GREW WINGS

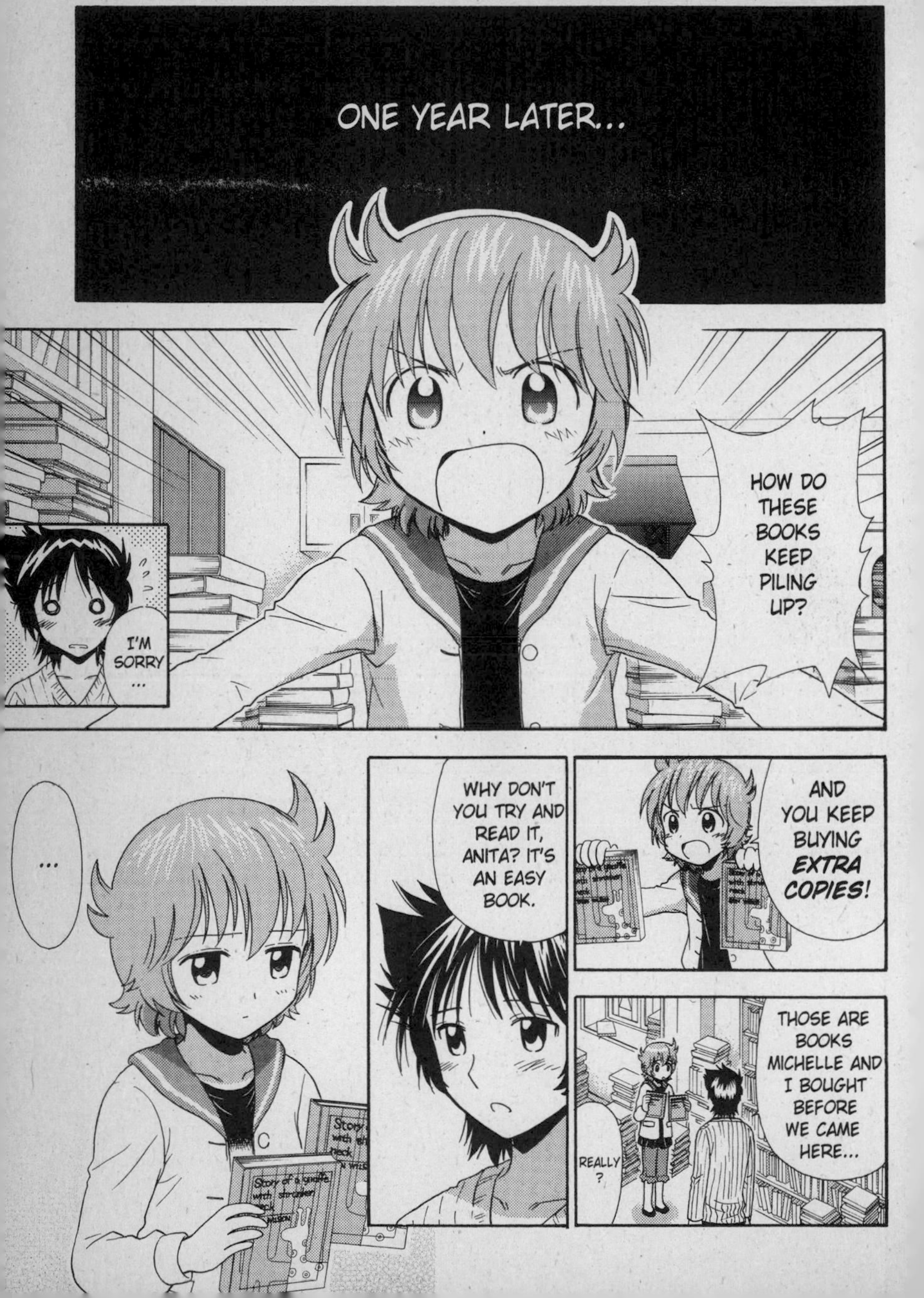

ONE YEAR LATER...
HOW DO THESE BOOKS KEEP PILING UP?
I'M SORRY...
AND YOU KEEP BUYING *EXTRA COPIES*!
THOSE ARE BOOKS MICHELLE AND I BOUGHT BEFORE WE CAME HERE...
REALLY?
WHY DON'T YOU TRY AND READ IT, ANITA? IT'S AN EASY BOOK.
...

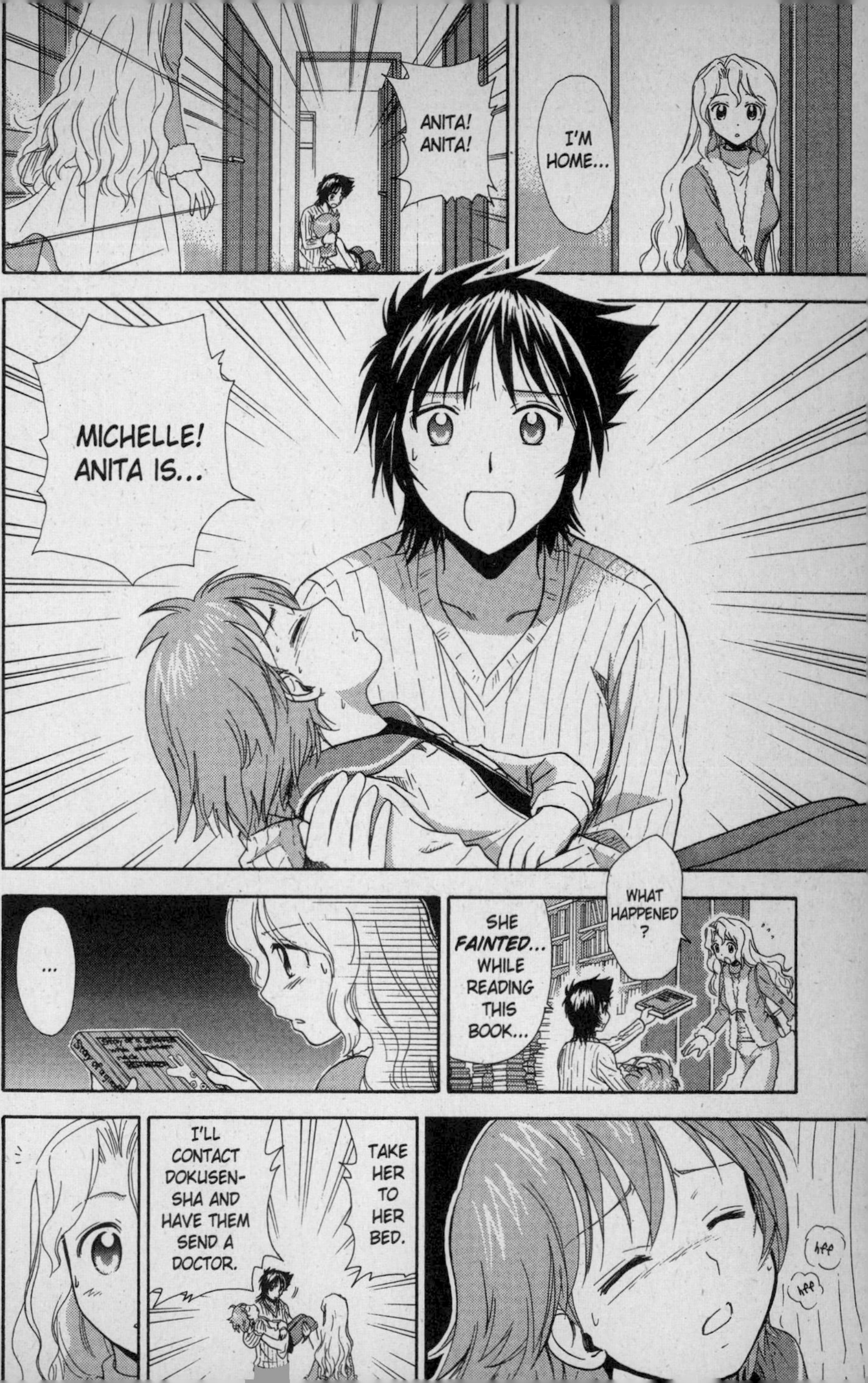
I'M HOME...
ANITA! ANITA!
MICHELLE! ANITA IS...
WHAT HAPPENED?
SHE FAINTED... WHILE READING THIS BOOK...
...
hff
hff
TAKE HER TO HER BED.
I'LL CONTACT DOKUSEN-SHA AND HAVE THEM SEND A DOCTOR.

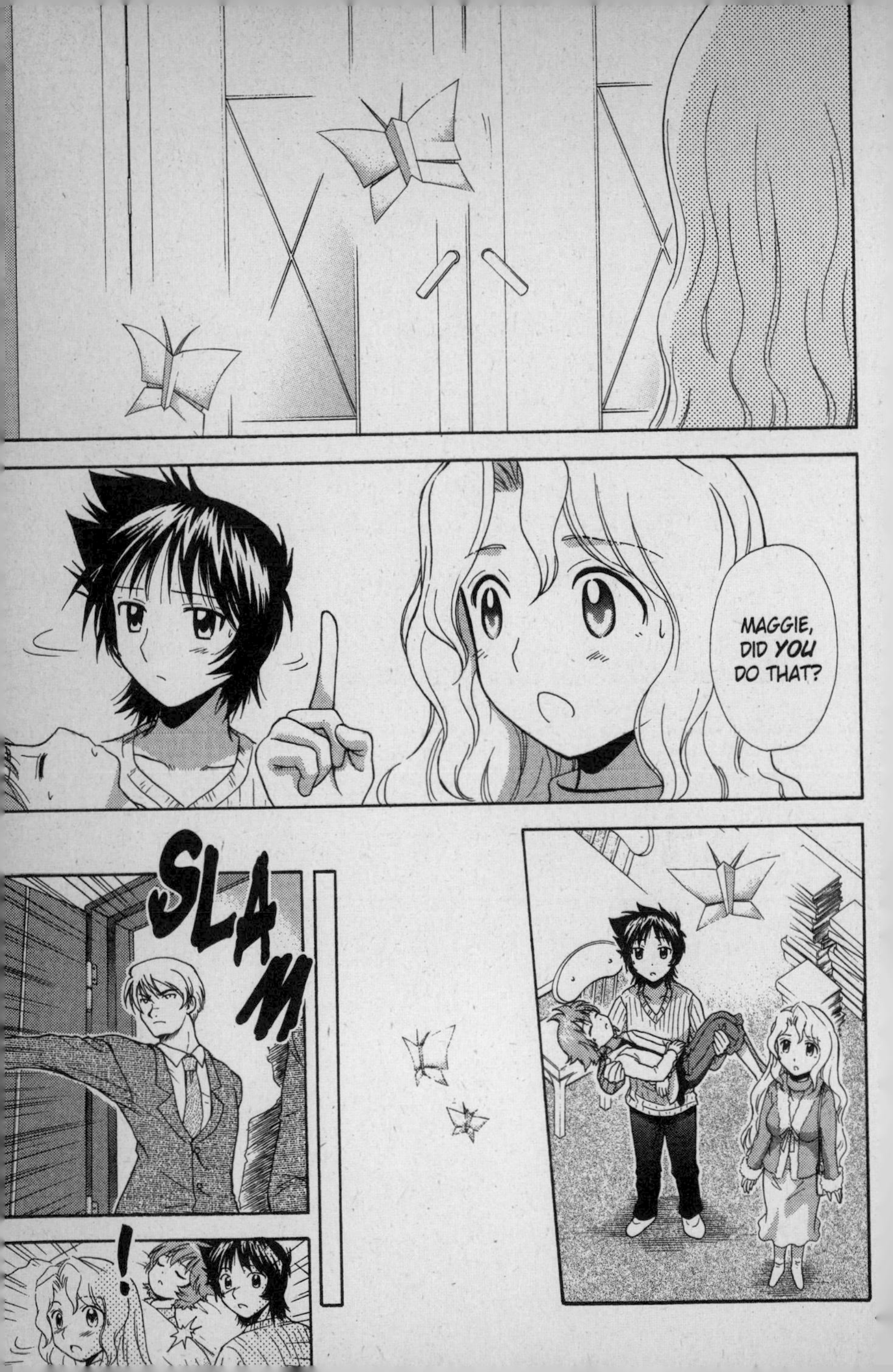
MAGGIE, DID *YOU* DO THAT?
SLAM
!

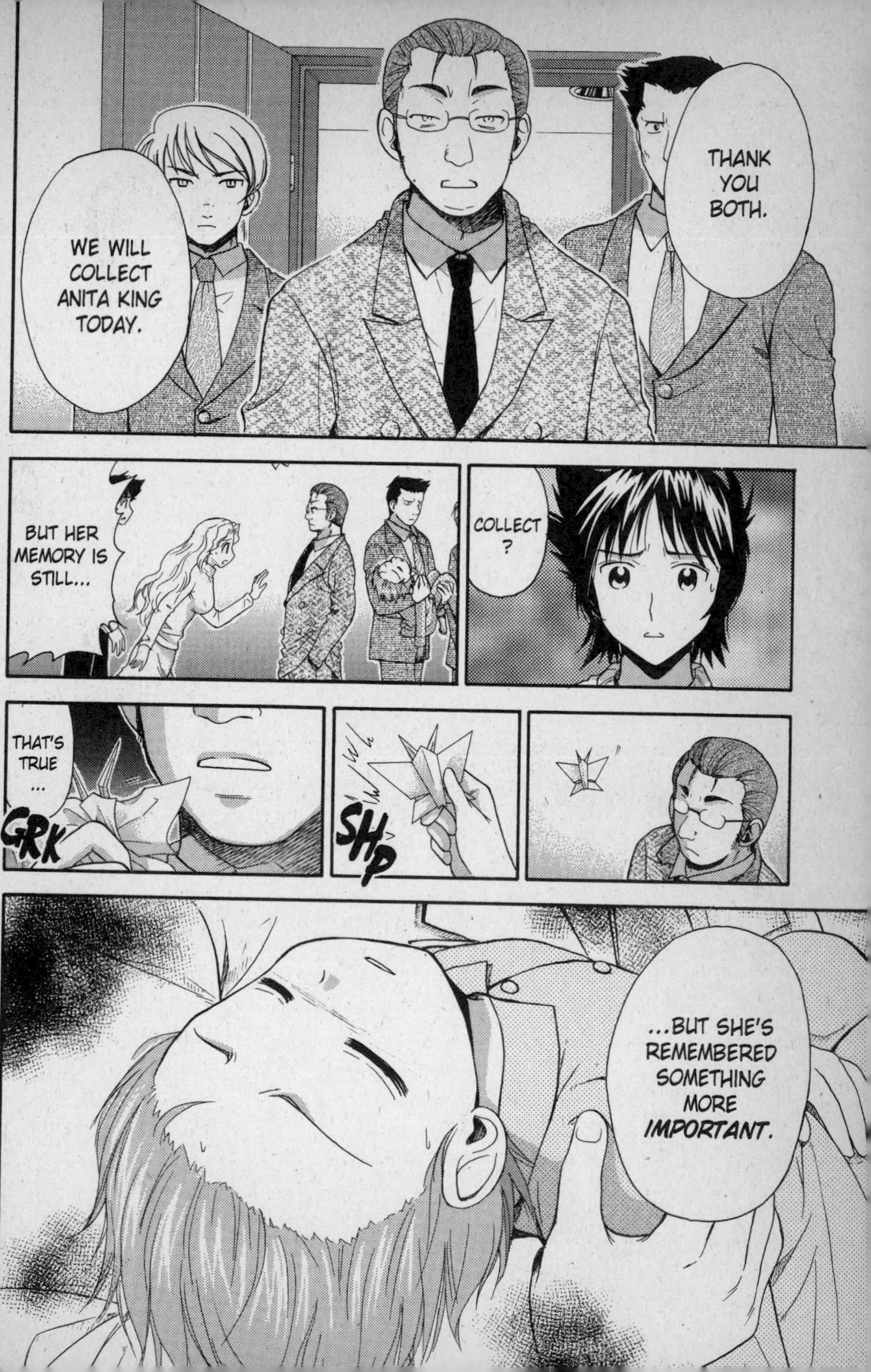
THANK YOU BOTH.
WE WILL COLLECT ANITA KING TODAY.
COLLECT ?
BUT HER MEMORY IS STILL...
SHP
THAT'S TRUE ...
GRK
...BUT SHE'S REMEMBERED SOMETHING MORE IMPORTANT.

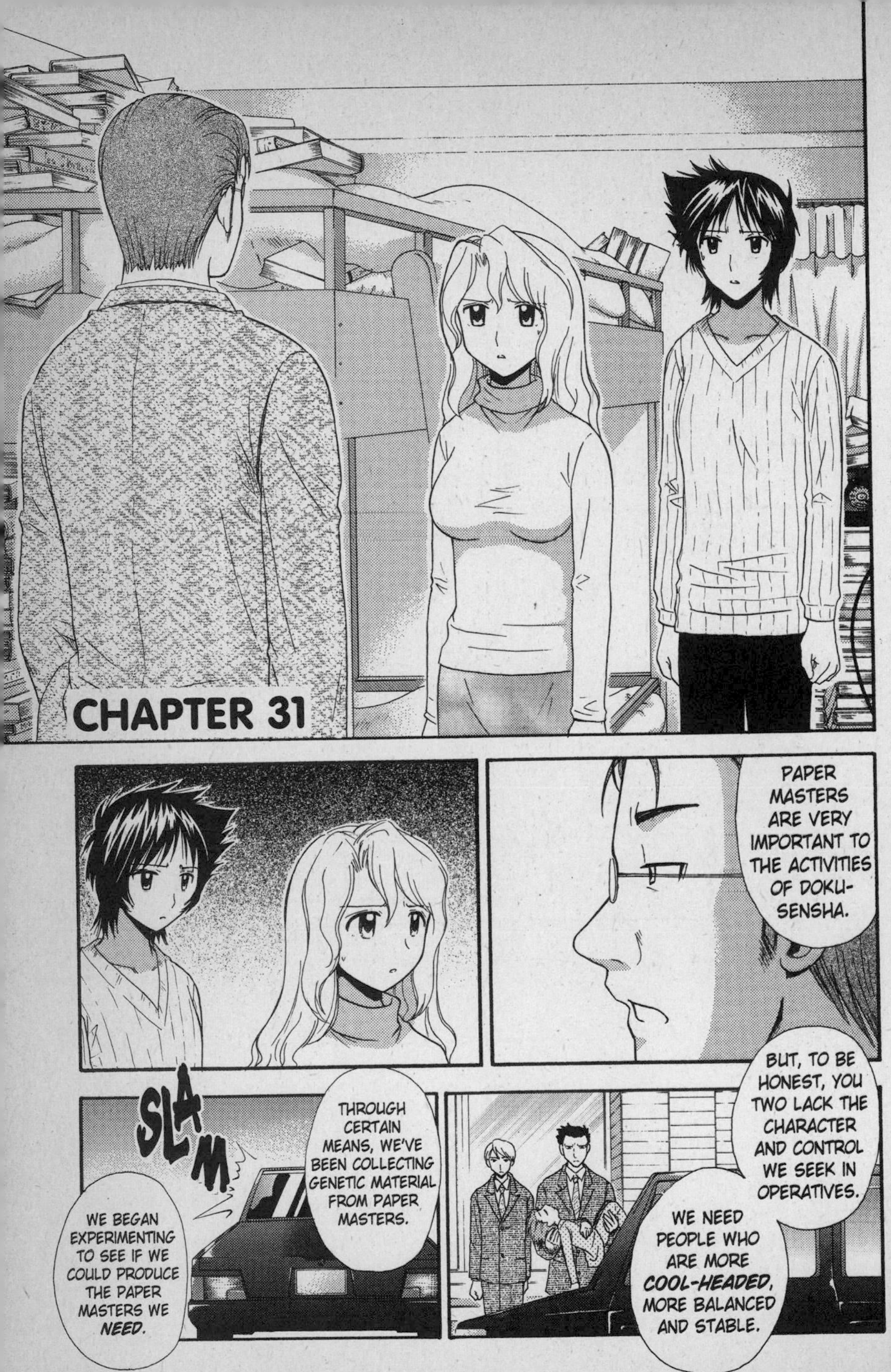
CHAPTER 31
PAPER MASTERS ARE VERY IMPORTANT TO THE ACTIVITIES OF DOKU-SENSHA.
BUT, TO BE HONEST, YOU TWO LACK THE CHARACTER AND CONTROL WE SEEK IN OPERATIVES.
WE NEED PEOPLE WHO ARE MORE *COOL-HEADED*, MORE BALANCED AND STABLE.
THROUGH CERTAIN MEANS, WE'VE BEEN COLLECTING GENETIC MATERIAL FROM PAPER MASTERS.
SLAM
WE BEGAN EXPERIMENTING TO SEE IF WE COULD PRODUCE THE PAPER MASTERS WE *NEED*.

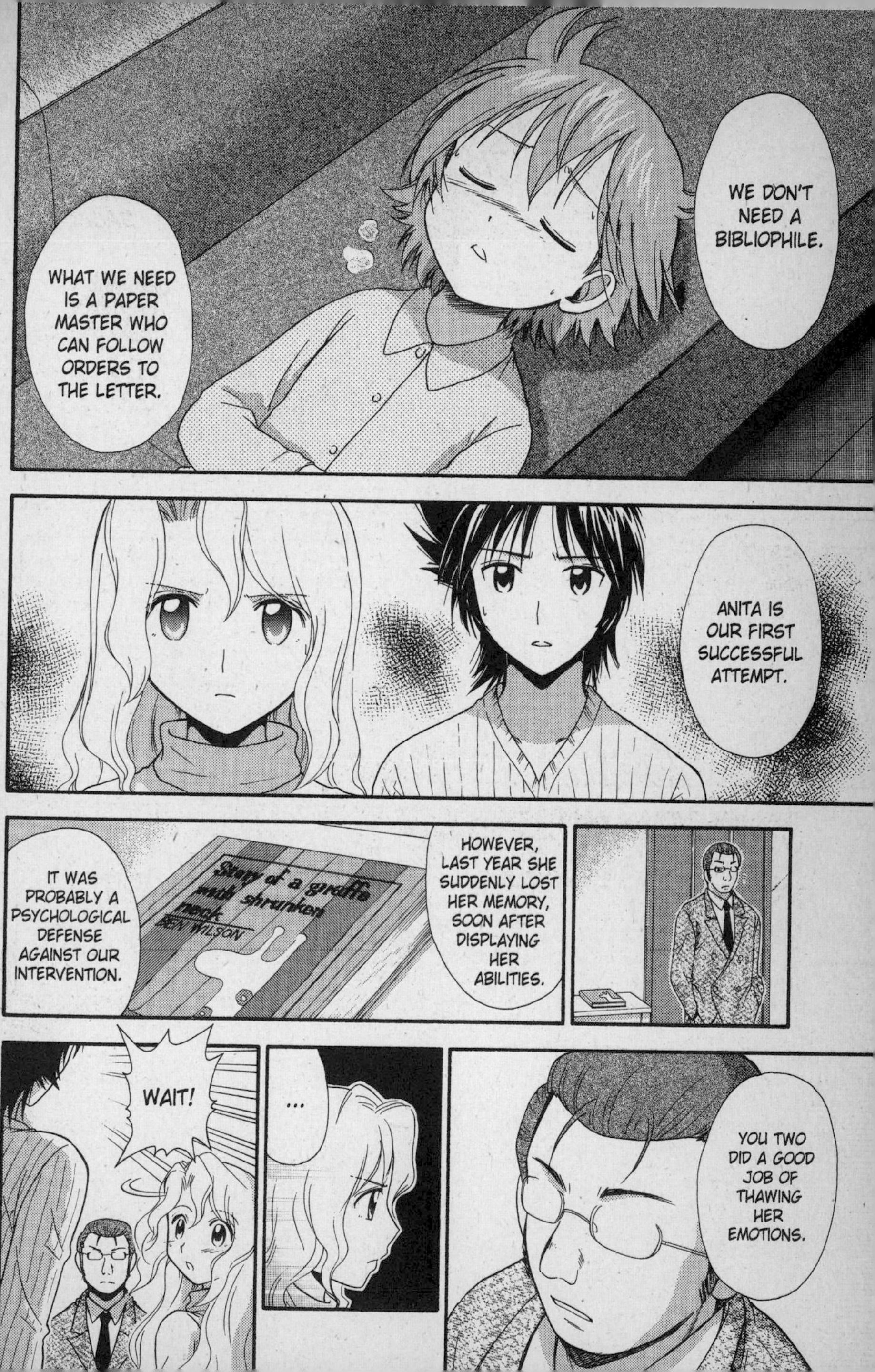
WE DON'T NEED A BIBLIOPHILE.
WHAT WE NEED IS A PAPER MASTER WHO CAN FOLLOW ORDERS TO THE LETTER.
ANITA IS OUR FIRST SUCCESSFUL ATTEMPT.
HOWEVER, LAST YEAR SHE SUDDENLY LOST HER MEMORY, SOON AFTER DISPLAYING HER ABILITIES.
Story of a giraffe with shrunken neck
BEN WILSON
IT WAS PROBABLY A PSYCHOLOGICAL DEFENSE AGAINST OUR INTERVENTION.
YOU TWO DID A GOOD JOB OF THAWING HER EMOTIONS.
...
WAIT!

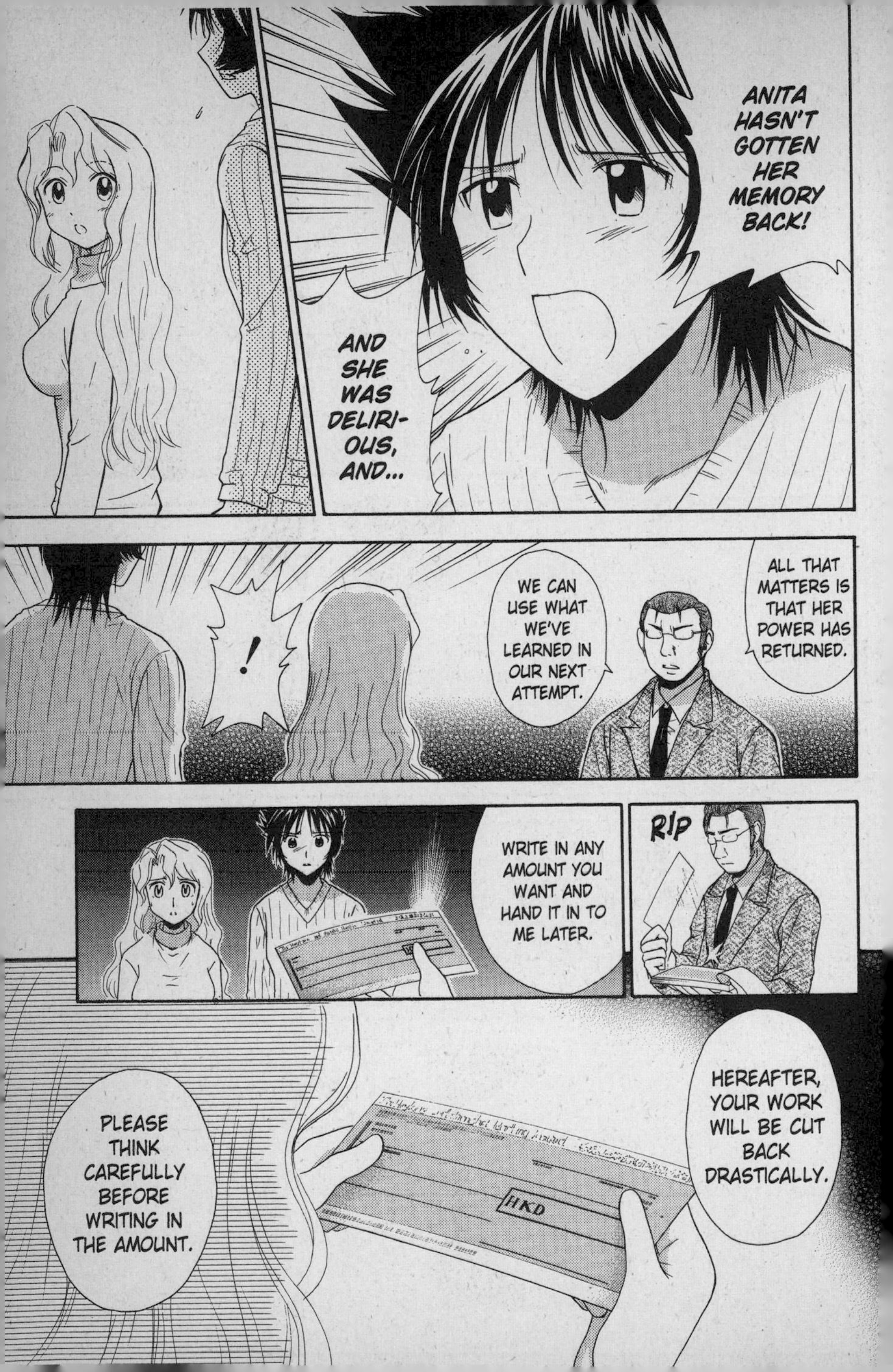
ANITA HASN'T GOTTEN HER MEMORY BACK!
AND SHE WAS DELIRI-OUS, AND...
ALL THAT MATTERS IS THAT HER POWER HAS RETURNED.
WE CAN USE WHAT WE'VE LEARNED IN OUR NEXT ATTEMPT.
!
R!P
WRITE IN ANY AMOUNT YOU WANT AND HAND IT IN TO ME LATER.
HEREAFTER, YOUR WORK WILL BE CUT BACK DRASTICALLY.
HKD
PLEASE THINK CAREFULLY BEFORE WRITING IN THE AMOUNT.

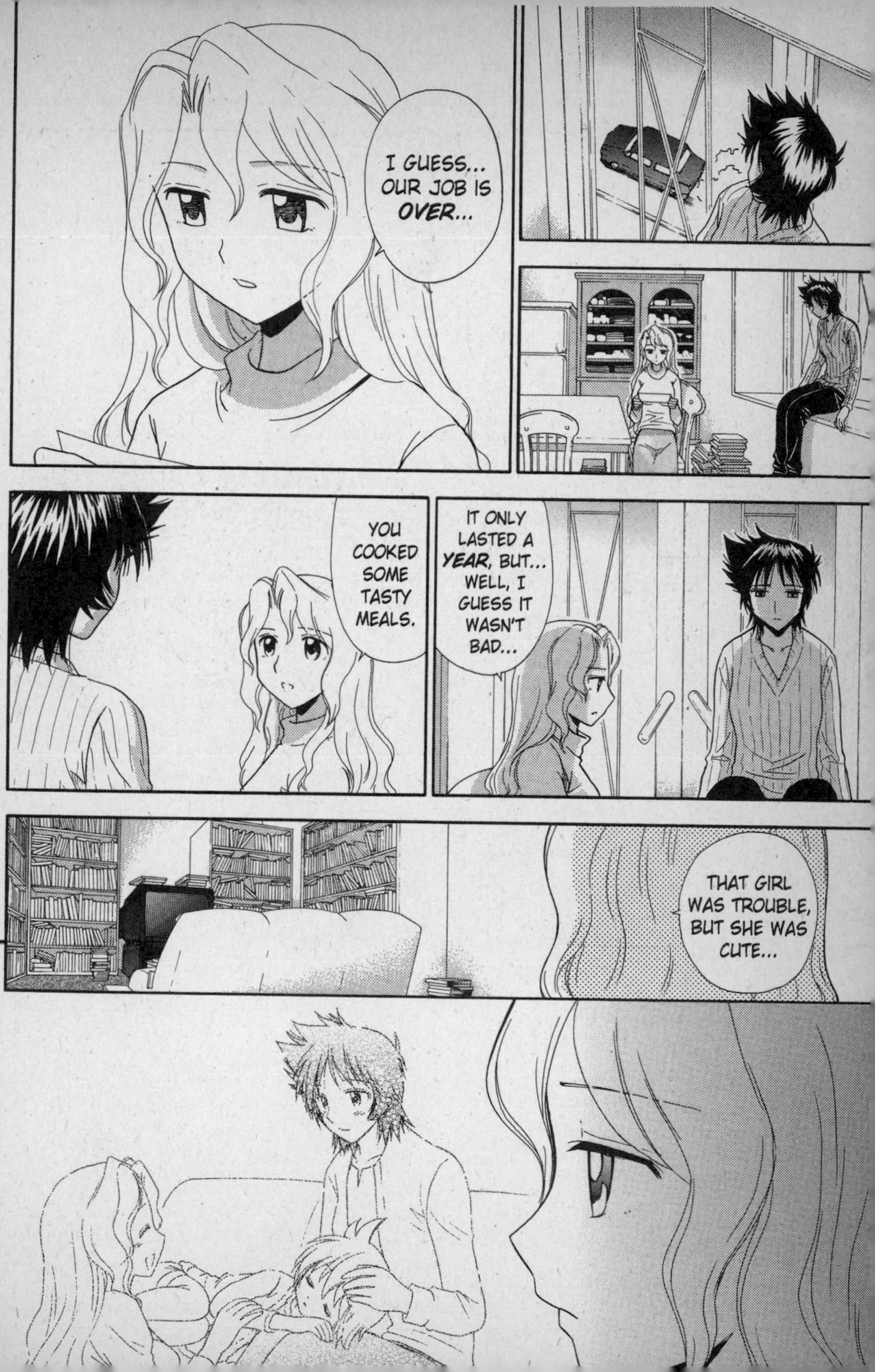
I GUESS... OUR JOB IS OVER...
IT ONLY LASTED A YEAR, BUT... WELL, I GUESS IT WASN'T BAD...
YOU COOKED SOME TASTY MEALS.
THAT GIRL WAS TROUBLE, BUT SHE WAS CUTE...

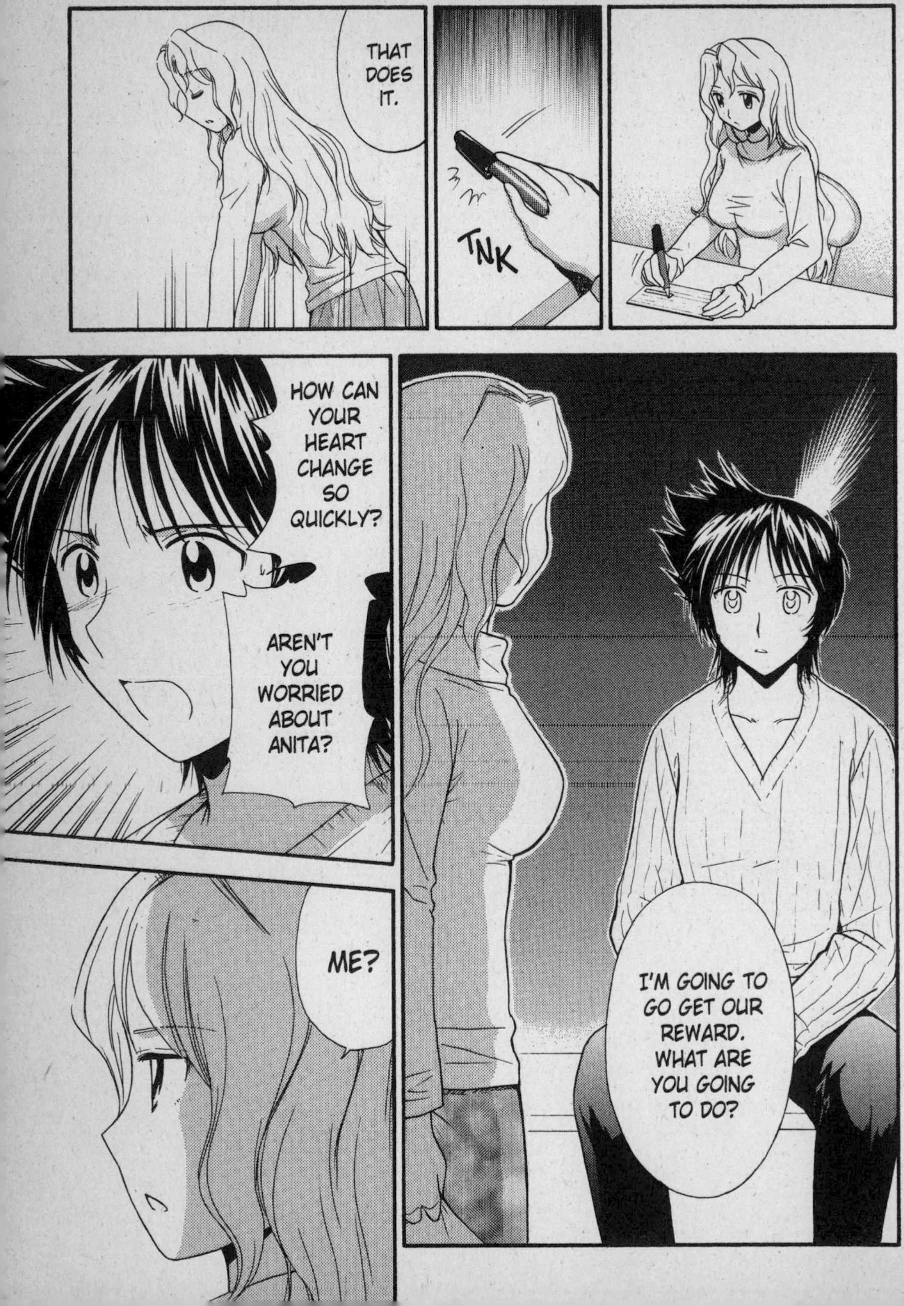
TNK
THAT DOES IT.
I'M GOING TO GO GET OUR REWARD. WHAT ARE YOU GOING TO DO?
HOW CAN YOUR HEART CHANGE SO QUICKLY?
AREN'T YOU WORRIED ABOUT ANITA?
ME?

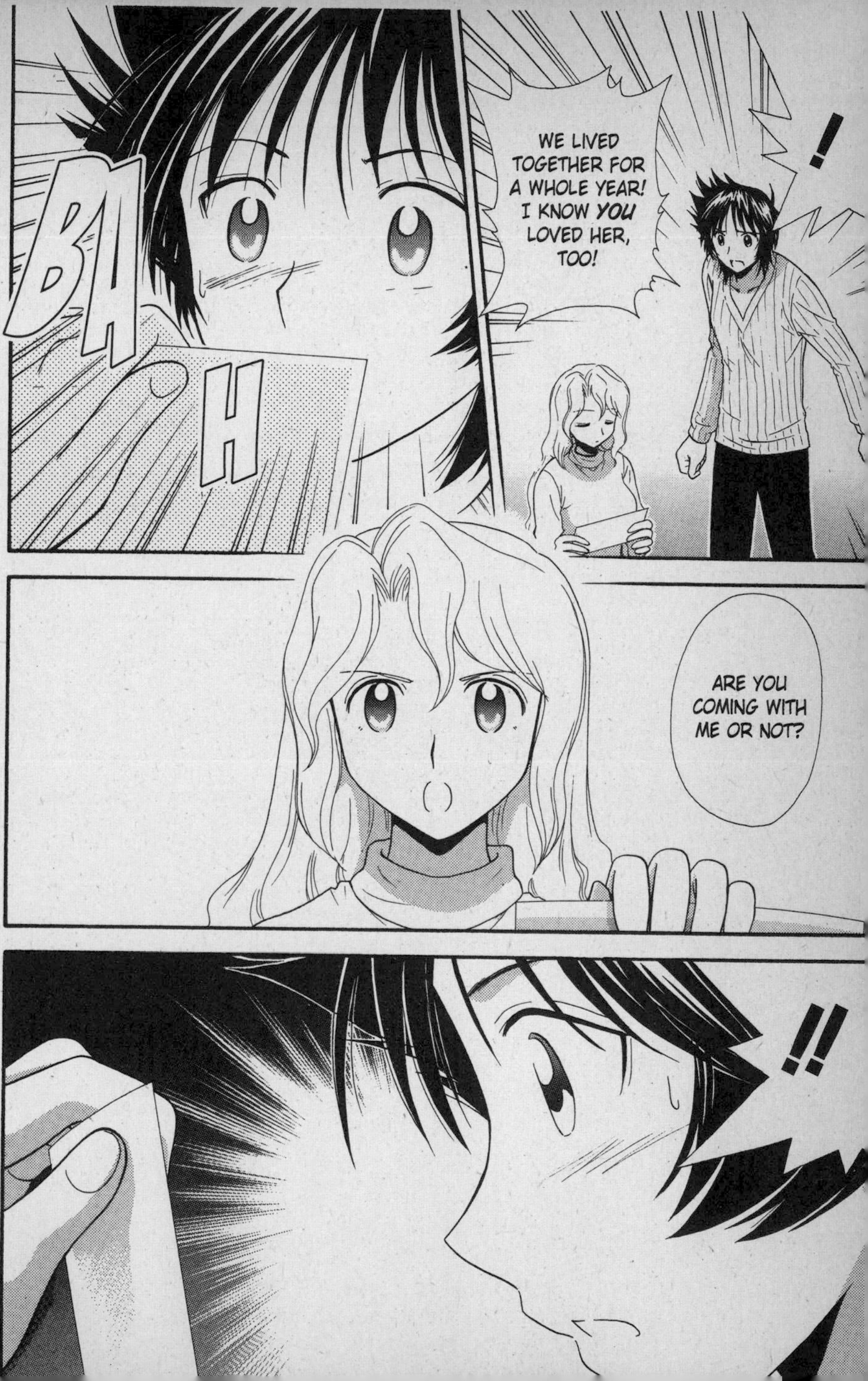
!
WE LIVED TOGETHER FOR A WHOLE YEAR! I KNOW *YOU* LOVED HER, TOO!
BAH
ARE YOU COMING WITH ME OR NOT?
!!

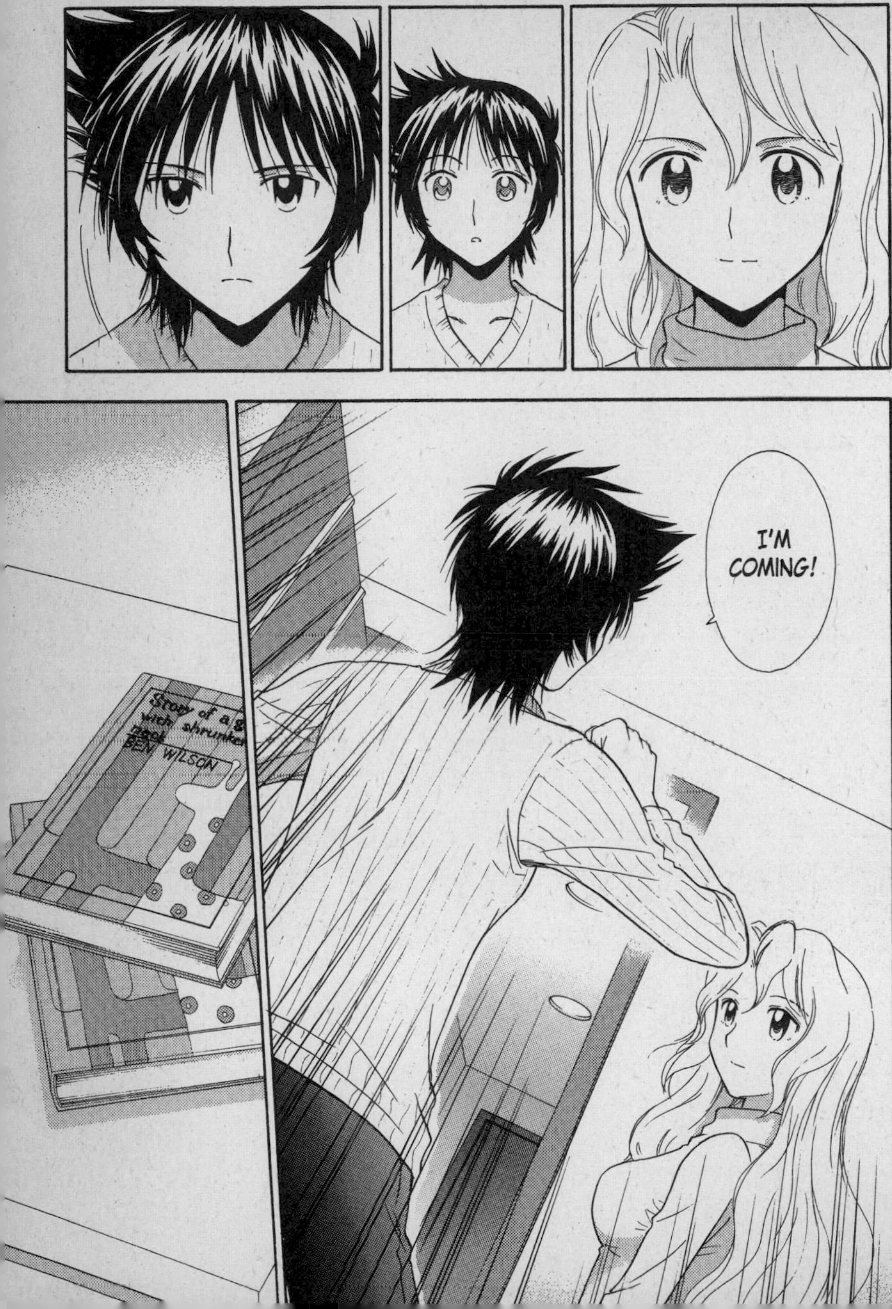
I'M COMING!
BEN WILSON

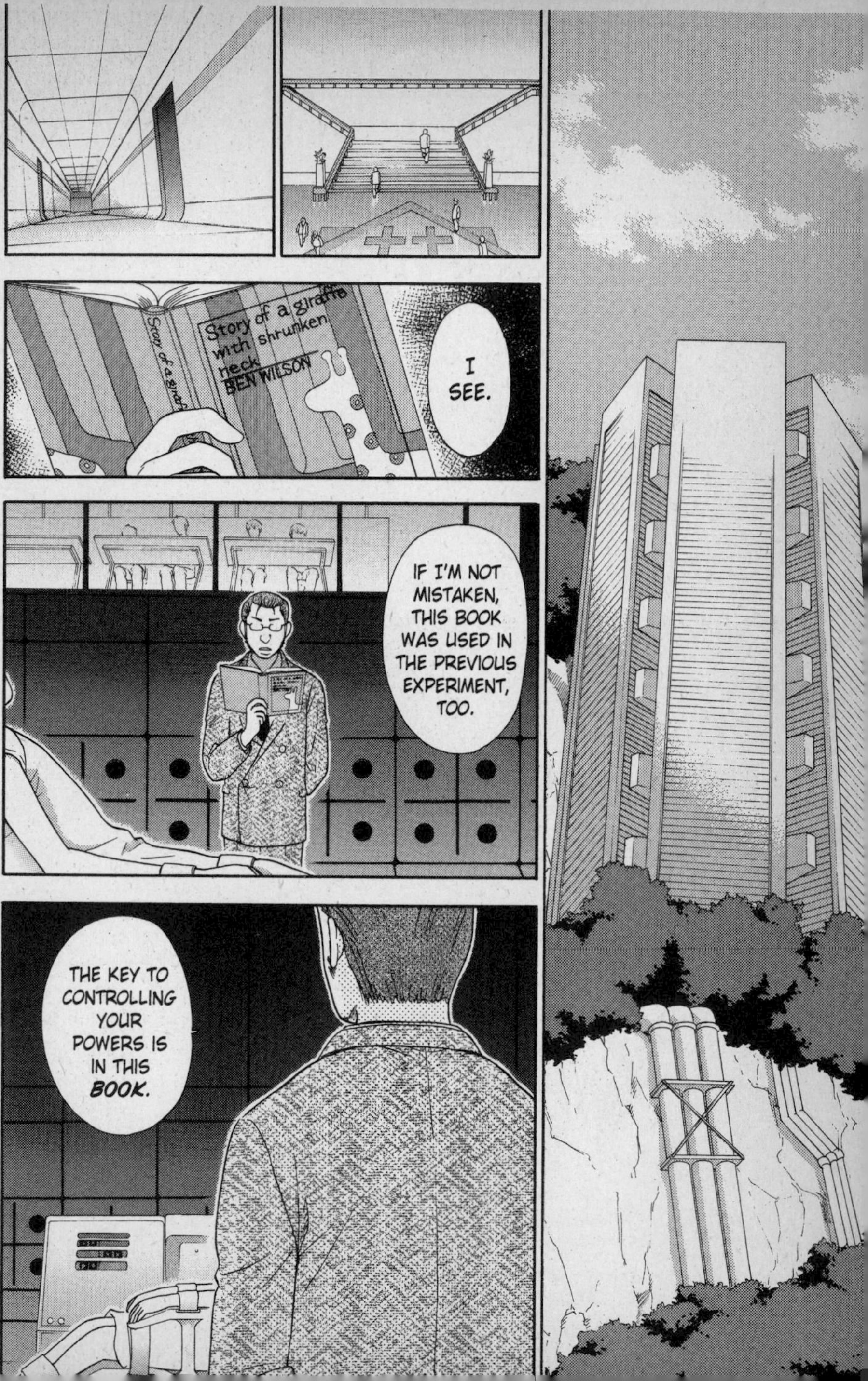
I SEE.
Story of a giraffe with shrunken neck
BEN WILSON
IF I'M NOT MISTAKEN, THIS BOOK WAS USED IN THE PREVIOUS EXPERIMENT, TOO.
THE KEY TO CONTROLLING YOUR POWERS IS IN THIS *BOOK*.

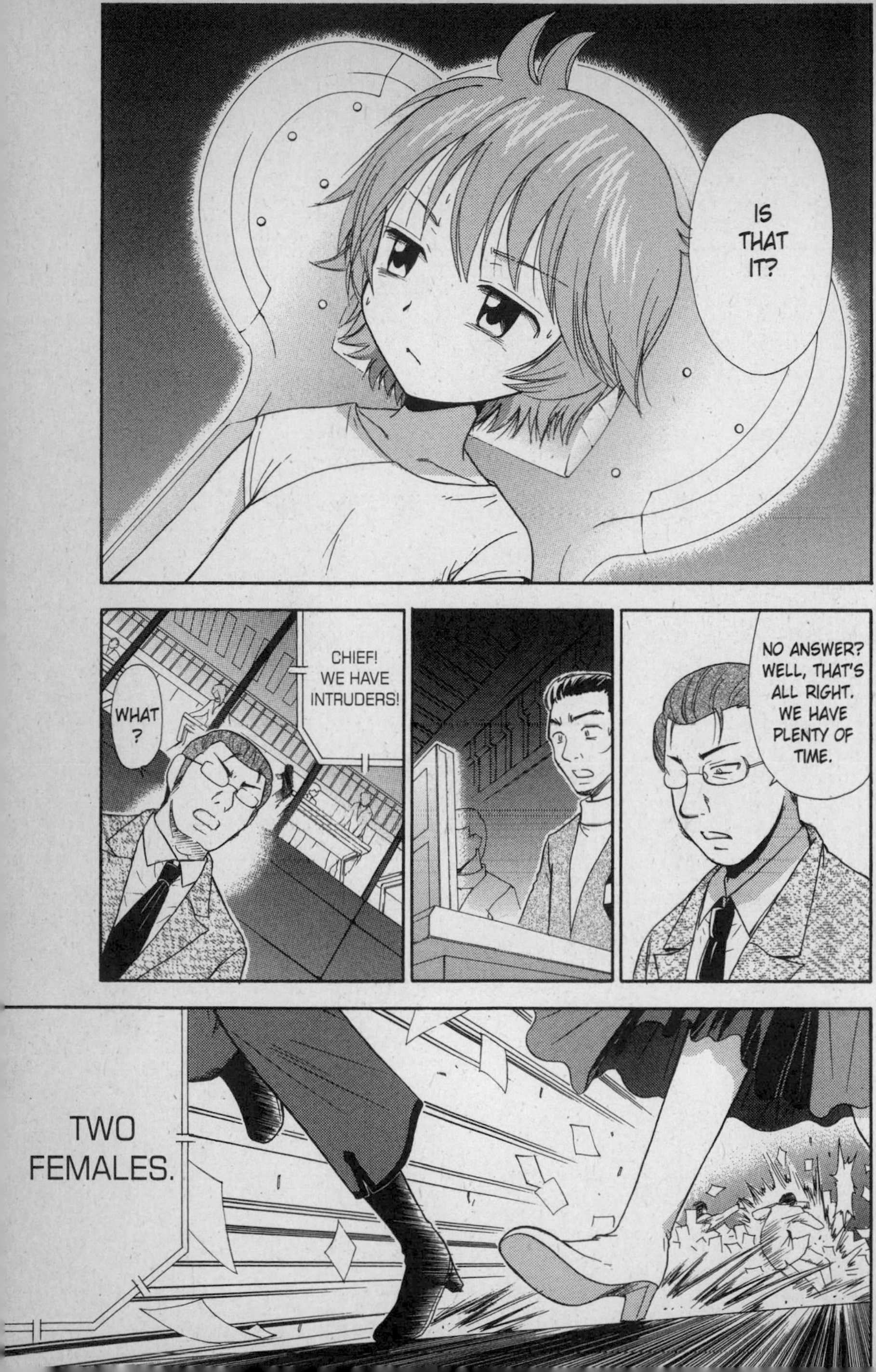
IS THAT IT?
NO ANSWER? WELL, THAT'S ALL RIGHT. WE HAVE PLENTY OF TIME.
CHIEF! WE HAVE INTRUDERS!
WHAT?
TWO FEMALES.

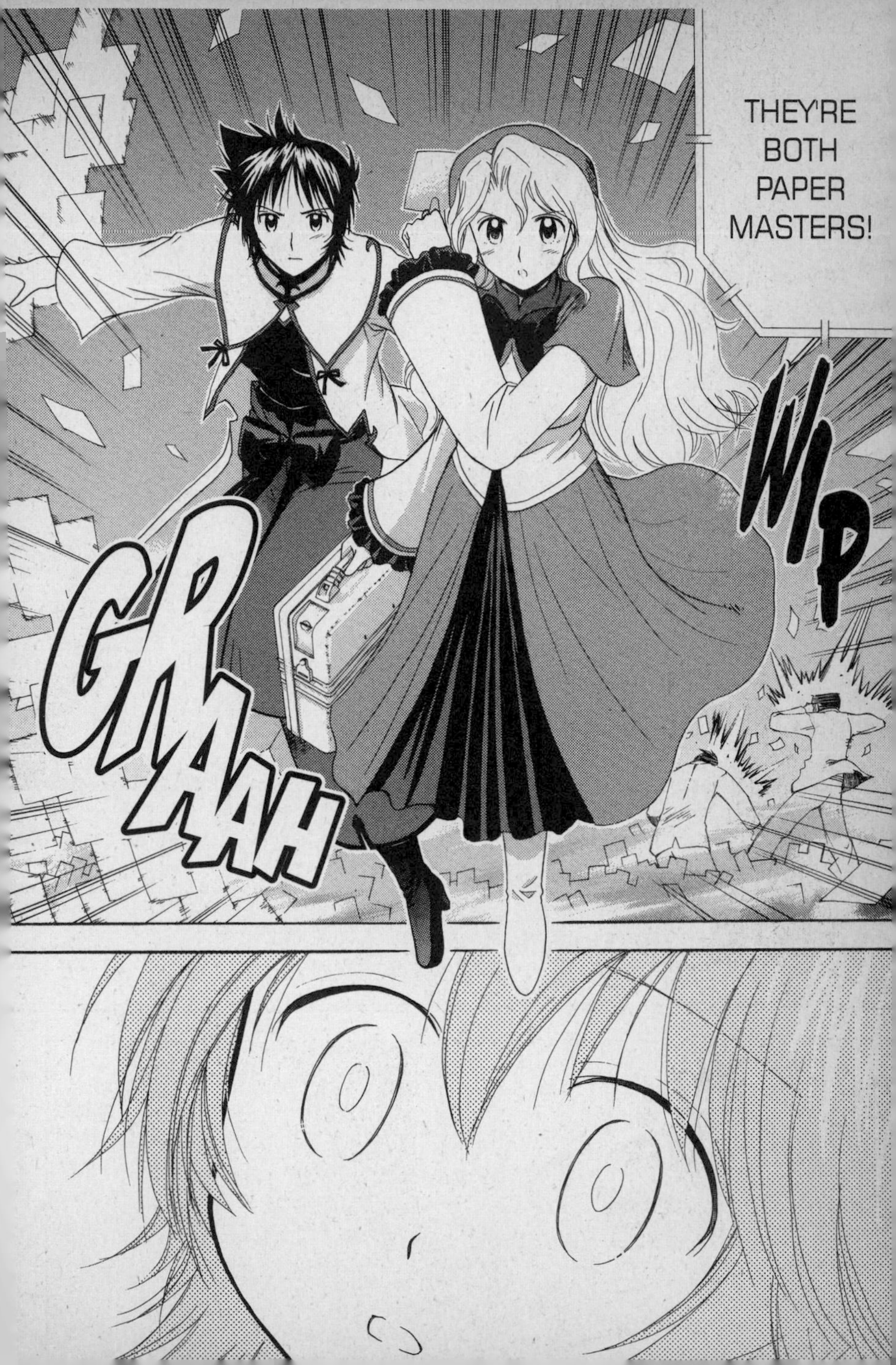
THEY'RE BOTH PAPER MASTERS!
WIP
GRAAH

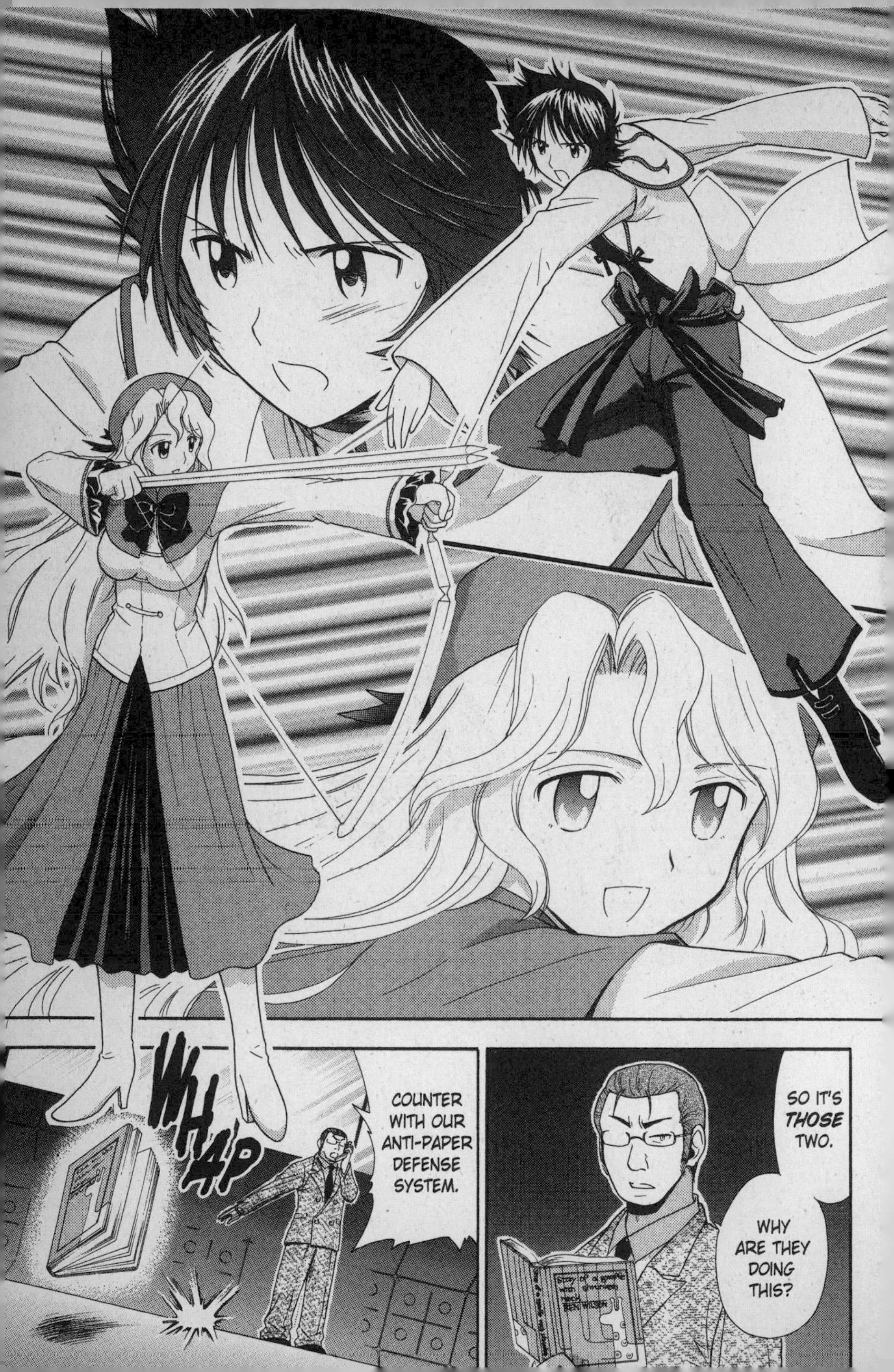
SO IT'S *THOSE* TWO.
WHY ARE THEY DOING THIS?
COUNTER WITH OUR ANTI-PAPER DEFENSE SYSTEM.
WHAP

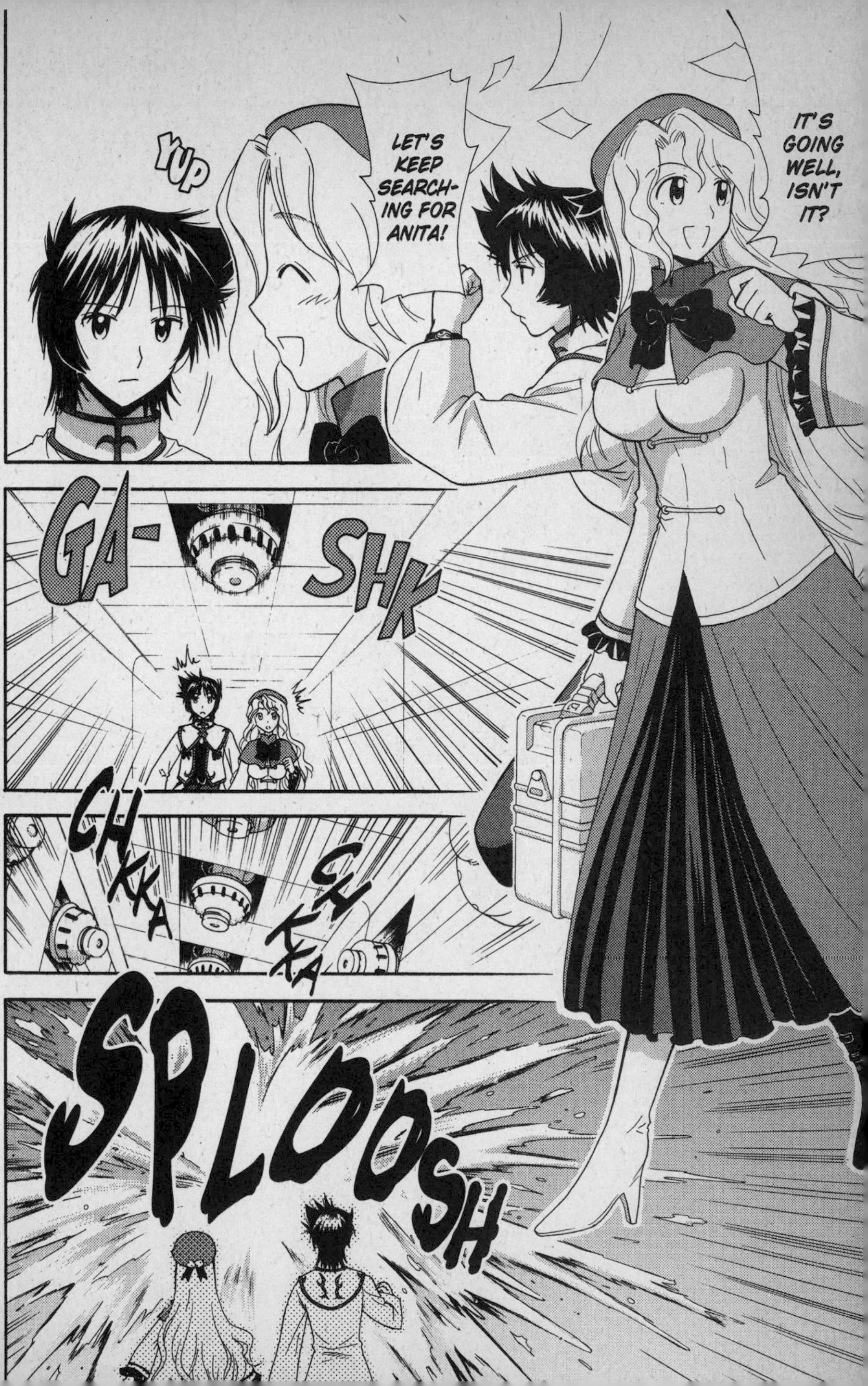
IT'S GOING WELL, ISN'T IT?
LET'S KEEP SEARCHING FOR ANITA!
YUP
GA-SHK
CHKKA
CHKKA
SPLOOSH

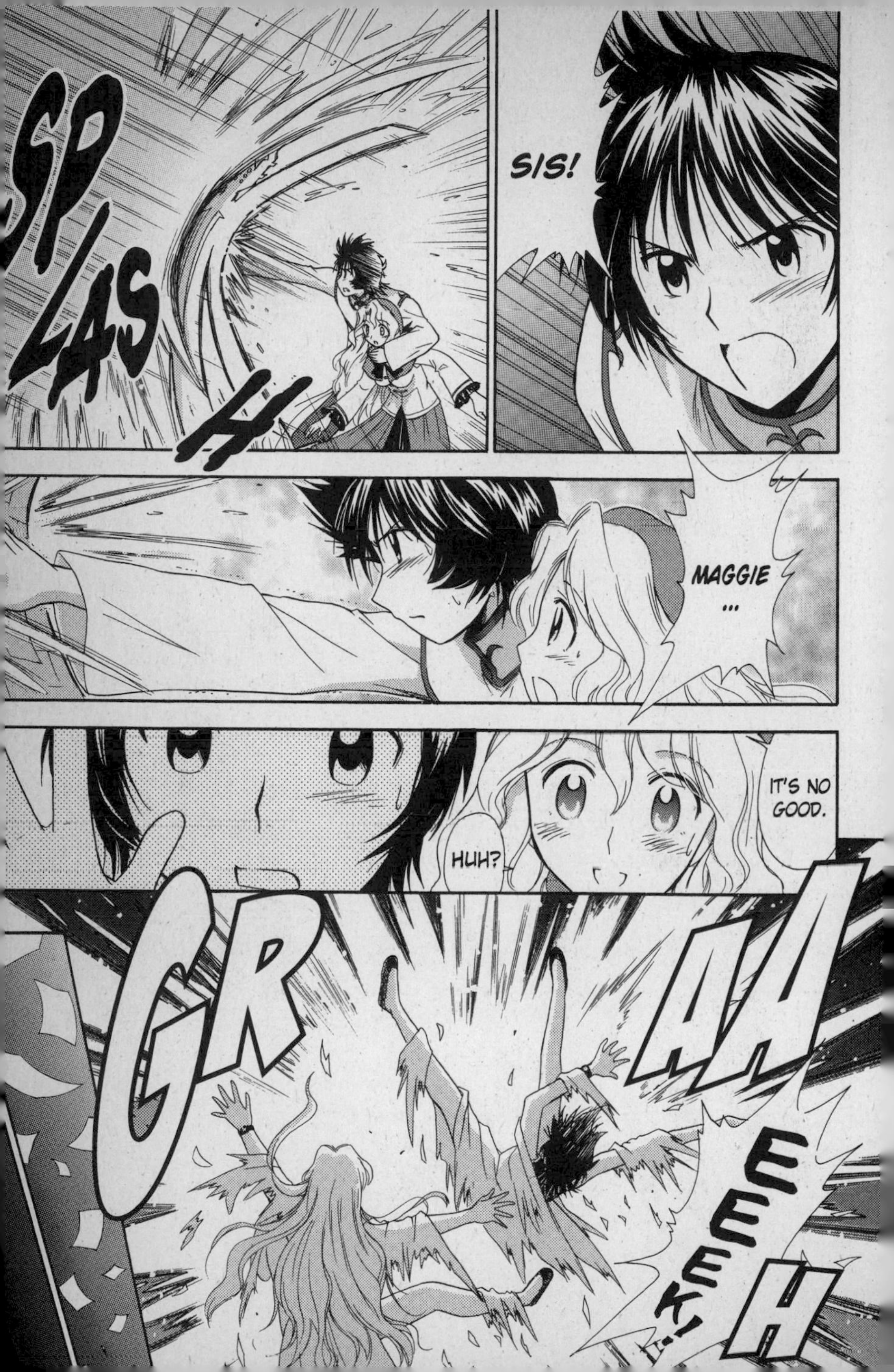
SIS!
SPLASH
MAGGIE ...
IT'S NO GOOD.
HUH?
CRAAAH
EEEK!

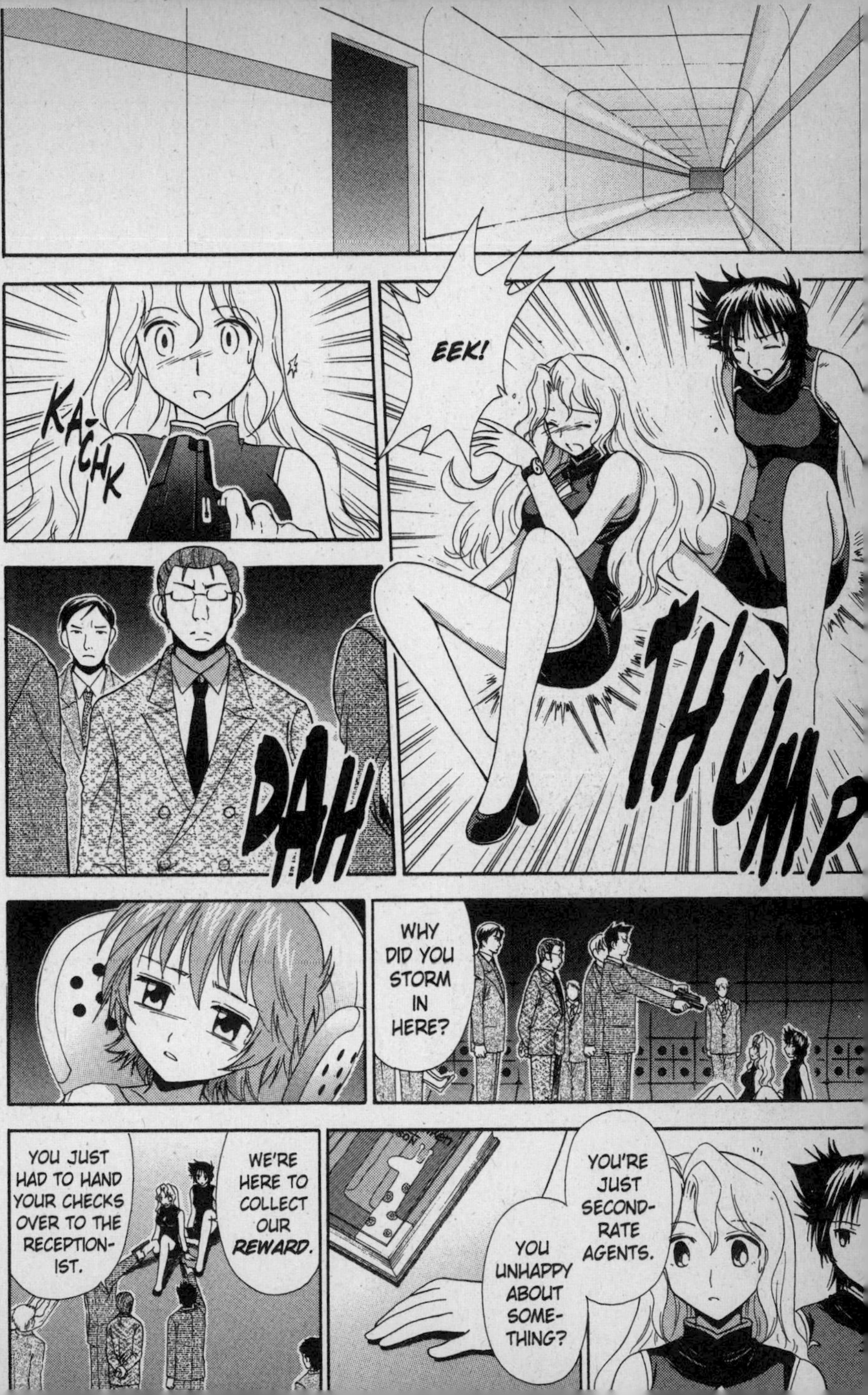
EEK!
THUMP
KA-CHK
DAH
WHY DID YOU STORM IN HERE?
YOU'RE JUST SECOND-RATE AGENTS.
YOU UNHAPPY ABOUT SOMETHING?
WE'RE HERE TO COLLECT OUR *REWARD*.
YOU JUST HAD TO HAND YOUR CHECKS OVER TO THE RECEPTION-IST.

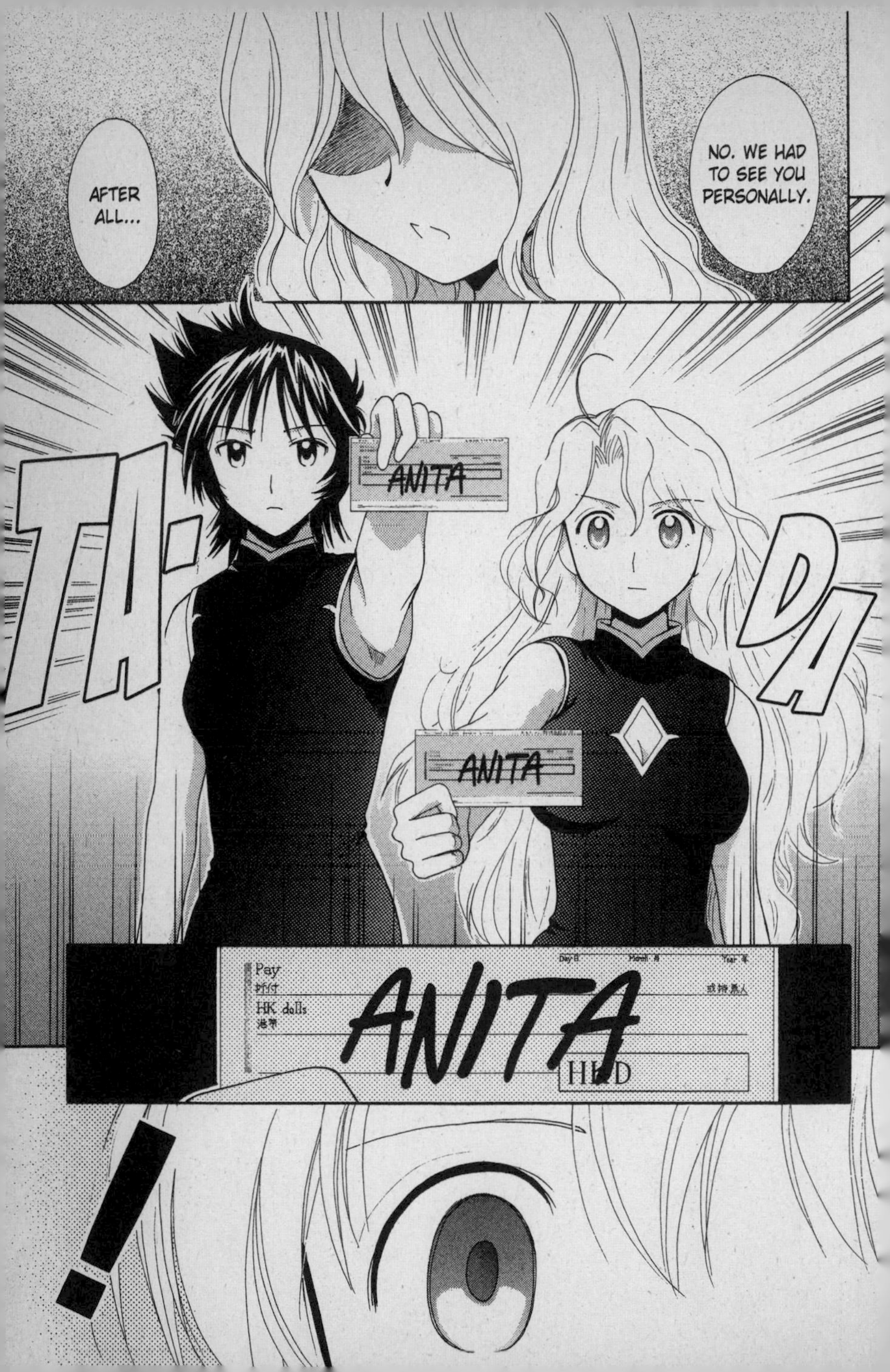
NO. WE HAD TO SEE YOU PERSONALLY.
AFTER ALL...
TA-
DA
ANITA
ANITA
Day 日
Month 月
Year 年
Pay
HK dolls
ANITA
HKD
!

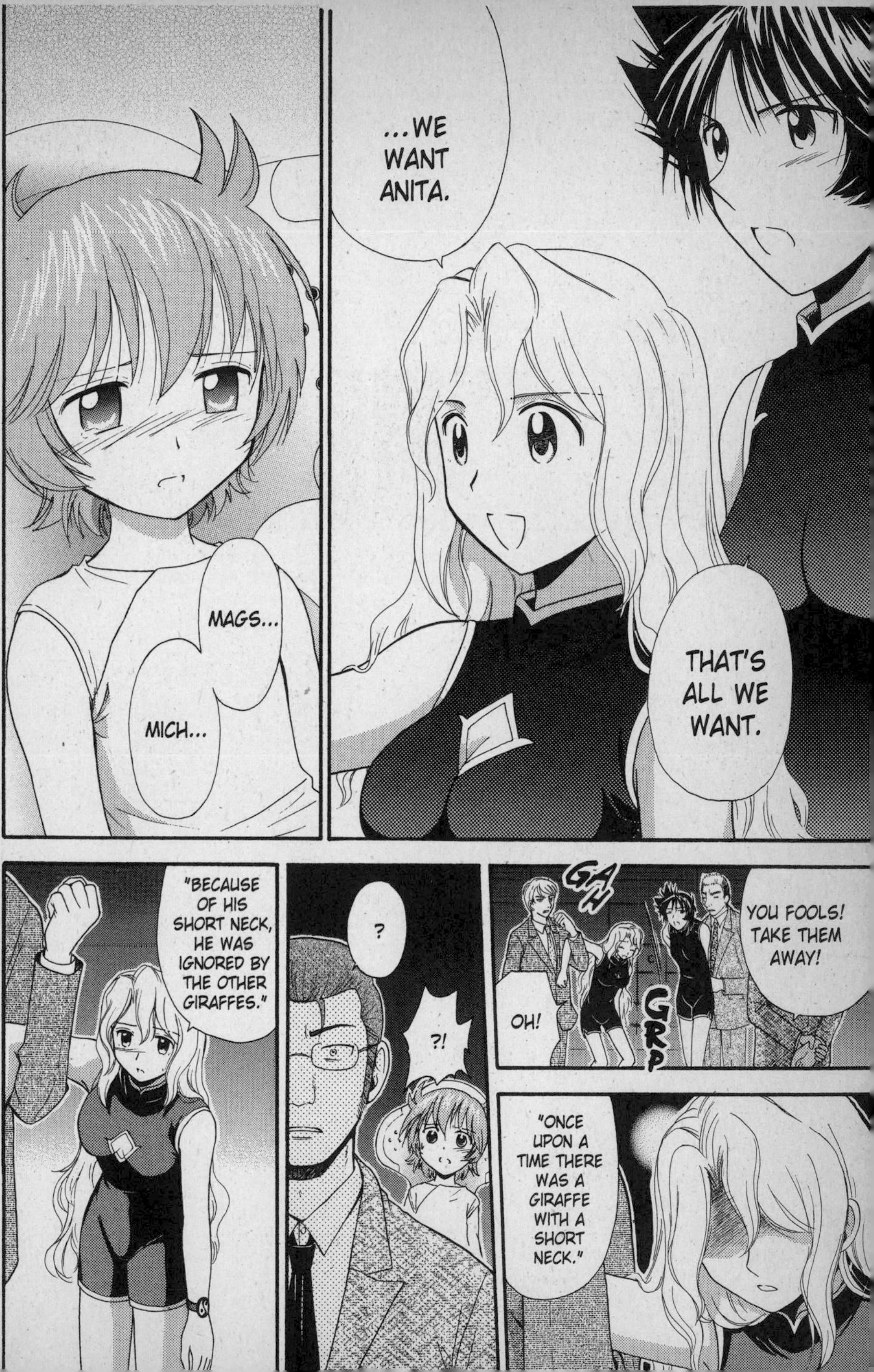
...WE WANT ANITA.
THAT'S ALL WE WANT.
MAGS...
MICH...
YOU FOOLS! TAKE THEM AWAY!
GAH
GRP
OH!
"ONCE UPON A TIME THERE WAS A GIRAFFE WITH A SHORT NECK."
?
?!
"BECAUSE OF HIS SHORT NECK, HE WAS IGNORED BY THE OTHER GIRAFFES."

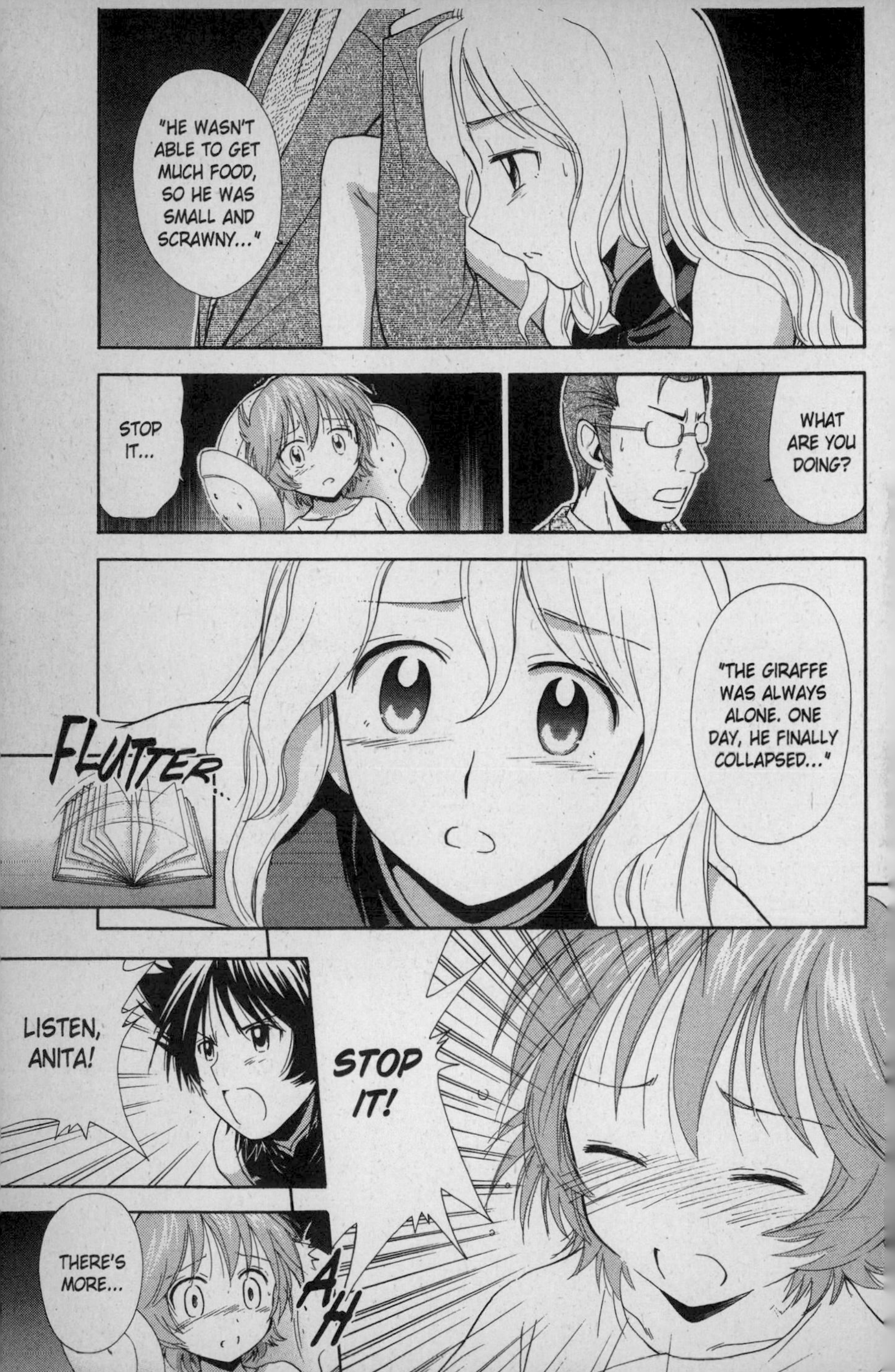
"HE WASN'T ABLE TO GET MUCH FOOD, SO HE WAS SMALL AND SCRAWNY..."
WHAT ARE YOU DOING?
STOP IT...
"THE GIRAFFE WAS ALWAYS ALONE. ONE DAY, HE FINALLY COLLAPSED..."
FLUTTER...
LISTEN, ANITA!
STOP IT!
THERE'S MORE...
AH

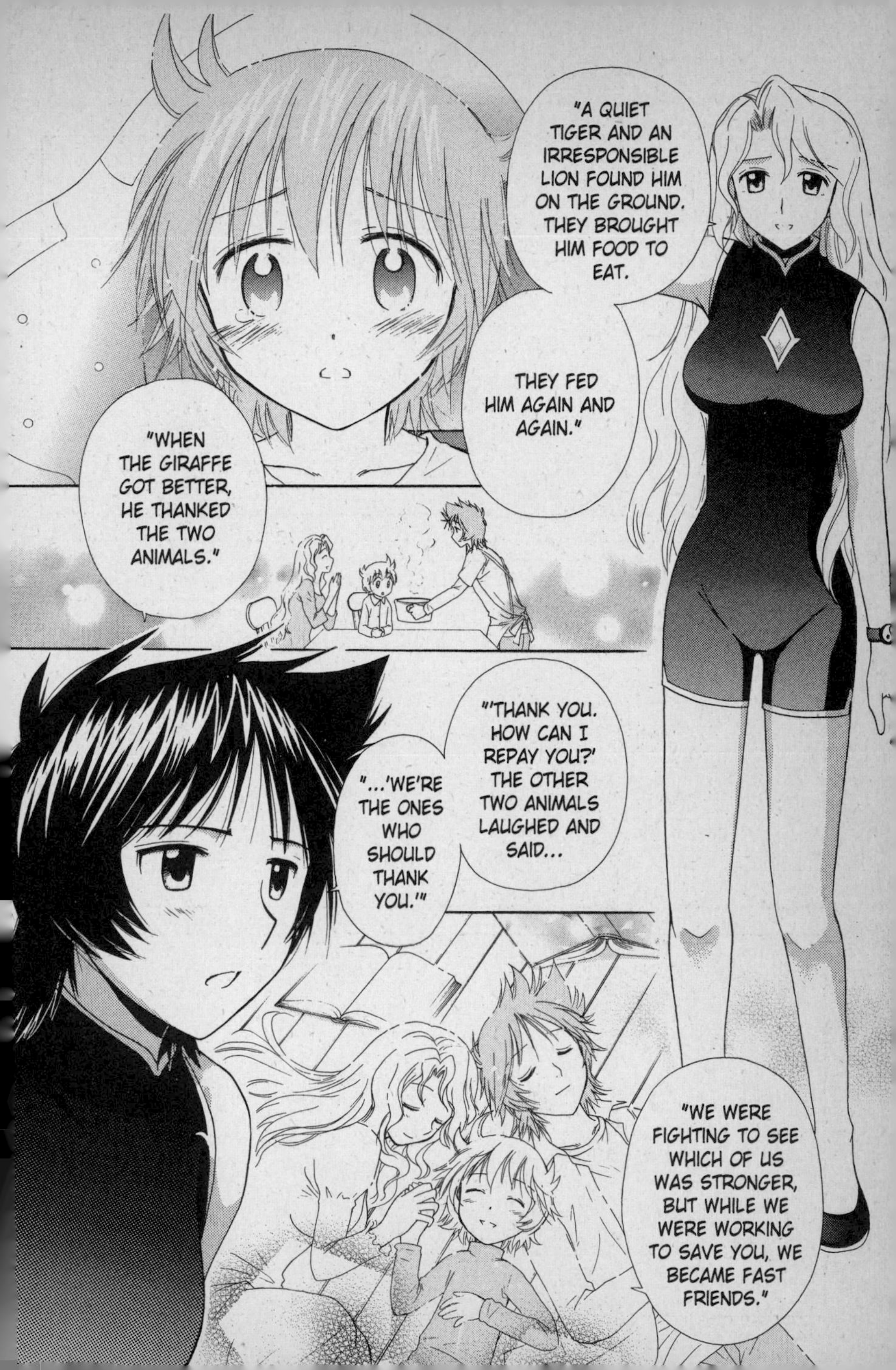
"A QUIET TIGER AND AN IRRESPONSIBLE LION FOUND HIM ON THE GROUND. THEY BROUGHT HIM FOOD TO EAT.
THEY FED HIM AGAIN AND AGAIN."
"WHEN THE GIRAFFE GOT BETTER, HE THANKED THE TWO ANIMALS."
"'THANK YOU. HOW CAN I REPAY YOU?' THE OTHER TWO ANIMALS LAUGHED AND SAID...
"...'WE'RE THE ONES WHO SHOULD THANK YOU.'"
"WE WERE FIGHTING TO SEE WHICH OF US WAS STRONGER, BUT WHILE WE WERE WORKING TO SAVE YOU, WE BECAME FAST FRIENDS."

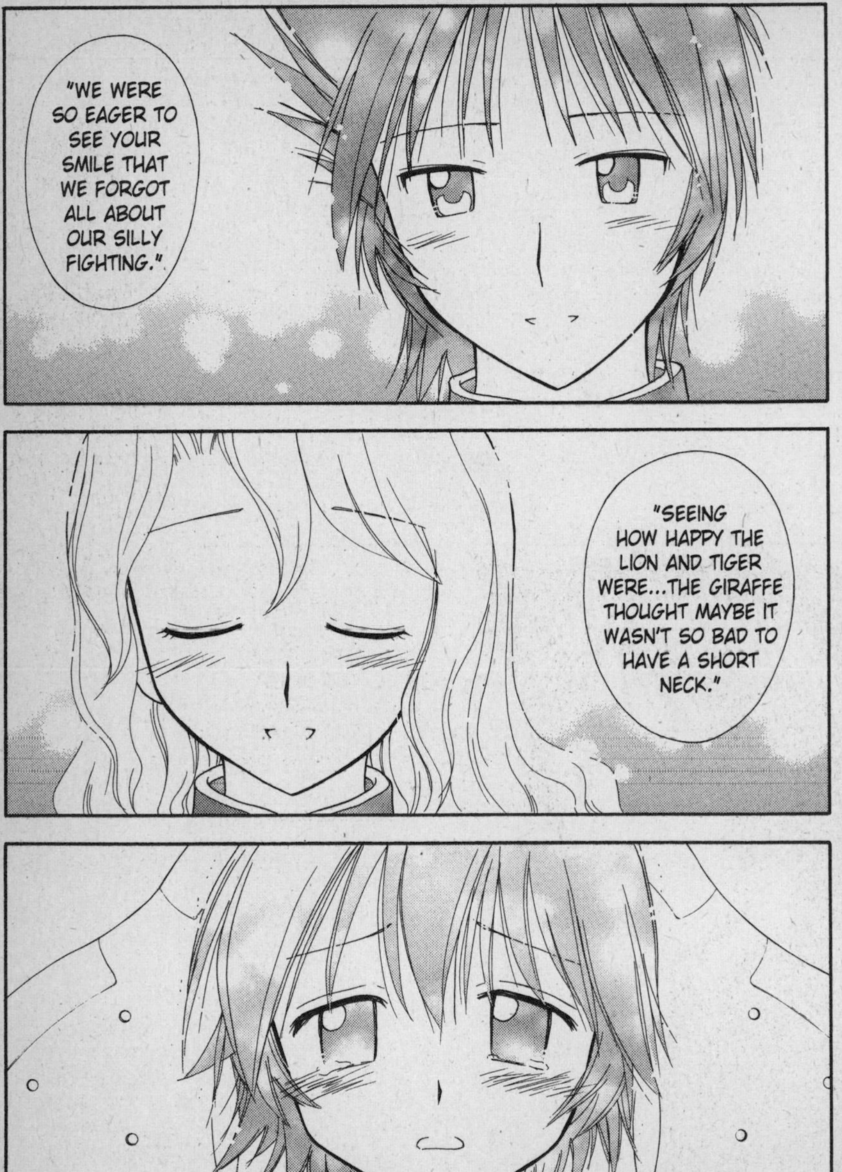
"WE WERE SO EAGER TO SEE YOUR SMILE THAT WE FORGOT ALL ABOUT OUR SILLY FIGHTING."
"SEEING HOW HAPPY THE LION AND TIGER WERE...THE GIRAFFE THOUGHT MAYBE IT WASN'T SO BAD TO HAVE A SHORT NECK."

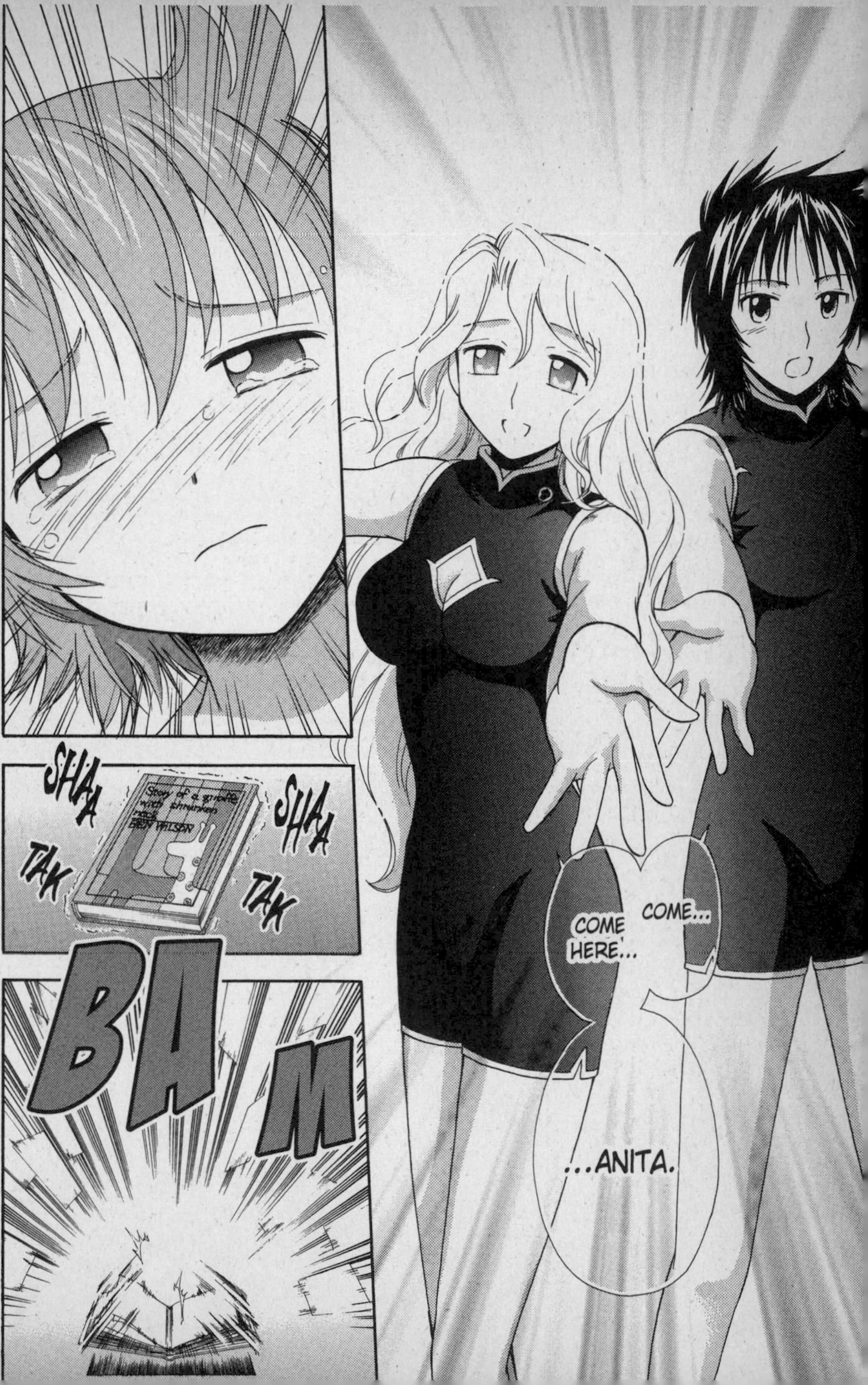
COME...
COME HERE...
...ANITA.
SHAA
SHAA
TAK
TAK
Story of a giraffe with shrunken neck
BEN WILSON
BAM

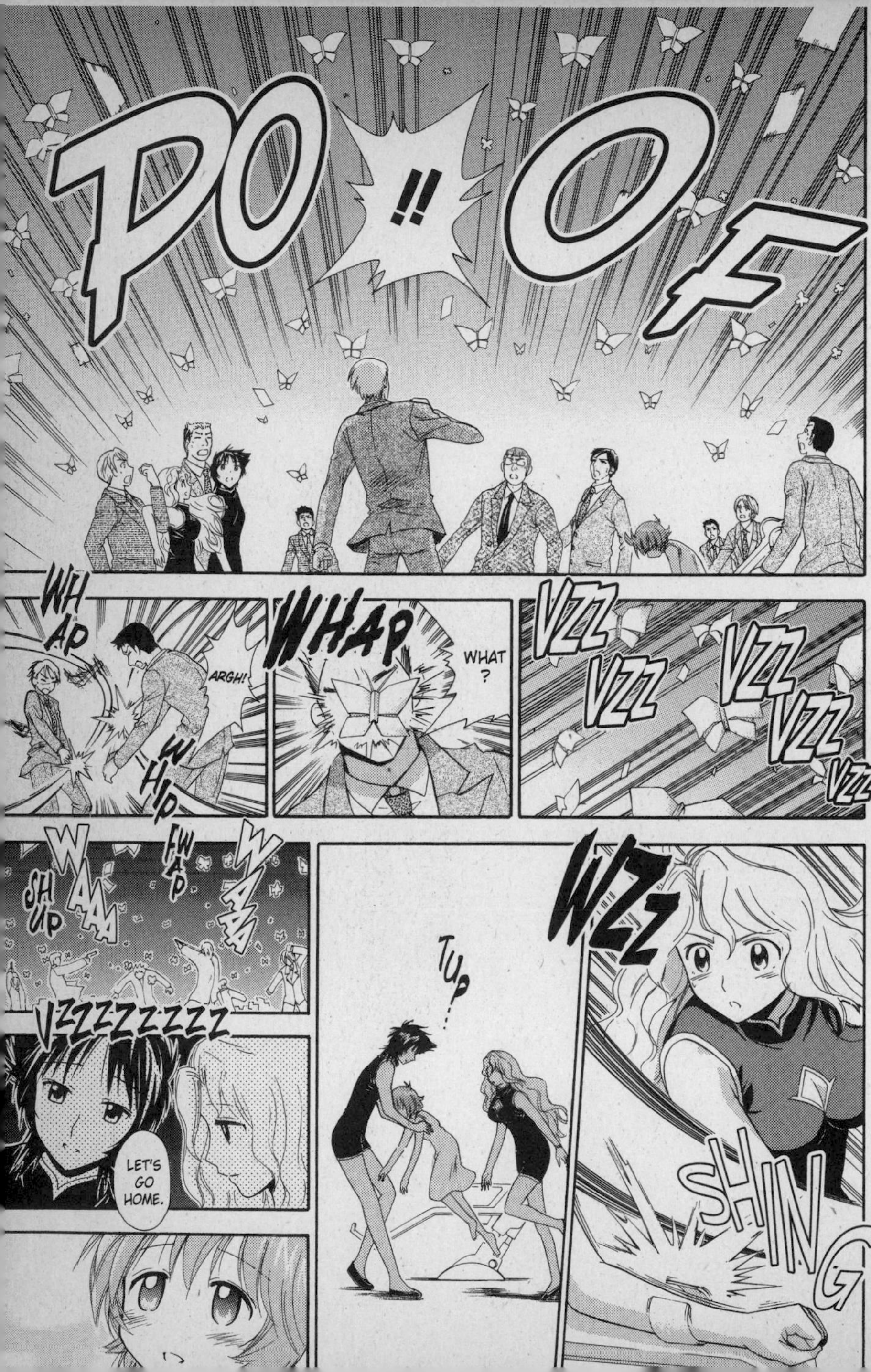
PO!!OF
VZZ
VZZ
VZZ
VZZ
VZZ
WHAP
WHAT?
WHAP
ARGH!
WHIP
WZZ
SHING
TUP...
WAAA
FWAP
WAAA
SHUP
VZZZZZZZZ
LET'S GO HOME.

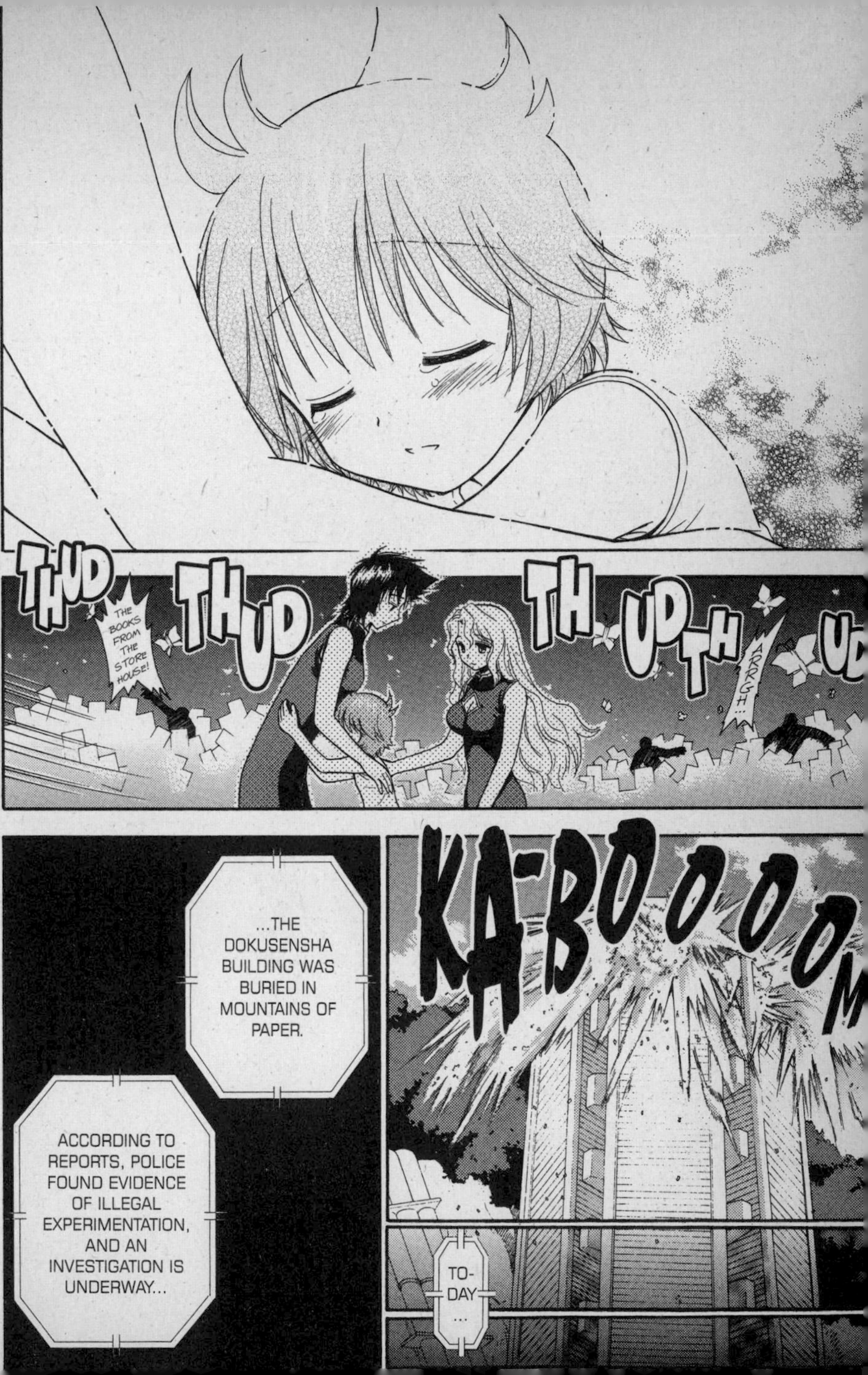
UD
ARRGH!!
THUD
THUD
THUD
THE BOOKS FROM THE STORE HOUSE!
THUD
KA-BOOOOOM
TO-DAY...
...THE DOKUSENSHA BUILDING WAS BURIED IN MOUNTAINS OF PAPER.
ACCORDING TO REPORTS, POLICE FOUND EVIDENCE OF ILLEGAL EXPERIMENTATION, AND AN INVESTIGATION IS UNDERWAY...

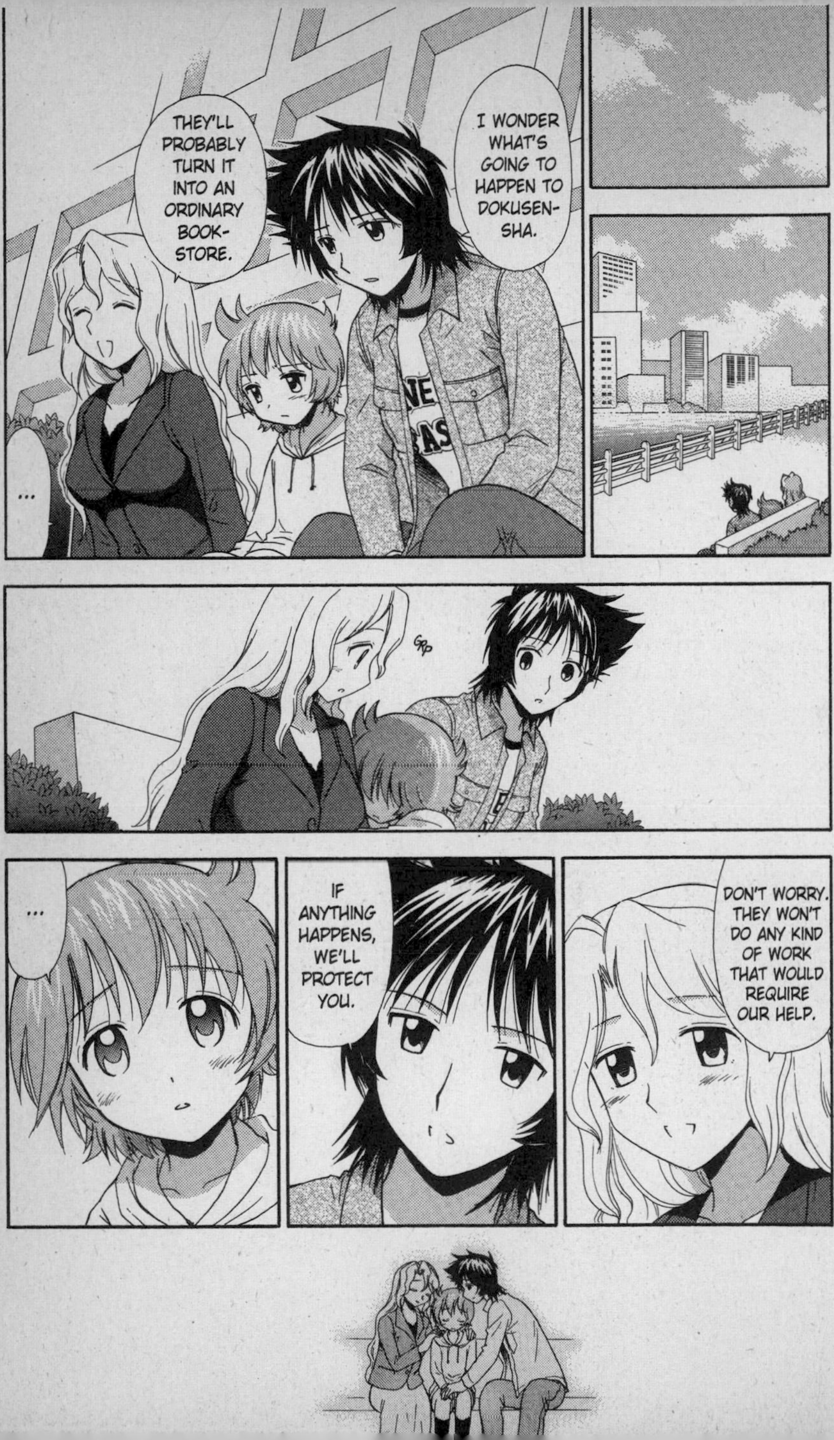
I WONDER WHAT'S GOING TO HAPPEN TO DOKUSEN-SHA.
THEY'LL PROBABLY TURN IT INTO AN ORDINARY BOOK-STORE.
...
GRP
DON'T WORRY. THEY WON'T DO ANY KIND OF WORK THAT WOULD REQUIRE OUR HELP.
IF ANYTHING HAPPENS, WE'LL PROTECT YOU.
...

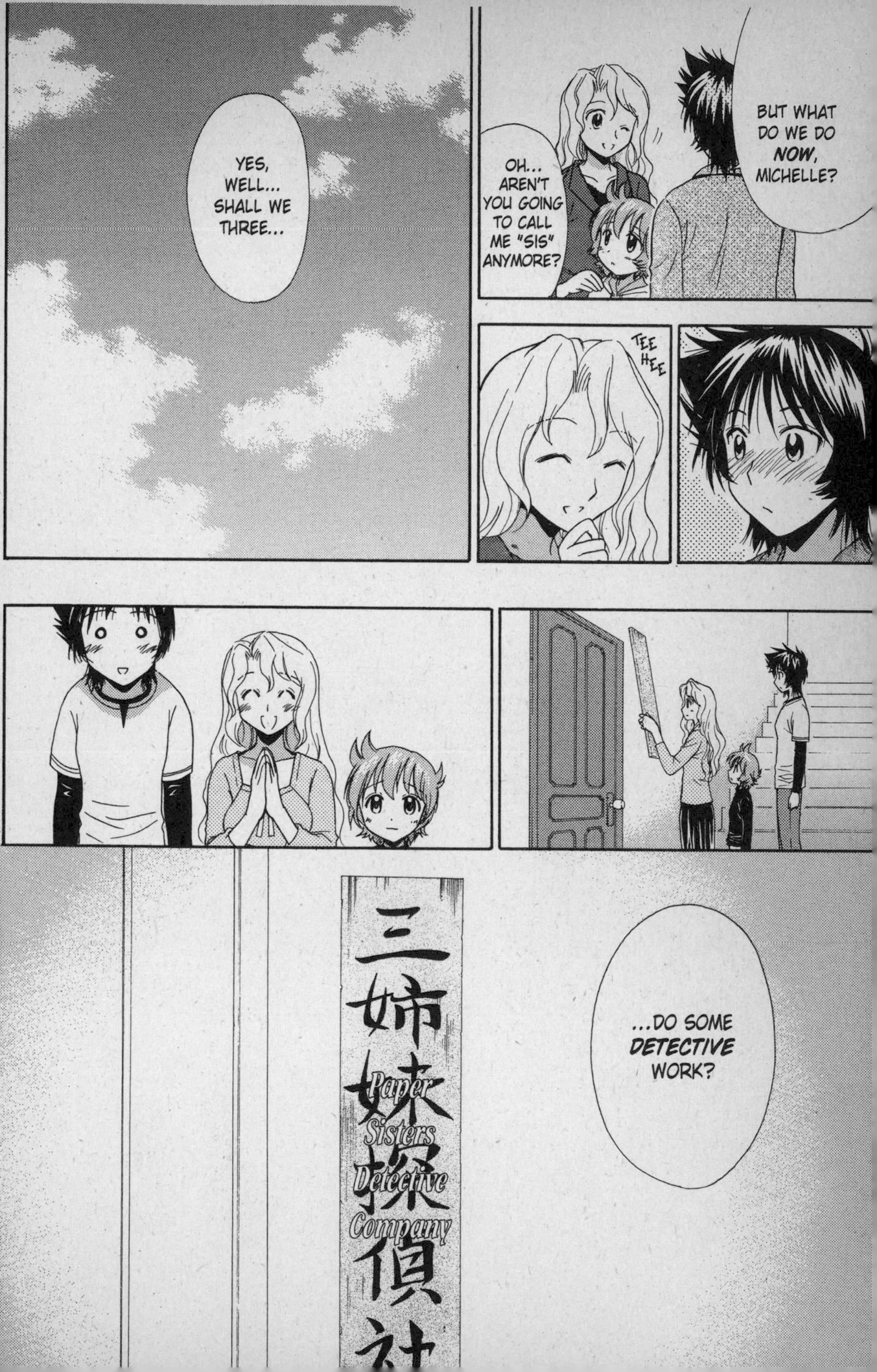
BUT WHAT DO WE DO **NOW**, MICHELLE?
OH... AREN'T YOU GOING TO CALL ME "SIS" ANYMORE?
TEE HEE
YES, WELL... SHALL WE THREE...
...DO SOME **DETECTIVE** WORK?
三姉妹探偵社
Paper Sisters Detective Company

THE FINAL CHAPTER

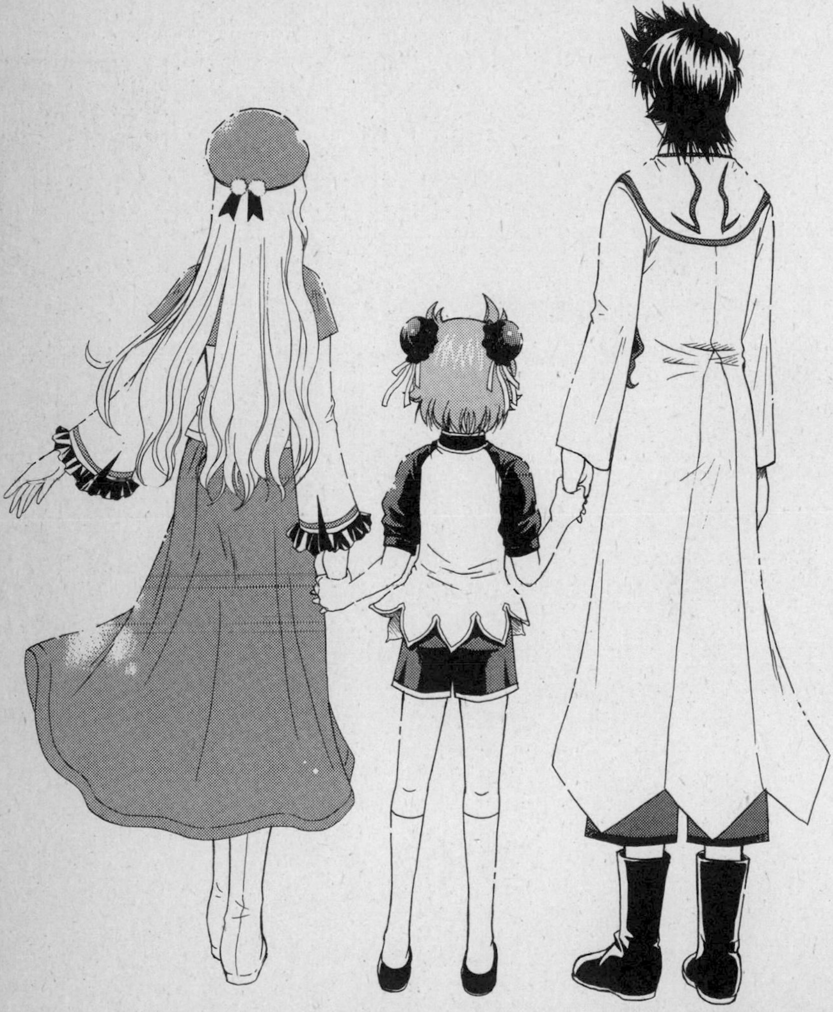

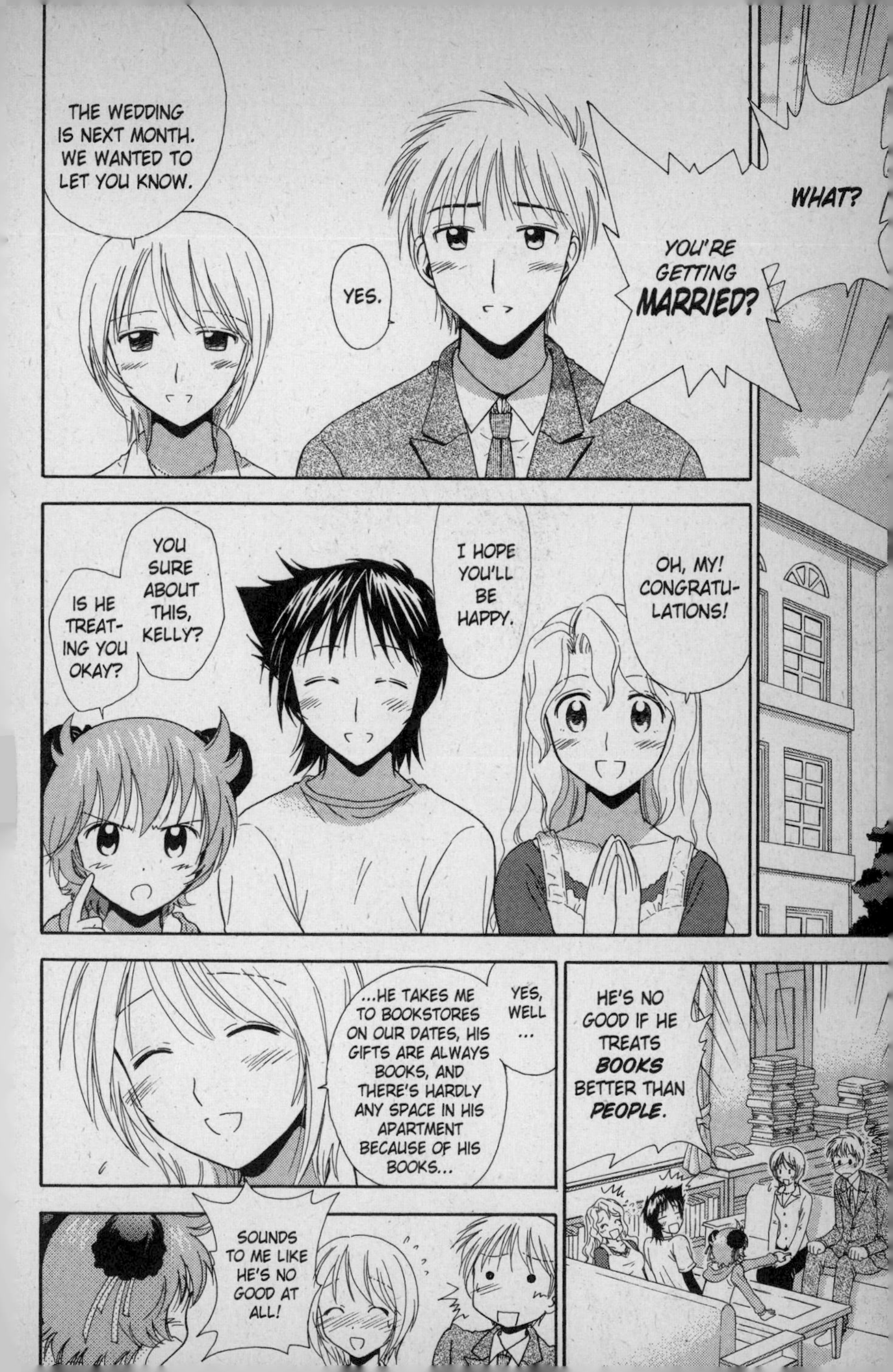

THE WEDDING IS NEXT MONTH. WE WANTED TO LET YOU KNOW.
YES.
WHAT?
YOU'RE GETTING MARRIED?
OH, MY! CONGRATU-LATIONS!
I HOPE YOU'LL BE HAPPY.
YOU SURE ABOUT THIS, KELLY?
IS HE TREAT-ING YOU OKAY?
HE'S NO GOOD IF HE TREATS BOOKS BETTER THAN PEOPLE.
YES, WELL ...
...HE TAKES ME TO BOOKSTORES ON OUR DATES, HIS GIFTS ARE ALWAYS BOOKS, AND THERE'S HARDLY ANY SPACE IN HIS APARTMENT BECAUSE OF HIS BOOKS...
SOUNDS TO ME LIKE HE'S NO GOOD AT ALL!

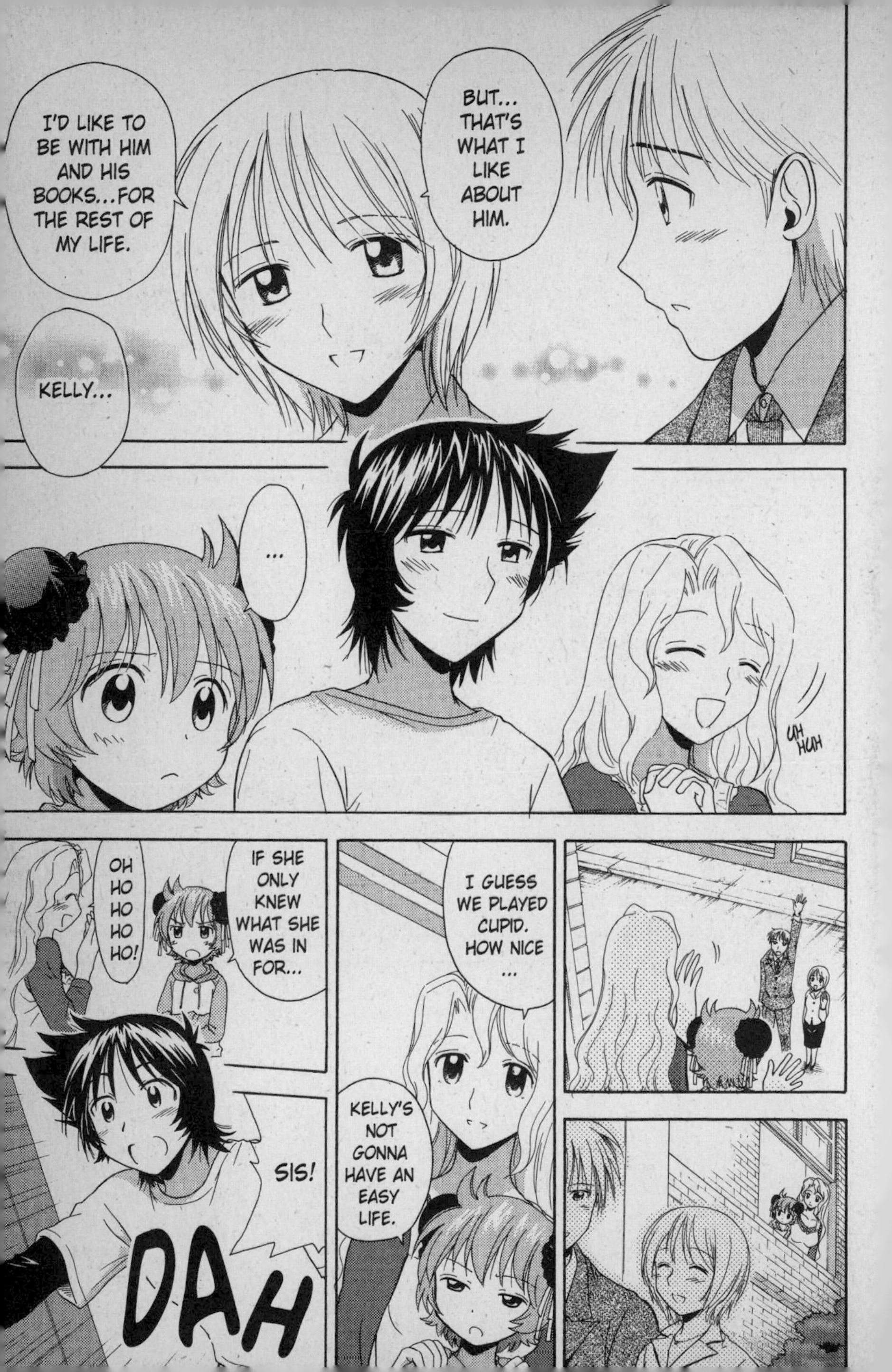
BUT... THAT'S WHAT I LIKE ABOUT HIM.
I'D LIKE TO BE WITH HIM AND HIS BOOKS...FOR THE REST OF MY LIFE.
KELLY...
UH HUH
...
I GUESS WE PLAYED CUPID. HOW NICE ...
KELLY'S NOT GONNA HAVE AN EASY LIFE.
IF SHE ONLY KNEW WHAT SHE WAS IN FOR...
OH HO HO HO HO!
SIS!
DAH

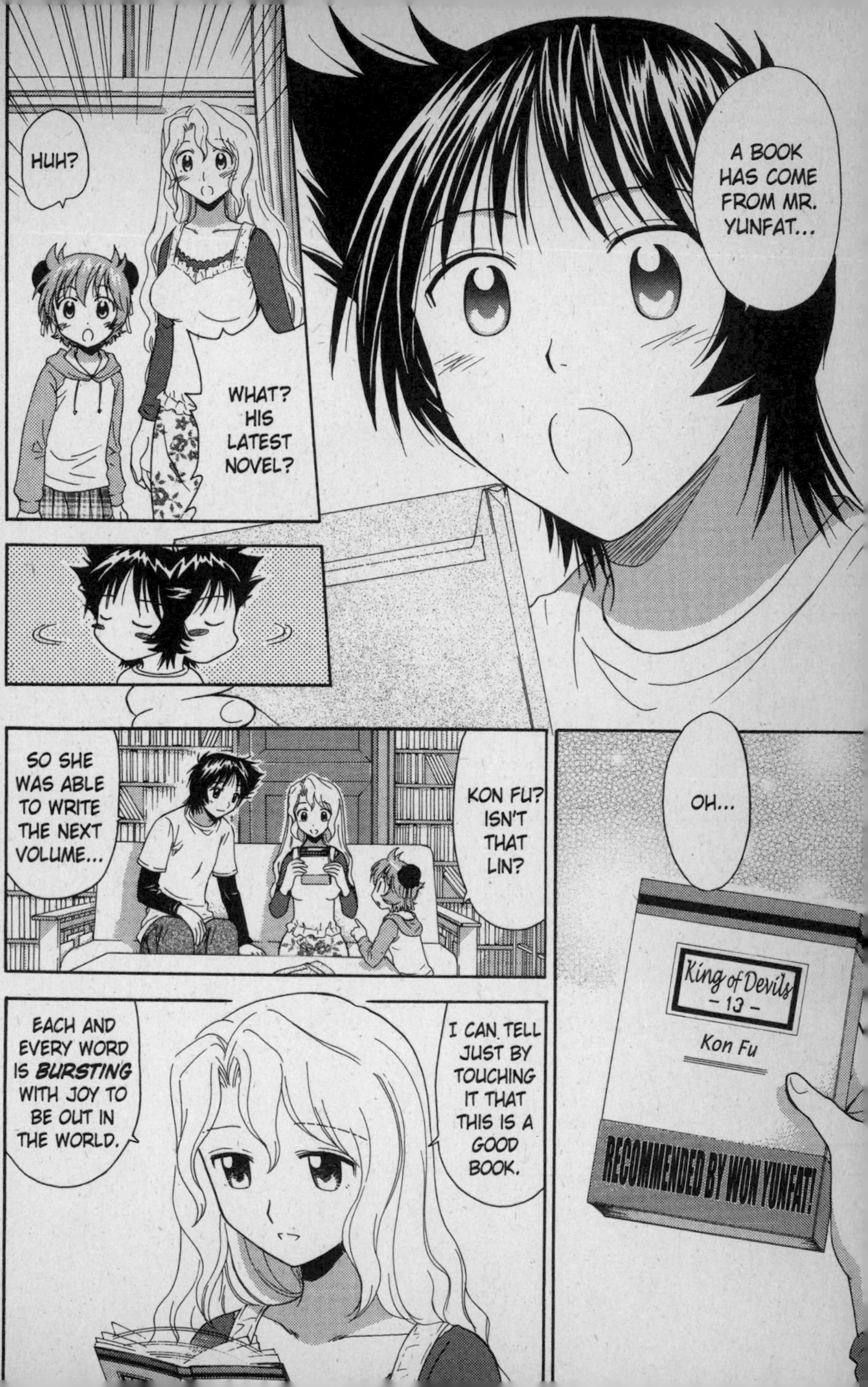
A BOOK HAS COME FROM MR. YUNFAT...
HUH?
WHAT? HIS LATEST NOVEL?
OH...
King of Devils
-13-
Kon Fu
RECOMMENDED BY WON YUNFAT!
KON FU? ISN'T THAT LIN?
SO SHE WAS ABLE TO WRITE THE NEXT VOLUME...
I CAN TELL JUST BY TOUCHING IT THAT THIS IS A GOOD BOOK.
EACH AND EVERY WORD IS BURSTING WITH JOY TO BE OUT IN THE WORLD.

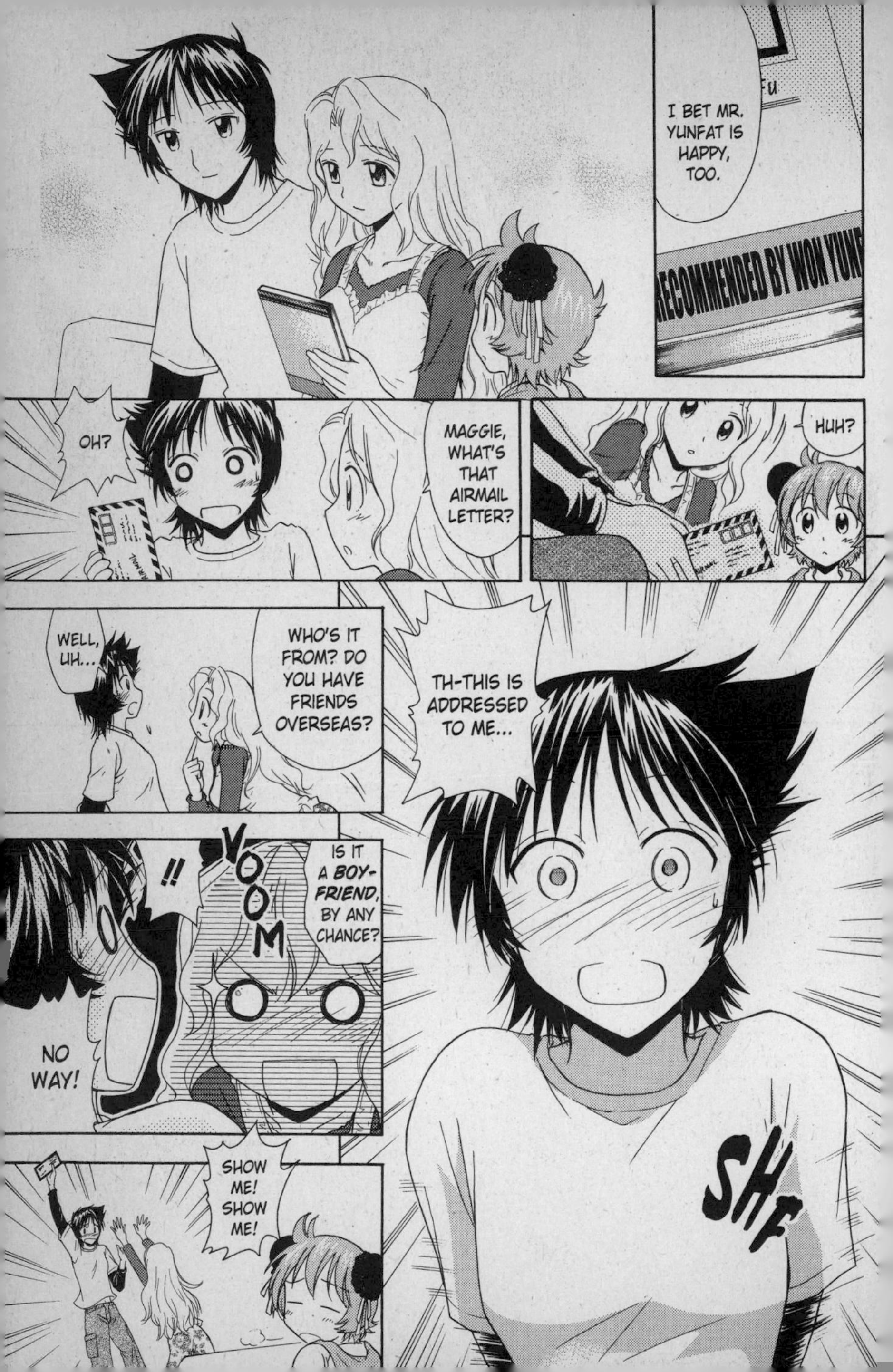
I BET MR. YUNFAT IS HAPPY, TOO.
RECOMMENDED BY WON YUN
HUH?
MAGGIE, WHAT'S THAT AIRMAIL LETTER?
OH?
TH-THIS IS ADDRESSED TO ME...
SHF
WHO'S IT FROM? DO YOU HAVE FRIENDS OVERSEAS?
WELL, UH...
IS IT A *BOY-FRIEND*, BY ANY CHANCE?
VOOM
!!
NO WAY!
SHOW ME! SHOW ME!

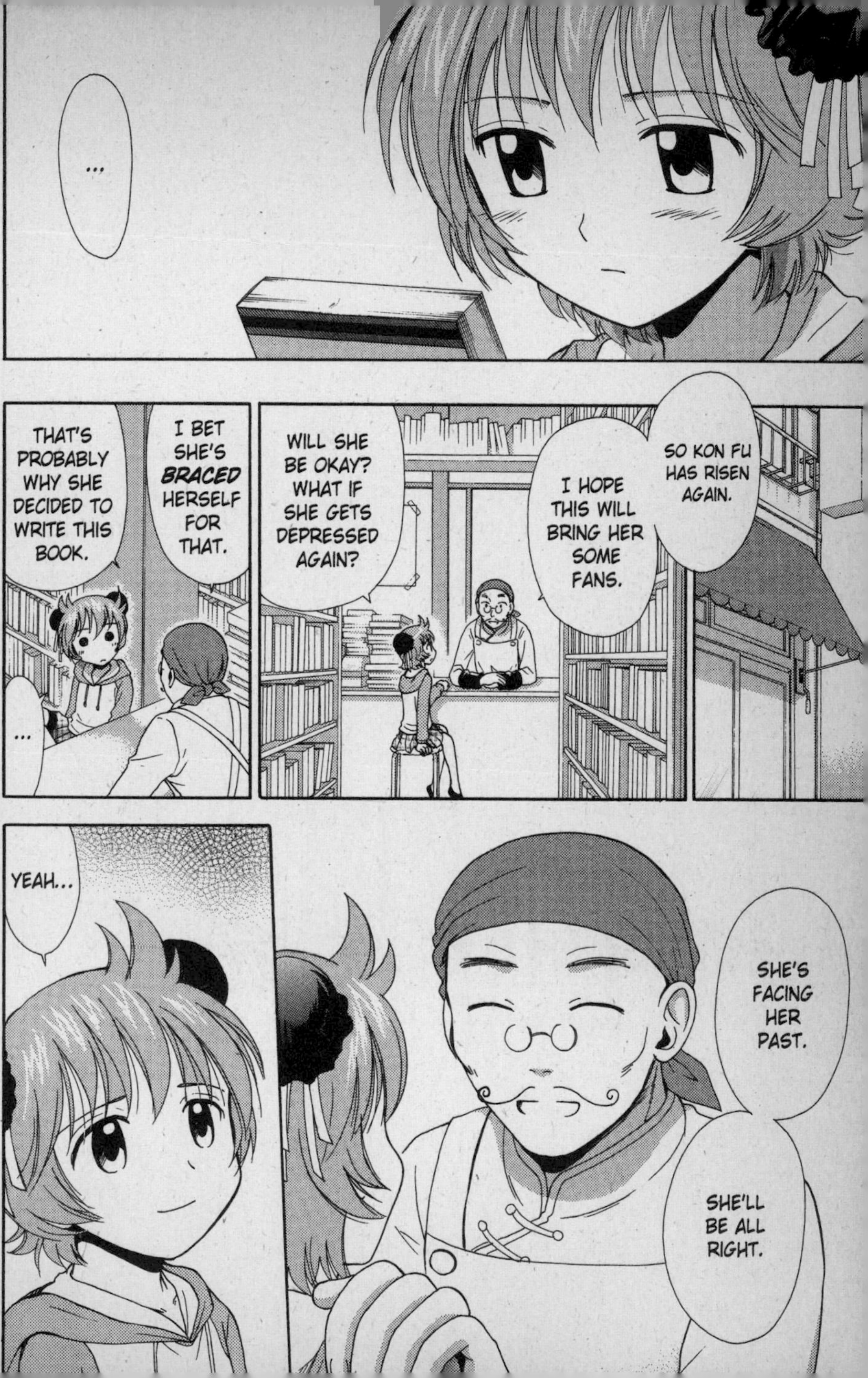

...,
SO KON FU HAS RISEN AGAIN.
I HOPE THIS WILL BRING HER SOME FANS.
WILL SHE BE OKAY? WHAT IF SHE GETS DEPRESSED AGAIN?
I BET SHE'S BRACED HERSELF FOR THAT.
THAT'S PROBABLY WHY SHE DECIDED TO WRITE THIS BOOK.
...
SHE'S FACING HER PAST.
SHE'LL BE ALL RIGHT.
YEAH...

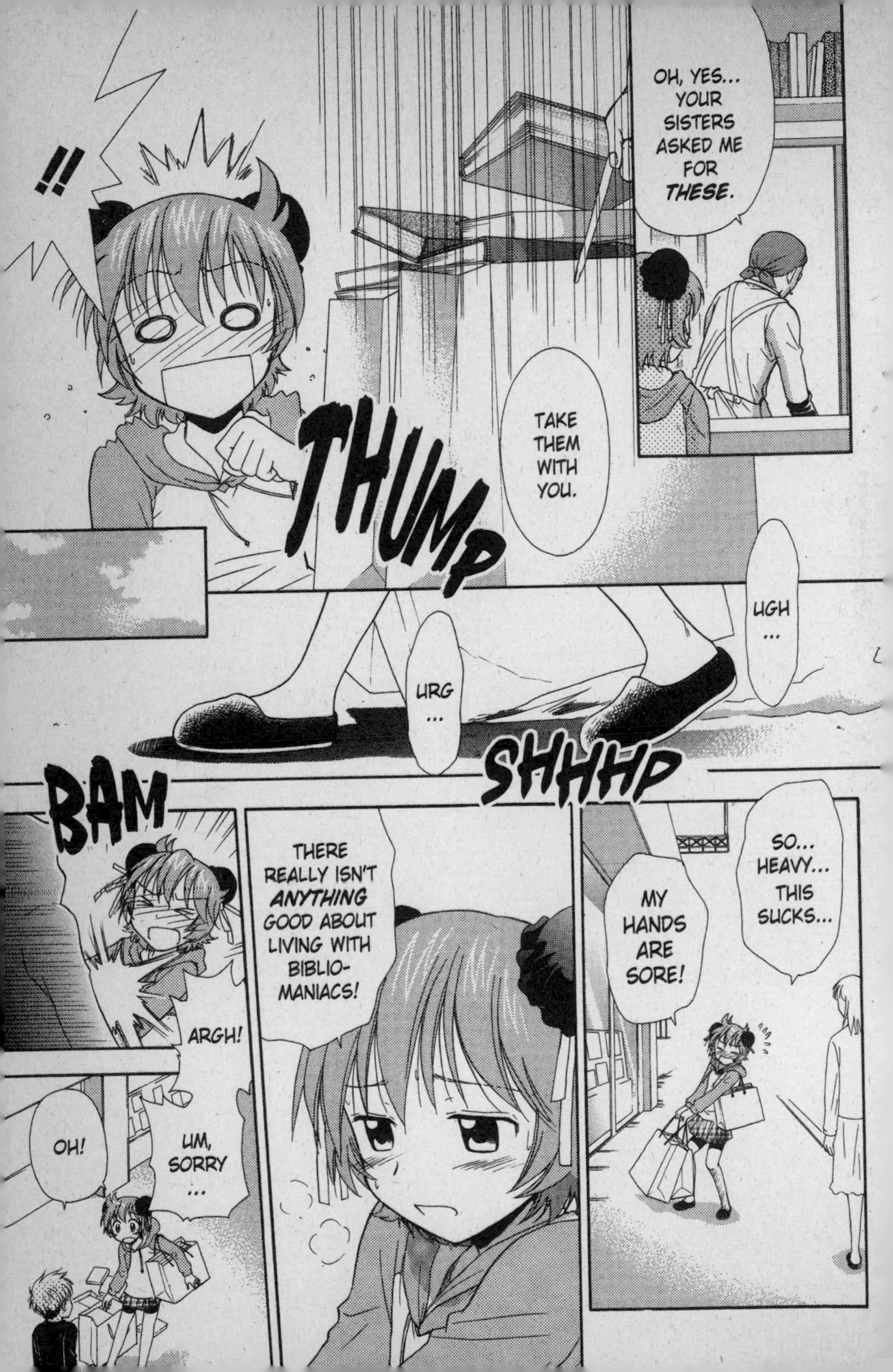
OH, YES... YOUR SISTERS ASKED ME FOR *THESE*.
TAKE THEM WITH YOU.
!!
THUMP
UGH...
URG...
SHHHP
SO... HEAVY... THIS SUCKS...
MY HANDS ARE SORE!
THERE REALLY ISN'T *ANYTHING* GOOD ABOUT LIVING WITH BIBLIO-MANIACS!
BAM
ARGH!
UM, SORRY...
OH!

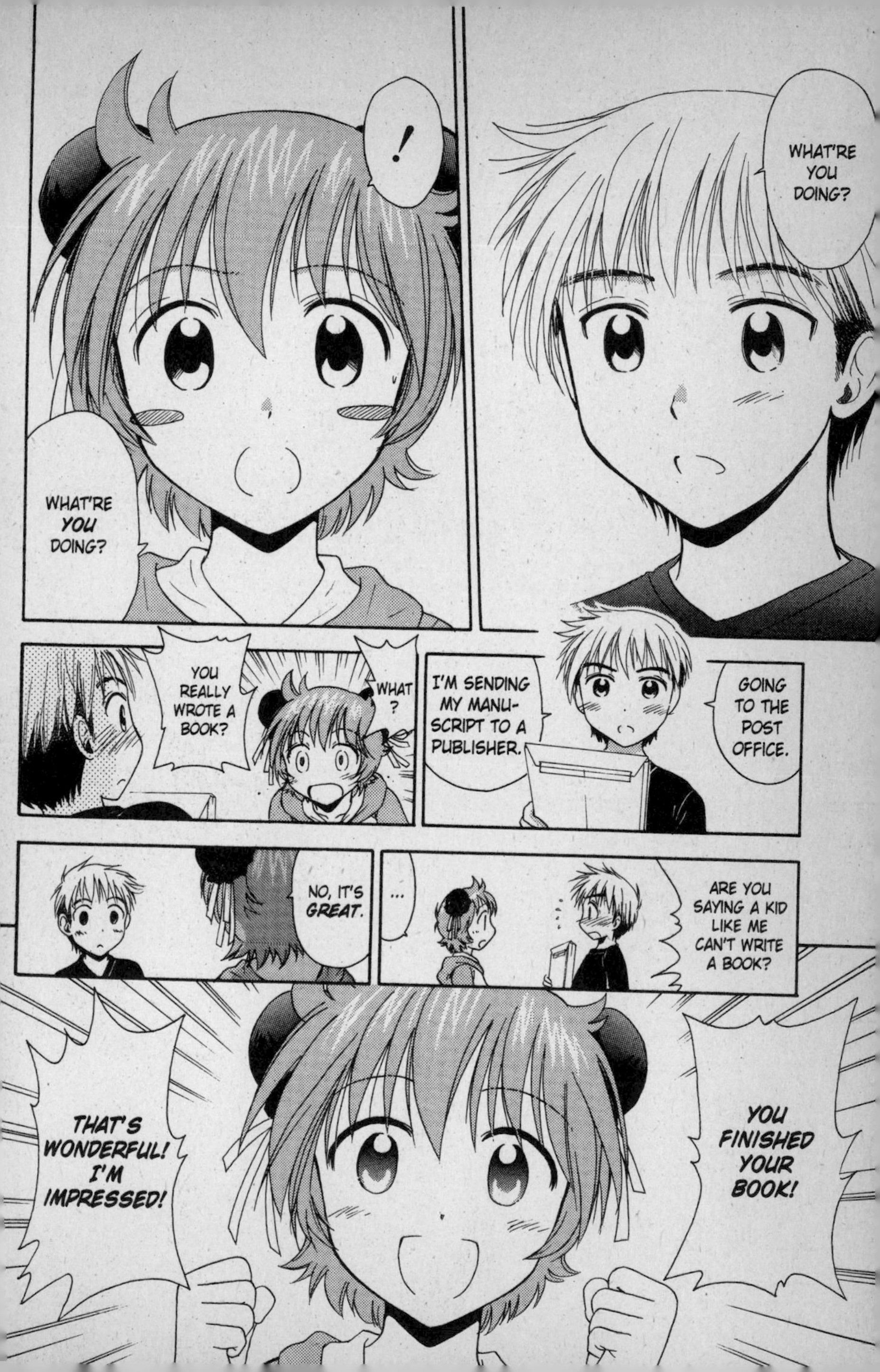
WHAT'RE YOU DOING?
!
WHAT'RE *YOU* DOING?
GOING TO THE POST OFFICE.
I'M SENDING MY MANU-SCRIPT TO A PUBLISHER.
WHAT?
YOU REALLY WROTE A BOOK?
ARE YOU SAYING A KID LIKE ME CAN'T WRITE A BOOK?
...
NO, IT'S *GREAT*.
YOU FINISHED YOUR BOOK!
THAT'S WONDERFUL! I'M IMPRESSED!

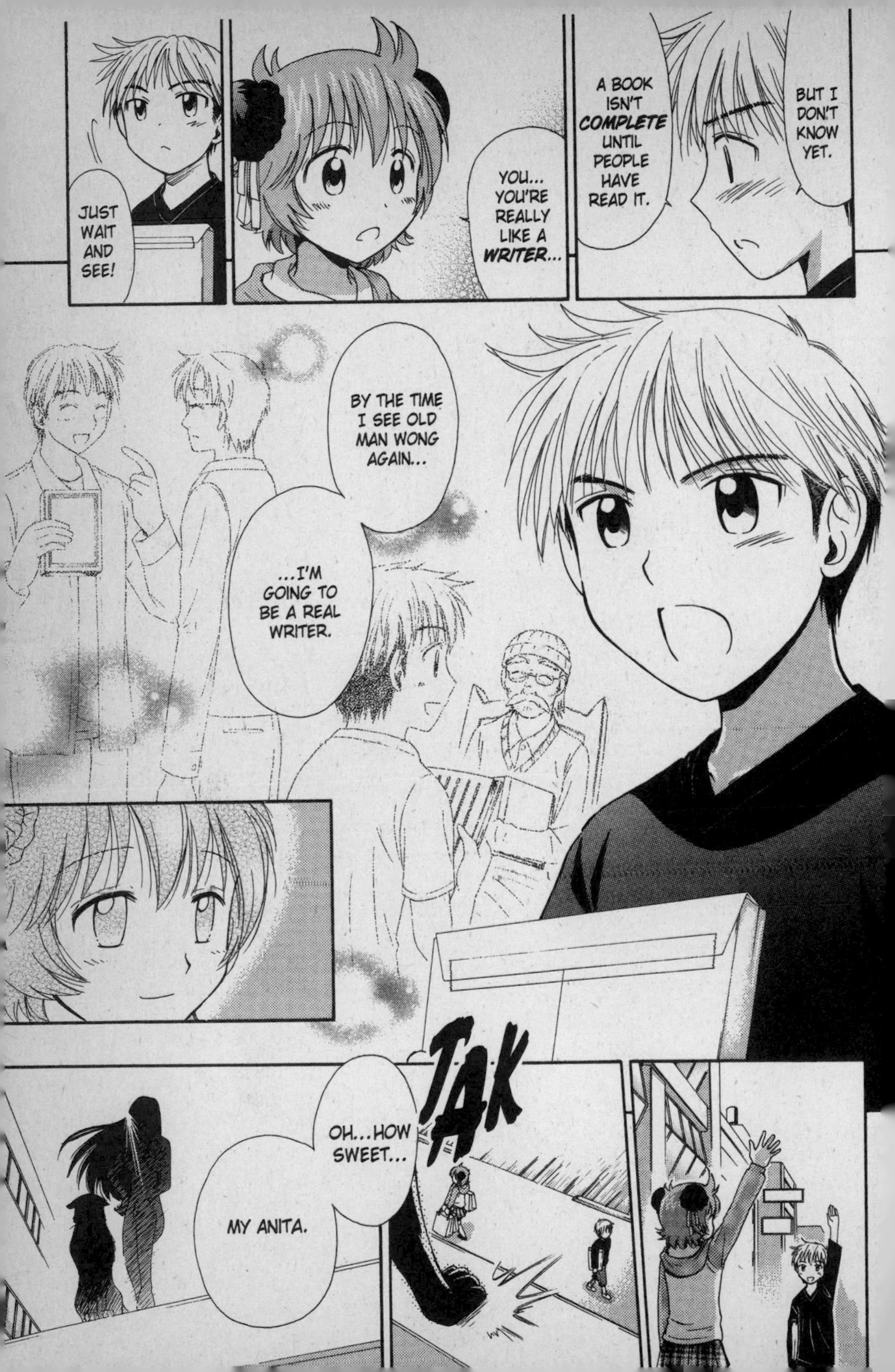
BUT I DON'T KNOW YET.
A BOOK ISN'T COMPLETE UNTIL PEOPLE HAVE READ IT.
YOU... YOU'RE REALLY LIKE A WRITER...
JUST WAIT AND SEE!
BY THE TIME I SEE OLD MAN WONG AGAIN...
...I'M GOING TO BE A REAL WRITER.
TAK
OH...HOW SWEET...
MY ANITA.

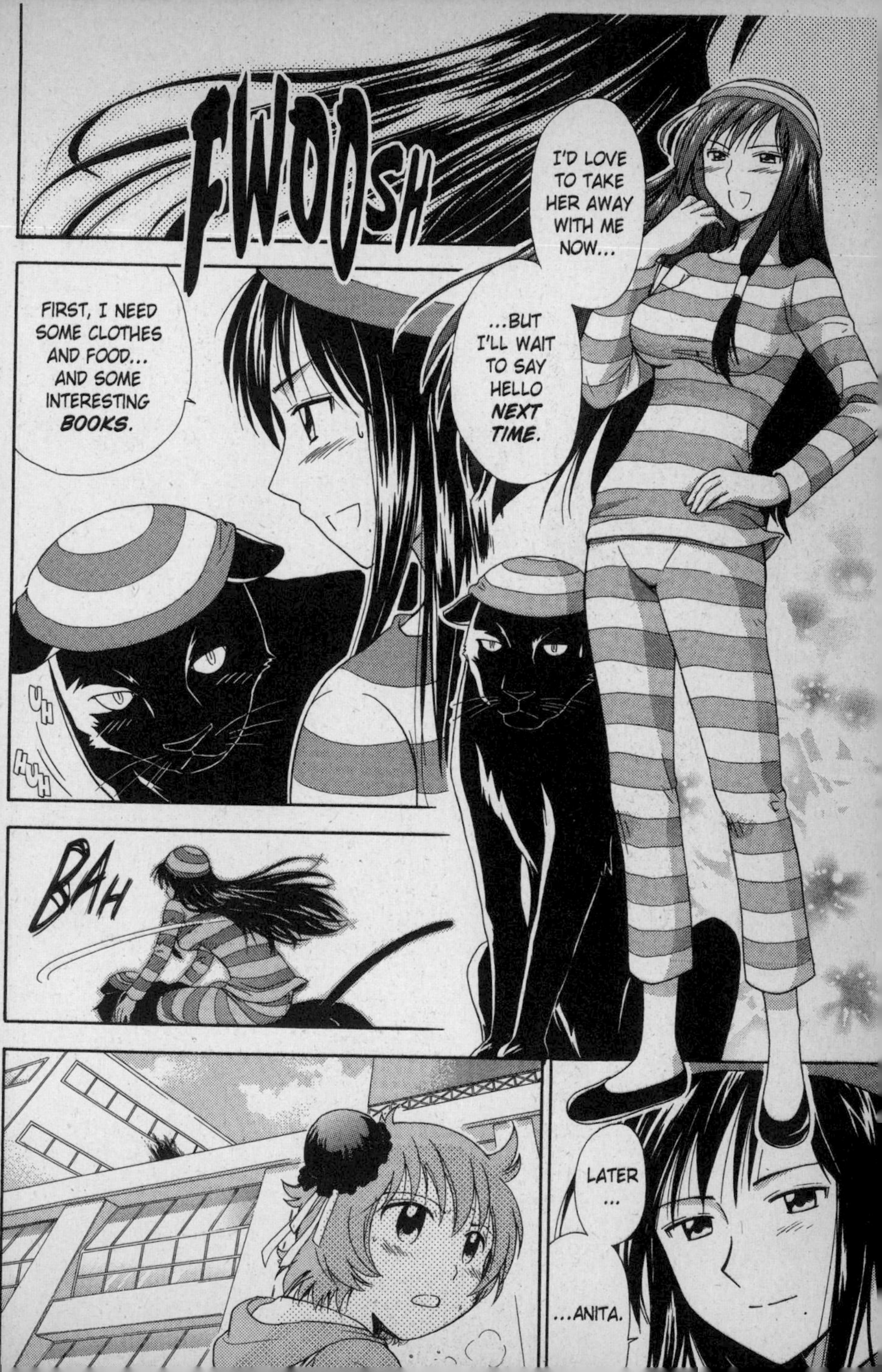
FWOOSH
I'D LOVE TO TAKE HER AWAY WITH ME NOW...
...BUT I'LL WAIT TO SAY HELLO *NEXT TIME*.
FIRST, I NEED SOME CLOTHES AND FOOD... AND SOME INTERESTING *BOOKS*.
UH HUH
BAH
LATER...
...ANITA.

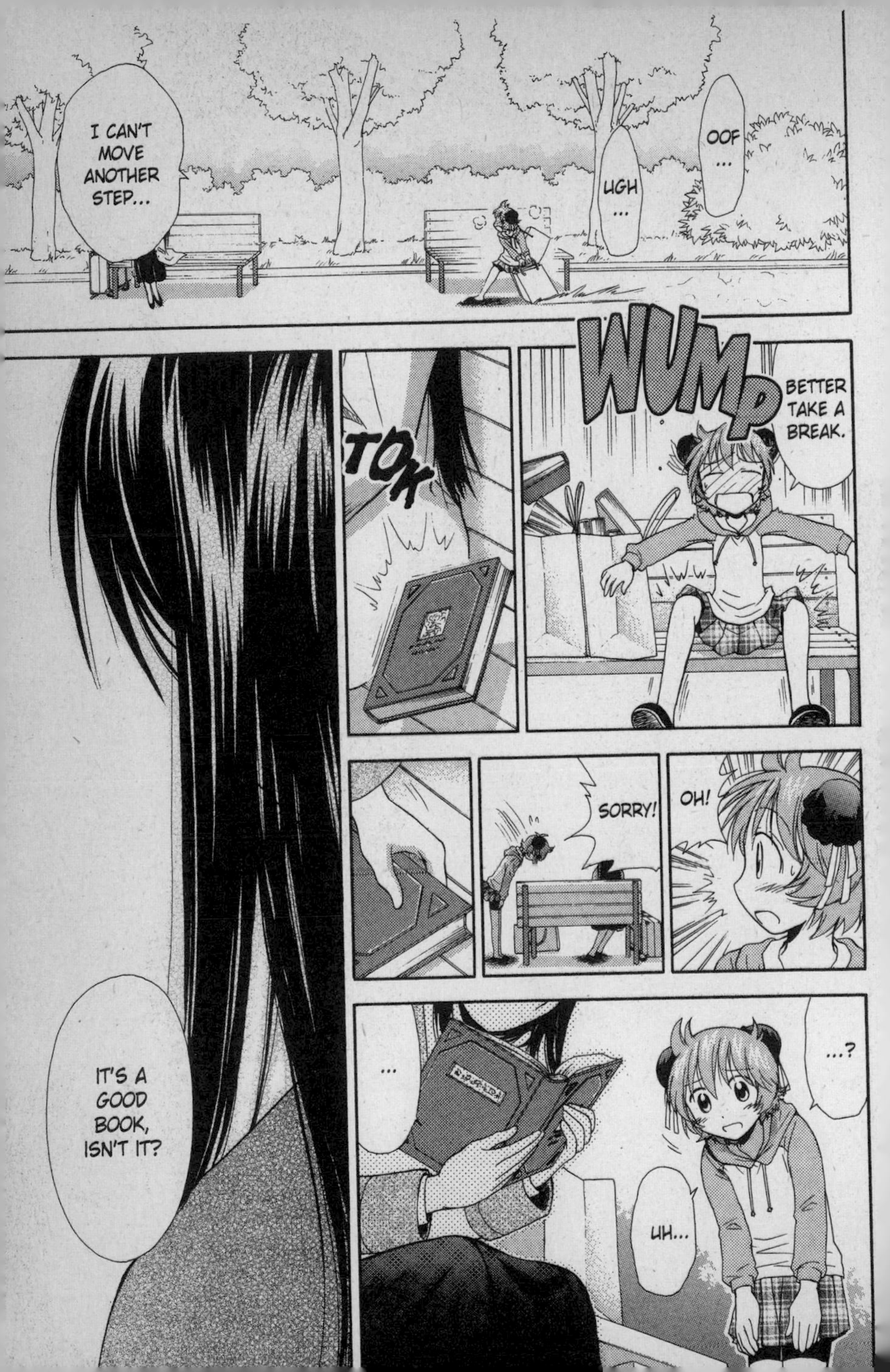
OOF ...
UGH ...
I CAN'T MOVE ANOTHER STEP...
WUMP
BETTER TAKE A BREAK.
TOK
OH!
SORRY!
...?
UH...
...
IT'S A GOOD BOOK, ISN'T IT?

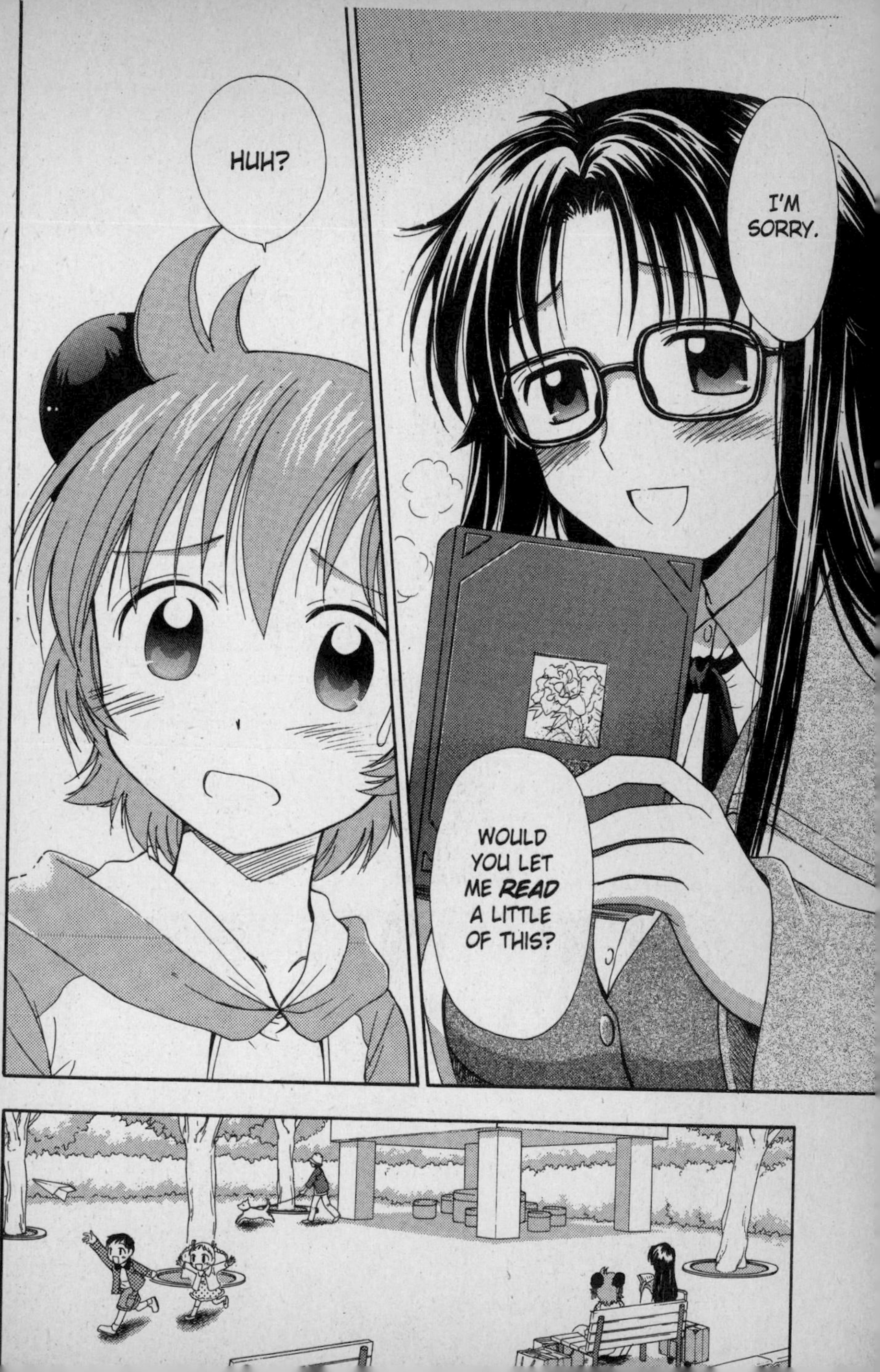
I'M SORRY.
WOULD YOU LET ME *READ* A LITTLE OF THIS?
HUH?

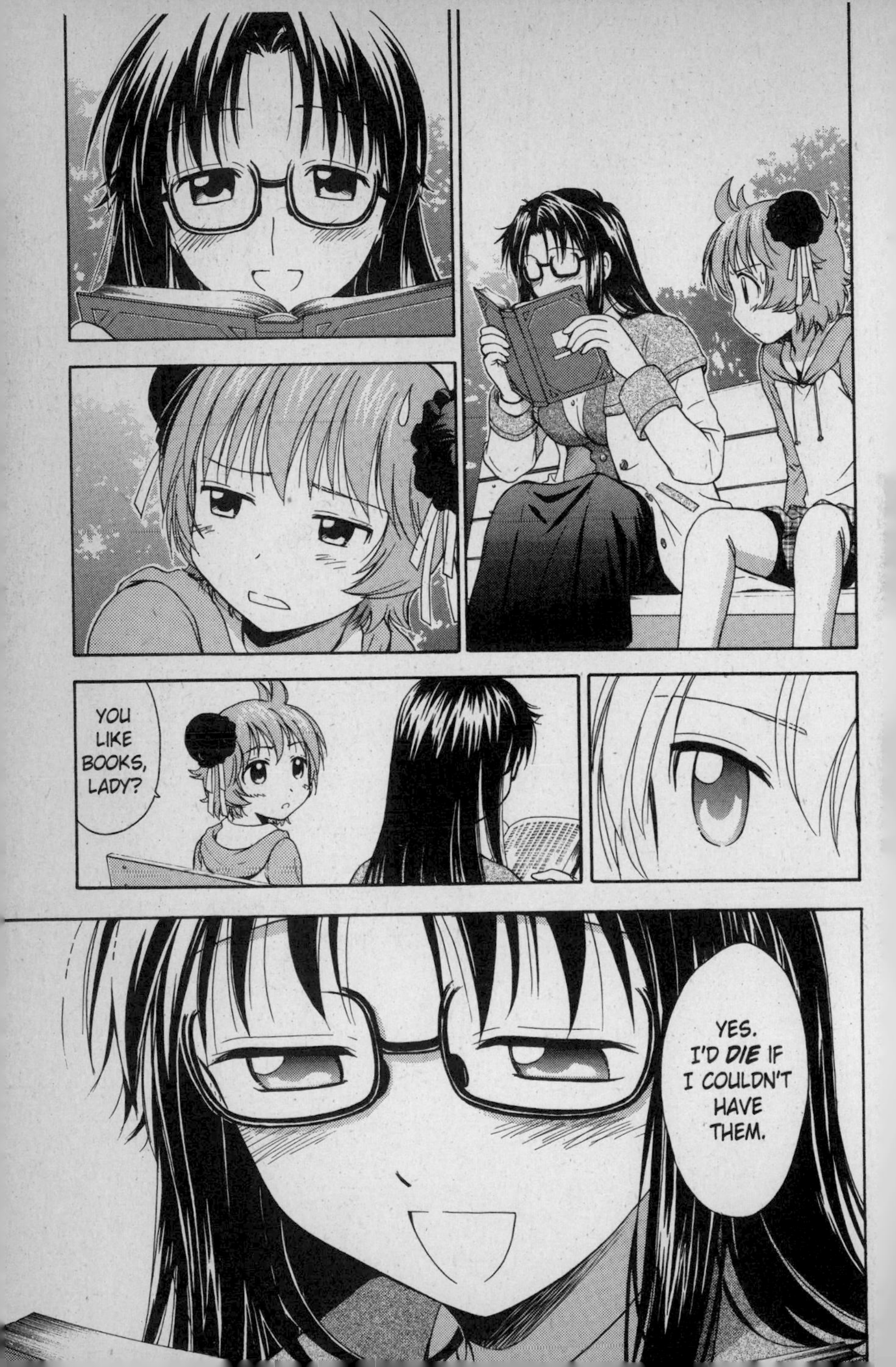
YOU LIKE BOOKS, LADY?
YES. I'D ***DIE*** IF I COULDN'T HAVE THEM.

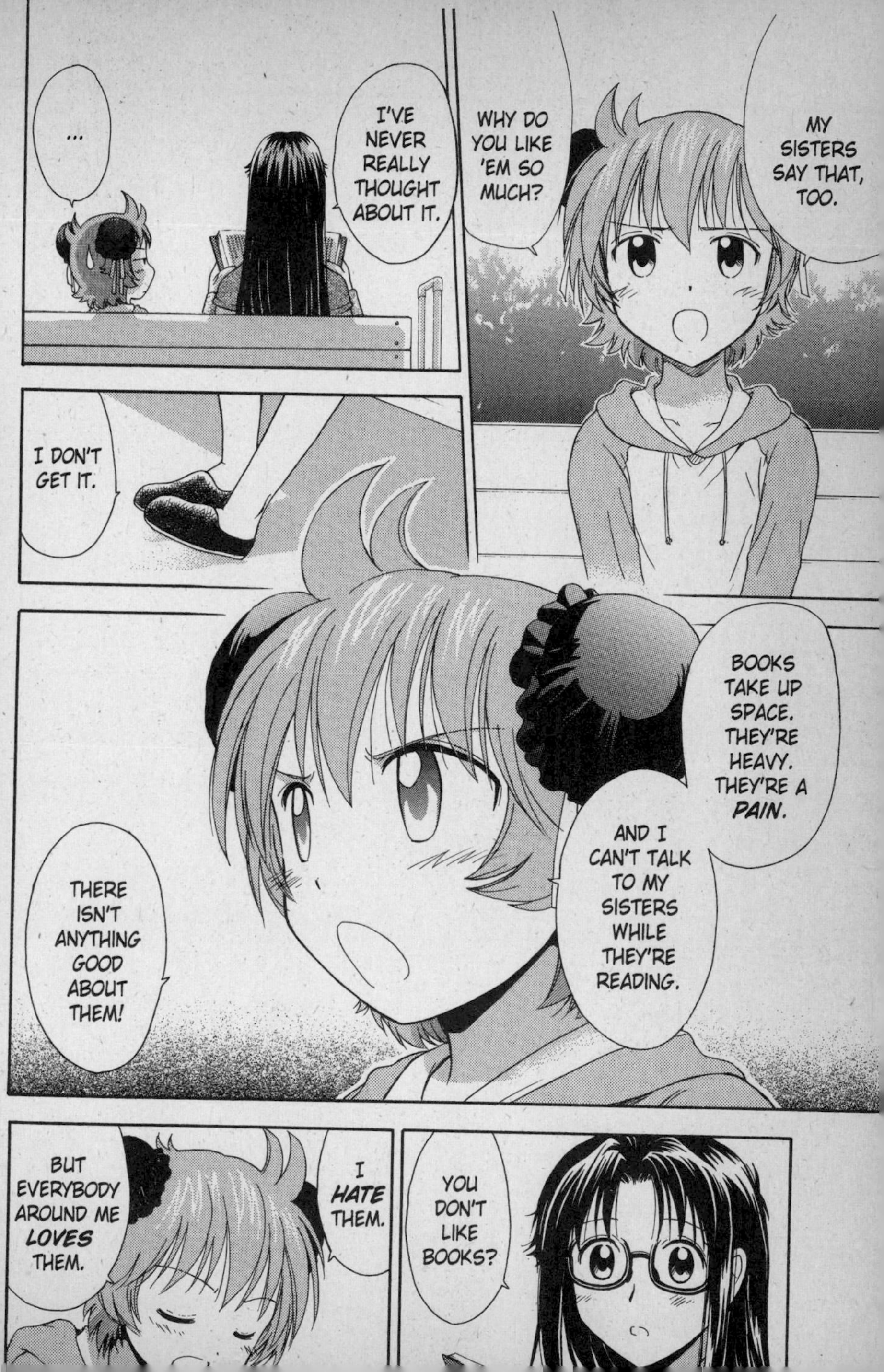
MY SISTERS SAY THAT, TOO.
WHY DO YOU LIKE 'EM SO MUCH?
I'VE NEVER REALLY THOUGHT ABOUT IT.
...
I DON'T GET IT.
BOOKS TAKE UP SPACE. THEY'RE HEAVY. THEY'RE A ***PAIN***.
AND I CAN'T TALK TO MY SISTERS WHILE THEY'RE READING.
THERE ISN'T ANYTHING GOOD ABOUT THEM!
YOU DON'T LIKE BOOKS?
I ***HATE*** THEM.
BUT EVERYBODY AROUND ME ***LOVES*** THEM.

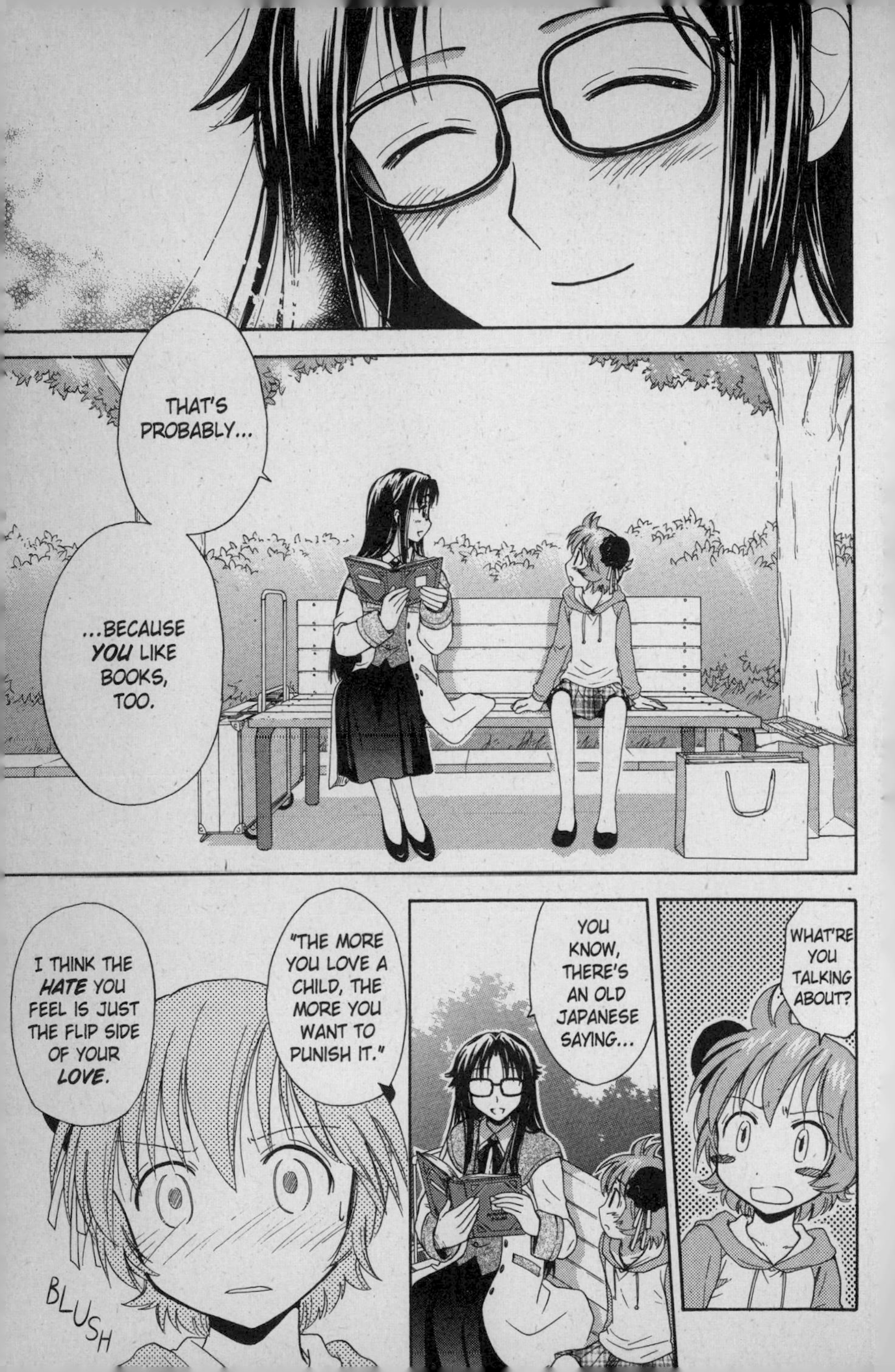
THAT'S PROBABLY...
...BECAUSE YOU LIKE BOOKS, TOO.
WHAT'RE YOU TALKING ABOUT?
YOU KNOW, THERE'S AN OLD JAPANESE SAYING...
"THE MORE YOU LOVE A CHILD, THE MORE YOU WANT TO PUNISH IT."
I THINK THE HATE YOU FEEL IS JUST THE FLIP SIDE OF YOUR LOVE.
BLUSH

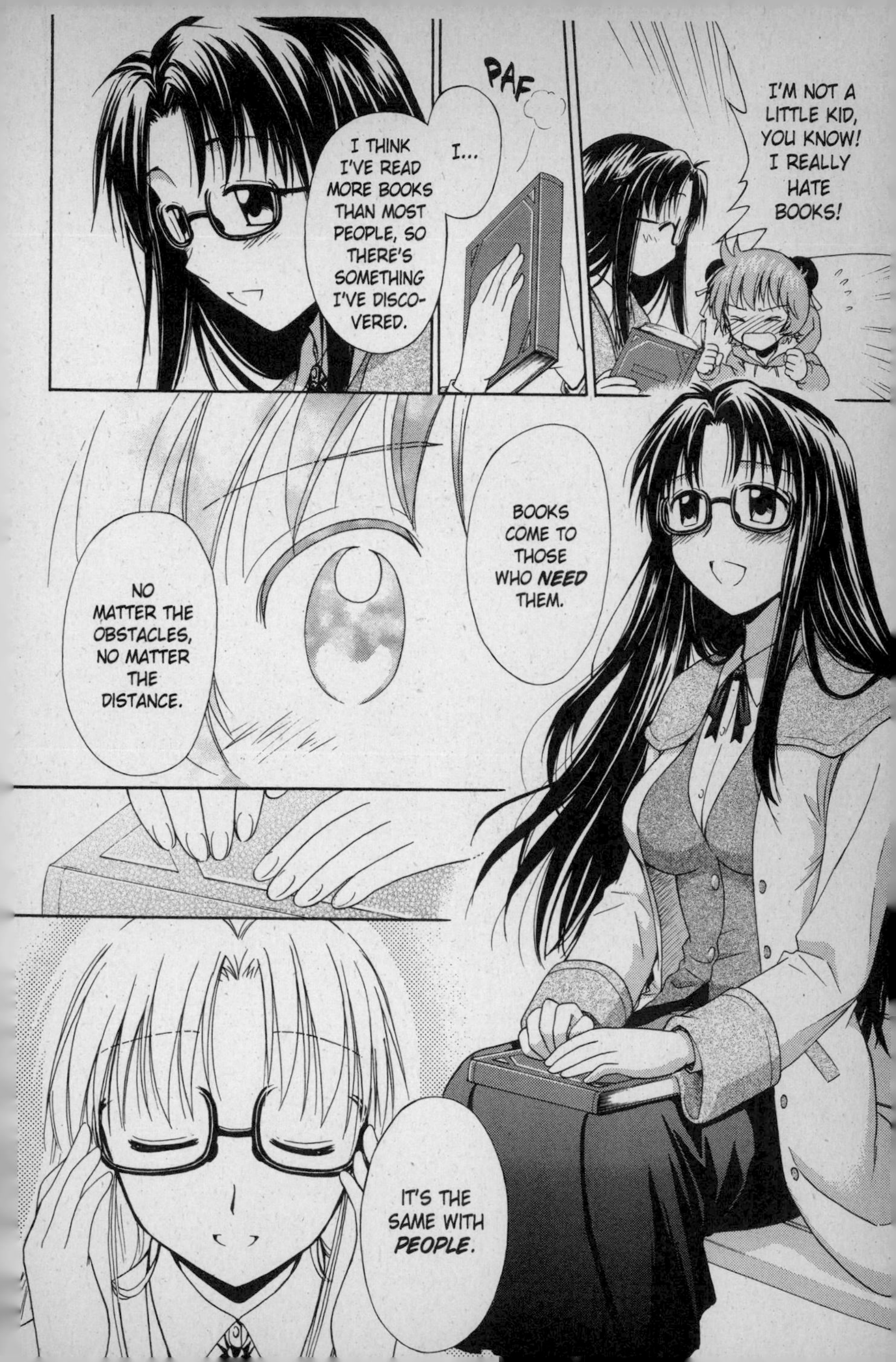
I'M NOT A LITTLE KID, YOU KNOW! I REALLY HATE BOOKS!
PAF
I...
I THINK I'VE READ MORE BOOKS THAN MOST PEOPLE, SO THERE'S SOMETHING I'VE DISCOVERED.
BOOKS COME TO THOSE WHO *NEED* THEM.
NO MATTER THE OBSTACLES, NO MATTER THE DISTANCE.
IT'S THE SAME WITH **PEOPLE**.

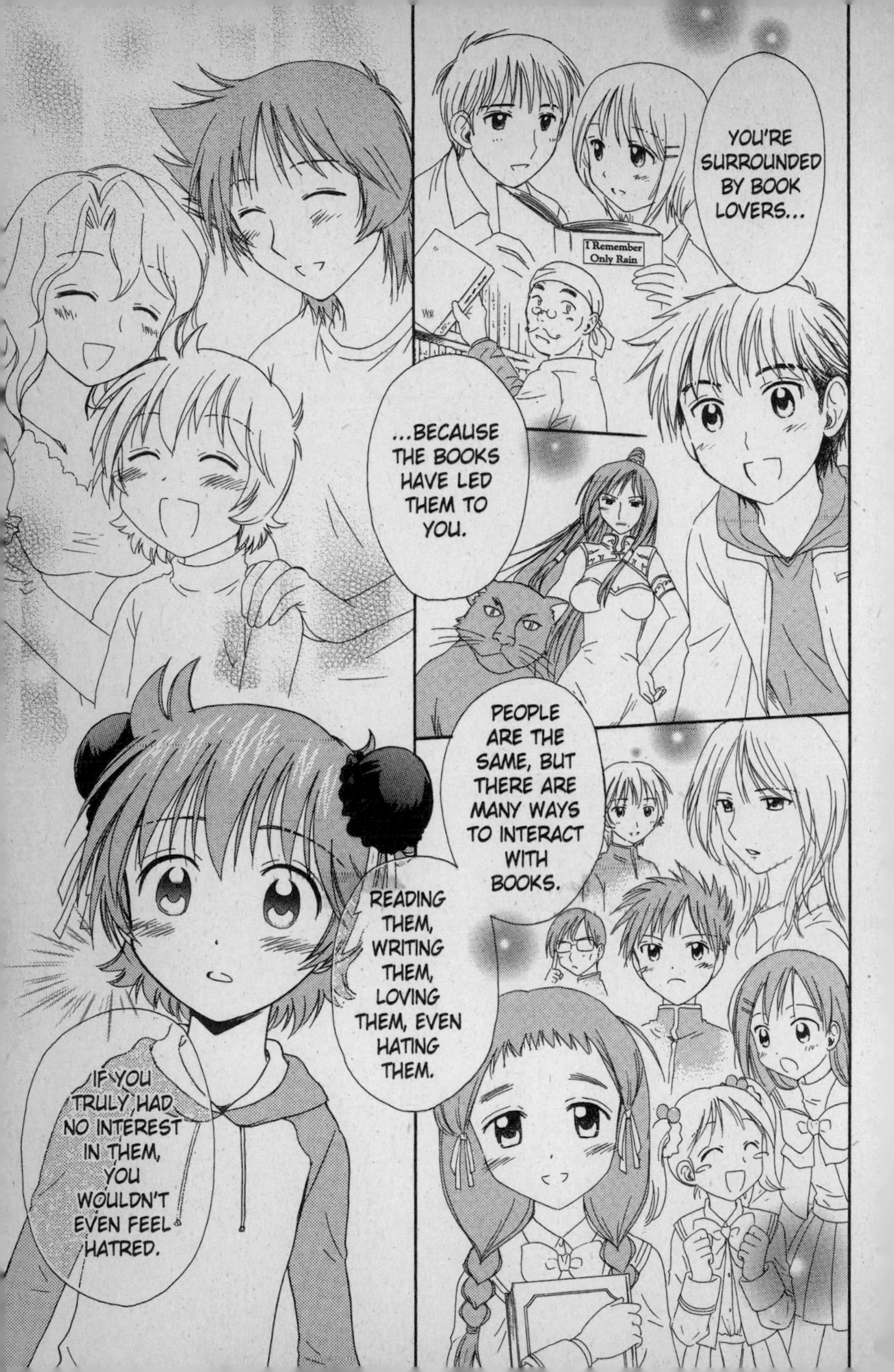
YOU'RE SURROUNDED BY BOOK LOVERS...
I Remember Only Rain
...BECAUSE THE BOOKS HAVE LED THEM TO YOU.
PEOPLE ARE THE SAME, BUT THERE ARE MANY WAYS TO INTERACT WITH BOOKS.
READING THEM, WRITING THEM, LOVING THEM, EVEN HATING THEM.
IF YOU TRULY HAD NO INTEREST IN THEM, YOU WOULDN'T EVEN FEEL HATRED.

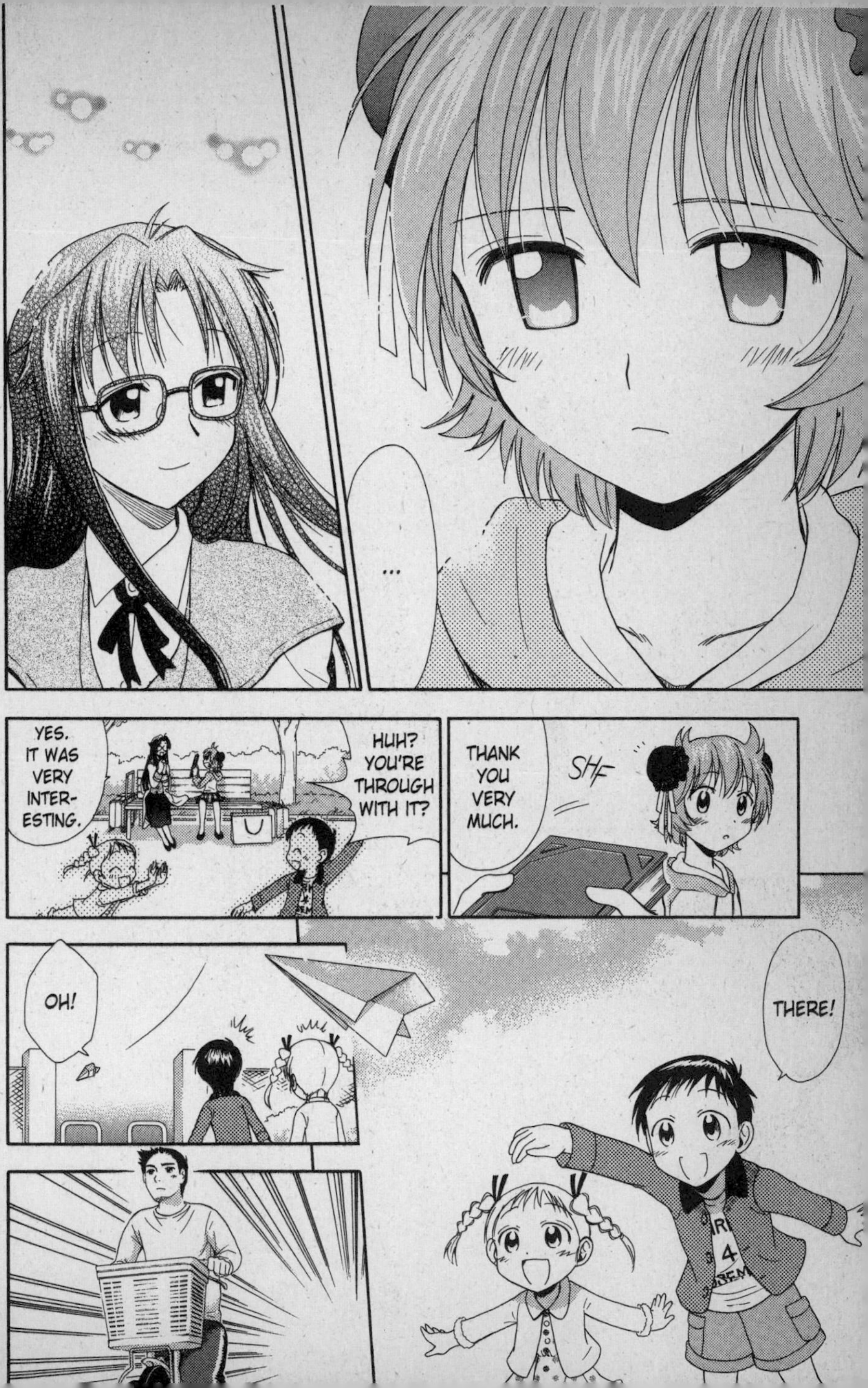
...
THANK YOU VERY MUCH.
SHF
HUH? YOU'RE THROUGH WITH IT?
YES. IT WAS VERY INTER-ESTING.
THERE!
OH!

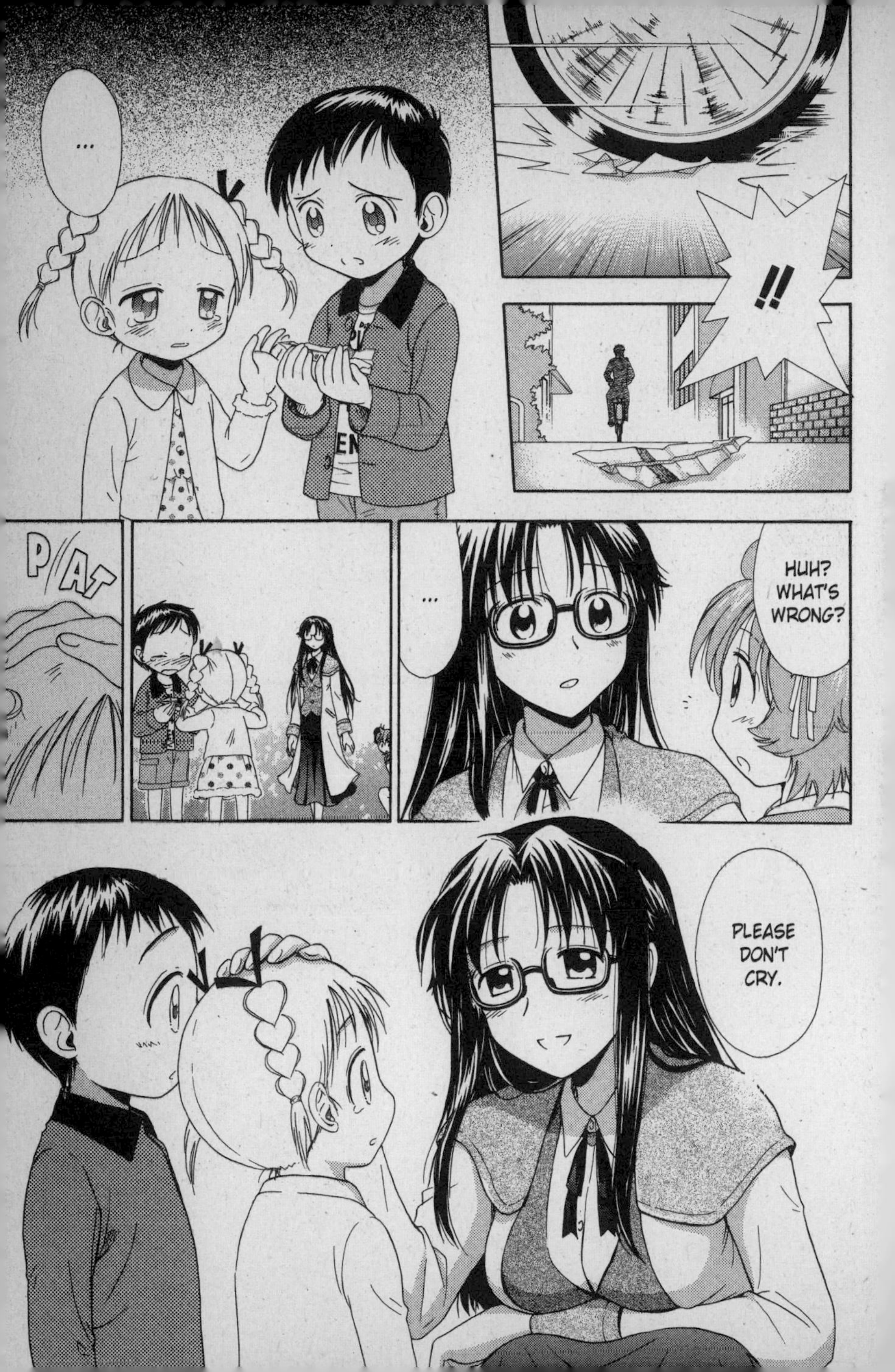
!!
...
HUH? WHAT'S WRONG?
...
PAT
PLEASE DON'T CRY.

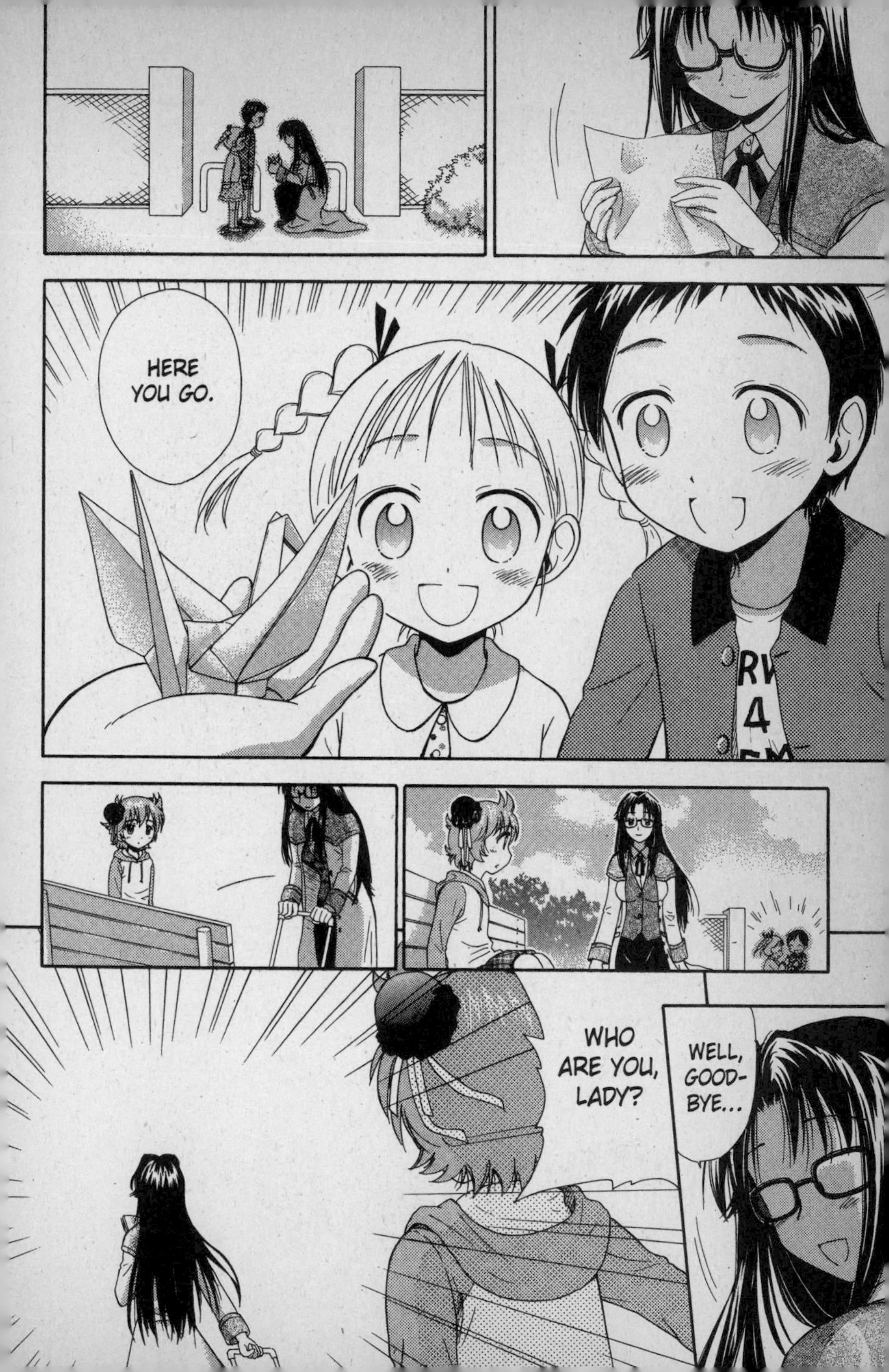
HERE YOU GO.
WELL, GOOD-BYE...
WHO ARE YOU, LADY?

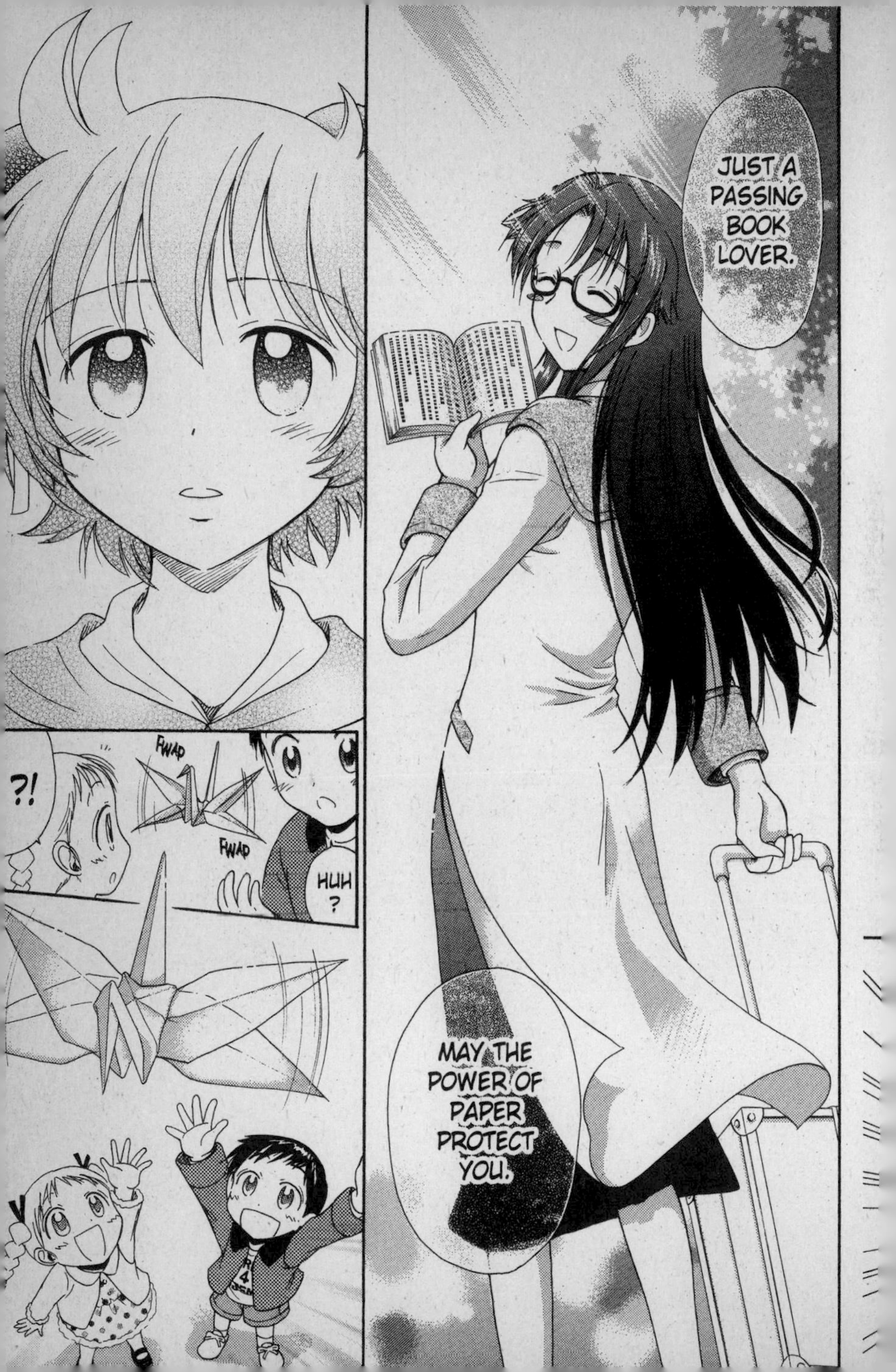
JUST A PASSING BOOK LOVER.
MAY THE POWER OF PAPER PROTECT YOU.
FWAP
HUH ?
FWAP
?!

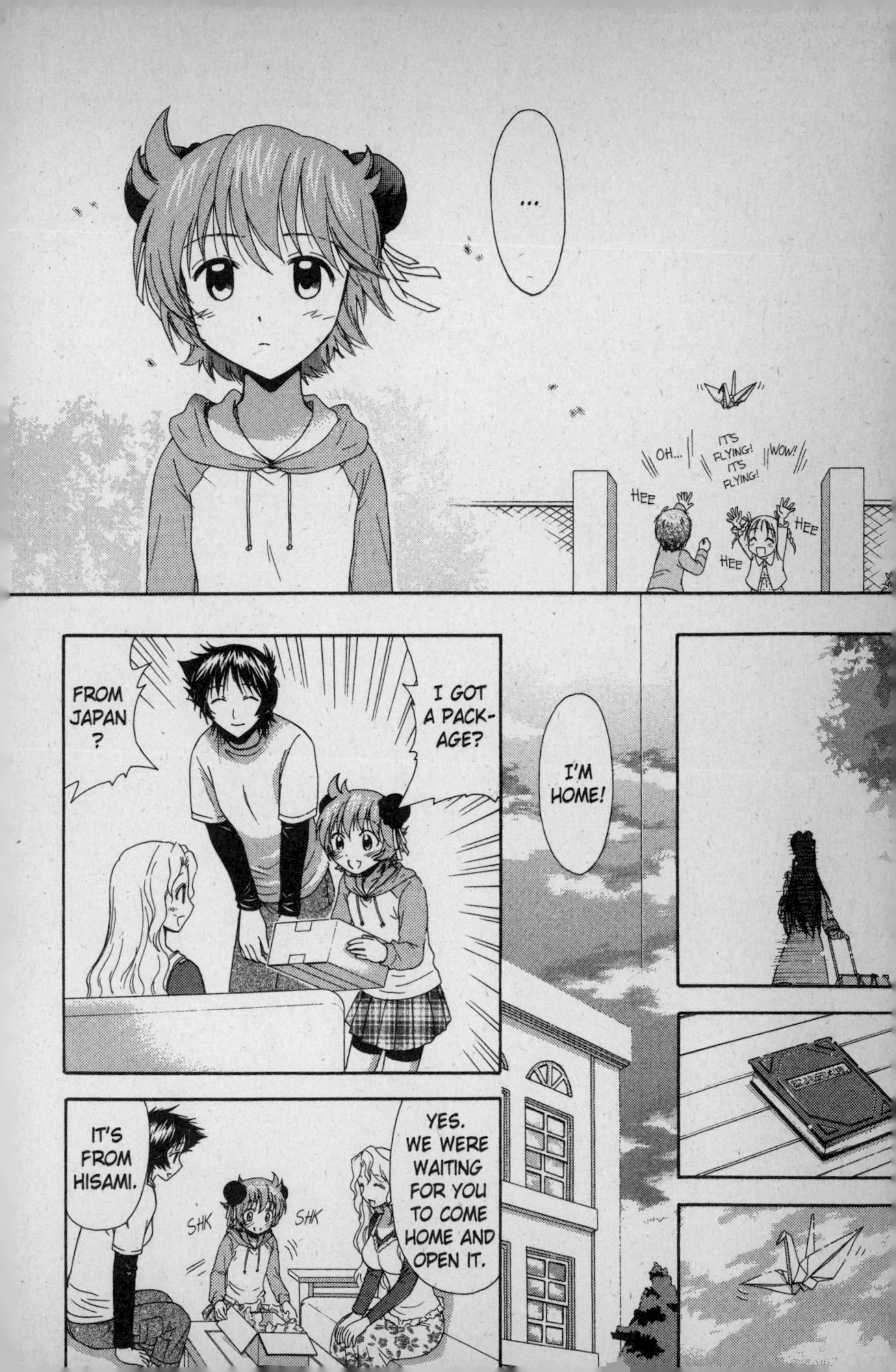
...
WOW!
IT'S FLYING! IT'S FLYING!
OH...
HEE
HEE
HEE
I'M HOME!
I GOT A PACK-AGE?
FROM JAPAN?
YES. WE WERE WAITING FOR YOU TO COME HOME AND OPEN IT.
SHK
SHK
IT'S FROM HISAMI.

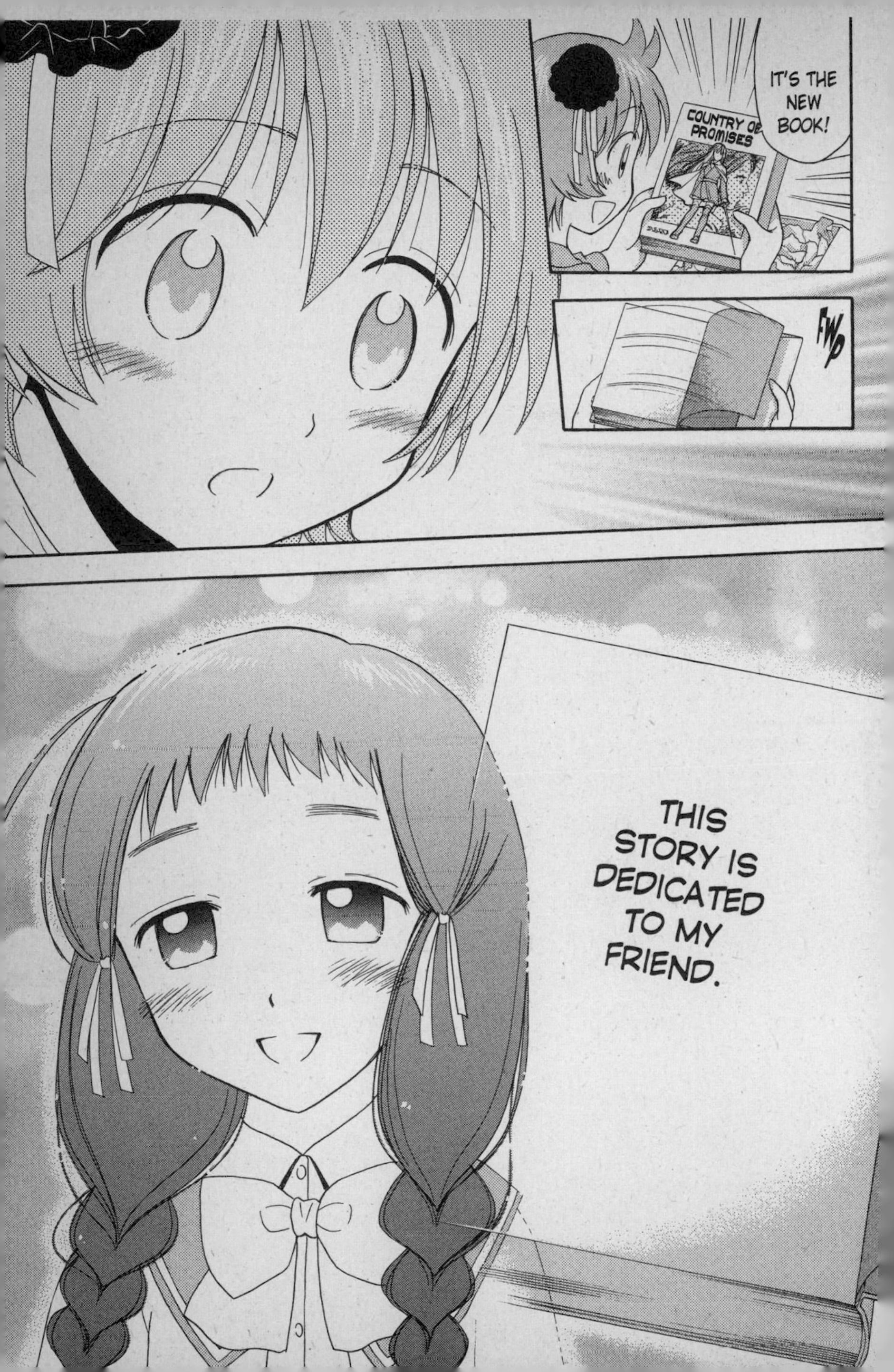
COUNTRY OF PROMISES
IT'S THE NEW BOOK!
FWP
THIS STORY IS DEDICATED TO MY FRIEND.

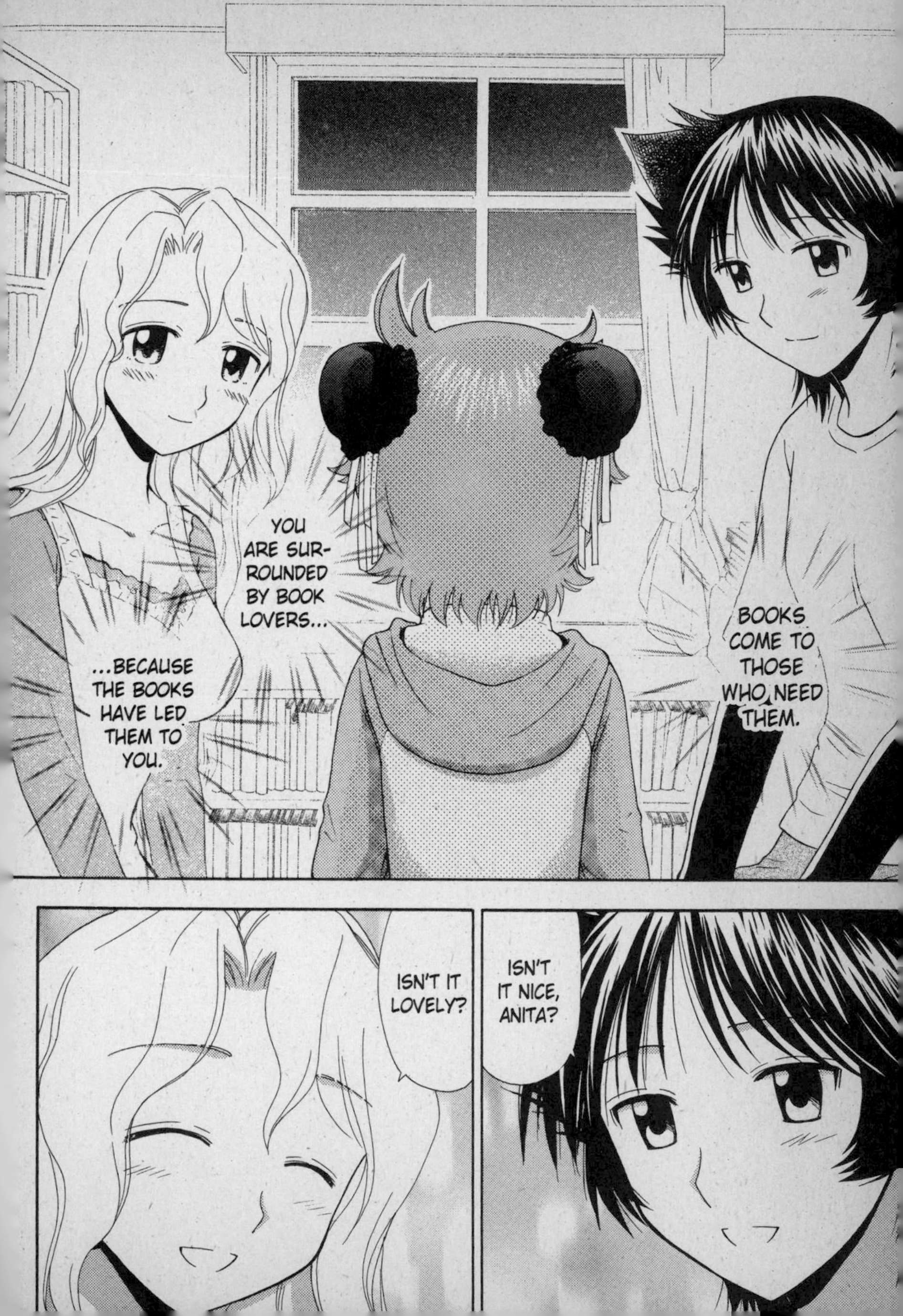
BOOKS COME TO THOSE WHO NEED THEM.
YOU ARE SUR-ROUNDED BY BOOK LOVERS...
...BECAUSE THE BOOKS HAVE LED THEM TO YOU.
ISN'T IT NICE, ANITA?
ISN'T IT LOVELY?

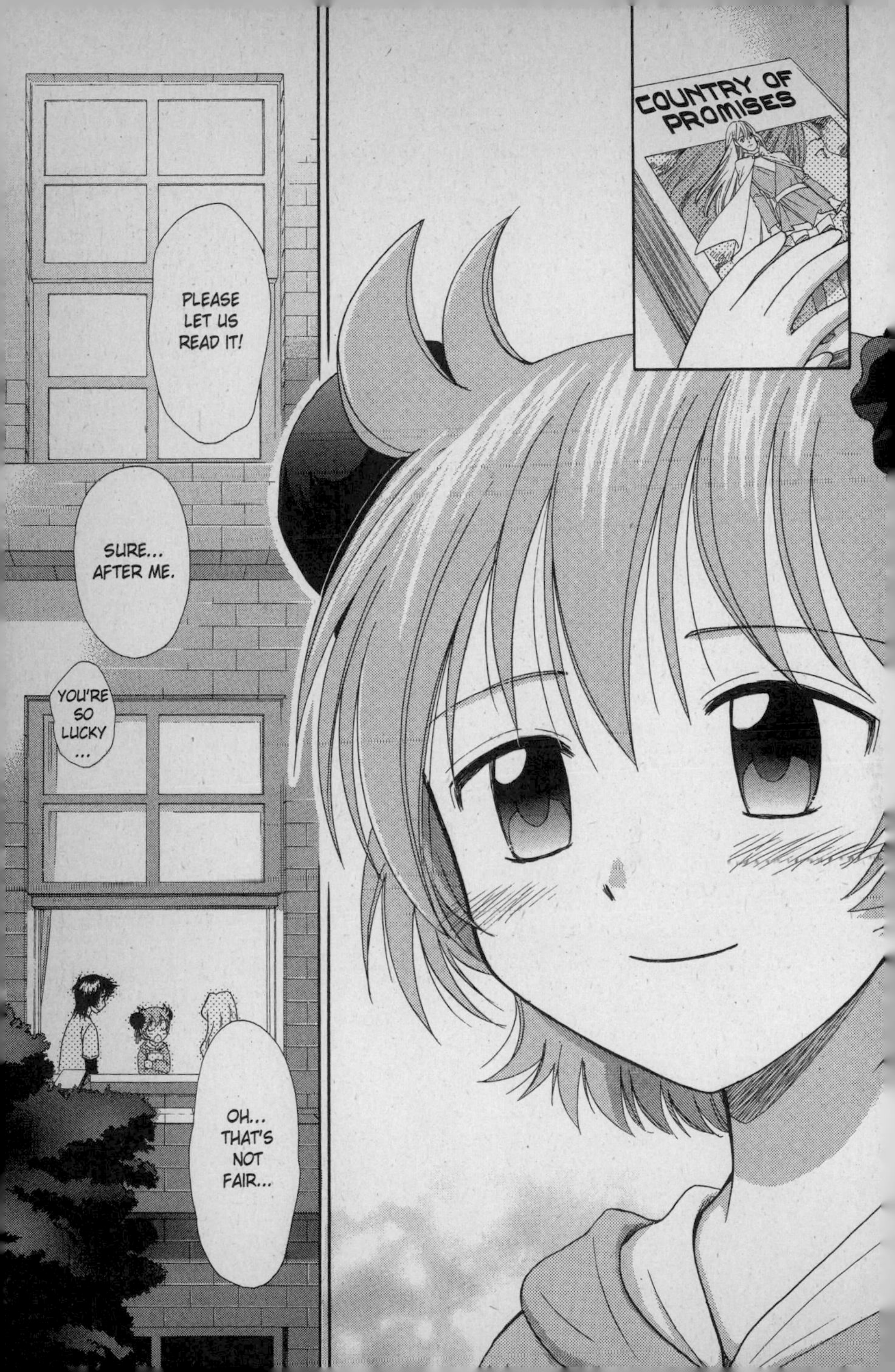
COUNTRY OF PROMISES
PLEASE LET US READ IT!
SURE... AFTER ME.
YOU'RE SO LUCKY...
OH... THAT'S NOT FAIR...

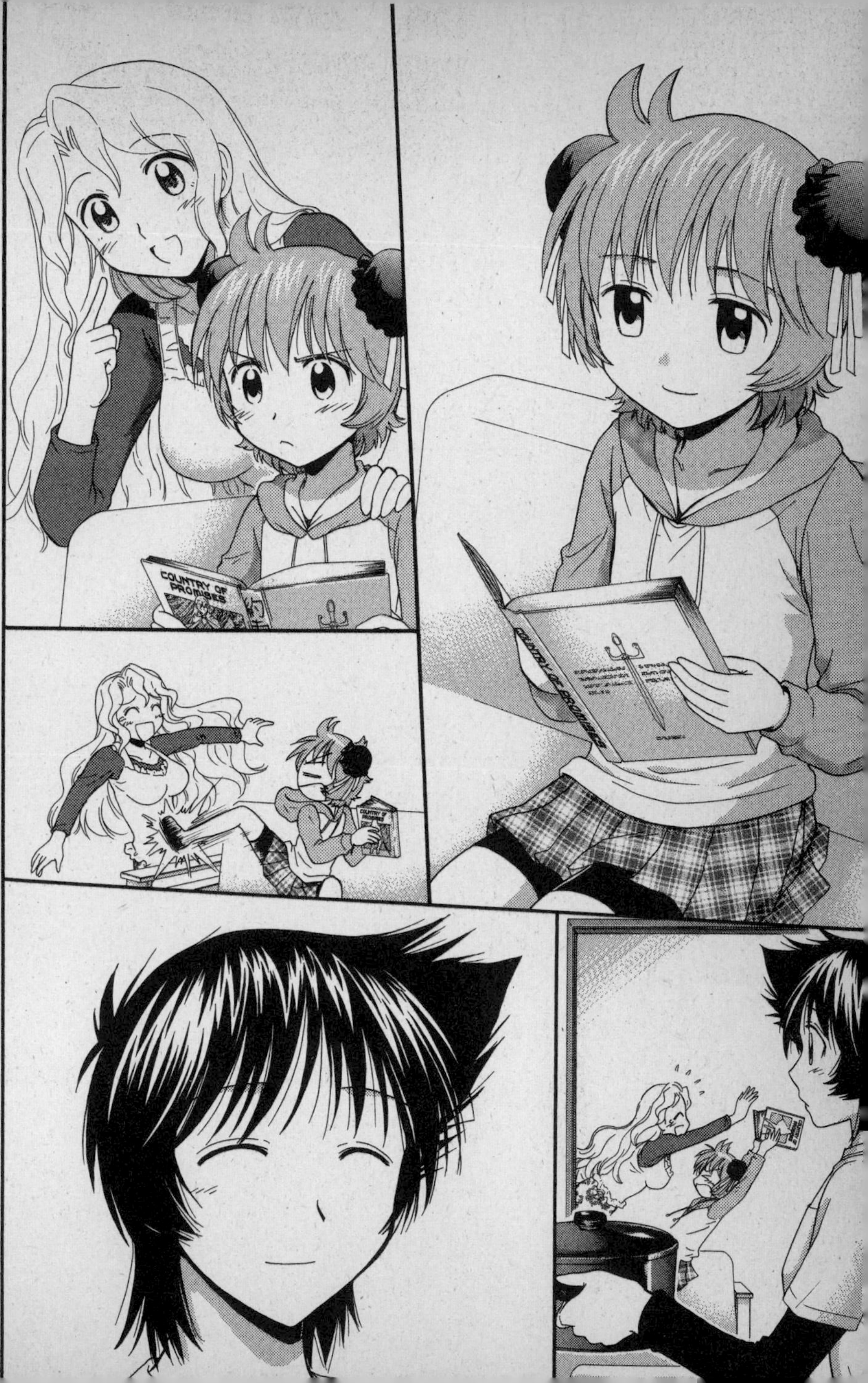
COUNTRY OF PROMISES
COUNTRY OF PROMISES
COUNTRY OF PROMISES

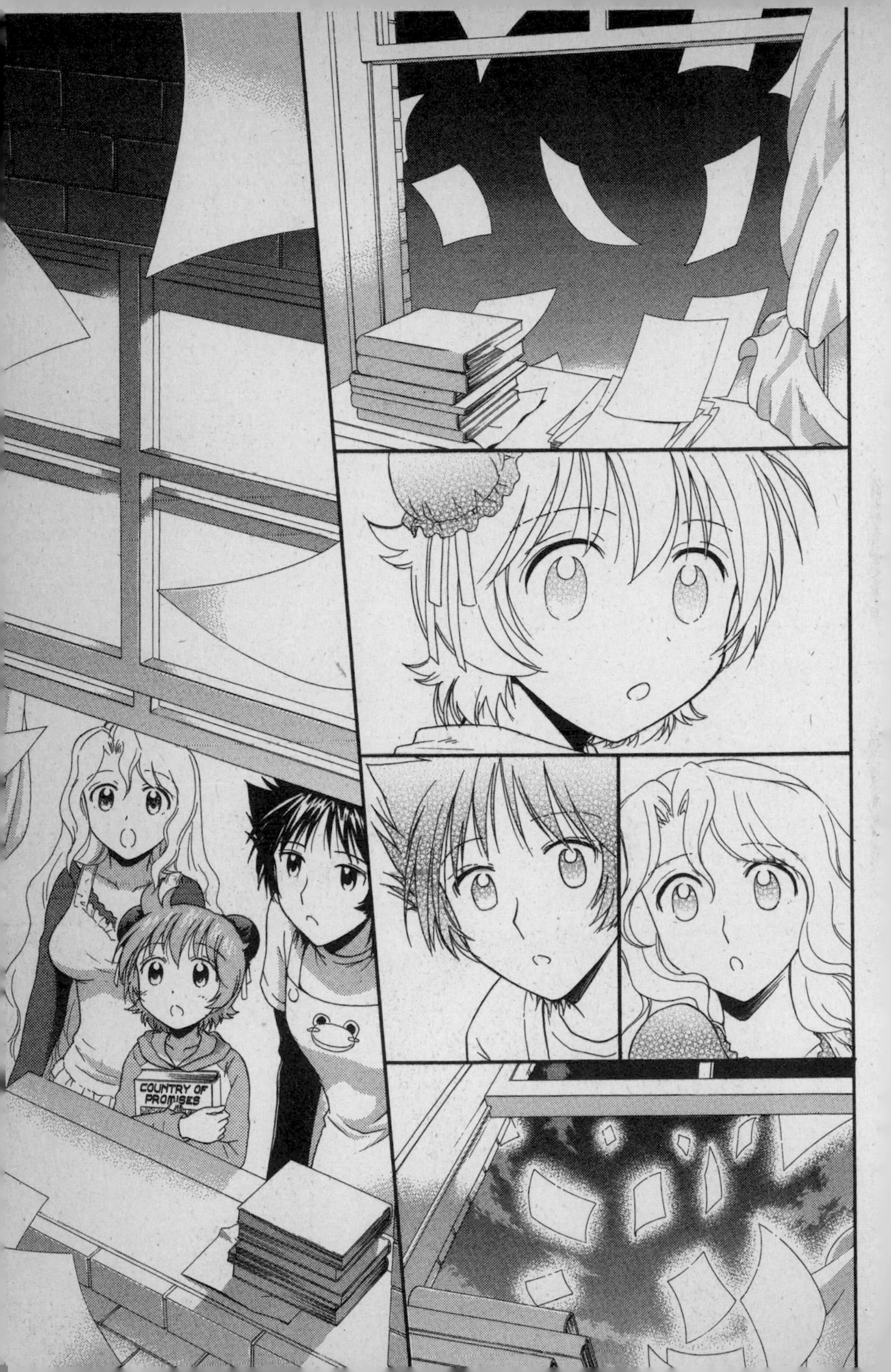
COUNTRY OF PROMISES

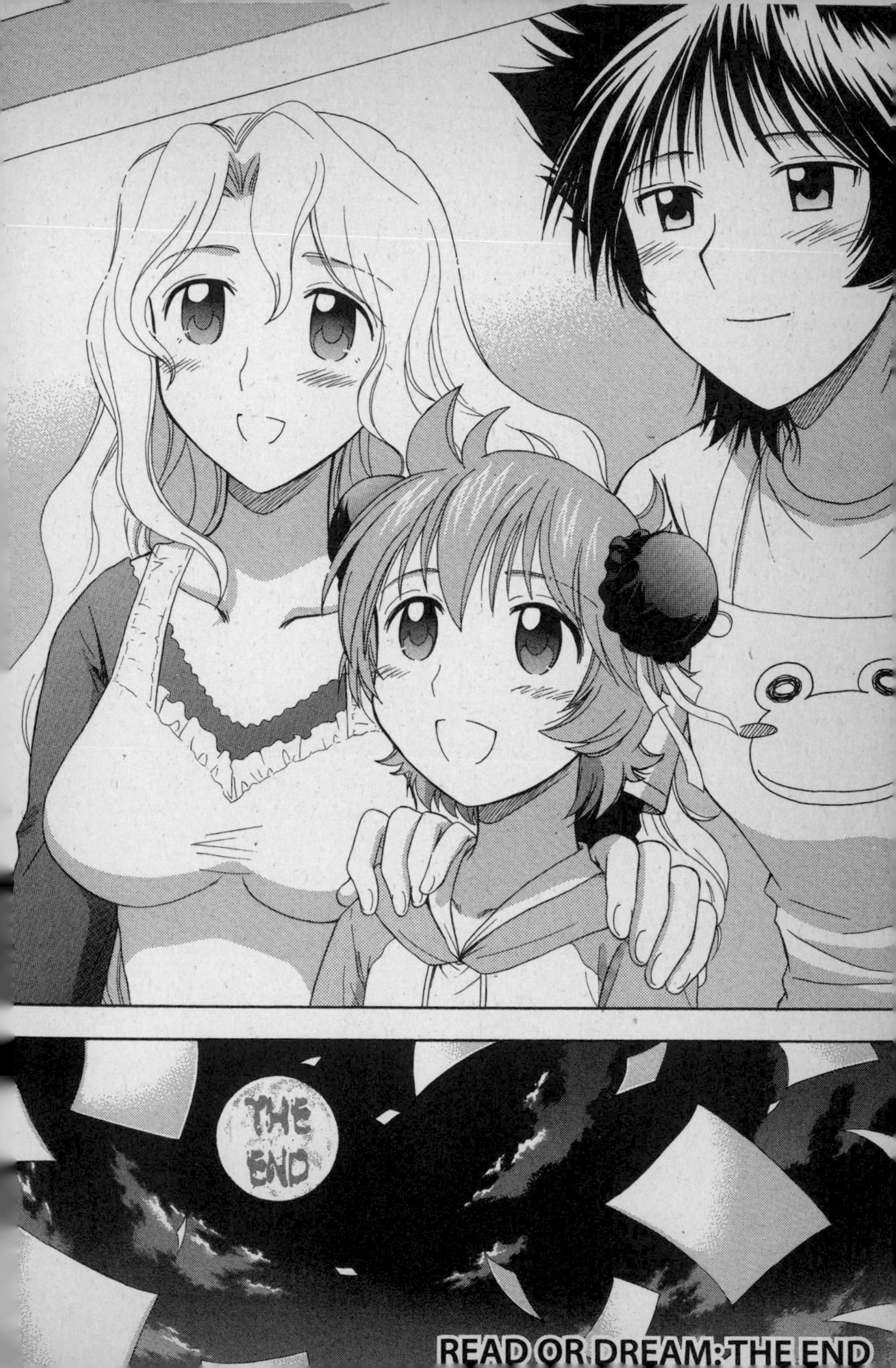
THE END
READ OR DREAM: THE END

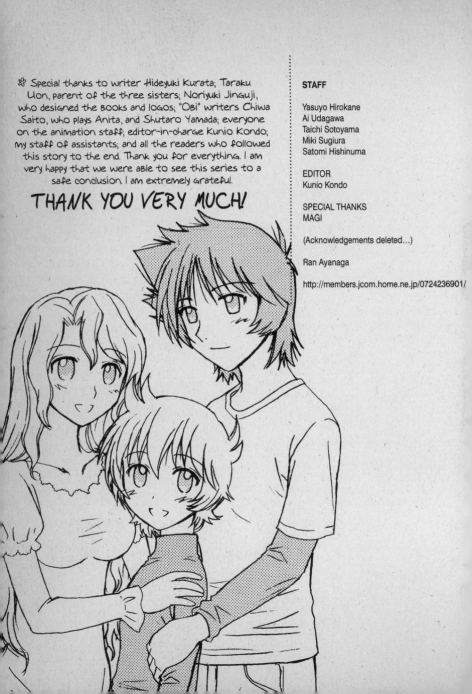

Special thanks to writer Hideyuki Kurata; Taraku Uon, parent of the three sisters; Noriyuki Jinguji, who designed the books and logos; "OBI" writers Chiwa Saito, who plays Anita, and Shutaro Yamada; everyone on the animation staff; editor-in-charge Kunio Kondo; my staff of assistants; and all the readers who followed this story to the end. Thank you for everything. I am very happy that we were able to see this series to a safe conclusion. I am extremely grateful.

THANK YOU VERY MUCH!

STAFF

Yasuyo Hirokane
Ai Udagawa
Taichi Sotoyama
Miki Sugiura
Satomi Hishinuma

EDITOR
Kunio Kondo

SPECIAL THANKS
MAGI

(Acknowledgements deleted...)

Ran Ayanaga

http://members.jcom.home.ne.jp/0724236901/

READER KING FINAL

HIDEYUKI KURATA X RAN AYANAGA

+ EDITOR-IN-CHIEF

NATURALLY, WE HAD TO MEET AT MR. KURATA'S HOME FOR OUR FINAL INTERVIEW. WE THEREFORE VISITED THE KURATA LIBRARY, A.K.A. HIS APARTMENT IN ARAIYAKUSHI.

THE PLACE IS AN URBAN JUNGLE.

After passing through a maze of books, going treasure-hunting behind stacks of books, and arguing about selling this book and dumping that one, we finally settled down in his living room.

Ayanaga: It's amazing. It's really filled with books, more than I imagined. It's like one of those used bookstores in Kanda.
Editor: What she said.
Kurata: Well, pardon me.
Editor: There are definitely more books here than when I came three years ago with Yamada.[1] Is this your legacy? One day you'll die in an avalanche of books.
Kurata: I'd be happy to die like that.
Ayanaga: But they're all very orderly. I'm amazed.
Kurata: Haven't you ever seen a room like this before, Miss Ayanaga? Aren't there people like me among your colleagues?
Ayanaga: Not among my female friends. They have some messy rooms, but none where their hobby gets in the way of their daily lives like this.
Kurata: I see...
Editor: To us, a woman's living quarters are a place of mystery. How many rooms of people of the opposite sex have you actually visited?
Kurata: What kind of question is that? Are you talking about our little-kid days, too?
Editor: No. Since becoming an adult.
Kurata: Maybe two or three.
Ayanaga: Me, too.
Editor: Oh. Okay, after this opening question verging on indecency, shall we begin the final installment of Reader King?
Ayanaga: Um, do coworkers count?

Let's learn more about Ran Ayanaga!

Editor: Well, now...All sorts of things have happened.
Kurata: We've worked together for nearly three years now.
Ayanaga: I enjoyed being able to experience new things, like the anime and the autograph session.
Kurata: Miss Ayanaga was so nervous at the autograph session.
Editor: That's right. "My hand is shaking so much I can't sign." I thought she was joking, but she really was so nervous she could hardly get the cap off the pen.
Ayanaga: I never want to work in front of people again.
Editor: Did you really hate it so much?
Kurata: Many fans began talking about wanting to see the real Miss Ayanaga.
Editor: Should she have worn something more revealing?
Ayanaga: That's not funny!
Kurata: That'd be hot.
Editor: Let me tell those who were unable to come to our only autograph session that Miss Ayanaga is a very proper young lady. Some people have said she looks a little like Yukie Naka[redacted]
Ayanaga: I look like who?
Editor: Just buttering you up.

The secret behind Anita's chest.

Editor: You also designed the characters for the anime, Miss Ayanaga.
Ayanaga: They let me do a little bit with characters like Hisami and Toru and the other classmates. It was a lot of fun to see my drawings move and talk.

Ayanaga: It was a good experience. I am truly grateful to Mr. Kurata and all the readers who gave me their support.

Editor: Anyway, it was smooth sailing, wasn't it?

Kurata: Well, my motto was, "Take it easy." We took it easy at the start and all the way to the end. That was good, I think. All we need is a little bit more happiness.

Ayanaga: I have lots of wonderful memories.

Kurata: I hope our readers feel the same way.

Editor: Um, taking it easy is good, but please give me your plans for your next project. Especially you, Miss Ayanaga.

Ayanaga: All right…

Finally…

Editor: Finally, do you have any complaints? Something off the record?

Kurata: Not really. I think it was best that everything ended cleanly. We didn't have any fights, and we had fun doing it.

Ayanaga: That's right. I'm not dissatisfied with anything.

Editor: Don't you have anything to make this more interesting?

Ayanaga: You want a shock ending?

Kurata: I just remembered something. Our editor missed our meeting for the final chapter.

Ayanaga: Oh, yes! I thought you were only late, but you actually forgot about it and didn't come at all.

Editor: Er…I guess that **did** happen.

Ayanaga: And it was a very important final meeting, too.

Kurata: Unfortunately, it wasn't until the final chapter that we realized we didn't need you at all.

Editor: Well…I'm glad that that's about the only trouble we had…

Kurata/Ayanaga: Who are you to say that?

We'll continue to take things easy. May happiness come along nice and easy for you, too.

1. **Yamada:** Shutaro Yamada, the artist for Kurata's previous manga, *Read or Die*.

Kurata: Because she'd already appeared in the anime, when we got ready for Hisami to appear in the manga, we gave it some thought. We thought we'd have some overlap with the anime, but make her a little different. In the anime, she's an ordinary schoolgirl, but for the manga we made her a young novelist. I wonder how it went over.

Editor: The manga delved deeper into her friendship with Anita, so a lot of people said they liked it.

Kurata: How did it feel to design your own characters, Miss Ayanaga?

Ayanaga: It was difficult. I know I did the original designs, but I had so much trouble making them look cute. I'm afraid I created problems for Ishihama, the animator. (Laughter.)

Kurata: Is that so? (Laughter.) Whom did you find easiest to draw?

Ayanaga: Maybe Anita. Then Michelle. It's easier to draw characters who have lots of facial expressions.

Kurata: The art changed over the course of the series, don't you think? The characters were drawn rather small and tight. (Laughter.)

Ayanaga: As I kept drawing, the characters kept changing.

Kurata: Perhaps Anita changed the most.

Ayanaga: Oh, that's right. Did you notice her chest? At first she hardly had any breasts, but when I saw how flat-chested she was in the anime, I decided to give her more of a figure. (Laughter.)

Kurata: So you answered the needs of the times?

Editor: I had no problem with it at all.

Ayanaga: By the way, I want to make it clear that I was just following Mr. Kurata's story to the letter when I drew Michelle getting fat or growing a mustache.

Kurata: Why do you say that?

Ayanaga: I don't want Michelle's fans to get angry with me. (Laughter.)

Kurata: But you seemed rather eager to draw her like that.

Ayanaga: I just have fun drawing Michelle. (Laughter.)

Let's take it easy.

Editor: Finally, let's get your impressions. Did anything change along the way?

Kurata: It was fun. And people around me started getting married.

BONUS STORY:
CLEANING UP DEMONS
WITH ANITA THE CLEANER

ANITA AND MICHELLE JUMPED INTO THE LIGHT THAT WAS LIFTING MAGGIE. THE FLYING SAUCER SWALLOWED ALL THREE OF THEM AND FLEW OFF INTO THE SKY.

"HMM...SO YOU TWO CAME ALONG, EH?"

AN ALIEN ENTERED THE SHIP'S BAY. HE GRIMACED AS HE SAW ANITA.

"OF COURSE! I WON'T LET AN OCTOPUS LIKE YOU GET THE BETTER OF ME!"

THE SPACEMAN LOOKED LIKE AN OCTOPUS OF GOOD LINEAGE. ANITA HAD SEEN A PICTURE OF A CREATURE LIKE HIM ON THE WALL OF A MOVIE THEATER SHE HAD CLEANED RECENTLY, SO SHE WASN'T AFRAID OF HIM AT ALL.

"ALIENS ARE SCIENTIFICALLY IMPLAUSIBLE," SNIFFED MICHELLE, KEEPING HERSELF WELL OUT OF RANGE. "ANITA, GET HIM!"

"SURE! TASTE MY MOP OF JUSTICE!" ANITA BEGAN TO WHACK THE SPACESHIP WITH ALL HER MIGHT.

"AAGH! WHAT ARE YOU DOING?" THE ALIEN FLAILED HIS LIMBS, TRYING DESPERATELY TO STOP HER. BUT THIS BEING WITH THE OVERDEVELOPED BRAIN WAS NO PHYSICAL MATCH FOR ANITA, WHO DID HARD WORK EVERY DAY.

"SPACEMEN SHOULD STAY IN SPACE," SAID ANITA. "YOU SHOULDN'T TRY TO STEAL MAGGIE AWAY. ANYWAY, YOU'RE JUST TOO COCKY FOR AN OCTOPUS. SPACE BELONGS TO US, THE PEOPLE OF EARTH!"

IRRITATED WITH ALL THIS OVERTIME WORK, ANITA ESCALATED HER DESTRUCTION OF THE SPACESHIP.

"UH-OH..." MICHELLE BROKE OUT IN A SWEAT. "DID I GIVE THAT MOP TOO MUCH MAGICAL POWER?"

"OH, NO!" THEY ALL SHOUTED.

VEERING WILDLY, THE SPACESHIP CRASHED ON THE MOON.

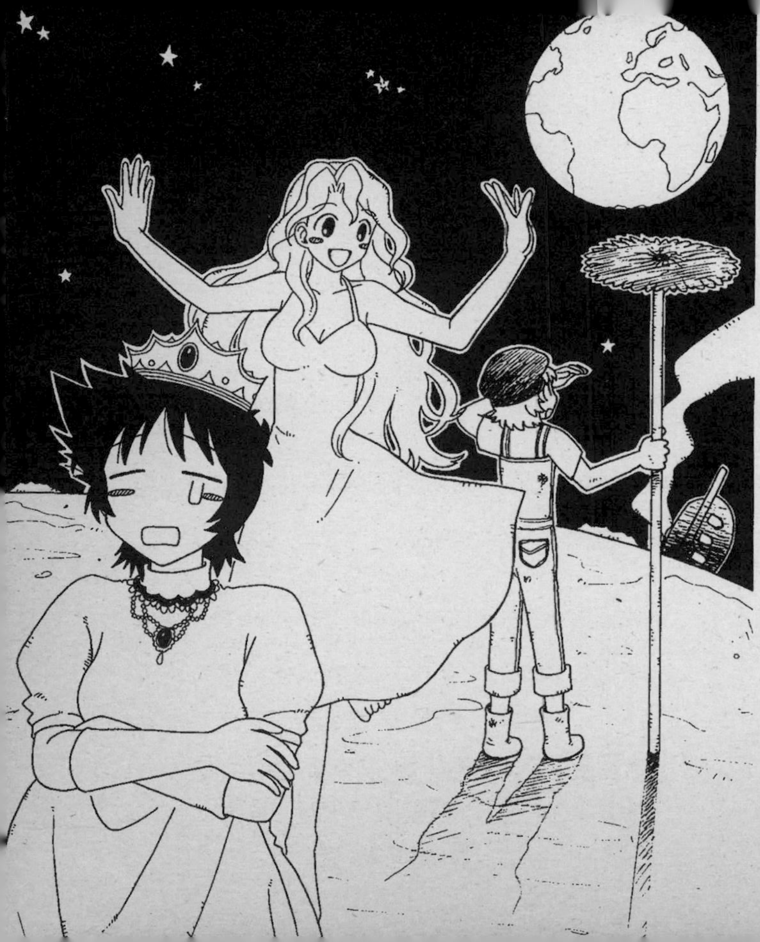

"OH, HOW WONDERFUL! I'VE GOT A NICE BODY!"

PERHAPS IT WAS CAUSED BY THE CHANGE IN GRAVITY, BUT MICHELLE SUDDENLY GREW LARGE. SHE BEGAN DANCING LIGHTLY AROUND.

"WHAT AM I DOING HERE?" MAGGIE AWAKENED AND LOOKED AROUND, PUZZLED.

"I GUESS I OVERDID IT A LITTLE..." REFLECTING ON THIS UNFORESEEN CHAIN OF EVENTS, ANITA BEGAN HAVING SECOND THOUGHTS. SHE LOOKED UP AT THE EARTH.

"OH, MY...WHEN YOU LOOK AT IT FROM A DISTANCE, EARTH SEEMS QUITE DIRTY."

SUDDENLY, ANITA UNDERSTOOD WHAT POLLUTION AND THE DESTRUCTION OF THE NATURAL ENVIRONMENT WERE ALL ABOUT. WITH MOP IN HAND, SHE WHISPERED, "I GUESS IT'S TIME TO DO SOME CLEANING."

AND THAT WAS THE BEGINNING OF THE MOON SISTERS' CLEANING INVASION BATTLES.

(THE END)

R.O.D
R E A D   O R   D R E A M
We are Paper Sisters Detective Company

VIZ Media Edition
Vol. 4

STORY BY HIDEYUKI KURATA
ART BY RAN AYANAGA

Translation/JN Productions
Touch-up Art & Lettering/Mark McMurray
Design/Amy Martin
Editor/Shaenon K. Garrity

Managing Editor/Annette Roman
Editorial Director/Elizabeth Kawasaki
Editor in Chief, Books/Alvin Lu
Editor in Chief, Magazines/Marc Weidenbaum
Sr. Director of Acquisitions/Rika Inouye
Sr. VP of Marketing/Liza Coppola
Exec. VP of Sales & Marketing/John Easum
Publisher/Hyoe Narita

T 251335

Printed in the U.S.A.

Published by VIZ Media, LLC
P.O. Box 77010
San Francisco, CA 94107

10 9 8 7 6 5 4 3 2 1

www.viz.com

store.viz.com

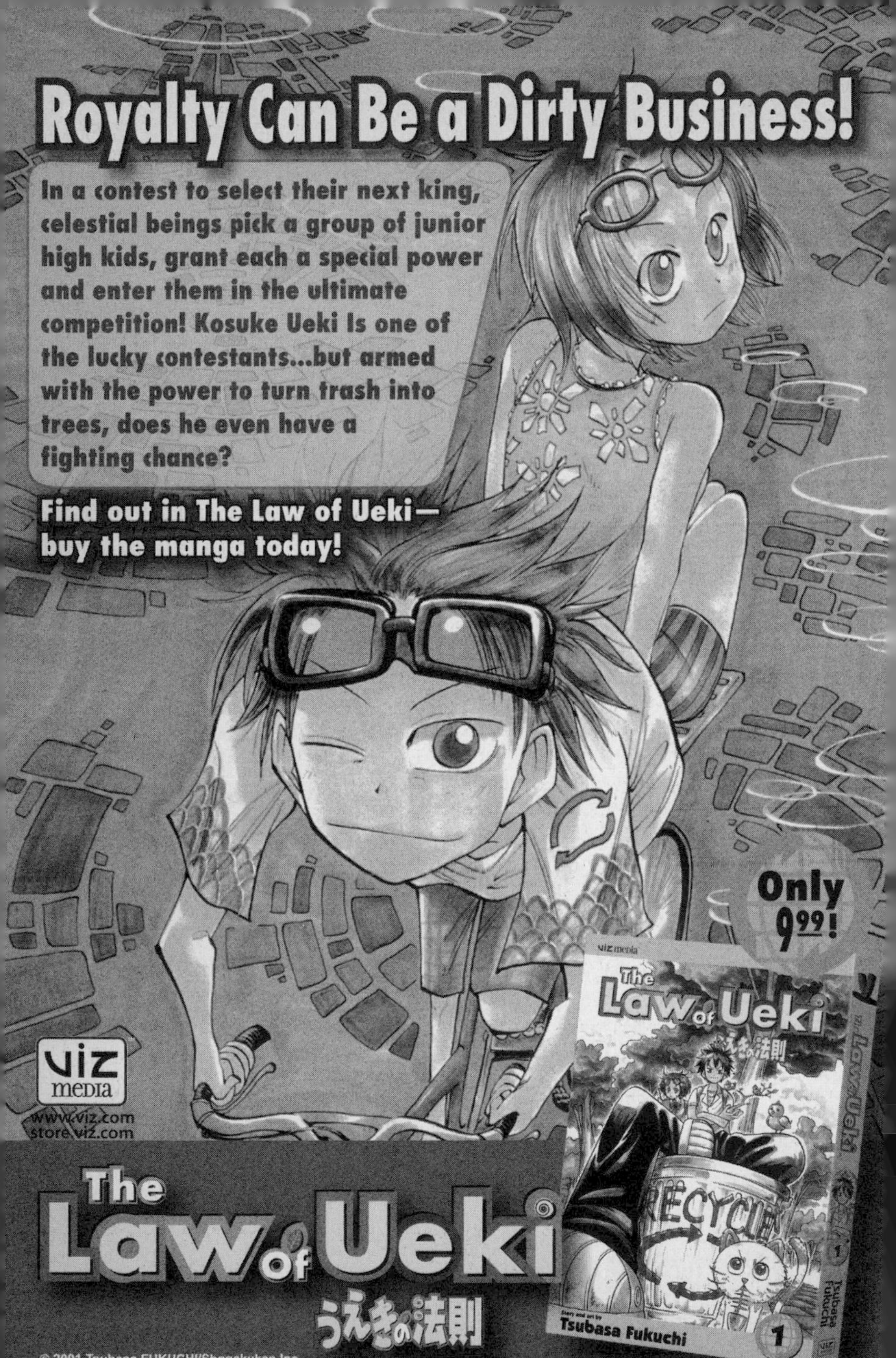
Royalty Can Be a Dirty Business!
In a contest to select their next king, celestial beings pick a group of junior high kids, grant each a special power and enter them in the ultimate competition! Kosuke Ueki Is one of the lucky contestants...but armed with the power to turn trash into trees, does he even have a fighting chance?
Find out in The Law of Ueki—buy the manga today!
Only 9.99!
viz media
www.viz.com
store.viz.com
The Law of Ueki
うえきの法則
Story and art by Tsubasa Fukuchi
1

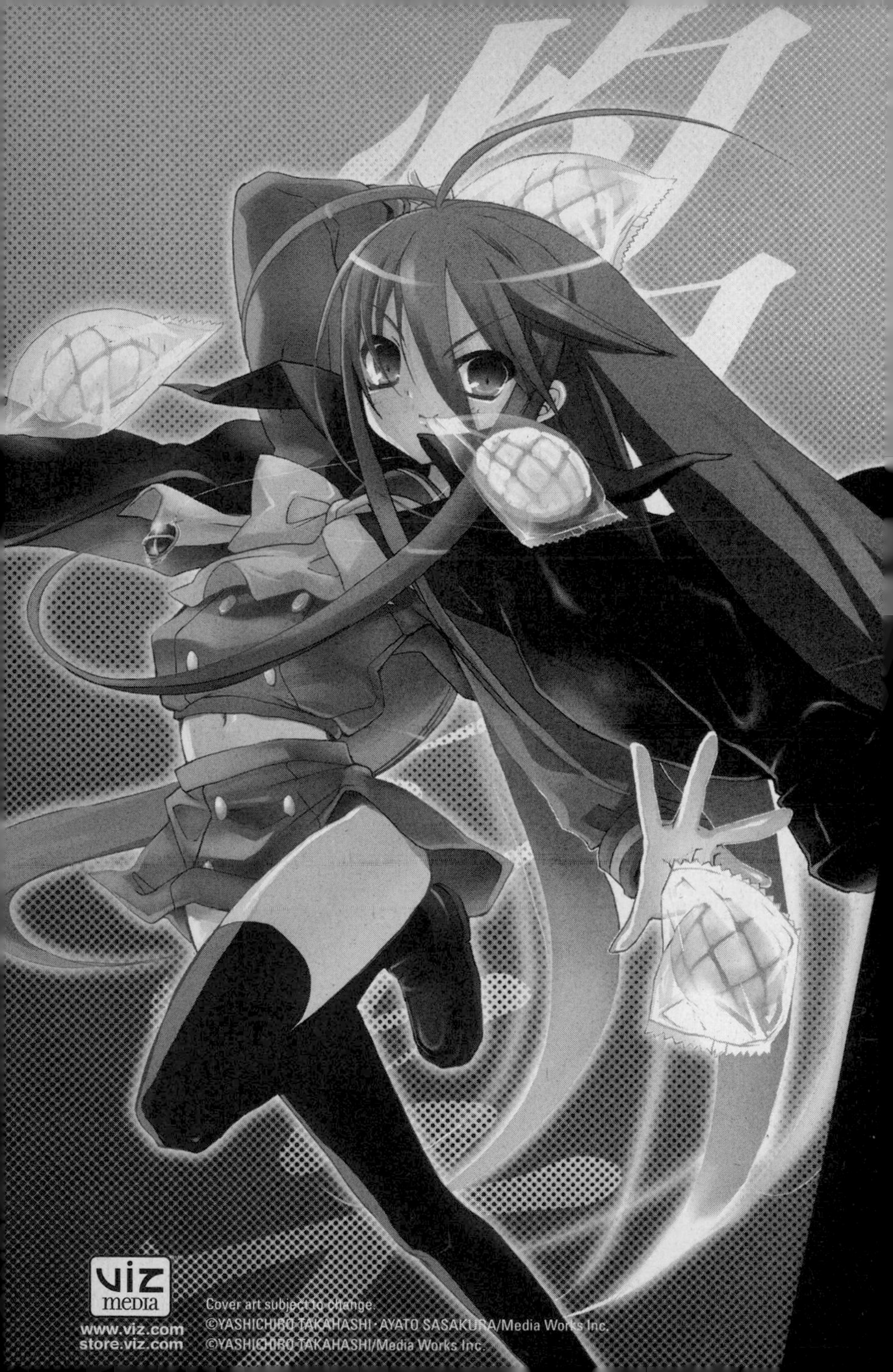

LOVE MANGA?
LET US KNOW WHAT YOU THINK!

OUR MANGA SURVEY IS NOW
AVAILABLE ONLINE. PLEASE VISIT:
VIZ.COM/MANGASURVEY

HELP US MAKE THE MANGA
YOU LOVE BETTER!

VIZ
MEDIA